THE HARBINGER THEORY

# The Harbinger Theory

## HOW THE POST-9/11 EMERGENCY BECAME PERMANENT AND THE CASE FOR REFORM

Robert Diab

OXFORD
UNIVERSITY PRESS

OXFORD
UNIVERSITY PRESS

*Oxford University Press is a department of the University of Oxford. It furthers the University's objective of excellence in research, scholarship, and education by publishing worldwide.*

Oxford New York
Auckland Cape Town Dar es Salaam Hong Kong Karachi Kuala Lumpur Madrid
Melbourne Mexico City Nairobi New Delhi Shanghai Taipei Toronto

With offices in
Argentina Austria Brazil Chile Czech Republic France Greece Guatemala Hungary
Italy Japan Poland Portugal Singapore South Korea Switzerland Thailand
Turkey Ukraine Vietnam



Published in the United States of America by
Oxford University Press
198 Madison Avenue, New York, NY 10016



Library of Congress Cataloging-in-Publication Data
Diab, Robert, author.
The harbinger theory : how the post-9/11 emergency became permanent and the case for reform / Robert Diab.
pages cm
Includes bibliographical references and index.
ISBN 978-0-19-024322-7 ((hardback) : alk. paper)
1. Terrorism—Prevention—Law and legislation. 2. Terrorism—Prevention—Law and legislation—United States. 3. Terrorism—Prevention—Law and legislation—Canada. 4. War and emergency powers. 5. War and emergency powers—United States. 6. War and emergency powers—Canada. I. Title.
K5256.D53 2015
344.7305'32517—dc23

9780190243227

**Note to Readers**

This publication is designed to provide accurate and authoritative information in regard to the subject matter covered. It is based upon sources believed to be accurate and reliable and is intended to be current as of the time it was written. It is sold with the understanding that the publisher is not engaged in rendering legal, accounting, or other professional services. If legal advice or other expert assistance is required, the services of a competent professional person should be sought. Also, to confirm that the information has not been affected or changed by recent developments, traditional legal research techniques should be used, including checking primary sources where appropriate.

*(Based on the Declaration of Principles jointly adopted by a Committee of the American Bar Association and a Committee of Publishers and Associations.)*

*For Wes Pue*

# Contents

# Acknowledgments

THIS BOOK HAS its origins in doctoral research in the Faculty of Law at the University of British Columbia, where I had the privilege of working with an outstanding legal historian and expert in civil liberties, W. Wesley Pue. Wes has been a mentor to me for over a decade and a constant source of inspiration and wise counsel, and by dedicating this book to him, I hardly begin to express the extent of my gratitude and indebtedness. I was also privileged to work at UBC with Ben Goold and Michael Burgess, who were unfailingly generous with their time and offered me much invaluable guidance and encouragement.

A portion of the research for this book was conducted as a visiting scholar at the Yale Law School, where Professor Paul Kahn was an exceptionally warm host and brilliant interlocutor. I also had the pleasure at Yale of working briefly with the late Jonathan Schell whose discussions with me about the literature on nuclear terror set me on the path that led to a larger body of skeptical literature on the threat of terror that would form the centerpiece of my inquiry.

I am indebted to the insights of Jonathan Simon of Berkeley Law in his role as external examiner of the dissertation, and to Craig Forcese of the University of Ottawa for comments on an earlier draft of this book. I thank Blake Ratcliff, my editor at Oxford University Press, for his enthusiasm and support of this project from its earliest stages. I also thank Alden Domizio at OUP and the anonymous referees.

Much of the research for this book was made possible through the generous funding of the Vanier Canada Graduate Scholarship and the Michael Smith Foreign Study Scholarship—neither of which I would have obtained without the diligent oversight of Joanne Chung at UBC.

Finally, I owe a deep debt of gratitude to my wife Ciara, and to Rosemary and Sean, for allowing me the time and space to work, and for their love and support throughout.

# 1

# Introduction

SINCE THE TERRORIST attacks on the United States in September 2001, North American law has been transformed in ways previously unimaginable. Measures that had once seemed extraordinary or even unthinkable in sophisticated Western democracies have now become permanently ensconced in our legal systems. Laws now authorize, and courts have affirmed the constitutionality of, indefinite detention without charge on secret evidence, mass secret surveillance, and a vastly expanded scope for the assertion of state privilege. The U.S. Congress has acquiesced in the President's claim of authority to carry out targeted killing of American citizens. Perhaps more strikingly, from a pre-9/11 perspective, large portions of the U.S. and Canadian public support many of these measures.

What seems just as striking as the nature of the shift is the sense of its possible permanence. Acting on powers conferred by Congress days after 9/11, the President continues to hold 149 detainees at Guantanamo on secret evidence, with an intention to imprison 48 "high value" detainees indefinitely and without charge.[1] Revelations of mass secret surveillance of telephone and Internet communications of unsuspecting civilians on an unprecedented scale are met with assurances by security officials of the legality and propriety of the measures, and acquiescence by a larger public.[2] The President continues every month to authorize scores of drone strikes of persons he alone deems to pose an imminent danger to the United States, asserting the power to target U.S. citizens without charge or judicial oversight, and to do so,

[1] Charlie Savage, *The Future of Guantanamo*, N.Y. TIMES, Aug. 31, 2014, and *US Government Releases Names of Indefinite Guantanamo Detainees*, jurist.org, June 19, 2013.

[2] *See* discussion of sources in Chapter 3.

if necessary, on American soil.[3] Canada has seen a similar entrenchment of powers to detain indefinitely without charge, to assert greater state secrecy, and to conduct new forms of secret surveillance.[4] Attempts to hold officials in both nations accountable for involvement in torture, rendition, or other violations of core human rights continue to be hindered by assertions of state privilege, with no change likely in the foreseeable future.[5]

How did this transformation occur? Was it simply an extension of an increasing "culture of control" or a trend toward greater "securitization" in North America that began two or three decades before 9/11?[6] Or has the embrace of extraordinary measures since 2001 been marked by the prevalence of a new and unique form of reasoning about law and security? And how will it end?

This book seeks to shift perspective in debates about counterterrorism measures in the post-9/11 period by revisiting the conceptual framework by which many extraordinary measures were initially justified and have now come to be entrenched. The book argues that we cannot begin to undo the many facets of the permanent emergency until this framework is better understood and arguments for reform are crafted to address it more effectively.

The central contention of this book is that in the wake of 9/11, a range of extraordinary measures have come to be entrenched in North American law largely as a consequence of a wider cultural and political embrace of what can be called the harbinger theory.[7] At the core of the theory is the assumption that 9/11 was not a profoundly anomalous event in the history of terror but the harbinger of a new order of terror—giving rise to the belief that at some point in the near future, an attack might occur in a large North American city on a scale similar to or greater than 9/11. More specifically, the theory assumes the form of a belief that al Qaeda, or an affiliated or analogous group, may soon make use of a weapon of mass destruction (WMD), with cataclysmic or possibly "existential" consequences for the state, or that terrorists without WMDs may soon carry out an attack on the scale of 9/11 or greater. Either form of attack would entail thousands or more casualties rather than tens or hundreds, as in earlier events (the Air India bombing, Oklahoma City), lending the prospect of terrorism a qualitatively different character from crime. Further terror on this scale is assumed to be likely either because WMDs are—so is the common refrain—"only

---

[3] Details of the President's practice of targeted killing are explored in Chapter 2.

[4] Chapter 2 provides a brief overview of the "security certificate" regime in Canada's Immigration and Refugee Protection Act, S.C. 2001, c. 27 and new powers of law enforcement, intelligence, and state secrecy in the Anti-terrorism Act, S.C. 2001, c. 41 and other legislation.

[5] *See* the discussion in Chapter 2 of El-Masri v. United States, 479 F.3d 296 (4th Cir. 2007); Mohamed v. Jeppesen Dataplan, No. 08-15693 (9th Cir., Sept. 8, 2010); and Arar v. Ashcroft, No. 06-4216 (2d Cir., June 30, 2008).

[6] David Garland, The Culture of Control: Crime and Social Order in Contemporary Society (Chicago: University of Chicago Press, 2001); Lucia Zedner, *Seeking Security by Eroding Rights: The Side-stepping of Due Process*, in Benjamin J. Goold & Liora Lazarus, eds., Security and Human Rights (Oxford: Hart Publishing, 2007); Jonathan Simon, Governing Through Crime: How the War on Crime Transformed American Democracy and Created a Culture of Fear (Oxford: Oxford University Press, 2007).

[7] For the use of the term "harbinger," I acknowledge a debt to John Mueller who analyzed early perceptions of 9/11 in *Harbinger or Aberration? A 9/11 Provocation*, Nat'l Interest, Fall 2002, at 45.

becoming more accessible and diffuse" or because today's terrorists are more skilled and ambitious, and 9/11 itself has demonstrated how readily and *easily* non-state actors can carry out an attack on that order. What is therefore at stake in the possibility of another attack is much more than the safety of a small number of civilians, but a much greater and more catastrophic disruption of both society and the state. These beliefs commonly form the basis of a larger claim, made in several contexts, that given the magnitude of the outstanding threat, more invasive measures have become necessary for the foreseeable future.

A key context is government itself. In numerous pronouncements and policy statements since 2001, and often at crucial moments, such as legislative debates around the passage of controversial measures, members of the executive and prominent security officials in both nations have defended the necessity of authoritarian measures continuously and at times exclusively by invoking the prospect of terror involving WMD or another attack on the scale of 9/11. For example, in his "National Security Strategy" of 2010, President Barack Obama affirmed a set of initiatives that include targeted killing and indefinite detention without charge in light of the prefatory comment that "[t]he American people face no greater or more urgent danger than a terrorist attack with a nuclear weapon..."[8] His 2011 "National Strategy for Counterterrorism,"[9] published after Osama bin Laden's death, reiterated that the "danger of nuclear terrorism is the greatest threat to national security." Terror groups including al Qaida, we were told, "have engaged in efforts to develop and acquire weapons of mass destruction—and if successful, they are likely to use them."[10] In March 2013, in a widely reported exchange with Senator Rand Paul, Attorney General Eric Holder rendered the opinion that the President maintains the authority to carry out targeted killing of U.S. citizens without charge on U.S. soil and defended such power as "necessary and appropriate" in the event of "a catastrophic attack like the ones suffered on December 7, 1941, and September 11, 2001."[11] In a speech in January 2014 in response to the report of the President's Review Group on Intelligence and Communications Technologies and following the Edward Snowden revelations, President Obama defended the use of mass secret surveillance by making several references to the prospect of another 9/11 or an attack involving WMDs. He claimed, for example, that "emerging threats from terror groups and the proliferation of weapons of mass destruction place new, and in some ways, more complicated demands on our intelligence agencies"; and "[t]he men and women at the NSA know that if another 9/11 or massive cyberattack occurs, they will be asked by Congress and

---

[8] *The National Security Strategy of the United States of America* (Washington, D.C.: The White House, May 2010), at 23.

[9] *National Strategy for Counterterrorism* (Washington, D.C.: The White House, June 2011).

[10] Ibid. at 8.

[11] Holder set out this position in a letter in response to a query from Senator Paul Rand: http://www.paul.senate.gov/files/documents/BrennanHolderResponse.pdf. *See also* Charlie Savage, *Senators Press Holder on Use of Military Force on U.S. Soil*, N.Y. Times, Mar. 6, 2013.

the media why they failed to connect the dots…"[12] Similarly, in Canada, a host of policy statements and reports since 9/11, from the Ministry of Public Safety to the Canadian Security and Intelligence Service, have invoked the prospect of large-scale terror, and the possible use of WMDs.[13]

In addition to its role in political rhetoric, scholars and authorities in a number of fields have invoked the harbinger theory in work on terror threats of a specific nature (nuclear, biological, radiological), the history of terrorism, and other facets of security, including cyberterror.[14] A host of prominent public intellectuals and high-profile commentators, including Richard Posner, Alan Dershowitz, and John Yoo, have also sought to make the case for extreme measures on the basis of often vivid and stirring hypothetical scenarios consistent with the notion of 9/11 as a harbinger of the scale of future terror.[15]

The harbinger theory has thus been invoked with a prevalence and consistency in political and juridical defenses of extreme measures that places it at the center of political and public discourse on national security in North America. For this reason, it can be distinguished from other grounds of public support for extraordinary measures. Some have argued, for example, that to a significant extent popular support for the measures reflects a set of racist, imperialist, or jingoistic assumptions and beliefs about the nature

---

[12] Barack Obama, *Remarks by the President on Review of Signals Intelligence*, (Washington D.C.: Dep't of Justice, Jan. 17, 2014): http://www.whitehouse.gov/the-press-office/2014/01/17/remarks-president-review-signals-intelligence. Further examples are explored in Chapter 3.

[13] Ministry of Public Safety, Canada, *Building Resilience Against Terrorism: Canada's Counter-terrorism Strategy* (Ottawa: Ministry of Public Safety, 2012); Canadian Security and Intelligence Service, *2008–2009 Public Report* (Ottawa: CSIS, 2008). References to mass terror are explored in Chapter 3.

[14] Walter Laqueur, THE 9/11 NEW TERRORISM: FANATICISM AND THE ARMS OF MASS DESTRUCTION (Oxford: Oxford University Press, 1998); NO END TO WAR: TERRORISM IN THE TWENTY-FIRST CENTURY (New York: Continuum, 2004); Philip Bobbitt, TERROR AND CONSENT: THE WARS FOR THE TWENTY FIRST-CENTURY (New York: Knopf, 2008). On nuclear terror, see Graham Allison, NUCLEAR TERROR: THE ULTIMATE PREVENTABLE CATASTROPHE (New York: Henry Holt, 2005), Charles D. Ferguson and William C. Potter, THE FOUR FACES OF NUCLEAR TERRORISM (London: Routledge, 2005), Matthew Bunn, *Securing the Bomb 2010: Securing All Nuclear Materials in Four Years*, (Cambridge, Mass. and Washington, D.C.: Project on Managing the Atom, Belfer Center for Science and International Affairs, Harvard Kennedy School and Nuclear Threat Initiative, April 2010): www.nti.org/e_research/Securing_The_Bomb_2010.pdf. On biological terror, see Barry Kellman, BIOVIOLENCE: PREVENTING BIOLOGICAL TERROR AND CRIME (Cambridge: Cambridge University Press, 2007); Jim A. Davis, *A Biological Warfare Wake-Up Call: Prevalent Myths and Likely Scenarios*, in Jim A. Davis and Barry R. Schneider, eds., THE GATHERING BIOLOGICAL WARFARE STORM (Westport, CT: Praeger, 2004); and Frank Barnaby, HOW TO BUILD A NUCLEAR BOMB AND OTHER WEAPONS OF MASS DESTRUCTION (London: Granta Books, 2004). On cyberterror, see Sam Powers, *The Threat of Cyberterrorism to Critical Infrastructure*, E-International Relations, September 2013, *available at* http://www.e-ir.info/2013/09/02/the-threat-of-cyberterrorism-to-critical-infrastructure/; and Marie-Helen Maras, COMPUTER FORENSICS: CYBERCRIMINALS, LAWS, AND EVIDENCE (Sudbury, MA: Jones and Bartlett, 2012).

[15] See, e.g., Alan Dershowitz, PREEMPTION: A KNIFE THAT CUTS BOTH WAYS (New York: Norton, 2006); Richard Posner, NOT A SUICIDE PACT: THE CONSTITUTION IN A TIME OF NATIONAL EMERGENCY (Oxford: Oxford University Press, 2006); and John Yoo, WAR BY OTHER MEANS: AN INSIDERS ACCOUNT OF THE WAR ON TERROR (New York: Atlantic Monthly Press, 2006).

of terrorism or national security.[16] Or, as noted above, support may be grounded in earlier cultural trends toward greater control, risk management, and security.[17] The intent here is not to deny the presence of other grounds for support, but, rather, to highlight the degree to which the measures have been defended in official pronouncements by a wide range of institutional actors in the post-9/11 period consistently and almost exclusively in terms of a single articulable theory. A variety of motivations may or may not inform the politics of security, but members of the executive and key security officials in both nations have rarely if ever sought to justify the measures in terms other than a variation on the harbinger theory.

The theory has also characterized the prevailing public imagination of the threat of terror and beliefs about appropriate responses to it. For much of the post-2001 period, the prospect of further terror on the scale of 9/11 has been continuously affirmed for a wider public in various works of popular culture—from countless films and books to TV series, including *24*, *Zero Dark Thirty*, and *Homeland*—which often depicted terror plots involving WMDs or contemplated the imminent possibility of attack resulting in thousands of casualties rather than tens or hundreds. Many of these works have also endorsed a more aggressive and preemptive approach to national security by depicting the use of torture, rendition, or targeted killing as necessary, effective, and proportionate responses to the threat of terror.

Public opinion surveys over the course of the post-9/11 period in Canada and the United States suggest that large portions of the North American public have adopted beliefs consistent with the harbinger theory and its corollary assumptions about security. More recent polls confirm the currency of these beliefs, indicating that a large portion of the U.S. public continues to fear the future possibility of an attack on the scale of 9/11 or greater.[18] Recent polls also suggest that sizeable numbers still support a range of authoritarian measures including targeted killing, indefinite detention without charge, and mass secret surveillance. Poll data in Canada are less clear on the extent to which Canadians fear large-scale terror, but confirm the currency of such fears along with significant support for more invasive measures. Opinion data thus support the role of the harbinger theory as a social and cultural foundation for extreme measures.

Earlier approaches to post-9/11 policies and practices have therefore erred in assuming a continuity with an older rise of securitization. These approaches overlook the important question of what the security landscape would have been like had 9/11 not occurred, and what particular forms of reasoning about security 9/11 had made possible. Put otherwise, if 9/11 had not occurred, an increase in forms of security may have been likely, but not the

---

[16] *See,* e.g., Sherene Razack, CASTING OUT: THE EVICTION OF MUSLIMS FROM WESTERN LAW AND POLITICS (Toronto: University of Toronto Press, 2008); Judith Butler, PRECARIOUS LIFE: POWERS OF MOURNING AND LIFE (London: Verso, 2004) and FRAMES OF WAR: WHEN IS LIFE GRIEVABLE? (London: Verso, 2010).

[17] *See* Garland, Simon, and Zedner, *supra* note 6.

[18] Examples are explored in Chapter 3.

extraordinary measures that have in fact come about. And while fear and overreaction to the spectacle of 9/11 explain much, they do not explain the primary mode of argument by which the executive, courts, and prominent voices in public debate have justified authoritarian measures, or the basis on which a wider public has come to accept them.

There is of course nothing new in the claim that North Americans have embraced more invasive measures on the basis of growing fears about terrorism. But by probing this claim in more depth, this book will demonstrate that support for the measures has rested on a more specific and recurring logic that played an indispensable role in shaping law and policy precisely as a result of the absence of any prominent public critique of it. Seeking to address this gap, the book will explore expert opinion and evidence to advance arguments that may be used in law and policy debates to call the harbinger theory into question.

But before expanding upon this, the book also advances a further primary claim. I will argue that the impact of the harbinger theory has gone beyond shaping security law and policy to affect a deeper transformation in cultural perceptions of law itself. Understanding this shift is essential to the project of reform in large part because authoritarian measures are not seen to be emergency measures, but part of the fabric of a new and evolving idea of law—one in which vastly expanded state secrecy, indefinite detention, mass surveillance, and extra-judicial killing are consistent with law. These practices have become consistent with law, and not merely temporary exceptions, on the basis that the much greater threat that terrorism poses is permanent. And this logic can be discerned on both sides of the border.

The salient feature of the Bush administration's legal response to 9/11, a feature retained under Obama, was to frame the event as an act of war, conferring upon the President warlike powers. The legal centerpiece of the war on terror in this regard is the "Authorization to Use Military Force" (AUMF), a joint resolution of Congress passed on September 14, 2001.[19] Containing no explicit time limit, the AUMF states that "the President is authorized to use all necessary and appropriate force against those nations, organizations, or persons he determines planned, authorized, committed or aided the terrorist attacks that occurred on September 11, 2001, or harbored such organizations or persons... in order to prevent any future acts of international terrorism against the United States." Given its broad sweep, the AUMF has served as a continuous reference point for the President's legal authority to carry out a range of extraordinary measures, including indefinite detention without charge at Guantanamo, targeted killing, and certain forms of mass surveillance.

But, notably, the AUMF, and the larger framing of the threat of terror as tantamount to war, is premised on the harbinger theory and would be implausible without it. The preamble to the AUMF makes this explicit: "on September 11, 2001, acts of treacherous violence were committed against the United States... and such acts continue to pose an

[19] Authorization to Use Military Force, Pub. L. No. 107–40, 50 U.S.C. §1541 (2001).

unusual and extraordinary threat to the national security and foreign policy of the United States." To assert that al Qaida poses a continuing and extraordinary threat is to view 9/11 not as an anomalous and highly improbable event but as one that may be repeated at some point in the near future. It was also an open-ended threat, giving rise to a war of indefinite duration—or at least as long as the harbinger theory seemed plausible. When Congress reaffirmed the validity of the AUMF in 2012—effectively renewing it—it also reaffirmed its belief in the currency of the harbinger theory.[20]

For much of the post-9/11 period, as these legal developments have emerged, U.S. jurists, legal scholars, and rights advocates have been concerned primarily with debating the constitutionality of the war on terror or its consistency with the rule of law and the principles of human rights. Part of the problem is that the conduct of the war has not easily fit within the older paradigm of a liberal or humane law of war against a conventional territorial enemy. And yet core elements of the new preemptive regime have found a place in law, forcing an ever-expanding set of subtle but significant alterations, amendments, and qualifications to primary doctrines and principles of law. To take a notorious example, the Bush administration sought initially to deny detainees at Guantanamo the protections of the Geneva Conventions—including the duty to refrain from interrogation—preferring to subject these "enemy combatants" to coercive or "enhanced" interrogations. The Supreme Court then ruled otherwise in what appeared to be a victory for human rights; but it conceded that the President had the authority to detain terror suspects for the "duration of hostilities" in the war on terror, however long that might be.[21] It also allowed for a more restricted form of habeas corpus and the use of secret evidence in reviewing the detentions.[22] Later, the administration would insist on the legality of coercive interrogation bordering on torture, and the practice of "extraordinary rendition."[23] In response to revelations in 2005 of a secret National Security Agency mass surveillance program, Congress would amend the Foreign Intelligence Surveillance Act in 2008 to allow many of the same powers with limited judicial oversight or public accountability.[24] At a further extreme, the President claimed in 2013 the constitutional authority to carry out targeted killing of U.S. citizens either abroad or *in* the United States on the basis that although it may involve a deprivation of life without "judicial process," it does not deny a form of due process.[25] These various controversial measures may not easily fit into either conventional criminal law or law of war frameworks, but are now entrenched to a significant extent in law.

---

20 *See* discussion in Chapter 2 of the National Defense Authorization Act for Fiscal Year 2012, H.R. 1540, 112th Cong. (2011).

21 Hamdi et al. v. Rumsfeld et al., 542 U.S. 507 (2004).

22 Boumediene v. Bush, 476 F.3d. 981 (2008).

23 *See* discussion of these measures in Chapter 2.

24 Foreign Surveillance Intelligence Act, Pub. L. 95–511, 92 Stat. 1783 (1978); Foreign Surveillance Intelligence Act of 1978 Amendments Act of 2008, Pub. L. 110–261, 122 Stat. 2436 (2008).

25 Charlie Savage, *Senators Press Holder on Use of Military Force on U.S. Soil*, N.Y. Times, Mar. 6, 2013.

Canada, by contrast, is not engaged in a war on terror, and in many respects its legal response to 9/11 has been more restrained than that of the United States. Canada's Anti-terrorism Act, passed in December of 2001, added new terror-related offenses to the Criminal Code, and powers for preventive detention and judicial interrogation.[26] But the new offenses did not contain mandatory minimum sentences, and the new detention and interrogation powers include significant procedural limits. And although the government preferred the use of immigration detention powers over criminal prosecution as a counterterrorism measure in the early years after 9/11, it soon shifted emphasis back to prosecutions, demonstrating a measured use of that tool as well. Moreover, while Canada's immigration law allows for a form of indefinite detention without charge on secret evidence, the "security certificate" regime is fundamentally different from detention at Guantanamo by virtue of the fact that its primary purpose is to facilitate a detainee's secure deportation rather than indefinite detention per se. Canada has also demonstrated a significant measure of accountability for rights violations by holding two high-profile inquiries into the involvement of state officials in the deportation and torture of one of its citizens, Maher Arar, and in the torture of three other Canadians in Syria and Egypt.[27] The government also compensated Arar with $10.5 million and made an official apology.

Yet, in many respects, Canada's response to 9/11 raises similar questions about the nature and limits of the concept of legality at work in much of its security law after 2001. Terrorism offenses may contain important limits on their scope, but changes to the law of evidence allow the government to prosecute these offences with greater secrecy, or to limit accountability for its complicity in torture or other rights violations through significantly expanded forms of public interest privilege.[28] Though much of the information the government sought to redact from final reports of the Arar and Iacobucci inquiries noted above was ordered to be released, much of the evidence in both cases and significant portions of the final reports were still concealed from the public. The Supreme Court of Canada has also held that in extraordinary circumstances, the government may deport an immigration detainee despite a clear risk of torture in their state of origin—*without violating* the protection of "life, liberty, and security of the person" in the Charter of Rights and Freedoms.[29] The Court has also affirmed the constitutional validity of immigration law allowing for a prolonged detention without charge on secret evidence, despite the fact that the cause of the delay is a difficulty in carrying out the deportation.[30] Relying on these powers, Canada held five non-citizens suspected of involvement in terrorism without charge for periods ranging from two to seven years.

---

26 Anti-terrorism Act, S.C. 2001, ch. 41; Criminal Code, R.S.C. ch. C-46, §§83.3(2), (6) and (7) and §83.28.

27 The Arar and Iacobucci inquiries are discussed at greater length in Chapter 2.

28 *See* discussion in Chapter 2 of litigation involving Abousfian Abdelrazik.

29 Suresh v. Canada (Minister of Citizenship and Immigration), [2002] 1 S.C.R. 3, citing the Canadian Charter of Rights and Freedoms, Part I of the Constitution Act, 1982, being Schedule B to the Canada Act 1982 (U.K.), 1982, c. 11.

30 Charkaoui v. Canada (Citizenship and Immigration), 2007 SCC 9; Canada (Citizenship and Immigration) v. Harkat, 2014 SCC 37.

The prevailing response to these measures among law scholars in both Canada and the United States has been to frame them as facets of emergency government, or of moments of non- or extra-legality with debatable legitimacy.[31] A fascinating discussion centered upon the work of Italian philosopher Giorgio Agamben and the German legal theorist Carl Schmitt has sought to complicate the question of the legality of extreme measures by positing the indeterminate character of the state of emergency or exception on which they are premised. On this view, measures imposed pursuant to an exceptional instrument such as the AUMF are neither within nor beyond law, but blur the boundaries between law and sovereign power, or expose the irreducible indeterminacy of their borders.[32] This book argues, by contrast, that all such approaches that emphasize a non- or extra-legal aspect of the measures overlook one of the salient characteristics of a wide range of extraordinary counterterrorism law and policy after 9/11—from legislation authorizing targeted killing, to court decisions confirming the constitutionality of indefinite detention, to the torture memos: the prevalence of an insistence on legality.

By virtue of a common insistence on the part of government that various measures are legal, and a broad acceptance on the part of the public and the judiciary (with some qualifications), the measures can be understood collectively as marking a shift in the cultural currency of liberal legality to what can be called authoritarian legality—effecting a shift of a deeper, more pervasive character. This new concept of law can be understood in terms of its basic features, including a repudiation of absolute or "non-derogable" human rights (against torture or indefinite detention without charge); the expansion of seemingly unfettered state secrecy and surveillance; broad judicial deference to executive discretion; and a reluctance to remedy serious rights violations or to be held accountable for them.

In May 2013, President Obama gave a speech that signaled an intention to bring the war on terror to an end. But his vision for a postwar security policy offered evidence of how deeply rooted some of the hallmarks of authoritarian legality have become and how much longer they may remain. Obama said he would work with Congress to "refine and ultimately repeal" the AUMF, and the United States would eventually have to close Guantanamo. But it would continue to hold a number of high-value detainees without charge in supermax American prisons. The limits and rules around mass warrantless surveillance of phone and Internet data should be debated, and certain limits imposed, but the general practice would continue.[33] Targeted killing should be subject to greater accountability and perhaps some form of judicial oversight, but the power and practice

---

[31] *See*, e.g., Oren Gross, *Chaos and Rules: Should Responses to Violent Crises Always Be Constitutional?*, 112 Yale L. J. 1011 (2003) and Kent Roach, The 9/11 Effect: Comparative Counter-Terrorism (Cambridge: Cambridge University Press, 2011).

[32] Giorgio Agamben, State of Exception, Kevin Attell (trans.) (Chicago: University of Chicago Press, 2004); Carl Schmitt, Political Theology: Four Chapters on the Concept of Sovereignty, George Schwab (trans.), (Chicago: University of Chicago Press, 2005). Both works are discussed further in Chapter 2.

[33] Obama confirmed this intention in his speech of Jan. 17, 2014, *supra* note 12.

would persist. And there was no discussion of redress for victims of torture, rendition, or civilian casualties from drone strikes. Expanded state secrecy and limited oversight will therefore still function in ways that pose large obstacles to accountability.

Thus, without the harbinger theory and the war on terror as a justification, authoritarian measures become harder to rationalize—yet they remain entrenched, as Obama's vision demonstrates, on the assumption that they now form an essential part of a rational, contemporary legal order. In the wake of Obama's declaration of the imminent end of the war on terror, some have suggested that many of the measures (detention, surveillance) should also be brought to an end.[34] While the argument is plausible, meaningful reform seems unlikely until two things come to pass. First, the harbinger theory will need to be repudiated on a wider level, or rendered less plausible with time. The current administration has continued to invoke the harbinger theory as a defense of extraordinary measures. Other security officials and experts on the threat of terror in both Canada and the United States continue to do the same, and likely will for the foreseeable future. Second, the currency of an earlier liberal legality—a legal order that values non-derogable or core human rights, individual privacy, and limited government—must be restored.

This book will argue that the project of reform, the task of bringing an end to the permanent emergency, can be more effectively advanced if liberal jurists and rights activists were to focus not only on the validity of liberal ideals, but also on the invalidity of the harbinger theory and related arguments about security. For much of the period at issue, rather than seeking to challenge the harbinger theory, or the claim that terrorism had come to pose a much greater and imminent threat to national security, many if not most rights advocates, scholars, and jurists have been concerned primarily with questions of law and principle. In ways to be explored below, the prevailing approach to reform has not been to question common claims and assumptions about outstanding threats, but to show instead how new laws and policies are unconstitutional or in violation of core human rights. Liberal advocates have often, therefore, been silent, ambivalent, or deferential to claims about the nature of the threats that are said to justify more elaborate measures.

This is not say that rights advocates have never been skeptical or have not sought to cast doubt on inflated claims or fears about the threat of terror after 9/11. But reformers have tended to call the harbinger theory into question not by drawing on evidence of its implausibility but by suggesting that it reflects a form of psychological overreaction to the spectacle of 9/11.[35] Seldom have rights advocates or liberal jurists sought to critique the need for extraordinary measures by endeavoring to demonstrate in any detail why claims about the imminence of terror on the order of 9/11, or terror involving WMDs, are highly implausible.

---

[34] See, e.g., David Cole, *The End of the War on Terror?*, N.Y. Review of Books, Nov. 7, 2013.

[35] David Cole & Jules Lobel, Less Safe, Less Free: Why America is Losing the War on Terror (New York: The New Press, 2007), Ch. 8; Cass Sunstein, Worst Case Scenarios (Cambridge: Harvard University Press, 2009), Ch. 1; Oren Gross & Fionnuala Ni Aolain, Law in Times of Crisis: Emergency Powers in Theory and Practice (Cambridge: Cambridge University Press, 2006), at 103–09.

By exploring the specific claims that make up the harbinger theory, this book aims to provide liberal jurists and rights advocates with a clearer understanding of a set of common assumptions about terror and security that they might seek to challenge more directly. Thus they may be in a better position to effect a deeper shift in public opinion about the necessity and proportionality of invasive measures. The book will also demonstrate patterns in the recurring use of the harbinger theory that help to explain its foothold in a larger public conversation. Chief among these is the self-evident character with which aspects of the theory are frequently presented; including, as noted above, the oft-repeated claim that WMD terror is more likely because the weapons are "only becoming more accessible and diffuse" or that a 9/11-scale attack is likelier by virtue of the greater skill and ambition of today's terrorists—claims that are seldom supported by evidence or expert knowledge. The analysis set out here will demonstrate that greater measures are supported not in response to a general tendency to threat inflation, or vague fears of future terror attacks on a significant scale, but a specific set of claims and assumptions about the form that future attacks will take, coupled with a rhetorical approach to framing the theory that resists or discourages skeptical responses.

Finally, the book highlights a body of critical material that reform advocates can draw upon to make a potentially stronger case for reform. Reformers have thus far largely overlooked the possible usefulness of a large body of evidence and opinion as to why the likelihood of a large-scale attack involving WMDs at the hands of a non-state actor is, as one commentator has suggested, "vanishingly small," and why the threat posed more recently by offshoots of al Qaeda or by "lone wolf" terrorists employing conventional methods does not amount to a "significant threat" to Canadian or American national security as is often alleged. The book therefore proposes a different approach to advocating reform, one in which advocates are encouraged not simply to dismiss the harbinger theory as a form of psychological overreaction, or to demand evidence of its proof, but to actively refute the theory by demonstrating its implausibility.

Later portions of this book will model this form of argument by canvassing some of the ample evidence in support of the view that future attacks in North America are likely to be no more serious or frequent than earlier attacks (Oklahoma, Air India) that were effectively addressed through the criminal law and liberal legal principles. These arguments are important to make because authorities continue to rely on the harbinger theory in defense of extraordinary measures and assertions of the theory remain largely unanswered in public debate. This may be due in part to the fact that much of the skeptical opinion on certain forms of mass terror remains dispersed throughout the expert literature, waiting to be consolidated and made more accessible. At the least, by drawing upon this body of opinion, reformers could help a wider public call into question the seemingly self-evident nature of many of the claims and assertions made in support of the harbinger theory. A more informed public discussion about the nature of outstanding threats would be an important step in bringing an end to the seemingly endless post-9/11 emergency.

## An Overview of the Book

The inquiry begins with a chapter that surveys extraordinary measures in U.S. and Canadian counterterrorism law after 9/11, advancing the argument that, together, the measures can be seen as part of a deeper normative shift from a liberal to an authoritarian form of legality. Drawing on the work of Joseph Raz, Lon Fuller, and Ronald Dworkin,[36] Chapter 2 first defines liberal legality and explores how liberal values can be distinguished from legality as such. It then defines authoritarian legality in terms of its basic features. These include the repudiation of absolute or "non-derogable" human rights in practices such as torture, rendition, targeted killing, and indefinite detention without charge. It also entails the expansion and increased use of state secrecy and surveillance; judicial deference to executive discretion; and a reluctance to remedy serious rights violations, or to be held accountable for them. The remainder of the chapter provides examples of these elements in both U.S. and Canadian law.

The third and fourth chapters explore beliefs and assumptions about the threat of terror and their role in the defense of extreme measures in law and policy. Chapter 3 focuses on the role of the harbinger theory in political discourse and public opinion, looking first at how members of government, security officials, and other policymakers have relied, and continue to rely, on claims about mass terror in defense of extreme measures. It draws on statements by members of the executive and submissions to congressional or parliamentary committees, as well as policy statements, such as the bi-annual U.S. *National Security Strategy*, and Canadian equivalents. The chapter then traces manifestations of the harbinger theory in popular media and cites public opinion surveys in both nations to highlight the link between a widespread fear of mass terror and a high degree of public support for invasive counterterror measures.

Chapter 4 turns from the world of politics and public opinion to an examination of the harbinger theory in three fields of scholarship: expert opinion on the prospect of terror involving WMDs and cyberterror; the history of terrorism; and legal scholarship in support of authoritarian measures. The aim in exploring these fields in a single discussion is to show that experts on WMDs and historians of terror helped to legitimize a belief in the imminent prospect of mass terror, which in turn bolstered the credibility of its use by law scholars arguing in support of extreme measures.

Experts on the use of WMDs and historians of terror advance a common set of arguments for the imminent prospect of nuclear, biological, or radiological terror that it may help to identify before giving an overview of later portions of the book.[37] Briefly,

---

[36] Joseph Raz, THE AUTHORITY OF LAW, 2d ed (Oxford: Oxford University Press, 2009); Lon Fuller, THE MORALITY OF LAW (New Haven: Yale University Press, 1964); Ronald Dworkin, TAKING RIGHTS SERIOUSLY (Cambridge, MA: Harvard University Press, 1977).

[37] *See*, e.g., Laqueur, Bobbitt, Allison, Bunn, Ferguson and Potter, Kellman, Davis, and Barnaby, *supra* note 14.

the case for why nuclear terror is a real possibility in the near future often begins with the collapse of the Soviet Union and the proliferation of nuclear technology in recent decades. Both have given rise to a copious supply of what is often thought to be poorly guarded fissile material, or fully functional bombs. At some point soon, a terror group will either steal a bomb or obtain the material to build one. And since, in the view of some experts, the task of building a nuclear bomb is not thought to be onerous, stealing the necessary material overcomes the greatest hurdle. As for the task of building a bomb, plans are readily available in the public domain, and constructing a crude but reliable "gun-type" nuclear weapon would not involve much technical expertise. Finally, an act of nuclear terror has seemed likely for much of the post-9/11 period given the fact that al Qaeda and other groups were known to be seeking weapons of this nature.

Experts offer a similar set of arguments about bio-terror. A number of known toxins offer the most lethal potential weapons in existence. Many can be produced with limited knowledge or equipment, from natural or readily accessible sources. Samples can be easily dispersed—at least in theory—to cause mass casualties. Others have made analogous arguments in relation to radiological terror. Building and deploying a radiological or "dirty bomb" is relatively simple. Radioactive material is available in countless commercial and industrial settings. Constructing and using a dispersal device would not be too complicated. The weapon would likely cause fewer deaths than a nuclear or biological attack, but could easily cause large-scale disruption—for example, large portions of a major city becoming uninhabitable for decades.

A small but prominent group of jurists has drawn on these arguments to advance a credible and compelling case for a deeper preemptive turn in the law. John Yoo, Richard Posner, and Alan Dershowitz, among others, have invoked—with some frequency—images of nuclear explosions in Manhattan or Chicago, or aerosol dispersions of anthrax or radiological particles in large airports or subway stations, causing tens or hundreds of thousands of casualties. In light of the danger, each has made the case that one set of extraordinary measures or another has become necessary, including torture, targeted killing, or indefinite detention without charge. And while members of this group may represent a fringe element in the North American legal academy, each also enjoys a public profile that has helped contribute a measure of legitimacy to the case for extreme measures among a wider public.

Chapter 5 considers the work of liberal jurists and rights advocates in countering extraordinary measures. It begins by acknowledging that liberals have made a number of strong arguments in defense of rights. Key among them is the claim that there ought to be clearer proof that certain measures are necessary, proportionate, and effective—which is seldom seen, if ever. But while making these and other powerful arguments, liberals have also tended to be less inclined to challenge beliefs about the gravity of current threats, or the claim that they *compel* the state to adopt a more preemptive approach. To demonstrate this, the chapter briefly surveys different forms of rights advocacy, including reports by nongovernmental organizations (NGOs) such as the International Commission of

Jurists and the International Committee of the Red Cross, and work by David Cole and Jules Lobel, Mark Danner, Ronald Dworkin, Michael Ignatieff, and Bruce Ackerman.

The survey demonstrates that liberal advocates have tended to fall within two camps. One group tends to downplay or ignore claims about the growing threat that terrorism poses, and often also the claim that it warrants the use of extraordinary measures. The other group highlights or pays deference to either or both claims. Both groups therefore demonstrate a tendency on the part of rights advocates in the post-9/11 period to avoid unsettling a deeper set of beliefs essential to authoritarian legality: namely, that current threats are catastrophic in nature, and as a result, a deeper "preemptive turn" is in order, involving more invasive or possibly extreme measures of one kind or another.

Chapter 6 proposes an alternative approach to advocating reform and comprises three parts. The first part challenges the strong form of the harbinger theory by canvassing skeptical opinion on the likelihood of terror involving WMDs. It does not, however, attempt to set out the case against WMD terror conclusively. It seeks instead to *model* the form of argument that advocates for reform might advance to call claims about WMD terror into question. The model centers on technological and scientific evidence as to why nuclear and biological terror in particular are not likely to occur soon, if at all. This part highlights a contrary body of opinion to that explored in Chapter 4.

But rather than saving this analysis for the final portion of the book, given its importance to the skeptical position taken throughout much of what follows, it may help to summarize the argument against WMD terror here briefly. The case for the imminence of nuclear terror often rests, as noted, on a claim about the abundance of poorly guarded material; the simplicity of building and deploying a bomb; and al Qaeda's ambitions in this regard. In response, a body of skeptical experts, including Michael Levi,[38] Steven Younger,[39] and co-authors Christoph Wirz and Emmanuel Egger,[40] argue that in the various stages of acquiring or building, and then deploying a bomb, terrorists would face a host of significant challenges.[41] Together, they render the prospect of a nuclear attack far more complicated and improbable than is often assumed in both casual assertions and in the scholarship warning of the likelihood of WMD terror. First, both nuclear terror alarmists and skeptics agree that the production of fissile material is beyond the capacity of a non-state actor. Acquiring a fully functional nuclear bomb, by theft or other means, is unlikely because most are stored disassembled or with elaborate codes closely guarded by a small few. In the 70-year history of the bomb, no nuclear power has ever shared the

---

38 Michael Levi, On Nuclear Terrorism (Cambridge, MA: Harvard University Press, 2007).

39 Steven Younger, Endangered Species: How We Can Avoid Mass Destruction and Build a Lasting Peace (New York: Harper Perennial, 2008).

40 Christoph Wirz & Emmanuel Egger, *Use of Nuclear and Radiological Weapons by Terrorists?*, Int' Rev. Red Cross 87: 859, 497 (2005).

41 Other skeptical perspectives include the first report of the U.S. Congress' "Gilmore Commission" (Advisory Panel to Assess Domestic Response Capabilities for Terrorism Involving Weapons of Mass Destruction), *First Annual Report: Assessing the Threat*, Dec. 15, 1999 ["Gilmore Commission Report"], *available at*

technology with another state, let alone a non-state actor. And while there may be an abundance of fissile material, very little of it has been stolen. The danger posed by the occasional report of stolen fissile material, or a black market, is implausible for a host of reasons that range from better detection of radiological materials in transit to much increased security and surveillance around existing installations, and a high rate of success in arresting or tracking down such material in short order.

Yet, even if fissile material of a sufficient quantity could be obtained—a large hurdle in itself—non-state actors would confront several more challenges at the bomb-building stage. These include the task of shaping the material to be used in a bomb device and crafting the weapon itself. Creating a nuclear explosion involves not just the slamming together of two pieces of highly enriched uranium, as some have suggested, but slamming together two pieces of an appropriate size and shape, at the right speed.[42] The material would be highly challenging to shape or mold, requiring special expertise, equipment, and time. The tasks of crafting and transporting the bomb (and testing, if the group chose to do so) would furnish further opportunities for detection, accidents, or failure. Given all of these hurdles, concerns about the imminence of an act of nuclear terror on the part of al Qaeda, or one of its offshoots, seem largely overstated.

A number of experts have also advanced a skeptical view of the likelihood of large-scale biological terror, including William Clark,[43] Milton Leitenberg,[44] and Andreas Wenger.[45] They concede that certain biotoxins may be quite lethal, produced from natural materials, and widely dispersed to cause mass casualties. Yet, at each stage, the practical challenges are extensive—with no group ever succeeding in causing significant casualties, despite considerable effort in some cases, including and perhaps most notably the Japanese Aum Shinrikyo cult in the mid-1990s. A highly dangerous bio-toxin can indeed be produced from natural sources, or illicitly obtained from an industrial lab or other source. But the problem of cultivating it into sufficiently large quantities, and then stabilizing it, has proven exceedingly challenging to experts and military personnel in nations with the largest and most advanced militaries, including the United States and Russia.

If these hurdles can be surmounted, the act of dispersing the material in an effective manner presents a greater challenge still. The packaging, storage, and dissemination of a

---

www.rand.org/nsrd/terrpanel; and some of the contributions to Paul Leventhal & Yonah Alexander, eds, Preventing Nuclear Terrorism: the Report and Papers of the International Task Force on Prevention of Nuclear Terrorism (New York: Lexington Books, 1987), including J. Carson Mark, Theodore Taylor, Eugene Eyster, William Maraman, and Jacob Wechsler, *Can Terrorists Build Nuclear Weapons?*

42 Levi, On Nuclear Terrorism, *supra* note 38, at 36–42.

43 William Clark, Bracing for Armageddon: the Science and Politics of Bioterrorism in America (Oxford: Oxford UP, 2008).

44 Milton Leitenberg, *Evolution of the Current Threat*, in Andreas Wenger & Reto Wollenmann, eds., Bioterrorism: Confronting a Complex Threat (Boulder, CO: Lynne Rienner Publishers, 2007).

45 *Securing Society Against the Risk of Bioterrorism*, in Wenger & Wollenmann, ibid. See also the contributions to the same collection by Peter Lavoy and Marie Isabell Chevrier.

bioweapon would require considerable expertise in a range of fields, special equipment, and sufficient personnel and space in which to work. All of this would increase the prospect of detection, logistical error, or illness and death on the part of the participants. It would also entail a high likelihood of the material destabilizing or spoiling, or resulting in a much less lethal attack than planned. The Aum Shinrikyo group encountered all of these pitfalls, in ways that are instructive, including the key fact that the group did not succeed in producing a deadly strain of anthrax or any other bio-toxin. The sole example of a non-state actor's effective use of a deadly bio-toxin *in world history* was the 2001 congressional incident involving anthrax in letters addressed to Senators Tom Daschle and Patrick Leahy, which caused a total of five casualties.[46] An extensive FBI investigation concluded in 2010 that the likely source of the sample in this case was a senior bioweapons researcher in the U.S. military.[47]

Experts taking a critical view of radiological terror concede that it poses fewer hurdles than either nuclear or biological terror. Thus it may be more likely to happen. Yet, upon closer inspection, a wide gap exists here too between theory and practice. More specifically, there are varying degrees of probability involved in accomplishing varying degrees of destruction. In theory, large samples of radioactive material can be easily obtained from universities, hospitals, or other industrial sites. These can be used in a bomb that might not kill many people, but could render a good portion of Manhattan or Toronto uninhabitable for decades. But significant hurdles would be faced at two stages. Building a bomb, or an effective dispersal device, would require substantial expertise, equipment, and time—along with an adequate amount of material, and material of an appropriate kind for use in the chosen device.[48] Nuclear physicists Wirz and Egger contend that most of the material available in common industrial sources would be insufficient to cause extensive damage or disruption, due to the fact that they are found in metallic form and are thus not likely to be effectively dispersed by an explosive device.[49] In any case, the magnitude of the damage one might cause using a bomb or other dispersal method would still depend on a range of variables. In addition to the quantity and nature of the material used, much would depend on the quality of the device itself, meteorological conditions, and the speed of the natural decay of the material once dispersed. In theory, a simple bomb could cause mass disruption. In practice, several factors make it more likely that far less damage would be caused than is often feared.

The model for reform advocacy set out in the first part of Chapter 6 is thus meant to show how liberal jurists might have employed (and might still employ) a technologically

---

46 Leitenberg, *supra* note 44, at 65.

47 U.S. Dep't of Justice, *Amerithrax Investigative Summary*. Feb. 19 2010, *available at*, http://www.justice.gov/opa/pr/justice-department-and-fbi-announce-formal-conclusion-investigation-2001-anthrax-attacks.

48 Michael Levi & Henry Kelly, *Weapons of Mass Disruption*, SCIENTIFIC AMERICAN 77 (November 2002), 78; Peter Zimmerman & Cheryl Loeb, *Dirty Bombs: the Threat Revisited*, 1 DEF. HORIZONS 5 (January 2004) 5; Christoph Wirz & Emmanuel Egger, *supra* note 40, at 505–06.

49 Wirz & Egger, *supra* note 40, at 503.

informed skepticism about WMDs to challenge claims about the imminent threat they have often been said to pose. It also shows how a broader critical approach may be useful in debates about law and policy relating to what are believed to be new and unprecedented dangers brought about by the potential uses of new technologies.

The second part of Chapter 6 challenges a belief in the likelihood of large-scale terror not involving WMDs. It canvasses evidence to suggest that future acts of terror are likely to be no more frequent or greater in scale than events prior to 2001. This part draws primarily on the work of John Mueller and Mark Stewart, who have sought to assess the merits of U.S. security expenditures in light of the risk posed, over much of the post-9/11 period, by the core al Qaeda group (in Afghanistan and Pakistan) and more recently by its offshoots and "lone wolf" imitators.[50]

Writing in 2011, Muller and Stewart noted that in the decade following 9/11, the core al Qaeda group had not carried out a single attack in Canada or the United States.[51] No al Qaeda cell has since been discovered in either country.[52] And apart from seven Americans who were briefly persuaded to travel to a training camp in Afghanistan in the summer of 2001 (shortly after which six of them returned disillusioned), al Qaeda has failed to recruit anyone in either nation.[53] The few known cases in which Westerners have sought links with the group resulted in what can best be described as a limited threat. For example, U.S. citizen Najibullah Zazi, the would-be New York subway bomber (2008), and London-educated Umar Abdulmutallab, the underwear bomber (2009), were both involved in foiled plots that were much smaller in scale than 9/11 and much less skillfully attempted.[54]

Mueller and Stewart have also argued that what remains of the group is likely "a few dozen individuals," joined by "perhaps a hundred fighters left over from al-Qaida's golden days in Afghanistan in the 1990s." They note that every terror attack linked to al Qaida since 2001 appears to have been carried out by a group only tenuously connected to the core group in the Afghanistan–Pakistan region. Much of the focus of concern about international terrorism has thus shifted to what are described as offshoots of al Qaida elsewhere in Asia and Africa. Yet, as Mueller and Stewart contend, attacks from Morocco to Bali to Jordan exhibit a similar tendency to involve groups whose primary grievance is with regional governments and events.[55]

---

[50] John Mueller & Mark Stewart, TERROR, SECURITY, MONEY: BALANCING THE RISKS, BENEFITS, AND COSTS OF HOMELAND SECURITY (Oxford: Oxford University Press, 2011); *Civil Liberties, Fear, and Terrorism*, NOTRE DAME J. INT'L & COMP. LAW 2:2 (2012) 282; and *The Terrorism Delusion: America's Overwrought Response to September 11*, INT'L SECURITY 37:1, 81 (2012).

[51] Ibid., *Civil Liberties, Fear, and Terrorism*, at 285.

[52] Ibid.; *see also* Brian Ross, *Secret FBI Report Questions Al Qaeda Capabilities*, ABC NEWS ONLINE, Mar. 9, 2005 (cited in Mueller and Stewart).

[53] Mueller & Stewart, *The Terrorism Delusion, supra* note 50, at 93.

[54] John Mueller, ed., TERRORISM SINCE 9/11: THE AMERICAN CASES (Columbus, OH: Mershon Centre for International Security Studies, 2012): http://polisci.osu.edu/faculty/jmueller/since.html, at 19.

[55] Mueller & Stewart, TERROR, SECURITY AND MONEY, *supra* note 50, at Kindle edition, location 617.

Mueller and Stewart also observe that what remains of international terrorism has dwindled to "thousands of sympathizers and would-be jihadists spread around the globe who mainly connect in Internet chat rooms, engage in radicalizing conversations, and variously dare each other to actually do something."[56] Future attacks in North America are therefore likely to involve, as Brian Jenkins has put it, "tiny conspiracies, lone gunman, one-off attacks rather than sustained terrorist campaigns."[57]

The Boston bombing in April of 2013 is consistent with this analysis. It caused an enormous amount of fear and terror. But notably, it was carried out by a group of individuals not affiliated with a larger international organization. It involved the use of conventional explosives, and caused three deaths and 230 injuries—certainly a significant number, but closer in magnitude to attacks prior to 9/11. The act was also not prevented through the use of post-9/11 extraordinary measures, including mass secret surveillance.

In recent years, a number of commentators have also posited the use of cyberterror as a new means by which mass casualties might be carried out. Defense Secretary Leon Panetta warned in 2012 of the prospect of a "Cyber Pearl Harbor" in which terrorists might soon use computers to "gain control of critical switches" to "derail passenger trains" or "contaminate the water supply in major cities."[58] In light of these fears, Panetta and others have called for increased—though not necessarily extraordinary—measures around sensitive networks. Yet as Chapter 5 notes, a number of experts have questioned whether cyberterror scenarios leading to mass casualties are remotely plausible, given a host of potential impediments. These include the complex and diverse body of knowledge and expertise needed to create certain effects in a given setting once one "gains control of critical switches," such as how to control a nuclear reactor, a water supply facility, or a train system; and the limited computer skills most terror suspects have displayed relative to what would be entailed in such elaborate scenarios.

The third part of the chapter argues that in the absence of the harbinger theory, and in light of evidence that future acts of terror in North America are likely to be no more serious or frequent than events prior to 9/11, the case for authoritarian measures becomes more difficult to sustain. Yet advocates for reform might still face an obstacle among a wider public in a further form of reasoning not grounded on the harbinger theory. Authoritarian measures might still be justified on the basis that terrorism represents a special threat to public order. It may do so, for some, on the basis that even where casualties or injuries in a given attack are relatively low compared to 9/11, they will still seem striking, horrible, or tragic in a way that no other criminal activity would. The special emotive charge of terrorism, on this view, justifies a perception of acts of terror—such

56 Ibid., at location 698.

57 Brian Jenkins, Would-be Warriors: Incidents of Jihadist Terrorist Radicalization in the United States Since September 11, 2001 (Santa Monica, CA: Rand, 2010), at 4 (cited by Mueller & Stewart, *supra* note 50, at location 768).

58 Elisabeth Bumiller & Thom Shanker, *Panetta Warns of Dire Threat of Cyberattack on US*, N.Y. Times, Oct. 11, 2012.

as the Boston bombing or the bombing of a plane killing 200 to 300 passengers—as something greater than crime but less than war. On this reasoning, we might feel justified in having a lower tolerance for terrorism and curtailing certain liberties in an effort to address the special risk that we perceive it to pose.

The chapter offers two responses to this line of reasoning. One is to argue that we should resist lowering our tolerance of terrorism because the risk it presents is comparable to risks we readily accept in other facets of modern life. As Mueller and Stewart have suggested, a variety of assessments on hazardous risks indicates a consensus as to acceptable or manageable degrees of risk. Using these assessments, Mueller and Stewart have observed that the risk of terrorism is comparable to the threat posed by many other hazards of modern life—calling into question the basis for perceiving terrorism as a special form of risk.

The second argument against terrorism as a special risk—whatever its scale—is that terrorism is essentially criminal in nature and does not pose a much greater harm to the public than the threat posed by other forms of grave or egregious criminal conduct. This can be demonstrated by considering the impact that terrorism might have compared to a range of offenses such as serial murder, large-scale financial fraud, or cybercrime. As a consequence of both arguments, the chapter concludes that terrorism should be addressed as a form of crime rather than as war or a hybrid of the two. Conventional protections of the criminal law should apply in terrorism cases, and the focus of preventive efforts should shift to the regulation of sensitive sites and materials.[59]

The goal, then, for those who wish to see an end to the permanent emergency is to persuade a wider public that ample evidence supports the view that terrorism on the scale of 9/11, while still possible, is not inevitable, imminent, or likely to occur in the near future. Moreover, events on the scale of the Boston bombing or even another Air India ought to be understood primarily as a form of crime as opposed to war. To accomplish this goal, rights advocates might attempt to challenge common assumptions about current threats more directly. Thus far, much of the advocacy in favor of reforming security law has focused on larger liberal or constitutional principles and a call for clearer proof of the necessity and proportionality of invasive measures. By contrast, a more effective case might be made by attempting to demonstrate why the measures are *not* necessary.

The conclusion addresses three potential counter-arguments. One is that a mass terror attack may still be imminent, because it can be accomplished through simple technological methods (Molotov cocktails in the crowded subway, suicide bombers in a large, busy urban space). Or it might occur through several smaller attacks carried out simultaneously. The chapter concedes that many conventional methods of terror might be more readily employed than a weapon of mass destruction, and many are capable of inflicting large-scale harm or damage. But it argues that a technically informed skepticism is still

---

[59] I follow Kent Roach in this suggestion, SEPTEMBER 11: CONSEQUENCES FOR CANADA (Montreal: McGill-Queens University Press, 2003).

also helpful in this context. Upon closer inspection, a host of obstacles and technical issues make it more likely that the real extent of the damage in many of these scenarios would be limited. For this reason, these and other low-tech possibilities do not alter the assessment set out in Chapter 6 that mass terror—on the order of 9/11 or greater—is highly improbable.

The conclusion also considers two important alternative accounts of the cultural conditions for post-9/11 security policy. Instead of foregrounding the fear of mass terror as key, scholars in political theory, critical race theory, and postcolonialism, including Sherene Razack and Judith Butler, have pointed to larger social and historical forces.[60] For example, Razack argues that extreme measures became possible due in large part to an underlying racism, xenophobia, or fear of a Muslim, Arab, or foreign other. Analogously, for contemporary criminologists such as David Garland, Lucia Zedner, and Jonathan Simon, the measures were not only a response to fears about current threats, but also part of an older shift toward a "culture of control," a "pre-crime society," or a pattern of "governing through crime."[61] Lawmakers since at least the 1970s have engaged deeper fears about violence to impose greater forms of control, surveillance, and racial or class exclusion. The trend has also proven remarkably unreceptive to evidence-based reasoning, claims about equity, or appeals to liberal standards on appropriate limits as to the state's use of force.

These and other alternate explanations for the embrace of authoritarian measures after 9/11 offer important insights. They also point to large obstacles to reform. It is likely true, for example, that racist, imperialist, and xenophobic attitudes render much of the North American electorate unsympathetic or indifferent to the mostly Muslim or Arab subjects of extreme measures—and thus unlikely to mobilize in support of reform. It is also true that the thrust of criminal law reform in recent decades has clearly favored victims' rights over those of the accused. Thus, restoring fairness or due process for terror suspects in the current political climate is certainly a daunting challenge.

Yet it remains important to distinguish these various accounts of the larger shift toward more security from what might be called the official account. In ways to be explored throughout this book, the single recurring thread in the public and juridical defense of authoritarian measures—from the executive to lawmakers, judges, and security officials—is that the catastrophic nature of the threat that terrorism poses has made these measures necessary. The measures may therefore be part of a larger and older movement toward a culture of control. But they are not *justified* in this light. They may reflect racist or imperialist attitudes and beliefs. But they are not *defended* in this light. On the contrary, the argument to justify and defend the measures is consistent and specific. Therefore, while the argument in favour of the measures may be informed on some level

---

60 *Supra* note 16.

61 *Supra* note 6.

by other beliefs and assumptions, the single recurring form of the official argument serves as a compelling focal point for a direct response—which has not been forthcoming. This book will contend that by addressing the harbinger theory more explicitly and directly, liberal advocates would offer a more persuasive case in defense of rights going forward.

Finally, the book offers a sketch of recommended reforms and suggestions for how the approach to advocacy set out here might be applied in practical situations. It calls for a return to a more faithful adherence to absolute or non-derogable human rights—against extra-judicial killing, torture, and cruel or inhumane treatment. It recommends a stricter threshold for granting state privilege and greater limits to lawful surveillance. Finally, it calls for domestic law compensating victims of torture and other serious violations for state complicity in their injuries.

Advocates for reform can make the case against the harbinger theory in a number of places where key decisions are made about law and policy. One is in the course of submissions to parliamentary or congressional committees tasked with assessing new measures and their necessity in relation to perceived threats. Another is in constitutional litigation, when questions are raised about reaching a reasonable balance between rights to due process and public safety. A further place is in the work of NGOs, scholars, and activists, who might collectively make more frequent and effective use of expertise and evidence on current threats in the course of scholarship and public advocacy.

Both Canada and the United States continue to insist upon the validity of the measures based in large part on the gravity of current threats. Meaningful reform will therefore depend at least in part on the ability to unsettle this line of reasoning, which presents an opportunity for rights advocates, and a measure of hope for those committed to the future of constitutionalism and human rights.

# 2

## The Embrace of Authoritarian Legality

IN THE POST-9/11 period, few topics have garnered more attention among scholars and journalists in the fields of law and politics than national security. The thrust of the vast majority of the legal literature in this area is to point out the many ways in which security measures have marked a break from the principles of liberal legality, or a commitment to upholding constitutionalism, human rights, and the rule of law. In contrast to this approach, this chapter will argue that, taken together, by virtue of a common acceptance of their legality, many of the measures at issue are better understood as part of a deeper shift in the cultural currency of a liberal form of legality to what might be called authoritarian legality. The argument here is concerned, therefore, not with a break from legality as such but with a deeper shift in shared ideas of what *could* be lawful.

Later chapters will argue that this shift was made possible in large part by the prevalence of two beliefs: first, that 9/11 was the harbinger of a new order of terror, one in which North Americans now faced the imminent threat of an attack on the same scale as 9/11, or much greater, possibly involving WMDs but certainly posing an unprecedented danger to society or the state; and second, the need to embrace a new, more pre-emptive and extreme set of measures to avert this.

The chapter begins with a brief discussion of liberal legalism and its constituent principles. It then examines the emergence of authoritarian legality in U.S. and Canadian counterterrorism law and policy in terms of its four basic features: (i) the suspension of absolute or non-derogable rights; (ii) the legislative entrenchment of greater powers of secrecy and surveillance; (iii) judicial deference to the executive; and (iv) the state's reluctance to remedy past violations of core human rights.

The intent here is to highlight the way that governments have fashioned these laws and policies, and courts have accepted their necessity, as part of a single shift in outlook—one in which older assumptions about the appropriate limits on the state's use of force no longer seem valid. As this and later chapters will argue, the measures did not simply mark a temporary departure from a widely accepted set of liberal principles, but the embrace of a new concept of legality that has allowed for a deeper legal entrenchment of extraordinary measures. And as later chapters will further argue, understanding this process is an important step in advancing the goal of reform.

## Part 1. Defining Liberal Legalism

While there is no single, canonical definition of "liberal legalism" in legal scholarship, the phrase is often used to refer to procedures and principles that give legal expression to political and economic aspirations of liberalism.[1] It is used here in a broader sense to describe an approach to law that reflects a commitment to core philosophical as well as political precepts of Enlightenment liberalism; namely, the notion that each individual is to be treated humanely and with equal value in law, on the basis of the inherent dignity and equal value to be accorded to each human life. A liberal *legal* order seeks to foster these values by preserving the individual's liberty to pursue self-defined goals of the good life, so long as they do not infringe unreasonably upon the freedom of others. It also seeks to protect a sphere of individual dignity by respecting a person's privacy and asserting limits on inhumane treatment or punishment. It assumes that all persons, citizens and foreigners alike, are equally entitled to due process or "natural justice" when deciding questions that concern their core freedoms—so that truth rather than prejudice may form a basis for state action. Liberal legalism is therefore embodied in a commitment to democratic government, constitutionalism, human rights, and the rule of law—or, more fundamentally, the principle that government should not be arbitrary.

These commitments had become so central to modern conceptions of law that some had questioned whether legality itself could be conceived apart from them. The question became especially compelling for legal theorists in the wake of Nazi Germany and other modern fascist or totalitarian regimes. This gave rise to a debate about the nature of legality that preoccupied many seminal legal thinkers in the second half of the twentieth century. Aspects of this debate are worth canvassing briefly to lend a clearer sense of the

1 *See, e.g.*, Sanford Levinson, *Escaping Liberalism: Easier Said Than Done*, 96:6 HARV. L. REV. 1466 (1983); *see also* Robert Gordon's *Some Critical Theories of Law and Their Critics*, in David Kairys, ed. THE POLITICS OF LAW: A PROGRESSIVE CRITIQUE (New York: Basic Books, 1982). Reviewing this collection, Levinson, ibid., links liberal legalism to liberal individualism, the distinctions between the private and public sphere, and the notion of the rule of law as "a means for resolving the inevitable conflicts among the atomistic individuals who inhabit liberal society" (1467).

difference between legality and liberalism, and how liberal beliefs might inform a legal framework—or be notable by their absence.

For legal positivists, the rule of law, or legality as such, is indispensable to the notion of a liberal legal order, but is conceptually distinct from it. Joseph Raz, for example, conceives of the rule of law as a "neutral" instrument, the essential features of which are equally amenable to a totalitarian state as they are to a liberal state. He asserts:

> ... the rule of law is just one of the virtues a legal system may possess and by which it is to be judged. It is not to be confused with democracy, justice, equality (before the law or otherwise), human rights of any kind or respect for persons or for the dignity of man. A non-democratic legal system, based on the denial of human rights, on extensive poverty, on racial segregation, sexual inequalities, and religious persecution may, in principle, conform to the requirements of the rule of law better than any of the legal systems of the more enlightened Western democracies. It will be an immeasurably worse legal system, but it will excel in one respect: in its conformity to the rule of law.[2]

For Raz, then, the rule of law entails only two propositions: (a) "that people should be ruled by the law and obey it" and (b) "that the law should be such that people will be able to be guided by it."[3] It is thus distinct from the constellation of liberal ideas and principles we have come to associate with it, yet its value to us consists in its promotion and support of them.[4]

By contrast to Raz and other positivists, another tradition has come to view the essential hallmarks of legality as inextricable from liberal ideals. Key figures in this tradition include the Victorian constitutional scholar A. V. Dicey and American legal theorists Lon Fuller and Ronald Dworkin. In Dicey's work, the rule of law is defined by three basic assumptions that reflect a kind of liberal rationalism: (i) that discretion is the antithesis of law; (ii) that law should strive to protect individual rights through their application to all persons; and (iii) that disputes are to be resolved by courts rather than officials or councils exercising unreviewable administrative discretion.[5] For Dicey, the function of the rule of law as a guarantor of stability and order is one facet of a larger project of creating a liberal state regime, based on a notion of liberal citizenship. With no one person standing above the law, and authority never being exercised beyond the law, it becomes possible to protect a sphere of individual liberty from arbitrary state power and to govern the collective order through a set of laws democratically created and impartially enforced.

---

[2] Joseph Raz, The Authority of Law, 2d ed (Oxford: Oxford University Press, 2009), at 211. *See also* H. L. A. Hart, The Concept of Law (Oxford: Clarendon Press, 1965).

[3] Raz, ibid. at 213.

[4] Ibid. at 221.

[5] A. V. Dicey, Introduction to the Study of the Law of the Constitution (London: MacMillan and Co, 1889). *See also* H. W. Arthurs, *Rethinking Administrative Law: A Slightly Dicey Business*, 17 Osgoode Hall L.J. 1 (1979), at 22.

Writing in the wake of the Second World War, Lon Fuller sought to demonstrate the close connection of legality to liberal values by posing a question that took on a particular resonance after the Holocaust. What basic qualities must a legal system possess in order to be considered legitimate and just to contemporary observers?[6] Such a system would, in his view, abhor the practice of arbitrary rule, vested in a single, unaccountable individual or group that issued secret orders and applied the law selectively or retroactively. And it would also require instead that laws be, at the least, publicized, clear, coherent, general in nature, and non-retroactive.[7] Although he spoke of these as amounting to a distinct "morality of law," it is clear that the larger morality that law is meant to serve is liberal in nature. A system of secret, partial, or arbitrary law, as found in authoritarian or totalitarian states, would appear illegitimate to contemporary Western sensibilities due in part to its inconsistency with a larger liberal morality that values individual liberty and equality.

The link between liberal values and the notion of legality becomes more explicit in the work of Ronald Dworkin. In *Taking Rights Seriously*,[8] Dworkin asserts that in contemporary Western legal systems, "no ultimate distinction can be made between legal and moral standards, as positivism insists."[9] On the contrary, for Dworkin, we can neither create nor enforce law without reference to moral standards. Indeed, the very notion of constitutionalism "rests on a particular moral theory, namely that men have moral rights against the state." This is captured in "[t]he difficult clauses of the Bill of Rights, like the due process and equal protection clauses, [which] must be understood as appealing to moral concepts rather than laying down particular conceptions."[10] At the heart of this morality are concepts of freedom and equality deeply rooted in the liberal Enlightenment:

> Government must treat those whom it governs with concern, that is, as human beings who are capable of suffering and frustration, and with respect, that is, as human beings who are capable of forming and acting on intelligent conceptions of how their lives should be lived. Government must not only treat people with concern and respect, but with equal concern and respect.[11]

More recently, Dworkin has extended this logic to a theory of the nature and purpose of human rights. Such rights are, in his view, vehicles for preserving "two dimensions of human dignity."[12] Each human life has "intrinsic value" by virtue of its "potentiality," and

---

6 Lon Fuller, The Morality of Law (New Haven, CT: Yale University Press, 1964).

7 Ibid., ch. 2.

8 Ronald Dworkin, Taking Rights Seriously (Cambridge, MA: Harvard University Press, 1977).

9 Ibid. at 47.

10 Ibid. at 147.

11 Ibid. at 272–73.

12 Ronald Dworkin, Is Democracy Possible Here? Principles for a New Political Debate (Princeton, NJ: Princeton University Press, 2006), at 9.

each holds "personal responsibility" for "realizing the success of his or her own life."[13] We seek to uphold human rights on the assumption that to treat a person contrary to these principles is to offend their human dignity.

Thus, although recent legal theorists could not agree on whether legality can be distinguished in a meaningful sense from liberal values, a number of them could generally agree on the *content* of liberal legalism. The Canadian law scholar W. Wesley Pue has sought to distill these principles in a way that captures the broader scope of liberal legality:

a. All law should seek to attain minimal infringement of civil liberty.
b. There should be maximum clarity of definition regarding powers conferred, restrictions imposed, and offences created.
c. All exercise of governmental power should be accountable, visible, and reviewable by the ordinary courts in the ordinary ways. The *core* constitutional principle of responsible government requires clear and effective channels of political and legal accountability.
d. Secrecy should only be tolerated in the smallest possible zone, only as absolutely essential, and only for limited duration. Power exercised in secret is never accountable.
e. Where extraordinary powers are invoked in times of perceived crisis, they should be of limited duration, renewable only by full reconsideration and re-enactment by Parliament.[14]

To Pue's list, one might add two further propositions that are not essential to legality as such, but are commonly embraced in a liberal legal framework.

One is the notion of absolute limits on the state's use of force against an individual, or what are called "non-derogable" rights. As Jeremy Waldron, David Luban, and others have argued, the absolute prohibition on torture, cruel or degrading treatment is not simply an important facet of liberal legalism but almost its very essence—a kind of archetype for legality itself.[15] As Waldron writes, "in the heritage of Anglo-American law, there is a long tradition of rejecting torture and regarding it as alien to our jurisprudence.... Actually, a case can be made that torture is now to be regarded as alien to *any* system of law."[16] The prohibition on torture is recognized in a series of human rights instruments,

---

[13] Ibid.

[14] W. Wesley Pue, *The War on Terror: Constitutional Governance in a State of Permanent Warfare*, 41 OSGOODE HALL L.J. 267 (2003), at 270.

[15] Jeremy Waldron, *Torture and Positive Law: Jurisprudence for the White House*, 105 COLUM. L. REV. 1681(2005), at 1687: "the rule against torture operates in our law as an archetype—that is, as a rule which has significance not just in and of itself, but also as the embodiment of a pervasive principle." *See also* David Luban, *Liberalism, Torture, and the Ticking Bomb*, 91 VA. L. REV. 1425 (2005); Ronald Dworkin, IS DEMOCRACY POSSIBLE HERE?, *supra* note 12, ch. 2; and Tamar Meisels, *Torture and the Problem of Dirty Hands*, XXI:1 Can. J.L. & Jur. 149 (2008).

[16] Waldron, ibid. at 1719.

including the United Nations' Universal Declaration of Human Rights and the Geneva Conventions. The 1984 U.N. Convention Against Torture is categorical in its prohibition, stating that "[n]o exceptional circumstances whatsoever, whether a state of war or a threat or war, internal political instability or any other public emergency, may be invoked as a justification of torture."[17] Both Canada and the United States are signatories to the convention; yet the prohibition is also arguably implied in the U.S. Constitution and the Canadian Charter of Rights and Freedoms.[18]

A further aspect of liberal legality relates to the role of individuals in violent acts. Liberal jurists tend to assume that any violent act carried out by an individual or group of non-state actors in their capacity as such is best understood in terms of the criminal law rather than the law of war.[19] They also assume that even if actions by non-state actors are believed to amount to a threat of war, human rights and other international humanitarian laws still apply.[20] In short, neither framework—crime or war—entails a space beyond law, with the law at issue always conceived in liberal terms. Yet, it is precisely the lack of a middle ground, a concept other than crime or war, which serves as an opening for an authoritarian form of legality.

## Part 2. Defining Authoritarian Legalism

### I. QUALIFICATIONS AND ANTECEDENTS

To trace the basic contours of an emerging authoritarian legality, the focus in the remainder of the chapter will shift to laws and policies that have been extensively explored in earlier literature. But distinct from a common approach in those earlier studies, the intention here is not to show how some of the more salient measures mark a break with liberal legality, but to show instead how they contribute to a new conceptual formation. The analysis is thus premised on the Razian assumption that legality can be distinguished from liberal values. The intention here is to demonstrate that a pervasive assertion and acceptance of the legality of extraordinary measures is best understood as part of a wider shift in conceptions of legality itself.

However, before moving on to explore defining characteristics of this concept, it may be useful to first distinguish the concept from aspects of U.S. security law to which it may be reduced, and from earlier theoretical approaches to questions of security and legality.

---

17 United Nations Convention against Torture and Other Cruel, Inhuman or Degrading Treatment or Punishment, art. 2(2), 1465 U.N.T.S. 85 (entered into force 26 June 1987).

18 Canadian Charter of Rights and Freedoms, Constitution Act, pt. 1, Sched. B to the Canada Act 1982 (U.K.), 1982, ch. 11 (the Charter).

19 *See*, e.g., David Luban, *The War on Terrorism and the End of Human Rights*, 22 Philosophy & Pub. Pol'y Q 3, 9 (2002).

20 *See*, e.g., works by Ronald Dworkin, Jeremy Waldron, and David Cole & Jules Lobel explored in Chapter 5.

To begin with one obvious point of possible confusion, authoritarian legalism is not tantamount to an expanded concept of presidential powers or executive discretion. While these may contribute to it, it remains conceptually distinct and viable without them. Nor does the concept rely on the belief that the threat of terror after 9/11 amounts to a war rather than a crime, or, as John Yoo and others have argued (Chapter 4), that many of the controversial measures employed by Presidents Bush and Obama are incidental to their powers as commander in chief in time of war. These are further important facets of authoritarian legality, but not synonymous with it.

Authoritarian legality arises in the U.S. context in part as a result of the belief that the nation is at war and that the "enemy combatants" in this conflict are entitled to neither the full protections of the laws of war nor many of the basic privileges afforded by due process or natural justice.[21] But a more crucial assumption, current in both Canada and the United States, is that the nature of the threat that terrorism has come to pose after 9/11 is sufficiently grave that it makes the use of extraordinary measures both necessary and proportionate.

The various measures contribute to a form of *legality* precisely to the extent that officials, jurists, and commentators conceive of them as lawful. Scholars may therefore continue to debate their lawful character within a liberal legal framework, but approached in strictly positivist terms, the measures acquire a form of legality by a number of indicia. In ways to be explored below, many of the measures are entrenched in legislation. Many have been constitutionally challenged but upheld by supreme courts. Others assume the form of court decisions condoning significant departures from constitutional or human rights principles. And finally, other measures bear a kind of official legality by virtue of the executive's continuous insistence to this effect and the acquiescence of a sizeable portion of the electorate.[22] An authoritarian form of legality can therefore be seen to have emerged gradually, then, through law, jurisprudence, executive policy and practice, and a wider public or cultural acceptance.

The concept is also distinct from earlier theoretical approaches to post-9/11 security. A number of commentators have gestured in the direction of authoritarian legalism by referring to a deeper conceptual shift in thinking about law and security after 9/11 in

---

21 Gabriella Blum & Philip Heymann, Laws, Outlaws, and Terrorists: Lessons from the War on Terrorism (Boston: MIT Press, 2010), at 3.

22 Drawing on the work of Stephen Griffin, Tracey Lightcap argues that "actions by the executive in the United States can attain legal status in several ways. In the past, legal change has been straightforward; legislation is passed or the constitution revised. But this is not the only way legality can be established, especially in recent times. Actions taken by presidents exercising their executive discretion can also be informally legalized by becoming routine actions that are neither forbidden by specific legislation nor declared out of constitutional bounds by the courts." Tracey Lightcap, *Review of Kent Roach's* The 9/11 Effect: Comparative Counter-terrorism, 22 Law & Pol. Book Rev, 129, 132 (2012). *See also* Stephen M. Griffin, *Constitutional Change in the United States*, in Dawn Oliver & Carlos Fusaro, eds., How Constitutions Change: A Comparative Study (Oxford: Hart Publishing, 2011).

favor of preemption.[23] Other scholars have also grappled with the relationship of many of the measures at issue to legality as such.[24] But in both cases, theorists have tended to conceive of the measures as operating beyond law, being "extra-legal," or essentially illegal.

For example, in his work on U.S. counterterrorism law after 9/11, Kent Roach has characterized aspects of the executive's use of various measures in terms of the concept of "extra-legalism."[25] "The American approach," he writes, "was based not so much on explicit extralegal conduct but extra-legalism in which illegal conduct was defended through claims of legality including arguments designed to deprive courts of jurisdiction to decide whether the governmental conduct was illegal."[26] Roach also contends that "[i]t would be a mistake to think the American acceptance of extralegal approaches to emergencies was an invention of 9/11 of the Bush administration." [27] Rather, it has "deep roots in American history," including President Lincoln's suspension of habeas corpus in the Civil War, and President Franklin D. Roosevelt's preference to submit captured German soldiers to a military tribunal rather than allow access to habeas corpus in a U.S. court.[28] In Roach's view, Presidents Bush and Obama also extend a tradition of an "executive model of counter-terrorism as opposed to a legislative one,"[29] in a pattern that conforms in some respects to the conduct of Reagan and Clinton, including the capture and rendition of foreign terror suspects for trial in the United States,[30] or their rendition to torture abroad.[31] Both presidents also engaged in targeted killing as a response to terrorism, with strikes in Libya in retaliation for the 1986 murder of U.S. soldiers in Germany and in strikes in Afghanistan and Sudan in response to the 1998 embassy bombings in Africa.[32] But in each case, Roach notes, the United States was "prepared to engage in extra-legalism ... only if supported by dubious claims of legality."[33]

Roach's model of "extra-legalism" thus characterizes certain post-9/11 measures as essentially illegal, consistent with earlier examples of illegal executive conduct, and distinct from a remaining body of lawful measures. But this approach overlooks a number of

---

[23] *See*, e.g., Jane Mayer, THE DARK SIDE: THE INSIDE STORY OF HOW THE WAR ON TERROR TURNED INTO A WAR ON AMERICAN IDEALS (New York: Random House, 2008), referring to a "new paradigm" for the use of force in the wake of 9/11; and Alan Dershowitz, PREEMPTION: A KNIFE THAT CUTS BOTH WAYS (New York: Norton, 2006).

[24] Oren Gross, *Chaos and Rules: Should Responses to Violent Crises Always Be Constitutional?*, 112 YALE L.J. 1011 (2003); David Dyzenhaus, THE CONSTITUTION OF LAW: LEGALITY IN A TIME OF EMERGENCY (Cambridge: Cambridge University Press, 2006); Blum & Heymann, LAWS, OUTLAWS, *supra* note 21; Kent Roach, THE 9/11 EFFECT: COMPARATIVE COUNTER-TERRORISM (Cambridge: Cambridge University Press, 2011).

[25] Kent Roach, THE 9/11 EFFECT, ibid. at 164.

[26] Ibid.

[27] Ibid. at 163.

[28] Ibid.

[29] Ibid. at 165.

[30] Ibid. at 167.

[31] Ibid. at 168.

[32] Ibid. at 169.

[33] Ibid. at 167.

significant aspects of the use of the measures, or the broader shift in the culture of security after 9/11 of which they form a part. What fails to be captured in Roach's otherwise compelling and persuasive account is a qualitative difference between the United States' isolated, restrained, and often surreptitious use of rendition, detention, or targeted killing before 9/11, and the often overt, persistent, and copious use of some of the same measures after 2001. In that earlier period, the United States had plausibly sought to frame its attacks on military installations in Libya or active al Qaida operatives in the immediate wake of the 1998 embassy bombings as matters calling for a military response. But it would come to operate within a very different legal framework—not reducible to a mere pretense at legality—when Attorney General Eric Holder asserted before Congress, 12 years after 9/11, and without reservation, that the president possessed the authority to carry out targeted killing of U.S. citizens on American soil without judicial due process.[34]

To cast some of the measures as "extra-legal" is also to overlook the significant degree to which they would come to be sanctioned by courts or entrenched in legislation, or both. Examples to be canvassed below include, among others, the court decisions and legislation permitting the prolonged military detention of U.S. citizens not charged with an offense, diminished habeas corpus rights of Guantanamo detainees, and mass secret surveillance. Moreover, to isolate some of the measures from others as "extra-legal" overlooks their function as part of a larger cultural and political framework in which the measures are not seen as temporary aberrations from legal order, as in the pre-9/11 period, but as facets of a "new normal." In ways to be explored in Chapter 3, the pervasive claim as to the legality of many of the measures—and consistent support for or acceptance of this claim on the part of lawmakers and jurists—is closely related to the sizable and abiding support for the measures among the U.S. electorate.

## II. DISTINGUISHING AUTHORITARIAN LEGALITY FROM THE STATE OF EXCEPTION

A further useful distinction to draw pertains to how authoritarian legality differs from scholarship approaching post-9/11 measures through the idea of a state of exception or emergency. One of the purposes of framing the measures in terms of an emerging form of legality is to highlight a facet of their role in contemporary law that is not captured in the theory on states of exception. The difference can be illustrated in relation to the two main currents of this theory, beginning with the work of Clinton Rossiter on the one hand and Carl Schmitt on the other.

In *Constitutional Dictatorship* (1948),[35] Rossiter explored the question of whether dictatorial powers exercised in a moment of national crisis, such as Lincoln's suspension of

---

[34] Holder's exchange with Congress is explored in Part 3 below.

[35] Clinton L. Rossiter, CONSTITUTIONAL DICTATORSHIP: CRISIS GOVERNMENT IN MODERN DEMOCRACIES (Princeton, NJ: Princeton University Press, 1948).

habeas corpus during the civil war, could be consistent with constitutional government, by serving as a broader, unwritten principle of constitutional law. Rossiter argued that such powers could be consistent on the basis that "the constitutional state is essentially designed to function under normal, peaceful conditions, and is often unequal to the exigencies of a great national crisis."[36] In an emergency, he asserted, "constitutional government must be temporarily altered to whatever degree is necessary to overcome the peril and restore normal conditions."[37] But in the event, "the narrow duty to be pursued by this strong government" is strictly "to end the crisis and restore normal times." For Rossiter, constitutional dictatorship was marked by an important limitation:

> [t]he government assumes no power and abridges no right unless plainly indispensible to that end; it extends no further in time than the attainment of that end; and makes no alteration in the political, social and economic structure of the nation which cannot be eradicated with the restoration of normal times. In short, the aim of constitutional dictatorship is the complete restoration of the *status quo ante bellum*.[38]

By contrast, the concept of authoritarian legality posited here will seek to highlight how many of the measures entrenched in law in response to the perceived crisis are not understood as temporary. Nor have the measures been entrenched with the primarily goal of effecting a quick restoration of a prior status quo. Instead, the thrust of the measures to be canvassed below is to address a new status quo, with powers meant to persist indefinitely as part of a new normal.

Building on Rossiter's work, Oran Gross and Fionnuala Ni Aolain have developed a more extensive taxonomy of models of government in times of emergency.[39] They place Rossiter's constitutional dictatorship within what they call "models of accommodation." Jurists working within these models understand constitutional principles broadly enough to include the power to suspend certain rights in times of emergency, but argue that emergency powers are also subject to important limits.[40] Gross and Ni Aolain discern the accommodation model at work in Supreme Court jurisprudence and legislative debates that emphasize the role of judges and lawmakers in moments of crisis as a crucial "check and balance" on the "executive's assertions of emergency powers."[41] But in their view, and in ways evident in the post-9/11 period, the model is flawed due in part to the

---

36 Ibid. at 5.

37 Ibid.

38 Ibid. at 7.

39 Oran Gross & Fionnuala Ni Aolain, Law in Times of Crisis: Emergency Powers in Theory and Practice (Cambridge: Cambridge University Press, 2006).

40 Ibid. ch. 1.

41 Ibid. at 53. Among the examples Gross and Ni Aolain offer is Justice O'Connor's dicta in Hamdi v. Rumsfeld, 542 U.S. 507 at 536: "[A] state of war is not a blank check for the President when it comes to the rights of the Nation's citizens…in times of conflict [the Constitution] most assuredly envisions a role for all three branches when individuals liberties are at stake."

fact that "as a matter of practice neither domestic courts nor any legislature perform their checking and monitoring task particular well when claims of necessity are made by the executive... during a period of crisis and emergency."[42]

By contrast, a second group of theories conforming to what Gross and Ni Aolain call the "business as usual" model insists on "constitutional absolutism and perfection."[43] This model posits the need for governments in times of emergency to adhere strictly to constitutional norms and limits regardless of the nature of the emergency that might arise. Gross and Ni Aolain call this model into question by drawing upon an ample history of abuses of power in times of emergency from America's internment of Japanese-American citizens in the Second World War to those cited by Israel's Landau Commission of Inquiry into the interrogation techniques of the Israeli Defense Force in the late 1980s. "Adopting the Business as Usual model," they write, "means either being unaware of the reality of emergency management, or ignoring it and knowingly maintaining an illusory façade of normalcy."[44] Without referring to reports of "enhanced interrogation," or other measures employed by the Bush administration that began to come to light in the first few years after 9/11, Gross and Ni Aolain point indirectly at the failure of constitutional perfectionism to prevent the inevitable use of such measures.

As an alternative model of government in times of national crisis, Gross and Ni Aolain advocate the adoption of a framework that allows for the use of "extra-legal measures." On this model,

> public officials may act extra-legally when they believe that such action is necessary for protecting the nation and the public in the face of calamity, provided that they openly and publicly acknowledge the nature of their actions.... Once an extra-legal action is taken, it is then up to the people to decide, either directly or indirectly (e.g., through their elected representatives in the legislature), how to respond to such actions.[45]

Gross and Ni Aolain would prefer that certain extraordinary measures—torture, possibly targeted killing—neither be claimed as legal pursuant to a temporary constitutional dictatorship nor be hidden to avoid the censure of the constitutional purists, but instead be openly carried out as illegal, with questions of accountability and necessity to be addressed after the fact.[46] This would preserve the integrity of the law from its contamination by the arbitrariness and violence of constitutional dictatorship. It would also acknowledge the historical tendency of emergency powers to exceed the limits to which

---

[42] Ibid. at 53.

[43] Ibid. at 10 and ch. 2.

[44] Ibid. at 95.

[45] Ibid. at 11 and ch. 3.

[46] Ibid.; at 381, the text is careful to distinguish that only Gross takes the view that torture may be justified in "truly catastrophic cases."

courts and legislatures attempt to subject them in times of crisis, or the government's tendency to hide certain measures from public view.

Contrary to Gross and Ni Aolain's analysis, the concept of authoritarian legality explored below suggests that what has occurred in North American law and politics after 9/11 is best understood as a *conflation of all three* of their models of emergency government. The executive has asserted greater powers as part of an extraordinary set of circumstances not understood as temporary; courts and lawmakers have asserted some important limits on those powers, but also sanctioned the suspension of many others; and while some of the most extreme measures began in secret ("enhanced interrogation," targeted killing, mass secret surveillance), once revealed, they were carried on openly and embraced or entrenched as legal.

A second important current in the state of emergency literature involves the work of German legal theorist Carl Schmitt[47] and its development in the work of Italian philosopher Giorgio Agamben.[48] For Schmitt, the exercise of sovereign power marks a crucial theoretical limit on the rule of law in a constitutional state by virtue of the sovereign's need to decide in moments of genuine crisis whether the law should be suspended to take measures that might save the nation from dire peril. A key aspect of this decision for Schmitt is that it cannot be preempted by law—or limited by unwritten constitutional principle, as Rossiter would later posit. The sovereign or executive is unavoidably in a position in which he or she must *decide* whether the state faces a truly unique and pressing emergency, and which powers are necessary to address it. These questions can never be exhaustively anticipated or decided in advance. The need and power to decide them in a moment of perceived crisis therefore places the sovereign or executive unavoidably beyond or before the law.

Schmitt's theory of emergency government has enjoyed a degree of currency in debates about security after 9/11 that can be gleaned by the amount of space devoted to grappling with this theory in much of the scholarship on counterterrorism law.[49] The claim often debated is whether some of the more extreme measures—waterboarding, targeted killing, secret warrantless surveillance—ought simply to be characterized as essentially illegal but arguably necessary in light of perceived existential threats to the nation. Obama's later repudiation of some of these measures offers further support for the view that when Bush employed them, they served as illegal emergency measures in the Schmittian sense. But in ways explored below, the concept of authoritarian legality is meant to highlight

---

47 Carl Schmitt, Political Theology: Four Chapters on the Concept of Sovereignty, George Schwab (trans.) (Chicago: University of Chicago Press, 2005 [1922]); Carl Schmitt, Dictatorship: From the Origin of the Modern Concept of Sovereignty to Proletarian Class Struggle, Michael Hoelzl & Graham Ward (trans.) (Cambridge MA: Polity Press, 2014 [1921]).

48 Giorgio Agamben, *State of Exception*, Kevin Attell (trans.) (Chicago: University of Chicago, 2004).

49 See, e.g., contributions to Victor V. Ramraj, ed., Emergencies and the Limits of Legality (Cambridge: Cambridge University Press, 2012) and David Dyzenhaus, Constitution of Law: Legality in a Time of Emergency (Cambridge: Cambridge University Press, 2006), at 35–54.

another crucial aspect of the Bush administration's use of these measures—its resistance to characterizing them as illegal, temporary, or extreme. Similarly, the concept is meant to highlight the process by which secret warrantless surveillance and other measures (forms of indefinite detention without charge, targeted killing) assume a questionable legality at the outset, only to become clearly entrenched at some later point in legislation or at common law, and openly accepted.

Finally, Agamben has approached indefinite detention at Guantanamo and other post-9/11 measures as an occasion to revisit Schmitt's theory of the exception, along with a broader history of emergency power in Western political theory. Agamben's treatment differs from that of both Schmitt and Rossiter by describing the state of exception not as a suspension of law in favor of sovereignty or a temporary exercise of extraordinary power consistent with broader legal principle, but rather, as a moment that illustrates the impossibility of drawing a line between legality and illegality—a moment of indeterminacy:

> [t]he state of exception is neither internal nor external to the juridical order, and the problem of defining it concerns precisely a threshold, or a zone of indifference, where inside and outside do not exclude each other but rather blur with each other.[50]

For Agamben, the state of exception is marked by the recognition of the limited nature of law (in the impossibility of predicting the demands of every unique emergency) but also the attempt to encompass the emergency within the law (by virtue of the sovereign's extra-legal decision having "the force of law").[51] Agamben's purpose in theorizing the exception as a "threshold" between legality and illegality is part of a larger project that explores, as Stephen Humphreys puts it, "the systemic and ongoing expansion of law itself into every area of lived existence, and the coextensive capacity of legal regimes to embed zones of lawlessness within themselves."[52] In contrast to both Schmitt and Agamben, facets of what is termed authoritarian legality in this chapter are not understood by the executive, lawmakers, or courts as exceptional, outside law, or occupying a place at the threshold of legal and non-legal orders. They are understood, once again, as consistent with the constitution, presidential authority, the common law, and ordinary legislation.

Authoritarian legality thus seeks to highlight a facet of post-9/11 measures often overlooked in the state of emergency literature: the insistence on legality and the compatibility between certain extreme measures and conventional precepts of constitutional government. The concept can also therefore be distinguished from a body of scholarship that explores a broader global trend on the part of governments and juridical systems that

---

[50] Agamben, *supra* note 48, at 23.

[51] Ibid. at 38; *see also* the discussion in Stephen Humphreys, THEATRE OF THE RULE OF LAW: TRANSNATIONAL LEGAL INTERVENTION IN THEORY AND PRACTICE (Cambridge: Cambridge University Press, 2010), at 101.

[52] Humphreys, ibid. at 99.

combine facets of constitutionalism and the rule of law with authoritarian practices and principles.[53] Thus, for example, a salient feature of what has been called the "authoritarian rule of law" in states such as Singapore and China,[54] or, in part, the "constitutional theocracy" of Iran or Malaysia, is the emphasis on formal rather than substantive elements of Western constitutionalism.[55] As distinguished from these trends, authoritarian legality in the present context is defined by an insistence upon the compatibility of substantive facets of liberal constitutionalism (substantive due process, human rights, individual dignity and equality) with a range of extraordinary measures that include indefinite detention without charge, targeted killing, and mass surveillance.

Finally, it should be noted that authoritarian legality has not emerged in a vacuum and should not be understood exclusively as a response to 9/11. Its cultural and conceptual antecedents are indeed much wider in scope and far older than the events of 9/11 and the debates about counterterrorism policy that followed. I canvass them briefly here but return to them in the concluding chapter of this book.

## III. SOURCES IN EARLIER TRENDS TOWARD GREATER SECURITY

The emergence of authoritarian legality cannot be understood without reference to changing assumptions in Anglo-American criminology and crime prevention over the last third of the twentieth century. Tracing developments from roughly the 1970s onward, David Garland, Lucia Zedner, Jonathan Simon and others have noted a general shift in emphasis from a long-standing perception of crime as a social welfare problem, calling for the rehabilitation of disadvantaged populations, to one of risk and control of "dangerous predators" and "incorrigible career criminals."[56] Throughout this period, the fear of crime and the idea of security had become primary preoccupations of politics and culture. As a part of this process, a tradition of protecting individual rights and civil liberties had come to be eclipsed in the United States and Britain, and to a lesser extent in Canada, by a form of lawmaking in which the role of the victim had become central.

---

53 *See*, e.g., Jothie Rajah, AUTHORITARIAN RULE OF LAW: LEGISLATION, DISCOURSE, AND LEGITIMACY IN SINGAPORE (Cambridge: Cambridge University Press, 2012), Ran Hirschl, CONSTITUTIONAL THEOCRACY (Cambridge, MA: Harvard University Press, 2010), and Tom Ginsburg and Tamir Moustafa, eds., RULE BY LAW: THE POLITICS OF COURTS IN AUTHORITARIAN REGIMES (Cambridge: Cambridge University Press, 2008).

54 Rajah, ibid. at 3–4.

55 Hirschl, *supra* note 53. At 13, Hirschl makes clear that constitutional theocracy is not a mere variation on "rule by law," or a façade of constitutional government. Rather, constitutionalism in this context plays "a key role in curbing the spread and impact of theocratic governance, with its alternative worldviews, texts, and hierarchies of authority."

56 David Garland, THE CULTURE OF CONTROL: CRIME AND SOCIAL ORDER IN CONTEMPORARY SOCIETY (Chicago: University of Chicago Press, 2001), at 10.

Criminal codes and statutes began to expand rapidly with new law fashioned in what Kent Roach has described as a "narrative" style meant to "memorialize terrible crimes."[57]

As a corollary to the rising status of the victim, the figure of the prosecutor also became more central to the rhetoric of politics and government. As Simon has demonstrated, the role and identity of the stern and effective prosecutor had become an indispensible quality in perceptions of the able politician. Rather than seeking to strike a balance between public safety and civil liberties, presidents, governors, and other members of the executive were encouraged to foreground their earlier careers as prosecutors, or to embrace a kind of quasi-prosecutorial rhetoric in their approach to law and order. It had also become incumbent upon politicians of any political persuasion to emphasize a willingness to employ harsh measures—as either an expression of or a response to the public's fear, anger, and desire for retribution.[58]

At the same time, the scope of criminal law and policy had vastly expanded. Broader racial, class, and gender-based tensions would come to be addressed through penal and drug policies clearly discriminatory in their effects. There was also a growing criminalization of deviance in schools and of violence in family relations and in the workplace.[59] Zedner complements this analysis by exploring the emergence, before 9/11, of various "pre-crime" control measures, which seek to impose penal or other restrictive measures as a means of segregating and controlling disenfranchised, disadvantaged portions of the population.[60]

In short, the practice of using the criminal law or punitive measures as a response to a set of social tensions or fears had long pre-dated 9/11 and the various amendments to criminal and immigration law that followed. Authoritarian legal measures should therefore be seen at least in part as elaborations of these earlier tendencies. Later chapters will explore how the legacy of 9/11, and beliefs about terrorism in particular, have come to shape authoritarian legality in ways unique from this earlier "culture of control" or "governance through crime."

## IV. CATALYZING EVENTS

Two legal developments in the wake of 9/11 have served as catalysts for much of the law and policy that comprise authoritarian legality.

The first, pertaining to the United States, was Congress's passage of the "Authorization to Use Military Force" (AUMF) on September 14, 2001.[61] This "joint resolution" of both

---

57 Kent Roach, SEPTEMBER 11: CONSEQUENCES FOR CANADA (Montreal: McGill-Queen's University Press, 2003), at 25.

58 Jonathan Simon, GOVERNING THROUGH CRIME: HOW THE WAR ON CRIME TRANSFORMED AMERICAN DEMOCRACY AND CREATED A CULTURE OF FEAR (Oxford: Oxford University Press, 2007), ch. 2.

59 Ibid, chapters 5, 6 and 7.

60 Lucia Zedner, *Seeking Security by Eroding Rights: The Side-stepping of Due Process*, in Benjamin J. Goold & Liora Lazarus, eds., SECURITY AND HUMAN RIGHTS (Oxford: Hart Publishing, 2007).

61 AUTHORIZATION FOR USE OF MILITARY FORCE, Pub. L. No. 107-40, 115 Stat. 224 (2001).

houses of Congress functions as a declaration of war against the perpetrators of 9/11 and other possible targets. The document contains only a preamble and one substantive section. The preamble invokes the nation's right to self-defense in response to the "grave acts of violence" that occurred on September 11, and the fact that those responsible "continue to pose an unusual and extraordinary threat to the national security" of the United States. The main section is sweeping in its scope and not limited in duration:

> ... the President is authorized to use all necessary and appropriate force against those nations, organizations, or persons he determines planned, authorized, committed, or aided the terrorist attacks that occurred on September 11, 2001, or harbored such organizations or persons, in order to prevent any future acts of international terrorism against the United States by such nations, organizations or persons.[62]

The AUMF is worded broadly enough that it authorizes attacks against nations or groups that had not yet assisted terrorists in 2001, but may have begun to do so later (for example, groups operating in Yemen).[63] The scope of its most important phrase—the authority to use "all necessary and appropriate force"—is also left unclear. Both the Bush and Obama administrations have taken the view that this allows the President to detain indefinitely and without charge either foreigners or citizens; to try detainees in military tribunals; and to carry out secret domestic surveillance and targeted killing.[64]

There were, however, two limitations to the AUMF—but both appear to have been removed by recent legislation. The first limitation had to do with its open-ended nature. As some have argued, at some point, the Authorization would cease to be valid due to the passage of an implied time limit.[65] The second limitation was the nexus requirement. The president had to draw a connection between an individual, group, or nation and the attacks of September 11: i.e., detainees or targets must have "planned, committed, or aided the terrorist attacks that occurred on September 11, 2001, or harbored such organizations or persons...."[66] Both administrations had taken the view that if a person had not engaged directly in any of those acts, it would suffice if they were part of a group that did, or if they substantially supported such a group.[67] But in either case, the group itself had to be connected with the attacks of September 11.

---

62 Ibid. §2(a).

63 I am indebted to Oona Hathaway for noting this in a presentation at the Yale Law School, February 2011.

64 The use of the AUMF as a basis for these practices is discussed further below, and in later chapters.

65 See, e.g., Deborah Perlstein, *More on the New AUMF*, Opinio Juris, June 26, 2011); Bruce Ackerman & Oona Hathaway, *Did Congress Approve America's Longest War?*, The Guardian, Jan. 27, 2011; John Bellinger, *A Counterterrorism Law in Need of Updating*, Wash. Post, Nov. 26, 2010.

66 Oona Hathaway, Samuel Adelsberg, Spencer Amdur, Philip Levitz, Freya Pitts, & Sirine Shebaya, *The Power to Detain: Detention of Terrorism Suspects After 9/11*, 38 Yale J. Int'l L. 123 (2013), at 130.

67 Ibid. at 133.

In response to the first limitation, Congress debated explicitly renewing the powers contemplated in the AUMF in a bill passed in 2011, but chose not to do so. However, while the National Defense Authorization Act of 2012 (NDAA) does not explicitly renew the powers of the AUMF, it does affirm their continuing validity.[68] Section 1021 of the Act states:

> Congress affirms that the authority of the President to use all necessary and appropriate force pursuant to the Authorization for Use of Military Force (Public Law 107–40; 50 U.S.C. 1541 note) includes the authority for the Armed Forces of the United States to detain covered persons [...] pending disposition under the law of war.

The section is structured as a form of clarification—the AUMF "*includes*" the authority to detain a certain class of persons. But notably, the section speaks of the president's powers under the AUMF in the present tense. By implication, then, not only is the AUMF itself still valid, it would appear to remain so for the foreseeable future. A further key provision of the NDAA supports this reading.

The section at issue is one that expands the president's authority to detain.[69] Now, the president may detain not only those who planned, aided, or harbored those involved in the attacks of September 11, but also those who were "part of or substantially supported al-Qaeda, the Taliban or associated forces *that are engaged in hostilities against the United States or its coalition partners...*"[70] A nexus to September 11 is therefore no longer necessary. It will suffice if a person or group is substantially linked to an "associated force," or what is called a "co-belligerent" force.[71] The detainee may be either a foreigner or a U.S. citizen, and he or she can be detained "under the law of war without trial until the end of the hostilities authorized by the Authorization for Use of Military Force."[72]

The second measure serving as a catalyst for new counterterrorism law was the passage of Resolution 1373 by the United Nations Security Council, on September 28, 2001.[73] This called on member states of the UN to reform criminal law regimes to more

---

68 NATIONAL DEFENSE AUTHORIZATION ACT FOR FISCAL YEAR 2012, H.R. 1540, 112th Cong. (2011) [NDAA].

69 Ibid. §1021(b)(2).

70 Ibid.

71 *See* the discussion in Hathaway, et al., *supra* note 66, at 135, of Hamlily v. Obama, 616 F. Supp. 2d. As Hathaway and her co-authors note, the D.C. District Court in *Hamlily* made clear that co-belligerents "do not include terrorist organizations who merely share an abstract philosophy or even a common purpose with al Qaeda—there must be an actual association in the current conflict with al Qaeda or the Taliban." (*Hamlily* at 74.)

72 NDAA, *supra* note 68, §1021(c)(1).

73 S/Res/1373 (2001) [Resolution 1373]. On the role of this resolution as a primary impetus for legislative responses to 9/11 by the United States, Canada and other commonwealth nations, see Kent Roach, *Sources and Trends in Post-9/11 Anti-terrorism Laws,* in Benjamin J. Goold & Liora Lazarus, eds., SECURITY AND HUMAN RIGHTS (Oxford: Hart Publishing, 2007).

effectively prevent "those who finance, plan, facilitate or commit terrorist acts."[74] It also called on states to establish "terrorist acts... as serious criminal offences in domestic laws"; to accelerate the exchange of information or evidence relevant to terror investigations,[75] and to "prevent the movement of terrorists [...] by effective border controls."[76] Within a month, the U.S. government had passed the USA PATRIOT Act,[77] and two and a half months later, Canada enacted the Anti-terrorism Act.[78] Through these and other acts, both governments sought to meet the demand to introduce new terrorism offenses, but also took the opportunity to expand the scope of state secrecy and surveillance, and powers of detention, in ways to be explored below.

The remainder of the chapter defines authoritarian legality in terms of four basic elements. Given the wealth of commentary on these measures, the intention here is only to provide a basic overview of law, policies, or court decisions that support essential facets of the paradigm. A more detailed exploration of these developments can found in earlier studies of both U.S.[79] and Canadian law.[80]

One final note of caution. By surveying Canadian law alongside U.S. law in what follows, there is a risk of creating a misleading impression that Canada's legal response to 9/11 was comparable in many respects or as extreme as those of its southern

---

[74] Resolution 1373, ibid. §2(d), ibid.

[75] Ibid. §3.

[76] Ibid. §2(g).

[77] P.L. 107-56, 115 Stat. 272 (2001) [USA PATRIOT Act].

[78] S.C. 2001, ch. 41.

[79] *See, e.g.*, Jules Lobel, *The War on Terrorism and Civil Liberties*, 63 U. PITT. L. REV. 767 (2002); Patricia Mell, *Big Brother at the Door: Balancing National Security with Privacy Under the USA PATRIOT Act*, 80 DENV. U. L. REV. 375 (2002); Kim Lane Scheppele, *Law in a Time of Emergency: Terrorism and States of Exception*, 6 U. PA. J. CONST. L.1001 (2004); Stewart Baker & John Kavanagh, eds., PATRIOT DEBATES: EXPERTS DEBATE THE USA PATRIOT ACT (Chicago: American Bar Association, 2005); Mark Tushnet, ed., THE CONSTITUTION IN WARTIME: BEYOND ALARMISM AND COMPLACENCY (Durham, NC: Duke University Press, 2005); David Cole & Jules Lobel, LESS SAFE, LESS FREE: WHY AMERICA IS LOSING THE WAR ON TERROR (New York: New Press, 2007); Ronald Dworkin, *The Threat to Patriotism* 49:3 N.Y. REV. BOOKS (Feb. 28, 2002) and *Terror and the Attack on Civil Liberties*, 50:17 N.Y. REV. BOOKS (Nov. 6, 2003); and Gabriella Blum & Philip Heymann, LAWS, OUTLAWS, *supra* note 21, at 3.

[80] Commentary on Canada's primary legislative response to 9/11, the Anti-terrorism Act (S.C. 2001, ch. 41), includes Ronald Daniels, Patrick Macklem & Kent Roach, eds., THE SECURITY OF FREEDOM: CANADA'S ANTI-TERRORISM BILL (Toronto: University of Toronto Press, 2001); David Daubney, ed., TERRORISM, LAW AND DEMOCRACY: HOW IS CANADA CHANGING FOLLOWING SEPTEMBER 11? (Montreal: Themis, 2002). For commentary on Canadian counterterrorism measures of a wider scope, see Kent Roach, SEPTEMBER 11: CONSEQUENCES FOR CANADA (Montreal: McGill-Queen's University Press, 2003); W. Wesley Pue, *The War on Terror: Constitutional Governance in a State of Permanent Warfare?*, 41:2&3 OSGOODE HALL L.J. 267 (2003); Kent Roach, *Must We Trade Rights for Security? The Choice Between Smart, Harsh, or Proportionate Security Strategies in Canada and Britain*, 27 CARDOZO L. REV. 2151 (2006); W. Wesley Pue, *Protecting Constitutionalism in Treacherous Times: Why 'Rights' Don't Matter*, in A. V. Narsimha Rao, ed., CONSTITUTIONALISM: AN INTERNATIONAL PERSPECTIVE (Hyderabad: Amicus Books, 2008); and Robert Diab, GUANTANAMO NORTH: TERRORISM AND THE ADMINISTRATION OF JUSTICE IN CANADA (Halifax, NS: Fernwood Publishing, 2008).

counterpart—which is not the case. Canada's response was more restrained. Its primary counterterrorism law passed after 9/11, the Anti-terrorism Act[81] added new terrorism offenses to Canada's Criminal Code,[82] including the financing of terrorism, and "facilitating" or "participating in" terrorism. Yet the Supreme Court has crafted significant safeguards to restrict the scope of the latter two offenses by affirming a mens rea requirement consistent with other serious offenses in the Criminal Code.[83] The Anti-terrorism Act also lacked minimum penalties for any of its new offenses, and the Supreme Court has affirmed that rehabilitation continues to apply in terrorism sentencing, including in the most serious cases.[84] There is also no true parallel in Canadian law to the form of detention carried out at Guantanamo. Canada's closest equivalent, the "security certificate" regime, for indefinite detention without charge under immigration law (discussed below) is premised on the crucial qualification that the primary purpose of the detention is to facilitate a quick deportation due to security concerns. In cases where detainees cannot be deported due to concerns about torture in countries of origin, lengthy detention is an incidental effect of the legislation rather than its goal. There has also been more accountability for state complicity in human rights violations, with the government having generously compensated Maher Arar for its role in his deportation and torture in Syria, following an extensive inquiry into the matter. It also held an inquiry into the role of Canadian officials in the torture of three other Canadians in Egypt and Syria.[85] Finally, courts have also resisted a number of attempts by government to assert secrecy in national security cases, including the Arar and Iacobucci Inquiries and prominent terrorism prosecutions.[86]

Yet, in a number of ways to be explored, Canadian law and policy has succumbed to many of the same shifts toward authoritarian legality in evidence in the United States. Its highest court has affirmed the constitutionality of deportation to torture in extreme cases, and the use of secret evidence in what amounts to prolonged or indefinite detention without charge. The Court has also affirmed the constitutionality of significant expansions of the power to assert state secrecy. And in a number of cases, the government has invoked public interest privilege to avoid accountability for serious rights violations in the national security context.

---

81 S.C. 2001, ch. 41.

82 R.S.C. 1985, ch. C-46 [Criminal Code].

83 R v. Khawaja, 2012 SCC 69; Criminal Code, §§83.02, 83.18 and 83.19.

84 *Khawaja*, ibid. at ¶¶41–64.

85 See below for a discussion of the Arar and Iacobucci inquiries.

86 See the discussion below of Canada's involvement in the case of Abousfian Abdelrazik and of actions brought by subjects of the Iacobucci inquiry.

## Part 3. Defining Characteristics of Authoritarian Legalism

### I. THE ABANDONMENT OF THE CONCEPT OF ABSOLUTE OR NON-DEROGABLE RIGHTS

In authoritarian legality, there are no longer any non-derogable rights. Put otherwise, all constitutional and human rights have proven to be derogable, including rights against torture, cruelty, and "extra-judicial" killing. Yet in every case where a government or court violates an absolute prohibition, the violation is not acknowledged as such. That is to say, while the act or court decision may amount to a de facto violation of the prohibition, governments or courts have either ignored the fact or insisted upon the legality or reasonable character of their actions.[87] Therefore, despite the fact that both the U.S. and Canadian governments are constitutionally and by treaty bound to uphold the absolute prohibition on torture, cruelty, and extra-judicial killing, each government and each nation's courts have sanctioned the violation of these and other core human rights (with the exception of targeted killing in the case of Canada).

A series of specific examples follows.

#### Indefinite Detention in U.S. Law

With the AUMF as a backdrop, President Bush issued an order on November 13, 2001, purporting to give himself the power to detain, indefinitely, any individual who is not a citizen of the United States and who there is "reason to believe" has engaged in or aided or abetted a terrorist group—or, more generally, anyone whom "it is in the interest of the United States" to detain.[88] The order allows that detainees may be tried by a military tribunal for any violations of the laws of war, and if convicted could face the death penalty. Given the "danger to the safety of the United States" posed by terrorism, the order states that it is "not practicable to apply in military commissions under this order the principles of law and the rules of evidence generally recognized in the trial of criminal cases in the United States district courts."[89] The order also precludes a detainee's right to seek "any remedy or maintain any proceeding, directly or indirectly... in any court of any court of the United States,"[90] or any other nation or international tribunal. Thus, a conviction and

[87] By contrast, in November of 2001, when the United Kingdom sought to legislate the power to detain non-citizens without charge for extended periods under new immigration legislation, it invoked the emergency derogation clause under the European Convention on Human Rights, 213 U.N.T.S. 221. The measure was thus conceived of as a derogation from a core human right. The validity of the derogation, and thus the law on which it was based, was successfully challenged in A and Others v. Secretary of State for the Home Dep't, [2004] UKHL 56.

[88] Military Order of Nov. 13, 2001; 66 Fed. Reg. 57,833 (Nov. 16, 2001), http://georgewbush-whitehouse.archives.gov/news/releases/2001/11/20011113-27.html.

[89] Ibid. §1(f).

[90] Ibid. §7(b).

death sentence could follow from a split decision of a panel, and the only appeal would lie with the President or Secretary of Defense—the same officials carrying out the prosecution.[91] The order states that these measures are necessary given the fact that the attacks of 9/11 occurred "on a scale that has created a state of armed conflict that requires the use of the United States Armed Forces."[92] The measures were also appropriate considering the "magnitude of the potential deaths, injuries, and property destruction that would result from potential acts of terrorism against the United States, and the probability that such acts will occur."[93]

The day after the order was issued, Vice President Richard Cheney asserted that detainees in America's military initiative against al Qaeda and its affiliates did not "deserve to be treated as prisoners of war" and were not entitled to the protection of the Geneva Conventions.[94] In January of 2002, legal opinions corroborating this view were issued by Donald Rumsfeld, on behalf of the Department of Defense, and Jay Bybee, for the Department of Justice.[95] On February 7, President Bush gave these legal force by issuing an order stating "none of the provisions of Geneva apply to our conflict with al Qaeda in Afghanistan or elsewhere throughout the world because, among other reasons, al Qaeda is not a High Contracting Party to Geneva."[96]

As Jane Mayer notes, President Bush's February 2002 order marked the first time the United States had explicitly declined to uphold the Geneva Conventions for prisoners in an armed conflict.[97] During the Vietnam war, the Conventions were applied to detainees of the Viet Cong despite the fact that the Viet Cong had ignored them. Mayer also notes that in Vietnam, as with Guantanamo, there had been concerns that some of the detainees were innocent civilians, but in the earlier instance, the United States was able to devise a system of status hearings—known as "Article 5 tribunals"—to extend to prisoners the right to make a case against detention.[98] These tribunals were used again in Grenada, Panama, and the first Gulf War. In the latter case, as Mayer points out, among the 1,200 or so Iraqi combatants initially imprisoned, Article 5 tribunals would determine that only 310 detainees should be held as prisoners of war.[99] Among the many protections

---

91 Mayer, THE DARK SIDE, *supra* note 23, at 87.

92 Military Order of Nov. 13, 2001, *supra* note 88, §1(a).

93 Ibid. §1(g).

94 Barton Gellman & Jo Becker, *A Different Understanding with the President*, WASH. POST, June 24, 2007: http://blog.washingtonpost.com/cheney/chapters/chapter_1/.

95 Rumsfeld's Jan. 19 memo is available online at lawofwar.org: http://www.lawofwar.org/Rumsfeld%20Torture%20memo_0001.jpg; Bybee's> memo of Jan. 22: http://www.washingtonpost.com/wp-srv/nation/documents/012202bybee.pdf.

96 Section 2(a) of the order is available online at lawofwar.org: http://www.lawofwar.org/Bush_memo_Genevas.htm.

97 Mayer, THE DARK SIDE, *supra* note 23, at 121.

98 Ibid. at 121.

99 Ibid.

afforded by the Geneva Conventions is a right against punishment for refusing to cooperate with interrogators. The Third Convention also states that "No physical or mental torture nor any other form of coercion may be inflicted on prisoners of war to secure from them information of any kind whatever."[100]

In the post-9/11 period, the United States would detain thousands of terror suspects from battlegrounds in Afghanistan and Pakistan, and from a host of other Asian nations, and hold them at prisons in Iraq, Afghanistan, Guantanamo Bay in Cuba, and at various CIA "black sites." Many were interrogated and tortured.[101] To focus for the moment on detainees at Guantanamo, beginning in January of 2002, the United States would bring roughly 800 men to the base over the course of the past decade. While 7 have died in custody, 149 remain at the time of this writing.[102] With the base situated on foreign soil, the Bush administration assumed that detainees were beyond the jurisdiction of American courts or the U.S. Constitution, for the purpose of challenging the grounds of their detention under a writ of habeas corpus, or their prosecution using military tribunals.

Through a series of decisions of the U.S. Supreme Court, the scope of detainee rights has become clearer. The decisions can be roughly divided into two classes of cases. One set of cases concerns the right of detainees to habeas corpus, or some form of judicial review, to determine whether their detention is lawful. The question in these cases is whether a detainee is in fact the "enemy combatant" the government alleges he is, or an innocent bystander caught up in the initial sweep.[103] A second set of cases, dealing with a smaller group of detainees charged with war crimes, concerns the validity of the military tribunal scheme set up to try them. The question in these latter cases was whether the Geneva Conventions do in fact apply, along with any other, more stringent, U.S. laws dealing with the use of military tribunals.

With the exception of the U.S. Supreme Court's decision in *Hamdan v. Rumsfeld*,[104] holding that the Geneva Conventions do apply to detainees held at Guantanamo, the

---

100 International Committee of the Red Cross (ICRC), Geneva Convention Relative to the Treatment of Prisoners of War (Third Geneva Convention), Aug. 12,1949, 75 UNTS 135; art. 17: http://www.unhcr.org/refworld/docid/3ae6b36c8.html; noted in Mayer, The Dark Side, *supra* note 23, at 120.

101 The issue of torture is explored in more detail below.

102 On the deaths in custody, see Mayer, The Dark Side, *supra* note 23, at 333.

103 A 2006 report by scholars at Seton Hall School of Law found that "Only 8% of [Guantanamo] detainees were characterized as al Qaeda fighters. Of the remaining detainees, 40% have no definitive connection with al Qaeda at all and 18% have no definitive affiliation with either al Qaeda or the Taliban." It also found that "Fifty-five percent (55%) of the detainees are not determined to have committed any hostile acts against the United States or its coalition allies." Moreover, "[o]nly 5% of the detainees were captured by United States forces. 86% of the detainees were arrested by either Pakistan or the Northern Alliance and turned over to United States custody." Commenting on this report, Mayer, The Dark Side, *supra* note 23, at 184–85, suspects that many if not most of the detainees arrested by non-U.S. forces were handed over by bounty hunters. *See* Mark Denbeaux, Joshua Denbeaux, et al., *Report on Guantanamo Detainees: A Profile of 517 Detainees through Analysis of Department of Defense Data*, Seton Hall University School of Law, 2006: http://law.shu.edu/ProgramsCenters/PublicIntGovServ/policyresearch/Guantanamo-Reports.cfm.

104 415 F.3d 33 (D.C. Cir.), *reversed and remanded*, 548 U.S. 557 (2006).

courts have been largely deferential to the assertions of expanded executive authority. (The deferential role of the courts, as a key feature of authoritarian legality, is explored in more detail below. I canvass the cases briefly here to lend coherence to the present discussion of indefinite detention and torture.)

The first of these decisions involved the case of Yaser Hamdi, an American citizen who was captured in Afghanistan in late 2001 while fighting for the Taliban against Northern Alliance forces. The authorities initially brought him to Guantanamo for interrogation; upon learning of his citizenship, they moved him to a Naval brig in Virginia for a period, then to a brig in South Carolina. In the view of the Bush administration, Hamdi's involvement in Afghanistan qualified him as an "enemy combatant." On this basis, the United States could detain him indefinitely, as a lawful incident to the powers set out in the AUMF. But the United States also asserted the right to keep him in solitary confinement, with no contact with anyone apart from the military, and to deprive him of access to counsel and to any judicial review of his detention. On a petition for habeas corpus brought by his father, the case made its way to the U.S. Supreme Court.[105] A plurality of the court agreed with the government that the AUMF authorizes the detention of combatants captured abroad—including citizens—and that the detention could continue as long as hostilities lasted, which could be indefinitely. It also held that Hamdi was entitled to counsel and judicial review of his detention, but that the executive was entitled to considerable deference in the process. The standard of review could be lower, it could involve secret evidence or hearsay, and it could take place in a military tribunal rather than a civilian court.

In response to this decision, the U.S. military put in place "Combatant Status Review Tribunals" (CSRTs) to provide detainees with a process for review that accorded with the *Hamdi* decision. However, detainees were appointed counsel by the tribunal (limited to members of the military); the military controlled who could be called as a witness; and detainees (or their counsel) were not able to examine government witnesses.[106] Hearsay was also admitted, and factual assertions by the military were assumed valid unless rebutted.[107]

On the same day that *Hamdi* was decided, the Court issued its decision in *Rasul v. Bush*.[108] This case affirmed that a statutory right to bring a habeas corpus petition extended not only to those within the United States, but also to those held in territories under the authority or control of the United States.[109] In response, Congress passed the Detainee Treatment Act (2005),[110] which explicitly precluded detainees at Guantanamo

105 Hamdi et al. v. Rumsfeld, Secretary of Defense, et al., 542 U.S. 507 (2004).
106 Ronald Dworkin, *Why It Was A Great Victory*, N.Y. Rev. of Books, 16 July 16, 2008.
107 Ibid.
108 Rasul v. Bush, 542 U.S. 466 (2004).
109 Tit. 28, pt. VI, ch. 153, §2241.
110 Detainee Treatment Act of 2005, H.R. 2863, tt. X.

from seeking habeas corpus under the former statutory scheme.[111] The act also limited review of decisions from the Combat Status Review Tribunal to the Court of Appeal for the District of Columbia, on the narrow grounds that the decision was "consistent with the standards and procedures specified by the Secretary of Defense," and with the U.S. Constitution, to the extent that it applied.

Thus, by early 2006, detainees at Guantanamo seeking habeas corpus were limited to CSRTs, followed by an appeal to a single court in Washington, D.C. The validity of the President's military tribunals for those facing war crimes prosecutions under military tribunals remained unclear.

The latter question was addressed in *Hamdan v. Rumsfeld* (2006),[112] which dealt with a challenge to military tribunals brought by a detainee facing prosecution for the crime of conspiring to commit an act of terror against the United States. The majority in this case held that Common Article 3 of the Geneva Conventions applied to detainees at Guantanamo, setting out minimal standards the United States was obliged to uphold. This included a prohibition on "the passing of sentences and the carrying out of executions without previous judgment pronounced by a regularly constituted court affording all the judicial guarantees which are recognized as indispensable by civilized peoples."[113] The Bush administration's intended military tribunal scheme contravened Article 3, because it allowed for the admission of any evidence that, in the opinion of the presiding officer, "would have probative value to a reasonable person"; the accused and his counsel could be denied access to evidence; and the accused and his counsel could be excluded from and prevented from ever learning what evidence was presented during any part of the proceeding the presiding officer decides to "close."[114]

In response, Congress passed the Military Commissions Act of 2006.[115] This codified a revised scheme for *both* status review hearings and war crimes prosecutions. Statements obtained through coercive interrogations or torture could be admitted,[116] along with secret evidence, and detainees could be excluded from hearings altogether.[117]

While the validity of the new military commission scheme for those facing prosecution remained unclear—i.e., was it consistent with the Geneva Conventions?—detainees continued to litigate the issue of habeas corpus. In *Boumediene v. Bush* (2008),[118] the Court was asked the more expansive question of whether the Constitution's guarantee of habeas corpus extended to non-citizens held by the United States on foreign soil in its permanent control. And if so, was the scheme for review of detentions under the Detainee Treatment

---

111 Section 1005.
112 Hamdan v. Rumsfeld, 548 U.S. 557 (2006).
113 Geneva Convention Relative to the Treatment of Prisoners of War, Common art. 3, §2(d).
114 *Hamdan, supra* note 112, §vi(a).
115 Pub. L. 109–366, 28 U.S.C. §2241 (2006).
116 Ibid. §948r.
117 Ibid. §949.d(3)(f)(B).
118 Boumediene v. Bush, 476 F. 3d. 981 (D.C. Cir. 2007), *reversed and remanded*, 128 S. Ct. 2229 (2008).

Act of 2005 and in the Military Commissions Act of 2006 consistent with this right? The Court sided with the detainees, holding that they do have a constitutional right to seek habeas corpus in U.S. federal court, and that the legislative scheme for review under both acts was not an adequate substitute for this. However, the Court continued to sanction a form of habeas corpus favorable to the government (more on this below).

When Barack Obama campaigned for president, he expressed the intention to try prisoners at Guantanamo in U.S. civilian courts, for terrorism offenses or crimes under the international law of war. In 2009, facing strenuous resistance in Congress to holding trials in the United States, Obama reversed course and acquiesced in the plan to hold trials in military tribunals. In the Military Commissions Act of 2009,[119] Congress amended the scheme set out in the 2006 MCA to explicitly rule out the use of evidence obtained by torture or cruel treatment "whether or not under the color of law," but it continued to allow for the use of hearsay and secret evidence.[120]

To date, six detainees have been convicted in the military commission regime created by Bush and continued, in modified form, by Obama.[121] A further five are due to be prosecuted, including Abd al Rahim al Nashiri (for his role in the bombing of the U.S.S. *Cole* in Yemen in 2000) and Khalid Shaikh Mohammed (for involvement in 9/11).[122] The United States is seeking the death penalty in each of these pending cases. Only one detainee, Ahmed Ghailani, has been tried in a civilian court in New York for his involvement in the 1998 bombings of U.S. embassies in Kenya and Tanzania.[123]

The status of the other remaining Guantanamo detainees (some 149 men at present) remains unclear. The most recent explanation of the administration's policy with respect them was set out by Obama in a May 2009 speech at the National Archives in Washington. He spoke of the detainees as falling into one of four categories. Some of them, he said, would be tried for criminal offenses in American courts, for offenses committed in the United States (an option since abandoned). Others, detained on battlefields abroad and whose cases concern sensitive evidence, would be tried by military commissions where greater secrecy could be maintained. A third group of some 20 detainees would be released pursuant to habeas challenges (discussed below).

A fourth and final group, comprising some 40 to 50 detainees, posed the greatest challenge. These were men who "cannot be prosecuted yet who pose a clear danger to the American people."[124] For persons in this category, there may be no offenses against them to prosecute, or no untainted evidence on which to rely. These are people who may

---

119 Pub. L. 111–84, 123 Stat. 2574 (2009).

120 Ibid. §1802, (4), and (5) and (7).

121 Human Rights Watch, *The Guantanamo Trials* (Aug. 2014), http://www.hrw.org/features/guantanamo.

122 Reed Brody, *No Real Justice in Guantanamo*, Human Rights Watch, Apr. 19, 2012.

123 The conviction was handed down in November 2010; *see* the ACLU press release, http://www.aclu.org/national-security/former-guantanamo-detainee-found-guilty-conspiracy-federal-court-terrorism-trial.

124 *Text: Obama's Speech on National Security*, N.Y. Times, May 21, 2009, http://www.nytimes.com/2009/05/21/us/politics/21obama.text.html.

have "received extensive explosives training at al Qaeda training camps, or commanded Taliban troops in battle, or expressed their allegiance to Osama bin Laden, or otherwise made it clear that they want to kill Americans." The conundrum for Obama was how to reconcile the indefinite detention of these detainees with the rule of law. Seeking to distinguish his own approach from the over-reactive and "ad hoc" approach of the Bush administration, Obama stated that:

> [...] we must recognize that these detention policies cannot be unbounded. They can't be based simply on what I or the executive branch decide alone. That's why my administration has begun to reshape the standards that apply to ensure that they are in line with the rule of law. We must have clear, defensible, and lawful standards for those who fall into this category. We must have fair procedures so that we don't make mistakes. We must have a thorough process of periodic review, so that any prolonged detention is carefully evaluated and justified.

The President sought to clarify these terms in an executive order of March 7, 2011.[125] The order sets out a framework for annual review of a detainee's status, with a range of procedural protections. These include notice of the grounds for continued detention, the assistance of counsel, and the opportunity to make written and oral submissions. However, the information provided to the detainee is still to be limited to an "unclassified summary" of the material on which the person's detention is based. The board may order the person's continued detention on the vague standard that it is "necessary to protect against a significant threat to the security of the United States."[126] Thus, in both Obama's speech, and in his order, the rule of law here is conceived in terms that are compatible with the notion of *indefinite detention without charge on secret evidence*.

As a capstone to this long and tangled history of presidential powers to detain is Congress's endorsement of the President's March 2011 order in the National Defense Authorization Act of 2012, discussed earlier.[127] The order, and the provisions endorsing it, provide a way for detainees to seek periodic review of their detention. But a point of larger significance, noted at the outset of this book, is the fact that section 1021 of the Act codifies the President's authority to indefinitely detain without charge *any* person—citizen or foreigner—who aided in the 9/11 attacks, or who assists al Qaeda or *any* "associated forces that are engaged in hostilities against the United States or its coalition partners."[128]

---

125 Executive Order 13567, §3, F.R. v. 76, no. 47.

126 Executive Order 13567, ibid. §2.

127 In addition to endorsing the scheme, Section 1023 of the Act requires the administration to issue a report on the implementation of the scheme within 180 days of the enactment of the National Defense Authorization Act, *supra* note 68.

128 Sec. 1021(b)(2), National Defense Authorization Act, *supra* note 68. As Glenn Greenwald has noted, both Human Rights Watch and the American Civil Liberties Union observed in mid-December 2011, after Obama indicated a willingness to sign the NDAA into law, that the bill would mark the first time indefinite

This not only tacitly renews the powers of the AUMF, but also considerably extends the possible scope of the president's detention powers.

The USA PATRIOT Act provides one further notable means for indefinite detention. Section 412 allows the Attorney General of the United States to issue a certificate against an alien where there are "reasonable grounds to believe" that he or she has "engaged in activity that endangers the national security of the United States."[129] Once certified, the Act requires the Attorney General to detain the person. Within seven days, removal proceedings must be initiated, or the person must be charged with an offense or released. If removal proceedings have been initiated, or the person is charged, they can continue to be detained indefinitely, with review every six months. The person may continue to be held only if the Attorney General, or a court on a habeas corpus petition, finds that "the release of the alien will threaten the national security of the United States or the safety of the community or any person."[130] As Kent Roach notes, however, the provision has not been used due in part to the fact that the administration chose to employ other means to effect prolonged detention without charge.[131] As he and others have noted, in the two years following 9/11, upwards of 5,000 Arab and Muslim foreign nationals were detained through the use of greater vigilance over minor immigration law infractions and material witness warrants before a grand jury.[132]

## Indefinite Detention Without Charge in Canadian Law

While Canada opted in the fall of 2001 to send troops to Afghanistan, in support of the U.S.-led mission to defeat the Taliban and hunt down members of al Qaeda, it has not sought to detain terror suspects in a foreign base equivalent to Guantanamo.[133] It has, however, employed a set of immigration laws that allow for prolonged detention of non-citizens without charge on secret evidence. But a key difference between these laws and the Guantanamo framework is that detention in the Canadian context is meant strictly for the purpose of facilitating deportation. Therefore, unlike Guantanamo, where

---

detention has been entrenched in U.S. law since the Internal Security Act of 1950—an act that President Truman vetoed on the basis that it would "make a mockery of our Bill of Rights," and which Congress passed by overriding the veto. As Greenwald also notes, the ISA was overturned by the Non-Detention Act of 1971, 18 U.S.C. 4001(a). Glenn Greenwald, *Obama to Sign Indefinite Detention Bill into Law*, SALON.COM, Dec. 15, 2011.

129 USA PATRIOT Act, P.L. 107–56, 115 Stat. 272 (2001), §412(a), adding 236A(3)(A) to 8 U.S.C. 1101. The full title of the Act is: "Uniting and Strengthening America by Providing Appropriate Tools Required to Intercept and Obstruct Terrorism (USA PATRIOT ACT)."

130 For a more detailed examination of this provision, see Shirin Sinnar, *Note, Patriotic or Unconstitutional? The Mandatory Detention of Aliens under the USA Patriot Act*, 55 STANFORD L. REV. 1419 (2003).

131 Roach, THE 9/11 EFFECT, *supra* note 24, at 183, 187, and 188.

132 Roach, ibid, at 187, citing Cole & Lobel, LESS SAFE, LESS FREE, *supra* note 79, at 107.

133 Canada's handling of detainees in Afghanistan has been the subject of long-standing controversy, but lies beyond the scope of the present argument for authoritarian legality. In distinction to the measures canvassed here, such transfers have not occurred, explicitly or implicitly, for reasons that fall within a framework of belief about threats to national security and necessary measures.

the United States intends (as noted above) to detain almost a third of the remaining prisoners indefinitely without charge, the intention in every "security certificate" case is to deport the detainee. Canada's courts have yet to address the question of what to do in the event that deportation proves unfeasible. Yet, short of this, they have sanctioned the constitutional validity of significant alterations to older ideas about "natural justice" or procedural fairness.

The focus of these laws involves a scheme for the issuance of "security certificates," which act as warrants for the arrest and detention of persons pending their removal from Canada. The certificate regime has been a part of immigration law since the late 1970s. It was added to the Immigration Act in something close to its present form in 1988, and was carried over in substantially the same form in the Immigration and Refugee Protection Act of 2002.[134] Although certificates had been used in numerous cases prior to 2001, they became an important tool in Canada's counterterrorism policy in the first few years following 9/11—only to become less appealing due in part to the considerable litigation they have since generated. Between 2000 and 2003, the government issued certificates to arrest five Muslim men believed to be associated with terrorism and detained them for periods ranging from two to ten years—due in large part to the challenge of safely removing them.[135]

During the period when these detentions first occurred, the security certificate regime worked, in brief terms, as follows. Section 34 of the Immigration and Refugee Protection Act[136] (IRPA) stated that a permanent resident or foreign national is "inadmissible" to Canada "on security grounds" for a number of possible reasons, including "engaging in terrorism," or being involved with an organization that is engaged in terrorism, or simply "being a danger to the security of Canada." Section 77 ordered the Minister of Citizenship and Immigration and the Minister of Public Safety and Emergency Preparedness, together, to sign a certificate stating that a permanent resident or foreign national is inadmissible to Canada on grounds of "security" or "serious criminality," among others, and to refer the matter to Federal Court for review. Once signed, the certificate functioned as a warrant for the person's arrest and detention.

A hearing in Federal Court then had to be held within 48 hours of arrest in the case of a permanent resident, but for a foreigner, it could be as late as 120 days.[137] The question for the court on review of the certificate was whether, "on the basis of the information and evidence available," it was "reasonable."[138] If it were found reasonable, deportation proceedings would begin. In practice, however, where there were concerns

---

134 Kent Roach and Gary Trotter note that as of 2005, Canada had issued 27 security certificates: *Miscarriages of Justice in the War Against Terror*, 109 PENN ST. L. REV. 967 (Spring 2005).

135 For a discussion of these cases, see Roach, THE 9/11 EFFECT, *supra* note 24, at 395–406.

136 Immigration and Refugee Protection Act, S.C. 2001, ch. 27.

137 Ibid. the previous §77.

138 Ibid. §80(1).

that detainees would face the risk of torture or death if deported, deportation could be deferred indefinitely.

The process itself placed the detainee at a serious disadvantage. The court could conduct the hearing *in camera*; prevent the detainee from obtaining disclosure; consider information or evidence in private (and for up to seven days after the matter had been referred for determination); and could hear all or part of the evidence in the absence of the detainee.[139] The court could receive into evidence "anything that, in the opinion of the judge, is appropriate." The detainee received only a summary of the information or evidence against them sufficient to "enable them to be reasonably informed of the circumstances giving rise to the certificate"—but excluding anything which, if disclosed, would be "injurious to national security."[140] As Craig Forcese notes, in some cases, the summary provided was "of the most general sort."[141] He also points out that the framework did not call for a "balancing of the secrecy interest against the fair trial imperative"—as does the Canada Evidence Act.[142] And where the use of secret evidence did lead to a serious violation of procedural fairness, there was no provision for dismissing the government's case (as there is in the CEA, with a power to grant a judicial stay in criminal proceedings).[143]

Separately, the five men who had been detained from 2000 onward (for periods ranging from 2 to 10 years) brought a number of court challenges to the certificate regime.[144] The central question in these cases was whether the scheme violated the detainee's right in Section 9 of the Charter to be free from arbitrary detention, the right in Section 12 to be free from cruel and unusual treatment, and the broader and more comprehensive right in Section 7 to "life, liberty and security of the person and the right not to be deprived thereof except in accordance with the principles of fundamental justice."[145] In *Re: Charkaoui*[146] the Federal Court of Appeal upheld the constitutionality of the regime, and the decision was appealed to the Supreme Court of Canada, giving rise to the most significant judicial assessment of the certificate regime to date.[147]

A unanimous Court of nine justices held that the scheme was unconstitutional, but that with a few slight modifications, this could be rectified. First, the regime violated

---

139 Ibid. the previous §78(1).

140 Ibid.

141 Craig Forcese, *Assessing the Secrecy Rules*, 15:5 Inst. for Research on Pub. Pol'y: Choices, (2009) at 15; *available at* http://irpp.org/research-studies/choices-vol15-no5/.

142 Ibid. *See* discussion of §38 of the CEA below.

143 Ibid.

144 In addition to Adil Charkaoui, the following have been detained and have launched challenges to various aspects of the security certificate regime: Hassan Almrei, Mohammed Harkat, Mohammad Mahjoub, and Mahmoud Jaballah. See, e.g., Almrei v. Canada (Minister of Citizenship & Immigration), [2005] F.C.A. 54; Harkat v. Canada (Minister of Citizenship & Immigration), [2004] F.C.J. No. 1104; Canada (Minister of Citizenship & Immigration) v. Mahjoub, [2004] F.C. 1028; Re: Jaballah, [2005] F.C. 399.

145 Canadian Charter of Rights and Freedoms, Pt. I of the Constitution Act, 1982, being Sched. B to the Canada Act 1982 (U.K.), 1982, ch. 11.

146 Charkaoui (Re), [2004] F.C.A. 421.

147 Charkaoui v. Canada (Citizenship and Immigration), [2007] S.C.C. 9.

the right against arbitrary detention, because it lacked an immediate initial review in all cases (i.e., sooner than 120 days for foreign nationals), and timely reviews thereafter. Second, given the psychological stress caused by indefinite detention without timely review, the framework also violated the right against cruel and unusual treatment. The Court suggested that if Parliament amended the scheme to include timelier, periodic reviews, these violations could be remedied. Parliament took up this invitation in Bill C-3 a year later.[148]

However, the Court also held that the scheme violated Section 7 of the Charter because it failed to provide the detainee a fair hearing, as required by "the principles of fundamental justice" referred to in that section. A fair hearing is one held before an independent and impartial judge, and in which a detainee has the right to know the case he has to meet and is given an opportunity to respond. In this case, the judge presiding over a certificate hearing maintains independence and impartiality, but because of the provision for the use of secret evidence and *in camera* hearings that exclude the detainee, the right to know the case and to make full answer and defense is violated. The Court recognized the real danger that a judge could decide matters without all of the relevant information, precisely because the detainee was unable to speak to or contradict a point raised by the secret evidence. To satisfy the requirements of Section 7, the Court held, "either the person must be given the necessary information, or a substantial substitute for that information must be found."

The question, then, was whether a "substantial substitute" could be found. One possibility appealed to the Court: the use of "special advocates." These are lawyers with security clearances who would have access to both the detainee and the secret evidence, on the promise that in the process of obtaining instruction from detainees, they would not divulge the evidence. In this curious position, they should, in theory, still be able to carry out an effective cross-examination of government witnesses. And on this basis, the court found that a regime modified for the use of special advocates would indeed present a "substantial substitute" for full disclosure. Given the availability of this less intrusive way of breaching the right in question, the violation of Section 7 here could not be justified as a "reasonable limit" on the rights set out in Section 1 of the Charter. In Bill C-3, Parliament amended the certificate regime to include the use of special advocates.

Yet the decision, and the later amendments to the scheme, give rise to two general concerns. The first is that special advocates alone would not guarantee a fair hearing. The judge could still receive evidence, and hold hearings with respect to it, in the detainee's absence. Disclosure to the detainee would also continue to be as limited as before—indeed, in Bill C-3 (the act amending the certificate regime), after having seen the secret evidence,

---

148 Revisions were included in Bill C-3, An Act to amend the Immigration and Refugee Protection Act, ch. 3, S.C. 2008.

a special advocate may not disclose it to the detainee, and may not even speak to the detainee without the court's approval.[149] Commenting on the bill, Craig Forcese writes:

> A special advocate can never share the secret information with the interested person. Thus, there will never be a case in which that person can inform a special advocate that the government's chief witness (say, a secret detainee interrogated by an allied intelligence agency) has a personal animus prompting him to fabricate a story. For this reason, issues of credibility—the meat and potatoes of a fair trial—cannot be effectively raised by advocates.[150]

Forcese also notes that Bill C-3 fails to provide special advocates with a basis on which to "seek and review government records not already disclosed to the court." Advocates must therefore rely on the government's own decisions about what may or may not be relevant. This is a significant concern because, as Forcese writes,

> ... what the government considers "relevant" and what a special advocate charged with defending the best interest of the detained person considers "relevant" will not always correspond. This discrepancy of views has arisen in Britain, where the government has sometimes failed to give special advocates relevant (and exculpatory) information. It is also an observation affirmed by the Arar commission experiences: Commission counsel (because they were able to compel everything from the government) found information the government initially had declined to disclose.[151]

Forcese also raises the concern that Bill C-3 does not expressly affirm the "ability of the advocate to meet the interested person once the former has seen the secret information." A judge has the discretion to allow this, but as Forcese points out, a similar provision in Britain has resulted in "little or no contact, hurting the advocate's effectiveness."[152]

---

149 See Bill C-3, ibid. §85.2(c). The test for speaking to a detainee after seeing the evidence is whether the court finds it "necessary to protect the interests of the permanent resident or foreign national." Kent Roach notes: "This in itself is a fairly stringent standard that requires the judge to conclude that the requested power is necessary and not just advisable in order to protect the interests of the non-citizen." Kent Roach, Charkaoui *and Bill C-3: Some Implications for Anti-Terrorism Policy and Dialogue between Courts and Legislatures*, 42 SUP. CT. L. REV. (2d) 281 (2008), at 315.

150 Craig Forcese, *Is Bill C-3 the Security Way to Go?*, GLOBE & MAIL, Feb. 6, 2008.

151 Ibid. In Charkaoui v. Canada (Citizenship & Immigration), [2008] S.C.C. 38, at ¶¶62 & 63, the Supreme Court held that to ensure a detainee's right to procedural fairness, CSIS officers have a duty to retain and disclose to ministers reviewing a security certificate and to the court all "operational notes" gathered in the course of interviews and investigations. A judge reviewing the certificate must also disclose the information contained in the notes or a summary of them, subject to review and redaction of portions pursuant to provisions pertaining to public interest privilege, discussed below.

152 Ibid. Forcese and Roach have noted that Bill C-3 employs the most restrictive of the options before Parliament in terms of how to craft a scheme for the use of special advocates. Other models, including one employed by Canada's Security Intelligence Review Committee, allow special counsel the freedom to

Regardless of whether special advocates make the process fairer, a more serious concern remains. The Court's decision in *Charkaoui* has the effect of deeming the remainder of the scheme constitutional. With an earlier initial review, followed by periodic reviews, and the use of special advocates, all of the other issues raised about the scheme are consistent with "fundamental justice": namely, *indefinite detention, pending deportation, without charge on secret evidence.* The amending legislation, Bill C-3, confirms this inference by virtue of the fact that, with one exception, it deals only with the concerns raised by the court in *Charkaoui*.[153] This remains valid law in Canada, with ongoing consequences for the liberty interests of three of the five subjects of the certificates.[154]

Once again, the crucial caveat to security certificate detention is that it is meant primarily to enable the removal of persons who pose a danger to national security. The Supreme Court in *Charkaoui* was not therefore passing judgment on the constitutionality of indefinite detention per se, but only whether prolonged detention pending removal violated the Charter. But while the Court avoided the larger question of indefinite detention per se, it did note in passing that, in a particular case, where removal proved unfeasible, the prospect of a person's indefinite detention *could* be found to violate Section 7 or 12 of the Charter. This would, however, remain to be determined on a case-by-case basis.[155] As a consequence, the broader holding in *Charkaoui* is that a lengthy detention under the certificate regime may violate the constitution, but the fact that the regime *allows for this possibility* does not.

Following the passage of Bill C-3, a new certificate was issued in the case of Mohamed Harkat, which he then challenged under the Charter. The Supreme Court upheld the

---

communicate with clients after having seen secret information (with an obligation to maintain secrecy). As Forcese writes: "for reasons that have never been satisfactorily explained to this author, the government opted for the secrecy-maximizing and fair-trial-minimizing United Kingdom approach." Forcese, *Assessing the Secrecy Rules, supra* note 141, at 26. *See also* Roach, Charkaoui *and Bill C-3, supra* note 149, at 305.

153 Sec. 83(1.1) of the bill also includes a provision stating that the prohibition in §269.1 of the Criminal Code on the use of evidence obtained by torture or "inhuman or degrading treatment" also applies to security certificate hearings.

154 At present (mid-2014), Mohammad Mahjoub, Mahmoud Jaballah, and Mohamed Harkat remain subject to onerous terms of community supervision as part of their pending security certificates. In a June 2011 profile of Mahjoub, Sara Falconer writes: "Despite a recent detention review that relaxed his conditions slightly, Mahjoub is still held under surveillance that is completely unprecedented in the judicial system in Canada. He wears a GPS tracking bracelet at all times. A camera outside his door monitors his every move, and he is only permitted to leave the house for four hours a day, and only within a few blocks of his apartment. CSIS monitors every phone call—in fact, they were caught listening to protected solicitor-client phone calls between Mahjoub and his lawyer, contrary to a court order." Sara Falconer, *Mohammad Mahjoub: the Life of a Security Certificate Detainee*, RABBLE.CA, June 1, 2011.

155 McLachlin, C.J., at ¶123, *Charkaoui, supra* note 147: "I conclude that extended periods of detention pending deportation under the certificate provisions of the IRPA do not violate s. 7 or s. 12 of the Charter, provided that reviewing courts adhere to the guidelines set out above. Thus, the IRPA procedure itself is not unconstitutional on this ground. However, this does not preclude the possibility of a judge concluding at a certain point that a particular detention constitutes cruel and unusual treatment or is inconsistent with the principles of fundamental justice, and therefore infringes the Charter in a manner that is remediable under s. 24(1) of the Charter."

new scheme, but added a number of qualifications that bring the powers under the regime into closer conformity with the powers of a criminal trial judge in a case where public interest privilege is asserted under the Canada Evidence Act (discussed below).[156] Yet the thrust of the Court's ruling in *Charkaoui* is preserved.

Harkat had argued that the new scheme violates Section 7 of the *Charter* despite the provision for summaries of the closed record on which the government's case is based, and despite the provision for representation of his interests by special advocates.[157] A central issue was the fact that under the new scheme, where the court found that disclosure would be injurious to national security or to the safety of any person, the person subject to a certificate (the "named person") could not obtain disclosure at all.[158] By contrast, under a similar provision in the Canada Evidence Act allowing for the assertion of public interest privilege, the court is obliged to balance the public interest in non-disclosure with the public interest in disclosure.[159] The IRPA provision had thus violated the right to full disclosure under section 7 without minimally impairing it. On behalf of the Court on this issue, Chief Justice McLachlin dismissed the argument as premised on an erroneous reading of key provisions of the scheme in light of the whole. Section 83(1)(e) of IRPA requires the judge to

> ensure that the permanent resident or foreign national is provided with a summary of information and other evidence that enables them to be reasonably informed of the case made by the Minister in the proceeding, but that does not include anything that, in the judge's opinion would be injurious to national security or endanger the safety of any person if disclosed.

This sets out the mandatory requirement that injurious information not be disclosed, but it also requires that the subject of the certificate be "reasonably informed" of the government's case. This latter requirement appears to work in tension with Section 83(1)(i), which allows the judge to base his or her decision on the reasonability of a certificate on "information or other evidence even if a summary of that information or other evidence is not provided to the permanent resident or foreign national..." Justice Noel of the Federal Court had conjectured in earlier proceedings that a finding of reasonability might conceivably be made on the basis of a source that must be kept confidential, resulting in the named person receiving no meaningful summary.[160] But Chief Justice McLachlin disagreed. The requirement in Section 83(1)(e) that the named person be "reasonably informed," coupled with the Court's prior decision in *Charkaoui*, implied

---

156 Canada (Citizenship and Immigration) v. Harkat, [2014] S.C.C. 37.

157 Ibid. at ¶48.

158 Ibid. at ¶49; IRPA §83(1)(e).

159 Canada Evidence Act, R.S.C., 1985, ch. C-5, §38.06(2) [CEA].

160 *Harkat (Re)*, [2010] F.C. 1242, at ¶59; cited by McLachlin, C.J., at ¶53 of *Harkat, supra* note 156.

that "there is an incompressible minimum amount of disclosure that the named person must receive in order for the scheme to comply with s. 7 of the *Charter*. He or she must receive sufficient disclosure to know and meet the case against him or her."[161]

Chief Justice McLachlin further clarified that the named person "need not only be given sufficient information about the allegations against him, but also about the evidence on the record."[162] The judge would have to decide whether the test of being "reasonably informed" has been met in a given case, but at the least the named person "must know the essence of the information and evidence supporting the allegations."[163] This therefore excludes a case in which "the name person receives no disclosure whatsoever of essential information or evidence."[164] The Act is silent as to what should occur in that event, but given the clear requirement in Section 83(1)(e) that a person be "reasonably informed," if the test cannot be met, "the Minister must withdraw the information or evidence" preventing the named person from being reasonably informed, which may in turn "effectively compel the Minister to put an end to the proceedings."[165]

*Harkat* is the latest Supreme Court decision discussed in this chapter, and in many respects it marks an important limitation in the function of the certificate regime in accordance with liberal legal principles. Yet, despite this, it continues to pursue the broader goal in *Charkaoui* of reconciling extraordinary powers with constitutional guarantees. As the Chief Justice puts it at the outset of *Harkat*, the fundamental issue in the case is "how far the principle of full disclosure in an open court can be qualified in order to address the threat posed by non-citizens who may be involved in terrorism."[166] The language here reveals the conscious sense of extending limits, or of occupying the outer edges of earlier ideas of natural justice. *Harkat* may therefore qualify the certificate regime in important ways, but by affirming the core holding in *Charkaoui*, it also further entrenches the constitutionality of a law enabling a prolonged detention without charge on secret evidence.

## Torture or Cruel and Unusual Treatment in the American Context

The Bush administration has continuously denied ever having resorted to torture.[167] It has conceded the use of "special" or "enhanced" coercive interrogation methods, or "alternative procedures," including waterboarding, and has also admitted to the detention of

161 *Harkat, supra* note 156, at ¶54.
162 Ibid. at ¶57.
163 Ibid.
164 Ibid.
165 Ibid. at ¶59.
166 Ibid. at ¶3.
167 For example, in an interview with the New York Times, in January 2005, Bush stated that "torture is never acceptable, nor do we hand over people to countries that do torture"; cited in Jane Mayer, *Outsourcing Torture: The Secret History of America's "Extraordinary Rendition" Program*, The New Yorker, Feb. 14, 2005. In a speech on September 6, 2006, Bush described the detention and use by the CIA of an

prisoners at "black sites" run by the CIA.[168] Yet in each case that the use of these measures was conceded, the administration insisted that they never amounted to torture or cruel and unusual treatment.[169] President Obama has made numerous pronouncements to the effect that under his administration, the United States does not torture.[170] In one sense, then, torture, or cruel and unusual treatment, has played no part in official or explicit U.S. counterterrorism law or policy after 9/11, and strictly speaking forms no part of an authoritarian legal paradigm. On another reading, however, ample evidence suggests that the United States has resorted to, and continues to resort to, torture or cruel treatment—and that by seeking to inscribe the legality of its conduct through euphemistic phrases and concepts such as "enhanced," "robust," or "special" interrogation, its handling of torture and cruel treatment exemplifies authoritarian legality.

Evidence of the use of torture by U.S. officials, after 9/11, has been investigated by various rights groups, jurists, and journalists.[171] A 2011 report by Human Rights Watch,

---

"alternative set of procedures" in the interrogation of suspects at prisons in undisclosed places abroad and at Guantanamo. Bush insisted on the need to keep the specifics of the techniques used confidential, but affirmed that "the procedures were tough and they were safe and lawful and necessary." For the text of the speech, see the New York Times online: http://www.nytimes.com/2006/09/06/washington/06bush_transcript.html?pagewanted = all.

168 In addition to Bush's speech on Sept 6, 2006, ibid., in February of 2008, CIA Director Michael Hayden confirmed that Guantanamo detainees Khalid Sheikh Mohammed, Abu Zubaydah and Abd al-Rahim al-Nashiri were waterboarded in 2002 and 2003: *White House Defends Use of Waterboarding*, ASSOCIATED PRESS, Feb. 6, 2008. On February 7, 2008, White House spokesman Tony Fratto impliedly conceded the past use of waterboarding by describing it as a legal technique that the President might reauthorize "under certain circumstances," including when there is a "belief that an attack might be imminent" (cited in Greg Miller, *Waterboarding Is Still An Option*, LOS ANGELES TIMES, Feb. 7, 2008). In July 2008, Attorney General John Ashcroft affirmed that waterboarding, and other harsh interrogation techniques, had served a "valuable" purpose: *Ashcroft Defends Waterboarding before House Panel*, CNN.COM, July 17, 2008.

169 See, e.g., Bush's speech in February 2006, *supra* note 167, and the Hayden and Ashcroft appearances, *supra* note 168.

170 *See*, e.g., Obama's archive speech, *supra* note 124: "I can stand here today, as President of the United States, and say without exception or equivocation that we do not torture..." See also *Statement of President Barack Obama on Release of OLC Memos*, Apr. 16, 2009, http://www.whitehouse.gov/the_press_office/Statement-of-President-Barack-Obama-on-Release-of-OLC-Memos; Obama's speech in Cairo, "I have unequivocally prohibited the use of torture by the United States...," N.Y. TIMES, June 4, 2009, http://www.nytimes.com/2009/06/04/us/politics/04obama.text.html?pagewanted = all.

171 See, e.g., Human Rights Watch, *Getting Away with Torture: the Bush Administration and Mistreatment of Detainees*, July 2011, http://www.hrw.org/en/node/100262/section/1; The International Commission of Jurists, *Assessing Damage, Urging Action: Report of the Eminent Jurists Panel on Terrorism, Counter-terrorism, and Human Rights*, February 2009, http://www.refworld.org/docid/499e76822.html; International Committee of the Red Cross, *Report on the Treatment of Fourteen 'High Value' Detainees in CIA Custody*, February 2007, http://www.nybooks.com/media/doc/2010/04/22/icrc-report.pdf; United Nations Commission on Human Rights, *Situation of the Detainees at Guantanamo*, February 2006, UNHCR, E/CN.4/2006/120, http://www.refworld.org/docid/45377b0b0.html; Human Rights Watch, *By the Numbers: Findings of the Detainee Abuse and Accountability Project*, April 2006, http://www.hrw.org/en/node/11352/section/1. Mayer, THE DARK SIDE, *supra* note 23; Karen Greenberg, THE LEAST WORST PLACE: GUANTANAMO'S FIRST 100 DAYS (London: Oxford University Press, 2009); Cole & Lobel, LESS SAFE, LESS FREE, *supra* note 79.

drawing upon various earlier reports, alleges that "[a]s a direct result of Bush administration decisions, detainees in US custody were beaten, thrown into walls, forced into small boxes, and waterboarded—subjected to mock executions in which they endured the sensation of drowning. Two alleged senior al Qaeda prisoners, Khalid Sheikh Mohammed and Abu Zubaydah, were waterboarded 183 and 83 times respectively."[172] The report also alleges that other techniques used on prisoners at Guantanamo and at sites in Iraq and Afghanistan included "painful 'stress' positions; prolonged nudity; sleep, food, and water deprivation; exposure to extreme cold or heat"; and also "beatings, near suffocation, [and] sexual abuse."[173]

In a series of memos authored in 2002 and 2003,[174] the Bush administration took the position that conduct amounted to torture only if it caused *physical* pain "equivalent in intensity to the pain accompanying serious physical injury, such as organ failure, impairment of bodily function, or even death."[175] It also held the view that, given reservations and qualifications with which the United States had agreed to enter into the 1984 UN Convention Against Torture, the President remained free to determine acceptable interrogation techniques, to the limit of those that would "shock the conscience" of a court.[176] John Yoo, a lawyer in the Department of Justice, authored a memo in March of 2003 arguing for the legality of dousing a prisoner with "scalding water, corrosive acid, or [a] caustic substance," or even "slitting an ear, nose, or lip, or disabling a tongue or limb."[177] As late as the spring of 2005, Assistant Attorney General Steven Bradbury produced a memo for the Office of Legal Counsel purporting to endorse the legality of several techniques and their simultaneous use, including "waterboarding, head and belly slapping, sensory deprivation, sleep deprivation, temperature extremes, and stress positions."[178] Officials employing these techniques would be immune to criminal prosecution, or if prosecuted could avail themselves of the defense of necessity.[179] In short, the torture carried out by the Bush administration was either not torture in law, or if it was, it was a justifiable use of the President's power as Commander in Chief in a time of war.

A further aspect of U.S. counterterrorism policy that represents a suspension of the right against torture or cruelty is the practice of extraordinary rendition. This involves

---

172 Human Rights Watch, *Getting Away with Torture*, ibid. at 4.

173 Ibid.

174 The *New York Times* provides links to each memo, with a chronology and explanation, at: http://www.nytimes.com/ref/international/24MEMO-GUIDE.html.

175 *See*, ibid., the Aug. 1, 2002 memo from Office of Legal Counsel to Alberto Gonzales, Counsel to the President.

176 See, ibid. the memo of Mar. 14, 2003, from Office of Legal Counsel to William Hanes, General Counsel of the Department of Defense: http://www.aclu.org/pdfs/safefree/yoo_army_torture_memo.pdf.

177 Mayer, The Dark Side, *supra* note 23, at 230.

178 Memo of May 10, 2005, from Office of Legal Counsel to John Rizzo, Senior Deputy General Counsel, CIA: http://fas.org/irp/agency/doj/olc/techniques.pdf.

179 Further protections against criminal liability set out in the *Detainee Treatment Act of 2005* are explored below.

the kidnapping of suspects and their covert transportation either to third countries for imprisonment, interrogation and torture, or to CIA "black sites" for interrogation and torture by U.S. officials.[180] As Jane Mayer explains, the practice of kidnapping and covert transport has its roots in the Reagan administration, in a program "aimed at a small, discrete set of suspects—people against whom there were outstanding foreign arrest warrants."[181] After 9/11, "the program expanded beyond recognition," and would soon include "the wide and ill-defined population that the administration terms 'illegal enemy combatants.' "[182] In contrast to extradition, therefore, the rendition program would have the effect of "disappearing" detainees into secret CIA sites, or the hands of foreign governments, for torture and lengthy detention.

Among the most notorious and well-documented cases of rendition is that involving Canadian citizen Maher Arar. In 2003, the Canadian Security and Intelligence Service and the Royal Canadian Mounted Police had provided U.S. customs officials with erroneous information that tied Arar to a person of interest in Montreal. On his return from a family vacation in Tunisia, Arar was detained on a stopover in New York. After holding Arar for 13 days in an immigration detention center, initially without counsel, then with counsel who was provided almost no information, U.S. authorities rendered Arar to Jordanian custody, where he was interrogated and then turned over to Syria. There, he was interrogated further, tortured repeatedly, and imprisoned for a year. Months after news of the case had surfaced, Arar continued to languish in a small, damp, windowless underground cell. Due in large part to the persistent efforts of Arar's wife, the Canadian government eventually intervened and lobbied for his release.

One further case worth noting involved the CIA's kidnapping of a Muslim cleric, Abu Omar, from Milan in 2003. Upon detaining Omar, CIA operatives flew him from an American air base in Italy to a base in Germany, then to Egypt, where he was tortured and detained for *four* years. Following his release, the Italian government initiated a prosecution of the CIA base chief in Italy, and 22 others, mostly CIA operatives, on the charge of kidnapping. A trial in Italy was held with the accused *in absentia*, and in November of 2009, all were found guilty.[183]

---

180 Mayer, The Dark Side, *supra* note 23. At 320, Mayer notes that the existence and use of CIA Black sites was first reported in the American press in Dana Priest, *CIA Holds Terror Suspects in Secret Prisons*, Wash. Post, Nov. 2, 2005.

181 Mayer, The Dark Side, *supra* note 23, at 108. Human Rights Watch, *Getting Away with Torture, supra* note 171, at 33–38, lists a series of cases, including those involving the October 2001 arrest of Australian citizen Mamdouh Habib in Pakistan; the November 2001 arrest of German citizen Muhammad Zammar in Morocco; the December 2001 arrest of Egyptians Ahmed Agiza and Mohammed al-Zari in Stockholm; the November 2003 arrest of Italian citizen Osama Nasr ("Abu Omar") in Milan; and the January 2002 arrest of Pakistani citizen Muhammad Madni in Jakarta. *See also* Leila Sadat, *Extraordinary Rendition, Torture and Other Nightmares from the War on Terror*, 75 Geo. Wash. L. Rev. 101 (2007).

182 Mayer, The Dark Side, *supra* note 23, at 108.

183 Rachel Donadio, *Italy Convicts 23 Americans for C.I.A. Renditions*, N.Y. Times, Nov. 4, 2009.

In August of 2009, officials in the Obama administration confirmed that the United States would continue the practice of rendition, but with greater oversight of interrogations conducted abroad to ensure that detainees were not tortured.[184] The policy raises the obvious question of why the United States would continue to render suspects to other countries if not to avoid its obligation to comply with U.S. law. A report by *The Nation* supports this view, alleging that in July 2011, the CIA had set up a compound behind the presidential palace in Mogadishu, Somalia, in which it was running a "counterterrorism training program for Somali intelligence agents and operatives aimed at building an indigenous strike force capable of snatch operations and targeted 'combat' operations against members of Al Shabab, an Islamic militant group with close ties to Al Qaeda."[185] In the basement of the compound, prisoners were being held who have been "snatched off the streets of Kenya and rendered by plane to Mogadishu."[186] The report also alleges that prisoners were being interrogated and held in small, damp, windowless cells, some for well over a year, and none had been charged with an offense or provided any form of judicial process.

## Torture or Cruel and Unusual Treatment in the Canadian Context

A significant statement about torture was made in the unanimous 2002 decision of the Supreme Court in *Suresh v. Canada*.[187] The case concerned Manickavasagam Suresh, a Sri Lankan refugee whom the Canadian Security and Intelligence Service had believed to be a member of, and fundraiser for, a group known as the "Liberation Tigers of Tamil Eelam." The Canadian government believed this group to be involved in terrorism, but also knew that members of the group had been tortured in Sri Lanka.[188] Suresh had been detained on a security certificate in 1995 and was awaiting deportation.

Upon review of Suresh's detention in Federal Court, Justice Teitelbaum found that Suresh had been a member of the Tamil Tigers; the group had been involved in terrorist activities; and some members of the group had been subjected to torture by the Sri Lankan government.[189] Despite these findings, Justice Teitelbaum confirmed the validity of the certificate and ordered the deportation to proceed. Suresh's challenge to this decision at the Supreme Court of Canada raised a host of issues. Among them was the larger constitutional question of whether "returning a refugee to the risk of torture because of security concerns violates the principles of fundamental justice [in Section 7 of the Charter] where the deportation is effected for reasons of national security."[190]

---

184 David Johnson, *U.S. Says Rendition to Continue, But With More Oversight*, N.Y. TIMES, Aug. 24, 2009.
185 Jeremy Scahill, *The CIA's Secret Sites in Somalia*, THE NATION, July 12, 2011.
186 Ibid.
187 Suresh v. Canada (Minister of Citizenship & Immigration), [2002] 1 S.C.R. 3.
188 Ibid. at ¶11.
189 Ibid. ¶13.
190 Ibid. ¶49.

The Court surveyed a number of international law instruments and treaties to which Canada is a party, including the International Covenant on Civil and Political Rights (1966), and the Convention Against Torture (1984), and held that the Court's interpretation of Charter rights could be guided by these treaties, but was not determined by them. It also acknowledged that international law absolutely prohibited the practice of deporting people to face the risk of torture—a point on which the court below had disagreed. In its conclusions, however, the Court introduced a subtle twist in logic:

> ... both domestic and international jurisprudence suggest that torture is so abhorrent that it will almost always be disproportionate to interests on the other side of the balance, even security interests. This suggests that, barring extraordinary circumstances, deportation to torture will generally violate the principles of fundamental justice protected by s. 7 of the Charter.[191]

In other words, although the deportation to torture was generally prohibited under the Charter, it was not absolutely prohibited. Although no explanation was provided for the decision to introduce a measure of executive discretion here, the Court sought to confine this discretion to a small ambit of cases, yet to be encountered:

> We do not exclude the possibility that in exceptional circumstances, deportation to face torture might be justified, either as a consequence of the balancing process mandated by s. 7 of the Charter or under s. 1. [...] the fundamental justice balance under s. 7 of the *Charter* generally precludes deportation to torture when applied on a case-by-case basis. We may predict that it will rarely be struck in favour of expulsion where there is a serious risk of torture. However, as the matter is one of balance, precise prediction is elusive. The ambit of an exceptional discretion to deport to torture, if any, must await future cases.[192]

In short, the court held that in some cases, national security will trump a person's right to be free from torture—and the outcome would still be consistent with the Charter's guarantee of "fundamental justice."

The *Suresh* exception was applied by the Federal Court in *Nlandu-Nsoki v. Canada* (2005),[193] which suggests that it may become more than an academic curiosity. Nsoki was a refugee claimant from Angola who was found inadmissible to Canada on the basis of his membership in an Angolan terrorist group. He sought a stay of deportation on the basis of a risk of torture upon his return to Angola. An opinion issued by a "pre-removal risk-assessment officer" had concluded that there was in fact a "very serious risk of torture

---

191 Ibid. at ¶76.

192 Ibid. ¶78.

193 Nlandu-Nsoki v. Canada (Minister of Citizenship & Immigration), [2005] F.C. 17.

and severe sanctions" if he were returned. Nsoki brought a Charter challenge to the order, which Justice Shore dismissed, citing *Suresh* and its holding that deportation could proceed despite the risk of torture in "exceptional circumstances." What is notable about the decision, apart from its almost casual reliance on the *Suresh* exception, is how broadly the exception was conceived. As Justice Shore asserted, "[i]n this case exceptional circumstances do exist, namely the need to protect Canada's security."[194] In support of this, the decision cites a passage in the deportation order noting that the group to which Nsoki is alleged to be involved had tortured and killed unarmed civilians. Although Nsoki denied involvement, the panel had "serious reasons to believe that the claimant was complicit, that he had information and knew the plans of attack." No further argument was made about the danger he posed to the security of Canada.

One further example can be noted of a shift in Canada's policy in relation to torture. In December of 2010, Public Safety Minister Vic Toews issued a directive (uncovered by the Canadian Press) to the Canadian Security and Intelligence Service.[195] In "exceptional circumstances," its states, CSIS should "share the most complete information available at the time with relevant authorities, including information based on intelligence provided by foreign agencies that may have been derived from the use of torture or mistreatment."[196] Exceptional circumstances include "situations where a serious risk to public safety exists, and where lives may be at stake."[197] In such cases, the Minister states, "I expect and thus direct CSIS to make the protection of life and property its overriding priority, and share the necessary information—properly described and qualified—with appropriate authorities."[198] Prior to this directive, the ministry had taken the position that CSIS should discount any information known to have originated from torture,[199] and presumably to avoid sharing it. Although this policy shift relates only to the sharing of information in Canada's possession, the concern, as Alex Neve of Amnesty International Canada has pointed out, is that "as long as torturers continue to find a market for the fruit of their crimes, torture will continue."[200]

## Targeted Killing

The practice of targeted killing on the part of the US has roots that extend to at least the 1960s, with CIA plots to assassinate Cuban leader Fidel Castro, and later plots against leaders in Vietnam and Chile.[201] In the late 1990s, President Clinton approved the use of "lethal force in self-defense" against members of al Qaida, following attacks

---

194 Ibid. at ¶22.

195 Jim Bronksill, *Ottawa Tells Spies to Use Possible Torture Info in 'Exceptional' Cases*, GLOBE AND MAIL (Toronto), Feb. 7, 2012.

196 Directive, cited in Bronskill, ibid.

197 Ibid.

198 Ibid.

199 Ibid.

200 Cited in Bronskill, ibid.

201 Blum & Heymann, LAWS, OUTLAWS, *supra* note 21, at 73.

on U.S. embassies in Kenya and Tanzania.[202] After 9/11, President Bush would extend the scope of targeted killing to a wider class of targets, with attacks beginning at least as early as November 2002, in a strike on six al Qaida operatives traveling in Yemen, including a U.S. citizen known to be in the same vehicle.[203] Strikes were soon frequently carried out in Afghanistan, Iraq, Pakistan, and Yemen,[204] with administration officials claiming the AUMF as authority for the practice.[205]

The Obama administration would significantly escalate the use of targeted killing, and claim a broader scope for its lawful use. By 2014, the New America Foundation, which has tracked drone strike casualties since 2004, reported a total of 377 strikes in that 10-year period in Pakistan alone, resulting in up to 3,496 deaths, including as many as 307 civilians.[206] By the Foundation's count, the United States has carried out 110 strikes in Yemen in that same period, resulting in up to 1,029 deaths, including 81 to 87 civilians.[207] Numerous media sources confirm that strikes continue at present in both Pakistan and Yemen,[208] with 7 strikes and up to 68 casualties in Pakistan by mid-2014,[209] and 12 strikes and as many as 100 casualties in Yemen alone.[210]

Despite the frequency of attacks and numbers killed since 2002, the practice of targeted killing has garnered broad public attention on only a few occasions over the course of this period. Chief among them was the targeted killing of Osama bin Laden on May 1, 2011. Bin Laden had been a fugitive from U.S. justice since his indictment in 1998 for involvement in the U.S. embassy bombings in Tanzania and Kenya that year. After 9/11, one reading of the AUMF would suggest that he had become a legitimate target of assassination rather than arrest.

But the circumstances surrounding bin Laden's killing, and the more recent targeting of U.S. citizens (discussed below), have raised questions about the legality and necessity of the practice—even on the government's own terms. Official accounts of the event suggest that bin Laden could have been detained rather than killed during the raid on his compound, given the limited threat he posed to U.S. forces. At a late-night press conference, when President Obama first made the killing known, he said that U.S. forces

---

202 Ibid. at 74.

203 Ibid.

204 Ibid.

205 Eban Kaplan, *Q&A: Targeted Killing*, N.Y. TIMES, Jan. 25, 2006.

206 New America Foundation, *Drone Wars Pakistan: Analysis*, http://securitydata.newamerica.net/drones/pakistan/analysis.

207 New America Foundation, *Drone Wars Yemen: Analysis*, http://securitydata.newamerica.net/drones/yemen/analysis.

208 In addition to the New America Foundation, ibid., see also Associated Press, *Pakistan: 13 Killed as US Resumes Drone Strike Campaign*, THE GUARDIAN, June 12, 2014; and Ismail Khan & Declan Walsh, *Missile Strike by CIA Drone Kills at Least 4, Pakistan Reports*, N.Y. TIMES June 11, 2014.

209 New America Foundation, *Drone Wars Pakistan: Analysis; Year-by-Year Data*, http://securitydata.newamerica.net/drones/pakistan/2014.

210 New America Foundation, *Drone Wars Yemen: Analysis; Year-by-Year data*, http://securitydata.newamerica.net/drones/yemen/2014.

had located bin Laden in the compound and killed him "after a firefight"—suggesting a show of deadly resistance to being taken into custody.[211] But administration officials soon offered differing accounts of the capture, including one indicating that the firefight with U.S. forces had taken place earlier in the raid, in an adjacent guesthouse, and did not involve bin Laden.[212] And, on this account, when he was killed, bin Laden was said not to be in possession of a weapon, but "within reach of an assault rifle and pistol."[213] Some have therefore concluded that bin Laden was killed not by U.S. forces acting in self-defense but in a deliberate effort to assassinate him—an account that is not contradicted by the President's initial report.[214]

Jane Mayer offers a suggestive contrast between the Clinton and Obama approaches to the search for bin Laden that illustrates the extent of the shift in legal cultures between the two periods. In 1998, prior to bombings of the U.S. embassies in Kenya and Tanzania, CIA officials had approached then-Attorney General Janet Reno with a plan to locate bin Laden in Afghanistan and transport him to Egypt for "rough" interrogation that would likely result in his death. Reno is said to have balked at the proposal. Bin Laden was certainly thought to be dangerous and in urgent need of capture at the time, given his involvement in the 1993 attack on the World Trade Center and on U.S. servicemen in Somalia in the mid-1990s. But in Reno's view, any operation to capture and retrieve him from Afghanistan could be approved only if he were first indicted and the goal of the operation was to bring him to the United States to stand trial.[215] By contrast, there has been no discussion on the part of the Obama administration as to why it might have been preferable to capture rather than kill bin Laden.[216] The President's late-night announcement of the killing as having followed a "firefight" suggested a rationale for the killing, but notably, the President did not state this explicitly. A justification was thus implied here, and in later official accounts, but not offered. The administration appeared to be acting on the reasonable inference that for many Americans, a justification for killing rather than capturing was neither necessary nor expected—nor possibly even appropriate.

In September of 2011 another important threshold was crossed when the United States carried out the targeted killing of an American citizen, Anwar al-Awlaki—a person widely known to be targeted for over a year.[217] Following the event, the President described Awlaki as "the leader of external operations for al Qaeda in the

---

211 Peter Baker, Helene Cooper & Mark Mazzetti, *Bin Laden is Dead, Obama Says*, N.Y. TIMES, May 1, 2011.

212 Robert Booth, *The Killing of Osama bin Laden: How the White House Changed Its Story*, THE GUARDIAN, May 4, 2011.

213 Ibid.

214 *See also* Yochi Dreazen, Aamer Madhani & Marc Ambinder, *The Goal Was Never to Capture bin Laden*, THE ATLANTIC, May 4, 2011.

215 Mayer, DARK SIDE, *supra* note 23, at 38.

216 See Booth, *supra* note 212, on the administration's varying accounts of the deadly force that commandos encountered, which impliedly made the killing necessary.

217 Laura Kasinof, Mark Mazzetti & Alan Cowell, *U.S.-Born Qaeda Leader Killed in Yemen*, N. Y. TIMES, Sept. 30, 2011.

Arabian Peninsula" and claimed that he had taken "the lead role in planning and directing the efforts to murder innocent Americans abroad."[218] He also suggested that Awlaki had encouraged or inspired militants in several plots, including the attempt in December of 2009 by Umar Farouk Abdulmutallab to explode a passenger jet destined for Detroit, using a bomb in his underwear.[219] The strike also killed a second U.S. citizen, Samir Khan, with whom Awlaki had been traveling. Khan was the editor of a radical online news organ, but had been not explicitly targeted.[220] Weeks later, the United States carried out another drone attack in Yemen that killed Awlaki's 16-year-old son, Abulrahman, along with eight others.[221] The administration has not indicated whom it sought to target in the attack, and initially claimed that Abdulrahman was 21 years old at the time.[222] The *Washington Post* soon published the boy's Colorado birth certificate, dating to 1995.[223] Journalist Glenn Greenwald has suggested that the failure to disclose the target in this case indicates at least the possibility that Awlaki's son was explicitly targeted.[224]

In February of 2013, NBC News published a white paper from the Department of Justice defending the legality of the targeted killing of U.S. citizens on foreign soil, without referring to Awlaki specifically.[225] As the paper argued, the President is authorized to carry out such an operation if a U.S. citizen is a "senior operational leader of al-Qa'ida or an associated force"; he poses "an imminent threat of violent attack" against the United States, his "capture is not feasible," and the operation is conducted in a manner "consistent with applicable law of war principles."[226] The President is said to derive authority for this from the AUMF and "the inherent right of the United States to national self-defense under international law."[227] The memo does not explain the process by which the President decides whether a person fits the description of a "senior operational leader," or what standard of evidence is sufficient. Nor does it suggest the need for any independent oversight of the President's decision-making process. But perhaps most crucially, the memo asserts the need to employ a qualified definition of the word "imminent." The threat at issue, it states, "demands a broader concept of imminence in judgment when a

---

218 Mark Mazzetti, Eric Schmitt & Robert Worth, *Two-Year Manhunt Led to Killing of Awlaki in Yemen*, N.Y. TIMES, Sept. 20, 2011.

219 Ibid.

220 Ibid.

221 Peter Finn & Greg Miller, *Anwar al-Awlaki's Family Speaks Out Against His Son's Death in Airstrike*, WASH. POST, Oct. 17, 2011.

222 Ibid.

223 WASH. POST, at http://www.washingtonpost.com/wp-srv/world/documents/abdulrahman-al-awlaki-birth-certificate.html.

224 Glenn Greenwald, *The Killing of Awlaki's 16-year-old Son*, SALON.COM, Oct. 20, 2011.

225 Dep't of Justice White Paper: *Lawfulness of a Lethal Operation Directed Against a U.S. Citizen Who is a Senior Operational Leader of Al-Qa'ida or an Associated Force*, http://msnbcmedia.msn.com/i/msnbc/sections/news/020413_DOJ_White_Paper.pdf>.

226 Ibid. at 1.

227 Ibid.

person continually planning terror attacks presents an imminent threat... In this context, imminence must incorporate considerations of the relevant window of opportunity, the possibility of reducing collateral damage to civilians, and the likelihood of heading off future disastrous attacks on Americans."[228]

The paper drew upon an earlier legal memorandum produced by the Department of Justice's Office of Legal Counsel that dealt with the legality of targeting Awlaki in particular. But that memo had remained confidential until recently. The American Civil Liberties Union (ACLU) and the *New York Times* sought disclosure of the memo in application under the Freedom of Information Act,[229] which the U.S. District Court for the Southern District of New York dismissed in January of 2013.[230] In April of 2014, the Court of Appeals for the Second Circuit overturned this ruling, with Judge Newman holding on behalf of the court that whatever merit there may have been for preserving the secrecy of the legal analysis in the memo, it had been lost "by virtue of public statements of public officials at the highest levels and official disclosure of the D.O.J. White Paper."[231] The court ordered disclosure of a redacted version of the memo, concealing roughly a quarter of the text setting out factual details of Awlaki's activities in Yemen and proposed methods for his assassination.[232]

The focus in this earlier memo, authored by former OLC lawyer David Barron in 2010, was whether a targeted killing on the part of either the Department of Defense (DOD) or the CIA is prohibited under federal criminal law offenses against the murder of U.S. citizens abroad, conspiracy to commit murder, or war crimes.[233] The memo contends that the offense of "foreign murder of United States nationals" in Title 18 was not intended to exclude traditional justifications for and defenses to murder, including the "public authority" justification, or to exclude their application to agencies such as the DOD or CIA.[234] The same would apply to the offense of conspiracy.[235] The justification was thus applicable to those offenses generally, but also in particular to the targeted killing of a U.S. citizen by either agency "because the operation would constitute the 'lawful conduct of war'—a well established variant of the public authority justification."[236] Awlaki's "operational and leadership" role as a planner of an "abortive attack" (presumably the Christmas plot of December 2009), and other unspecified activities, rendered

---

228 Ibid. at 7.

229 5 U.S.C. §552.

230 New York Times Co. v. U. S. Dep't of Justice, 915 F. Supp. 2d 508 (S.D.N.Y. 2013).

231 New York Times Co. v. U. S. Dep't of Justice, Docket Nos. 13-422(L), 13-445(Con), (2d Cir. June 23, 2014), at 56.

232 Office of Legal Counsel, *Memorandum for the Attorney General* (Dep't of Justice, July 16, 2010) ["OLC memo"], appended to the end of the Second Circuit decision, ibid.

233 18 U.S.C., §§1119, 956(a) and 2441.

234 OLC memo, *supra* note 232, at 17.

235 Ibid. at 35.

236 Ibid. at 20.

him a "leader" of al Qaeda in the Arab Peninsula (AQAP) and thus a combatant falling within the scope of the AUMF.[237] Despite there being no armed conflict between the United States and Yemen itself, the laws of war were engaged due to AQAP's "significant and organized presence" in Yemen, and its conduct of "terrorist training in an organized manner," which render it "part of the non-international armed conflict between the United States and al-Qaida."[238]

The memo then drew upon earlier Supreme Court jurisprudence to address the question of whether a target's identity as a U.S. citizen raises due process issues under the Constitution. As Barron writes:

> In *Hamdi*, a plurality of the Supreme Court used the *Mathews v. Eldridge* balancing test to analyze the Fifth Amendment due process rights of a U.S. citizen captured on the battlefield in Afghanistan and detained in the United States who wished to challenge the government's assertion that he was a part of enemy forces, explaining that "the process due in any given instance is determined by weighing 'the private interest that will be affected by the official action' against the Government's asserted interest, 'including the function involved' and the burdens the Government would face in providing greater process."[239]

Barron argued that the *Mathews* test applied here in the government's favor. Given "the nature of the threat posed by al-Aulaqi's activities," and the assumption that his capture was not "feasible" at present, "the weight of the government's interest in using an authorized means of lethal force against this enemy are such that the Constitution would not require the government to provide further process to the U.S. person before using such force."[240]

Yet, as other commentators have observed, Barron's articulation of the *Mathews* test is incomplete.[241] In the passage cited above, Barron quotes Justice O'Connor's opinion in *Hamdi* summarizing the *Mathews* test, but omits O'Connor's citation of the next sentence in *Mathews* that qualifies the balancing test. A citizen's private interest must be weighed against the government's interests in avoiding undue burdens of providing greater process, but as O'Connor adds:

> The *Mathews* calculus then contemplates a judicious balancing of these concerns, through an analysis of "the risk of an erroneous deprivation" of the private interest

---

237 Ibid. at 21.

238 Ibid. at 27.

239 Ibid. at 39, citing Hamdi v. Rumsfeld, 542 U.S. 507 (2004), at 529 (plurality opinion), quoting Mathews v. Eldridge, 424 U.S. 319, 335 (1976).

240 OLC memo, *supra* note 232, at 40.

241 Deborah Pearlstein, *OLC Memo—the Due Process Piece*, Opinio Juris, June 24, 2014; on a similar omission in the White Paper, see Jameel Jaffer, *The Justice Department's White Paper on Targeted Killing*, ACLU.org, Feb. 4, 2013).

> if the process were reduced and the "probable value, if any, of additional or substitute safeguards."[242]

As Deborah Pearlstein has suggested, this additional consideration complicates the *Mathews* test considerably, and there is "no indication that the memo conducted this part of the analysis, not only because this part of the *Mathews* test is missing from the memo's summary, but also because there is no indication the memo undertakes the first necessary part of what this test would require—a description of what are the existing procedures."[243] The memo also fails to explain why Awlaki's activities amounted to an "imminent threat," and the facts that might explain why it was not feasible to capture him were redacted.

In March of 2013, the Obama administration went a step further by asserting the legal authority to carry out targeted killing of American citizens *in* the United States. Attorney General Eric Holder set out this position in a letter to Senator Rand Paul, Republican of Kentucky, who had asked whether "the President has the power to authorize lethal force, such as a drone strike, against a U.S. citizen on U.S. soil, and without trial."[244] Holder replied, "it is possible, I suppose, to imagine an extraordinary circumstance in which it would be necessary and appropriate under the Constitution and applicable laws of the United States for the President to authorize the military to use lethal force within the territory of the United States" against a U.S. citizen. The President may have "no choice," Holder suggested, "in the circumstances of a catastrophic attack like the ones suffered on December 7, 1941, and September 11, 2001." Yet Holder also indicated that such a possibility was "entirely hypothetical" and "unlikely to occur." Holder appeared that week before the Senate Judiciary Committee. Although Senators were critical of the scope of the authority Holder had asserted in the letter, as the *New York Times* notes, a number of Senators "defended the notion that some use of military force on United States soil would be lawful."[245] Senator Dianne Feinstein, Democrat of California, suggested it might be necessary to shoot down a plane hijacked by terrorists, one or more of whom might be Americans. Senator Lindsey Graham, Republican of South Carolina, asserted that the AUMF did not preclude operations on U.S. soil, and Holder agreed.[246]

Aside from the Court of Appeals' decision to order disclosure of the OLC's 2010 legal memorandum, courts have been reluctant to assert limits on the President's use of targeted killing—or assumptions about its legality. In August of 2010, acting on

---

242 *Hamdi, supra* note 239, at 529.

243 Pearlstein, *supra* note 241.

244 Letter of Mar. 4, 2013, from Attorney General Eric Holder to Senator Rand Paul; online: http://www.paul.senate.gov/files/documents/BrennanHolderResponse.pdf.

245 Charlie Savage, *Senators Press Holder on Use of Military Force on U.S. Soil*, N.Y. TIMES, Mar. 6, 2013.

246 Ibid.

public knowledge that his son was being targeted, Awlaki's father Nasser al-Awlaki, together with the ACLU, brought an action in the U.S. District Court for the District of Columbia to enjoin the killing as a violation of his son's right to due process under the Fifth Amendment. Nasser's counsel had argued that the killing would be unlawful in the absence of due process, defined to include notice and a fair hearing, unless Anwar al-Awlaki "presented a concrete, specific, and imminent threat of death."[247] In the course of its motion to dismiss the action, the administration invoked the state secrets doctrine (discussed further below), with supporting evidence that included confidential statements of James Clapper, Director of National Intelligence; Robert Gates, Secretary of Defense at the time; and Leon Panetta, who was then Director of the CIA.[248] Judge Bates dismissed the action not on grounds of state or military secrets, but on the grounds that al-Awlaki's father lacked standing to sue for his son's constitutional rights.[249]

In response to the 2011 targeted killing of Awlaki, and collateral killings of Awlaki's son Abdulrahman and Samir Khan, Nassir al-Awlaki and Khan's mother Sarah Khan, along with the ACLU, filed an action in the U.S. District Court for the District of Columbia against Leon Panetta and various other administration officials in their personal capacity on a number of grounds, including a violation of due process rights under the Fifth Amendment.[250] On behalf of Awlaki's son and Mr. Khan, the two individuals not directly targeted, counsel had argued that the government violated obligations under both the Constitution and international human rights law to take greater steps to avoid harming the deceased. In her decision in *Al-Aulaqi v. Panetta*, Judge Collyer dismissed the action against the two collateral victims in part on the basis that "[m]ere negligence does not rise to a constitutional deprivation."[251] On behalf of the estate of Anwar al-Awlaki, counsel had argued that the deceased's rights to procedural and substantive due process under the Fifth Amendment were violated because he was "executed without charge, indictment, or prosecution."[252] Judge Collyer agreed that Awlaki's estate had established a prima facie case for a violation of due process rights, but held that there was "no available remedy under U.S. law for this claim."[253] Counsel had relied on *Bivens v. Six Unknown Named Agents of Federal Bureau of Narcotics*,[254] which allowed for damages against federal officials for violating Fourth Amendment rights. Yet, as Judge Collyer noted, in the four decades since *Bivens* was decided, courts had been reluctant to extend the holding to new contexts, and there were compelling reasons not to do so here.[255] The killing in this case

---

247 Al-Aulaqi v. Obama, 727 F. Supp. 2d 1 (D.D.C. 2010), at 4.
248 Ibid. at 52–54.
249 Ibid. at 14–35.
250 Al-Aulaqi v. Panetta, No. 12-1192 (D.D.C Apr. 4, 2014).
251 Ibid. at 26.
252 Ibid.
253 Ibid. at 27.
254 403 U.S. 388 (1971).
255 Al-Aulaqi v. Panetta, *supra* note 250, at 28.

was authorized under the AUMF, given its application to al Qaida and affiliated forces, evidence of Awlaki's leadership role in AQAP, and the AUMF's lack of "geographic limits."[256] To extend *Bivens* to the present context would "require the Court to examine national security policy and the military chain of command as well as operational combat decisions regarding the designation of targets and how best to counter threats to the United States"—all of which were clearly beyond the purview of the court.[257] Extending *Bivens* would also hinder the executive in the future "to act decisively and without hesitation in defense of U.S. interests."[258]

To a significant degree, *Al-Aulaqi v. Panetta* affirms the administration's perspective on the legality of targeting killing in the case of US citizens, and in the case of foreigners, the practice continues, for the most part, without constraint from US courts. Yet many facts remain unclear that would assist the public to assess the program's practical and legal justification. As the ACLU has argued, an adequate assessment would require a disclosure of the countries in which the US has carried out targeted killings, the investigative reports or facts on which decisions in earlier strikes were based, a record of collateral casualties, and other OLC memos on targeted killing the administration has used for legal guidance.[259] Although the Court of Appeals decision noted above has ordered disclosure of further OLC memos, there is no indication that the administration intends to release the other information or lower the rate at which it presently engages in targeted killing abroad.

## II. LEGISLATIVE ENTRENCHMENT OF EXPANDED SECRECY AND SURVEILLANCE

In addition to a suspension of core human rights, authoritarian legality is marked by the entrenchment of a greater scope for state secrecy and surveillance. Canadian law provides a better example of the former, and American law a better example of the latter.

### Expanded Scope for Secrecy and Surveillance in U.S. Law

Soon after 9/11, the Bush administration sought to expand the scope of state secrecy and surveillance on several fronts. One notable early example concerns an order that then-Attorney General John Ashcroft issued in October of 2001, pursuant to federal legislation governing prisons and military tribunals.[260] The order authorizes the Attorney General to monitor communications between prisoners or detainees and their lawyers that would otherwise be private and subject to attorney and client privilege. It allows for

256 Ibid. at 34.

257 Ibid. at 36

258 Ibid.

259 Jameel Jaffer, *Obama's "Drone Memo" is Finally Public. Now Show Us the Library of Secret Law*, ACLU.ORG, June 24, 2014.

260 National Security; Prevention of Acts of Violence and Terrorism, 66 Fed. Reg. 55,062 (Oct. 31, 2001) (codified at 28 C.F.R. §§501.2, 501.3 (2003)).

such monitoring where "reasonable suspicion exists to believe that a particular inmate may use communications with attorneys or their agents to further or facilitate acts of terrorism."[261] The Attorney General may issue an order for monitoring without judicial approval, if notice is provided. But with a court's approval, a client's communication with his or her counsel could be monitored without either being aware of it. The order has been the subject of considerable opposition from civil liberties groups[262] and was challenged in two cases,[263] but remains in effect.

Under the USA PATRIOT Act, [264] U.S. lawmakers enabled a much broader expansion of state secrecy and surveillance. To place these reforms into context, it may help to note that prior to the passage of the Act, there were three primary sources of authority by which the federal government could compel disclosure of third-party records or intercept private calls or e-mails of any person inside or outside the United States.[265] First, in a criminal investigation targeting any person inside the United States, authorities could obtain a warrant under the Wiretap Act of 1968 (Title III)[266] from a federal judge on the basis of reasonable grounds to believe that a crime has been committed, or is about to be, and that the search or surveillance is likely to yield relevant evidence.[267] Second, for the purpose of gathering "foreign intelligence" defined to include matters pertaining to international terrorism, agencies could obtain an order under the Foreign Intelligence Surveillance Act of 1978[268] (FISA) pursuant to a secret, ex parte hearing before the Foreign Intelligence Surveillance Court (FISA court). To compel disclosure of a third-party record, the government would have to show "specific and articulable facts giving reason to believe that the person to whom the records pertain is a foreign power or an agent of a foreign power." [269] For interceptions of electronic communications entirely or partly within the United States, the government would have to show probable cause to believe that the targeted person is an agent of a foreign power or engaged in international terrorism.[270] Finally, for surveillance of electronic communications that took place

261 §501.3(d) of the order, ibid.

262 Ellen Podgor & John Wesley Hall, *Government Surveillance of Attorney-Client Communications: Involved in the Name of Fighting Terrorism*, 17 Geo. J. Legal Ethics 145 (2003–2004), at 148.

263 Ibid. at 150.

264 USA PATRIOT Act, *supra* note 129, §§206, 207, 214, & 216.

265 The President's Review Group on Intelligence and Communications Technologies, *Liberty and Security in a Changing World: Report and Recommendations of The President's Review Group on Intelligence and Communications Technologies*, White House, Dec. 12, 2013, http://www.whitehouse.gov/sites/default/files/docs/2013-12-12_rg_final_report.pdf [Review Group Report], at 131.

266 18 U.S.C. §2518.

267 Ibid. §2518(3); Review Group Report, *supra* note 265, at 131.

268 50 U.S.C. ch 36.

269 Intelligence Authorization Act for Fiscal Year 1999, Pub. L. 105–272, §602, 112 Stat. 2396, 2410 (1998), adding the now rescinded section 1862 of FISA; *cited in* Review Group Report, *supra* note 265, at 80. A version of the Act containing the rescinded provision is available at http://epic.org/privacy/terrorism/fisa/FISA_since_911.pdf.

270 FISA, *supra* note 268, §1805(a)(3)(A); discussed in Review Group Report, *supra* note 265, at 131.

entirely outside the United States, limited authority could be found in President Reagan's Executive Order 12,333 of 1981.[271] This had been issued to address a gap left by FISA's drafters, who chose to defer the issue of what limits to place on surveillance outside the United States to later legislators dealing with individual agency powers, or to the constitutional powers of the executive.[272] The order required the various agencies to formulate policies and protocols for intelligence gathering, but did not set out a clear test governing when surveillance could occur involving either foreigners or Americans abroad. The order instead affirms that such collection should be "pursued in a vigorous, innovative and responsible manner that is consistent with the Constitution and applicable law and respectful of the principles upon which the United States was founded."[273]

The USA PATRIOT Act expanded the scope of the availability of warrants under the first two of these authorities, FISA and the Wiretap Act.[274] As noted, FISA had offered a limited exception to the Title III standard by allowing a warrant for surveilling a person in the United States to be issued on the lower threshold of probable cause to believe that the target of surveillance is a "foreign power" or an agent of a foreign power.[275] The USA PATRIOT Act expanded the scope of FISA warrants to allow for the surveillance of a person of unknown identity and to track their movement across jurisdictions, communication instruments, and providers ("roving wiretaps").[276] The scope for FISA warrants was also expanded to allow for wiretapping, electronic surveillance and physical searches of the property of both citizens and foreigners within the United States where "foreign intelligence" is not the primary purpose of an investigation, as before, but where it is only a "significant purpose."[277] A FISA warrant could thus be issued in many more domestic criminal cases than before. In addition, the USA PATRIOT Act amended the Wiretap Act to allow law enforcement or other government officials to access information gleaned under a Title III search carried out for some other purpose, if the information relates to "the ability of the United States to protect against" a potential terrorist attack.[278]

Yet among the most contentious of the USA PATRIOT Act's new surveillance powers were those found under Sections 213 and 215. Under Section 213, where a warrant is issued for the search of a premises, for electronic surveillance, or for the seizure of material, notice of the warrant may be withheld if it would otherwise risk destroying evidence, result in bodily injury, or jeopardize an investigation. Notice of the warrant must be provided "within a reasonable period of its execution"; however, this period "may thereafter

---

271 Executive Order 12,333, *United States Intelligence Activities*, Dec. 4, 1981, 46 Fed. Reg. 59941, 3 C.F.R. 1981 Comp., at 200: <http://www.archives.gov/federal-register/codification/executive-order/12333.html>.

272 Review Group Report, *supra* note 265, at 131.

273 Executive Order 12,333, *supra* note 271, at §2.1; *see also* discussion in Review Group Report, *supra* note 265, at 132.

274 *See* §§206, 207, 214, and 216 *USA* PATRIOT Act, *supra* note 129.

275 FISA, *supra* note 268, §1805(a)(2).

276 PATRIOT Act, *supra* note 129, §206.

277 Ibid. §218.

278 Ibid. §203.

be extended by the court for good cause shown." The section therefore contemplates a person's indefinite surveillance without their knowledge. Section 215 amended FISA to allow intelligence agencies to apply to the FISA court for an order requiring:

> the production of any tangible things (including books, records, papers, documents, and other items) for an investigation to protect against international terrorism or clandestine intelligence activities, provided that such investigation of a United States person is not conducted solely upon the basis of activities protected by the first amendment to the Constitution.[279]

This was a sweeping power that authorized the FISA court—a court that issues secret orders, following secret hearings—to order the disclosure of records of electronic and other communications of U.S. citizens without the need to establish reasonable and probable grounds or even reasonable suspicion that the items sought might afford evidence of an individual's involvement in terrorism. All that was required was to demonstrate that the record was sought as part of an "investigation to protect against international terrorism or clandestine intelligence activities." The target of the order need not be specified or confined to a *specific* group of people, nor would the target(s) need to be notified of the order after the fact. In response to criticism of the provision, Congress amended FISA in 2005 to provide that a Section 215 order could not be issued unless the government provided the court with a "statement of facts showing that there are reasonable grounds to believe that the tangible objects sough are *relevant*" to an investigation concerning a foreign power or its agent—"or to protect against international terrorism."[280]

However, as President Obama's Review Group on surveillance issues has noted, from 2006 onward, the FISA court took a broad interpretation of the meaning of "relevance" in this context.[281] The court might have assumed that the need to show the "relevance" of a record to an investigation required the government to show reasonable grounds linking a particular individual or group to which a record pertained with a specific suspect of a terror investigation—or to limit an order to records pertaining to any persons who called the suspect within a reasonable period.[282] But beginning in 2006, and in more than 35 decisions since, the court interpreted the term "relevant" broadly enough to authorize orders requiring U.S. telecommunication companies to provide to the FBI and NSA "on an ongoing daily basis" for 90 days "all call detail records or 'telephony meta-data' created by [the provider] for communications

279 Ibid. §215.

280 USA PATRIOT Improvement and Reauthorization Act of 2005, §106, 120 Stat. 196 (codified as amended at 50 U.S.C. §1861(b)(2)(A)) (emphasis added). *See also* Review Group Report, *supra* note 265, at 81.

281 Review Group Report, ibid. at 94.

282 Ibid.

(i) between the United States and abroad; or (ii) wholly within the United States, including local telephone calls."[283]

Yet well before the FISA court took this expansive approach, and before changes to Section 215 were made in 2005, the Bush administration saw the need to circumvent *FISA* altogether. In late 2001 or early 2002, the President issued a secret Executive Order authorizing the National Security Agency (NSA) to wiretap or monitor phone calls and other electronic communication between individuals *in* the United States and persons abroad, without a FISA order, or a warrant under any other legislation, where there was a basis to believe that one party was associated with al Qaida.[284] The program, and the order authorizing it, came to light in an article in the *New York Times* in 2005.[285] The Bush administration claimed that the President possessed the implied authority to issue the order under the powers set out in the AUMF, and the direct authority as Commander in Chief of the Armed Forces in Article 2 of the U.S. Constitution.[286] Critics of the program argued against this view on the basis that the U.S. federal criminal code explicitly states that the surveillance provisions of the code and FISA are the "exclusive means by which electronic surveillance... may be conducted."[287] In 2006, a member of a Muslim charity and two of his lawyers filed a tort claim against the government for its warrantless surveillance of them under the secret program. A U.S. district court in California ruled in the plaintiffs' favor in March of 2010, dismissing the government's claim to authority for warrantless surveillance, but the decision was overturned on appeal on other grounds.[288]

FISA was amended in 2008 to make clear that the President does not have the authority to carry out warrantless surveillance directed at "United States persons," defined as citizens or permanent residents, when situated in the United States.[289] The amendments also made clear that when the government targets a U.S. person outside the United States, it must meet the older requirement under FISA of showing probable cause to

---

283 In re Application of the Federal Bureau of Investigation for an Order Requiring the Production of Tangible Things from [Undisclosed Service Provider], Docket No. BR 13-109 (FISC Oct. 11, 2013) (hereinafter FISC order 10/11/2013). Cited in Review Group Report, *supra* note 265, at 95. For the original order, see In re Application of the Federal Bureau of Investigation for an Order Requiring the Prod. of Tangible Things from [Telecommunications Providers] Relating to [Redacted version], Order No. BR-05 (FISC May 24, 2006).

284 Jennifer Wispinski, The USA PATRIOT Act and Canada's Anti-terrorism Act: Key Differences in Legislative Approach, (Ottawa: Parliamentary Information and Research Service, 2006), at 11. *See also* Review Group Report, *supra* note 265, at 133.

285 E. Lichtblau & J. Risen, *Bush Lets U.S. Spy on Callers Without Courts*, N.Y. Times, Dec. 16 2005; *cited in* Wispinski, ibid.

286 Wispinski, *supra* note 284, at 11.

287 18 U.S.C., §2511(2)(f), *cited in* Ronald Dworkin, Kathleen Sullivan, Laurence Tribe, David Cole, & Curtis Bradley et al., *On NSA Spying: A Letter to Congress*, N.Y. Rev. of Books, Feb. 9, 2006.

288 Al-Haramain Islamic Foundation, Inc. v. Obama, 690 F.3d 1089 (9th Cir 2012), reversing In re Nat'l Sec. Agency Telecomms. Records Litig., 700 F.Supp.2d 1182 (N.D.Cal.2010).

289 Foreign Surveillance Act of 1978 Amendments Act of 2008, H.R. 6304 (FISA Amendment Act).

believe that the target is an agent of a foreign power.[290] But in Section 702 of the FISA Amendment Act, Congress established that in the case of a non-U.S. person who is "reasonably believed to be located outside the United States," the government need not show probable cause to believe the target is an agent of a foreign power, or obtain an individual warrant, *even if the interception is carried out in the United States.*[291]

Moreover, in the case of non-U.S. persons believed to be outside the United States, Section 702 authorizes a form of mass surveillance by allowing the NSA to submit to the FISA court for approval a general description of the *class* of persons it seeks to surveil for an entire year.[292] The primary requirement in Section 702 is for the government to show that "a significant purpose" of the surveillance is the gathering "foreign intelligence information,"[293] which is defined broadly in FISA to include information "relating to" potential attacks by a foreign power, international terrorism, or simply "the conduct of the foreign affairs of the United States."[294] Therefore, as long as the "significant purpose" test is met, and there is a reasonable belief that a targeted class of persons is located outside the US, a mass interception can be carried out *inside* the US and may involve communications with US persons. And more crucially, the surveillance in these cases is not limited to metadata, but also includes the *content* of the communication.

Thus, as the ACLU has observed, when approving an order under Section 702, the court "may not know who, what, or where will actually be tapped, thereby undercutting any meaningful role for the court and violating the Fourth Amendment."[295] Margot Kaminski adds that the new provision also "does not require the government to identify its targets; it does not require the government to identify the monitored facilities; and the purpose of foreign intelligence gathering attaches to the whole surveillance program, not the individual investigation."[296] As a result of the 2008 amendments to *FISA*, the government can now obtain "a single court order through which it can monitor thousands, or even millions, of people."[297] The ACLU has argued that in a broader sense, FISA now permits the state to "conduct mass, untargeted surveillance of all communications coming into and out of the United States, without any individualized review, and without any finding of wrongdoing."[298]

---

290 Ibid. §702, substantially codified as amended in FISA §1805(a).

291 FISA, *supra* note 268, §1805(a); *see also* Review Group Report, *supra* note 265, at 135.

292 FISA, ibid. §1805(c)(3); *see also* Glenn Greenwald, NO PLACE LEFT TO HIDE: EDWARD SNOWDEN, THE NSA, AND THE U.S. SURVEILLANCE STATE (New York: Metropolitan Books, 2014) at 74.

293 FISA Amendment Act, *supra* note 289, §702(g)(2)(A)(v).

294 FISA, *supra* note 268, §§1805(a)(4) & 1801(e).

295 American Civil Liberties Union, *Vote No on H.R. 6304, the FISA Amendments Act—Oppose Warrantless Surveillance and Immunity for Telecommunications Companies*, June 25, 2008 (ACLU letter), at 3: https://www.aclu.org/sites/default/files/images/general/asset_upload_file902_35782.pdf.

296 Margot Kaminski, *PRISM's Legal Basis: How We Got Here, and What We Can Do to Get Back*, THE ATLANTIC, June 7, 2013.

297 Ibid.

298 ACLU letter, *supra* note 295, at 3.

A crucial element in Section 702 is the possibility of incidental surveillance of U.S. persons, including the content of their communications with targeted foreigners. Jameel Jaffer of the ACLU questions whether this incidental character should be taken here to mean unintentional. As Jaffer notes:

> [w]hen the Bush administration officials asked Congress for this new surveillance power, they said quite explicitly that Americans' communications were the communications of most interest to them. See, for example, "FISA for the 21st Century," Hearing Before the S. Comm. on the Judiciary, 109th Cong. (2006) (statement of Michael Hayden) (stating, in debate preceding passage of FAA's predecessor statute, that certain communications "with one end in the United States" are the ones "that are most important to us").[299]

The primary purpose of the FISA Amendment Act was, in Jaffer's view, to "make it possible for the government to collect *Americans'* international communications" regardless of whether "any party to those communications was doing anything illegal."[300] Despite the focus in Section 702 on surveilling persons outside the United States, the section makes clear that "the government doesn't need to target Americans in order to collect huge volumes of their communications."[301]

Reports in the *Guardian* and the *Washington Post* in June of 2013 appeared to confirm the validity of concerns on the part of the ACLU and others.[302] Acting as a conduit for disclosures made by a 29-year-old NSA contractor, Edward Snowden, the papers revealed the existence of two secret NSA programs of considerable sweep. Under the authority of Section 215 of the Patriot Act, the NSA had been collecting phone records from all customers of the cell phone carrier Verizon in the United States for three months, including information about who was calling, where they were, and the duration of the calls.[303] The FISA court had secretly directed a subsidiary of Verizon to provide the NSA "on an ongoing daily basis" logs of communications "between the United States and abroad," or "wholly within the United States, including local telephone calls."[304] Senator Diane Feinstein, chair of the Senate's Select Committee on Intelligence, then confirmed that the order was one of several similar orders issued in the past seven years.[305]

---

299 Cited in Glenn Greenwald, *FISA Court Oversight: a Look Inside a Secret and Empty Process*, GUARDIAN (U.K.), June 19, 2013.

300 Ibid.

301 Ibid.

302 *See, e.g.*, Glenn Greenwald, *NSA Collecting Phone Records of Millions of Verizon Customers Daily*, THE GUARDIAN. June 6, 2013; and Glenn Greenwald & Ewan MacAskill, *NSA Prism Program Taps in to User Data of Apple, Google and Others*, THE GUARDIAN, June 7, 2013. For context on the disclosures, see Greenwald, NO PLACE LEFT, *supra* note 292, chs. 1–3.

303 Greenwald, *NSA Collecting Phone Records*, ibid.

304 Ibid.

305 Charlie Savage, Edward Wyatt & Peter Baker, *U.S. Confirms That It Gathers Online Data Overseas*, N.Y. TIMES, June 6, 2013.

Snowden also revealed the existence of the NSA's secret "Prism" program, which had been running at that point for six years and involved the collection of Internet data of foreigners outside the United States in relation to companies including Google, Facebook, Skype, AOL, YouTube, and Apple.[306] The program had been authorized under Section 702 of the FISA Amendment Act, pursuant to a series of orders that the FISA court had repeatedly renewed. The orders allowed for surveillance of both metadata and the content of e-mails, stored data, file transfers, and log-ins. The *Guardian* reported that the program involved U.S. calls and e-mails being "collected in large quantities... either deliberately because the individual has been in contact with a foreign intelligence target or inadvertently because the NSA is unable to separate out purely domestic communications."[307]

In the immediate wake of the Snowden revelations, James Clapper, Director of National Intelligence, issued a press release defending the legality of PRISM program and its necessity in light of grave threats to national security. The government was not "unilaterally" obtaining data from service providers, but acting pursuant to a FISA court order, under powers clearly set out in Section 702. The section also contains adequate protections, he asserted, given its restriction on disclosure to cases where there is "an appropriate, and documented, foreign intelligence purpose for the acquisition (such as for the prevention of terrorism, hostile cyber activities, or nuclear proliferation) and the foreign target is believed to be outside the United States."[308] He also asserted that the surveillance at issue had "directly and significantly contributed to successful operations to impede the proliferation of weapons of mass destruction and related technologies."[309]

In response to a broader public debate sparked by the Snowden revelations, President Obama convened a panel of experts to examine federal surveillance policy and make recommendations for reform. The President's Review Group on Intelligence and Communications Technologies included Richard A. Clarke, a former National Coordinator for Security, Infrastructure Protection, and Counterterrorism under Presidents Bush and Obama, and Cass Sunstein, a former member of the White House Office of Information and Regulatory Affairs and law professor at the University of Chicago and Harvard. Reporting in December of 2013, the Group took issue with the broad scope for surveillance under both FISA and the PATRIOT Act.[310] It asserted the view that, "as a general rule... government should not be permitted to collect and store

---

306 Greenwald, *NSA Prism Program*," *supra* note 302.

307 Ewan MacAskill, *NSA Paid Millions to Cover Prism Compliance Costs for Tech Companies*, GUARDIAN (U.K.), Aug. 22, 2013.

308 James Clapper, Director of National Intelligence, *Facts on the Collection of Intelligence Pursuant to Section 702 of the Foreign Intelligence Surveillance Act*, June 8, 2013, at 1, http://www.dni.gov/index.php/newsroom/press-releases/191-press-releases-2013/871-facts-on-the-collection-of-intelligence-pursuant-to-section-702-of-the-foreign-intelligence-surveillance-act.

309 Review Group Report, *supra* note 265.

310 Ibid. at 2.

mass, undigested, non-public personal information about US persons for the purpose of enabling future queries and data-mining for foreign intelligence purposes."[311] To this end, it recommended that Section 215 be amended to allow the court to authorize disclosure of the records only with "reasonable grounds to believe the particular information sought is relevant to an authorized investigation intended to protect against 'international terrorism or clandestine intelligence activities' " and the order is "reasonable in focus, scope, and breadth."[312]

Yet, to be clear, the Group was not endorsing an end to the bulk collection of personal data altogether. It called for an end to bulk collection on the part of government in light of an acknowledgement that under existing law, telephone companies and other third parties are required to retain much of the same information gathered under Section 215 for certain periods, and that many other companies do the same voluntarily. The Group thus recommended that government stop collecting and retaining directly, and that new law be passed to *require* third parties to collect and retain much of the same data in its stead.[313] The issue for the group was not therefore whether such information should be collected, but when the NSA should have access to it. Its recommendations for reform of Section 215 should thus be read in tandem with its recommendations for third-party retention rules.

The Review Group was also critical of the powers under section 702 of the FISA Amendment Act. These, it suggested, should be amended so that any information belonging to or pertaining to a U.S. person gleaned in the course of surveillance of a foreigner should be "purged upon detection unless it either has foreign intelligence value or is necessary to prevent serious harm to others."[314] The information also should not be used as evidence in any proceeding against a U.S. person. And more broadly, the provision should be amended to limit government access to the content of any communication by a U.S. person to cases where it was necessary to prevent "a threat of death or serious bodily harm," or where a warrant is obtained on probable cause to believe the person is

---

311 Ibid., at 17.

312 Ibid. at 24.

313 Ibid. at 25; *see also* discussion at 119, noting:

> Congress might enact legislation requiring relevant telephone providers to retain the data for a specified period of time to ensure that it will be available if and when the government needs to query it. In that case, the government should reimburse the providers for the cost of retaining the data. Based on our review, an appropriate period of time would seem to be no more than two years. A Federal Communications Commission (FCC) regulation already requires providers to hold such information for 18 months, so it seems feasible to change the retention period for telephone records. The FCC's rule on retention of telephone toll records is 47 C.F.R. §42.6: "Retention of telephone toll records. Each carrier that offers or bills toll telephone service shall retain for a period of 18 months such records as are necessary to provide the following billing information about telephone toll calls: the name, address, and telephone number of the caller, telephone number called, date, time, and length of the call. Each carrier shall retain this information for toll calls that it bills whether it is billing its own toll service customers for toll calls or billing customers for another carrier." 60 Fed. Reg. 2d 1529 (1986); 51 FR 32651, corrected, 51 FR 39536.

314 Ibid. at 146.

"planning or is engaged in acts of international terrorism."[315] But aside from these important suggestions, the Group affirmed the need to retain the broad power for surveillance of entire classes of foreign targets in Section 702, including communications with such persons that originate in the United States itself.

President Obama responded to the Review Group's recommendations in a speech in January 2014.[316] He began by affirming the need for more extensive surveillance powers by invoking the harbinger theory and returning to it at numerous points. He claimed, for example, that "emerging threats from terrorist groups and the proliferation of weapons of mass destruction place new and, in some ways, more complicated demands on our intelligence agencies" and that "the men and women at the NSA know that if another 9/11 or massive cyber-attack occurs, they will be asked, by Congress and the media, why they failed to connect the dots." He also conceded that although "[t]hose who are troubled by our existing programs are not interested in repeating the tragedy of 9/11," U.S. surveillance practices ought to be subjected to greater scrutiny and oversight as the Review Group had suggested. He immediately declassified 40 some opinions and orders of the FISA court and ordered the Attorney General and Director of National Intelligence to annually review for declassification "any future opinions of the court with broad privacy implications." He also called on Congress to create a panel of special advocates to "provide an independent voice in significant cases" before the FISA court.

However, in response to the most contentious aspects of U.S. surveillance policy, Obama was less eager to embrace substantial reform. He agreed that the government should no longer hold "bulk metadata" it collects under Section 215, but would seek to "establish a mechanism that preserves the [same] capabilities." This would not, however, involve new law mandating collection and retention by third parties, as the Review Group had recommended. In the President's view, delegating storage to third parties would only raise a new set of privacy concerns as companies would be "carrying out what's essentially a government function, but with more expense, more legal ambiguity, [and] potentially less accountability." In the absence of a better alternative, he would ask the Attorney General and the intelligence community to "develop new options for a new approach that can match the capabilities and fill the gaps that the Section 215 program was designed to address." In the meantime, he would direct the NSA to "pursue phone calls that are two steps removed from a number associated with a terrorist organization, instead of the current three."

In response to concerns raised about Section 702, Obama was prepared to make few if any significant changes. He would ask the Attorney General and Director of National Intelligence to "institute reforms that place additional restrictions" on the use of evidence

---

315 Ibid.

316 President Obama, *Remarks by the President on Review of Signals Intelligence*, Dep't of Justice, Washington, D.C., Jan. 17, 2014, http://www.whitehouse.gov/the-press-office/2014/01/17/remarks-president-review-signals-intelligence.

in criminal cases involving Americans in relation to whom Section 702 information had been gathered incidentally. A presidential directive issued that day required the government to use data gathered under Section 702 only for "legitimate national security purposes and not for the purpose of indiscriminately reviewing the emails or phone calls of ordinary folks." But the directive itself is aimed not primarily at limiting the scope of surveillance under Section 702 but affirming a set of general principles that should govern the bulk collection of data under the provision—such as the proposition that "privacy and civil liberties shall be integral considerations in the planning of U.S. signals intelligence activities" and that such activities will not be conducted "for the purpose of suppressing or burdening criticism or dissent, or for disadvantaging persons based on their ethnicity, race, [and] gender..."[317]

Thus, both the Review Group and the President affirmed the need for reform of U.S. surveillance law and policy, but neither contemplated an end to the bulk collection and storage of metadata under Section 215. They agreed that government should neither collect nor retain it, but that *someone* should. The primary question was how and when the government could access it, thus retaining the thrust of the power contemplated in Section 215. And both also agreed that despite new limits on the powers in Section 702, mass surveillance of broadly defined classes of foreigners should continue, along with the possibility of incidental capture of communications with U.S. citizens.

Whether Congress will take a substantially different approach is yet to be seen. In the months following the Snowden revelations, several bills were proposed. The most successful of these at present is the USA Freedom Act,[318] a bill that passed the House in May of 2014 and, at this writing, is before the Senate. There has been much support for the bill among civil libertarians, touting its ostensible end to bulk collection of metadata, but a more cautious reading is warranted.

As initially tabled, the bill adopted many of the Review Group's recommendations.[319] It purported to end the NSA's bulk collection and retention of phone records under Section 215 of the PATRIOT Act by authorizing disclosure to the NSA on reasonable grounds to believe in the possible relevance of a record linking an individual to a specific terror suspect or investigation. The bill was intended to restrict searches under Section 702 of FISA to prevent "reverse targeting," or incidental interceptions of communications between foreigners and Americans in the United States. The bill allowed third parties such as Internet Service Providers or phone companies subject to FISA disclosure orders to share information about those orders with the public, including how many they have received or complied with. The bill also introduced a special or "constitutional"

---

317 Presidential Policy Directive/PPD-28, Jan. 17, 2014, §1(b), http://www.whitehouse.gov/the-press-office/2014/01/17/presidential-policy-directive-signals-intelligence-activities.

318 USA Freedom Act, or the Uniting and Strengthening American by Fulfilling Rights and Ending Eavesdropping, Dragnet-Collection and Online Monitoring Act, H.R. 3361 (113th Cong. 2013).

319 Rep. Jim Sensenbrenner, *USA Freedom Act*, online, http://sensenbrenner.house.gov/legislation/theusafreedomact.htm; *see also* Jim Sensenbrenner, *The USA Freedom Act of 2013: Section-by-Section Analysis*, http://sensenbrenner.house.gov/uploadedfiles/usa_freedom_act__-_section_by_section.pdf.

advocate to argue for privacy interests in closed-door hearings before the FISA court. And the bill required greater disclosure of the court's activities to both Congress and the public, including the number of orders issued and persons affected.

However, before the House passed the USA Freedom Act, the Obama administration insisted on a number of changes, including some that would preserve a wide scope for surveillance under Section 215 of the PATRIOT Act. The bill had proposed to restrict those searches for a "specific selection term," defined as "a term used to uniquely describe a person, entity, or account."[320] The administration preferred to define a "specific selection term" as one that would simply "limit the scope of the information or tangible things sought."[321]

The Senate's version reasserts a narrower limit on the scope of Section 215 orders in part by precluding selection terms based on a geographic region or the name of a data provider.[322] But it also allows for such orders on reasonable suspicion of their possible relevance to a foreign power engaged in terrorism, rather than "reasonable grounds to believe."[323] More crucially, the Senate's version abandons most of the proposed revisions to Section 702. As the authors of a report from Human Rights Watch published in July of 2014 observe, "[m]any of the bill's original sponsors and supports now question whether the current version would prevent large-scale collection of business records or metadata in practice, defeating the objective of the bill."[324] Both bills "fail significantly to address U.S. surveillance under authorities other than Section 215."[325] The report concludes that "[e]ven were the USA Freedom Act to become law in some form, massive and largely indiscriminate collection of content appears set to continue under Section 702."[326]

## Expanded Scope for State Secrecy and Surveillance in Canadian Law

The Anti-terrorism Act of 2001 amended the Canada Evidence Act,[327] and other legislation, to expand considerably the scope of the assertion of public interest privilege, and curtail the right to appeal it.[328]

---

320 Jonathan Weisman & Charlie Savage, *House Passes Restrains on Bulk Data Collection*, N.Y. TIMES, May 22, 2014.

321 Ibid.

322 Press release, Sen. Patrick Leahy, *Leahy Introduces Historic Bill to Ban NSA's Dragnet Collection of Americans' Electronic Communications*, July 29, 2014, http://www.leahy.senate.gov/press/leahy-introduces-historic-bill-to-ban-nsas-dragnet-collection-of-americans-electronic-communications.

323 Draft of Leahy's version of the bill (August 2014), §101(a)(3), http://www.leahy.senate.gov/download/hen14602.

324 Human Rights Watch & American Civil Liberties Union, WITH LIBERTY TO MONITOR ALL: HOW LARGE-SCALE US SURVEILLANCE IS HARMING JOURNALISM, LAW AND AMERICAN DEMOCRACY (New York: Human Rights Watch, 2014), at 17.

325 Ibid.

326 Ibid.

327 CEA, *supra* note 159.

328 For this portion of the chapter, I draw upon Hamish Stewart, *Rule of Law or Executive Fiat? Bill C-36 and Public Interest Immunity*, in R. Daniels & P. Macklem, eds., THE SECURITY OF FREEDOM: ESSAYS ON CANADA'S ANTI-TERRORISM BILL (Toronto: University of Toronto Press, 2001), and Hamish Stewart,

The new provisions replaced the earlier statutory scheme for the state's assertion of "public interest immunity" and qualifies aspects of the common law doctrine on point.[329] Before the bill was enacted, Sections 37 to 39 of the Canada Evidence Act allowed for a process by which the Crown could object to requests for disclosure, or the requirement that a witness answer certain questions, on the basis that disclosure would be contrary to the public interest—or that the information was a cabinet secret. If it belonged to the former category, the court would adjudicate the claim, balancing the public's general interest in disclosure with the specific public interest at issue in the claim for protection. One of the possible grounds of public interest was that "the disclosure would be injurious to international relations or national defence or security."[330] A considerable body of case law had evolved over time, and it tended to demonstrate less deference toward the executive when balancing these interests.[331]

If the information belonged in the second category (a cabinet secret), the Clerk of the Privy Counsel for Canada could issue a certificate, pursuant to Section 39 of the Canada Evidence Act, declaring the information to be a cabinet confidence, and the assertion was beyond review. It was an extraordinary power, but was limited to cabinet secrets.[332]

The Anti-terrorism Act amended Sections 37 and 38 of the Canada Evidence Act in a number of ways. The former procedure for adjudicating claims of privilege is mostly intact in the new version of Section 37, but it is now subject to the procedure contemplated in Sections 38 to 38.16.[333] Those sections feature two new and broad categories of information: "potentially injurious information," which is defined as information that, if disclosed, "could injure international relations or national defence or national security"; and "sensitive information," which is defined as information "relating to international relations or national defence or national security that is in the possession of the Government of Canada, whether originating from inside or outside Canada, and is of a type that the Government of Canada is taking measures to safeguard."[334]

In the earlier version of the Act, the government official involved in a proceeding was the person responsible for asserting privilege. This is also the case in the new scheme, but in addition, "participants" in proceedings, whoever they may be, now have a positive

---

*Public Interest Immunity after Bill C-36*, 47 CRIM. L.Q. 249 (2003). On other legislation amended by the Anti-terrorism Act to allow for expanded state secrecy, see Craig Forcese, *Canada's National Security Complex: Assessing Secrecy Rules*, 15:5 Inst. for Research on Pub. Pol'y: Choices (2009).

329 Stewart, *Rule of Law or Executive Fiat?*, ibid. at 217.

330 Ibid. at 220. *See also* former §37(1). An attempt to assert privilege on that ground could be adjudicated only by the Chief Justice of the Federal Court, or his or her designate (*see* former §37(2)).

331 Stewart, *Rule of Law or Executive Fiat?*, *supra* note 328, at 219.

332 Stewart, ibid.; *see also* former §39.

333 CEA, *supra* note 159, §37(1).

334 Ibid. §38.

obligation to bring to the attention of the Attorney General (or the Crown) the fact that they possess sensitive or potentially injurious information that may be disclosed, or that they are seeking to have disclosed.[335] A person possessing such information is prohibited from disclosing that information except in accordance with the scheme set out in the section.[336]

Once the Crown receives notice of potentially injurious or sensitive information in the hands of a party to a proceeding, or if the Crown possesses such information and seeks to have it declared privileged, it may apply for an order under Sections 38.04 to 38.06. As was the case in the past, the matter is to be heard by a judge of the Federal Court. This means that a separate proceeding must begin if the matter arises out of a case already in progress—for instance, a civil or criminal case in the superior court of a Canadian province. Once before the Federal Court, the test for privilege is found in Section 38.06, which gives the court the discretion to grant privilege if the court concludes that the disclosure of the information would be "injurious to international relations or national defence or national security." If the court concludes that the information falls within any of these categories, all or some of it may still be disclosed—subject to conditions where appropriate—*if* the court decides that "the public interest in disclosure outweighs in importance the public interest in non-disclosure."[337]

The test itself is not new. What is new is the fact that if the court has considered a matter under Section 37 or 38 and decides that information should be disclosed, the Attorney General of Canada has the power under Section 38.13 to issue a certificate that prohibits the disclosure. The certificate effectively trumps the decision of the court, or, as Hamish Stewart has put it, it "permits the federal Attorney General to second-guess the result of any judicial determination concerning disclosure."[338] In an earlier draft of the bill, the issuance of a certificate under this section marked the end of the process. This provoked considerable criticism by a number of commentators, including Hamish Stewart and Kent Roach.[339] The final version of the bill subjects the Crown's certificate to what Roach has called a "light form of judicial review"[340] by a single judge in the Federal Court of Appeal.[341] The test on appeal is whether *any* of the information has been "obtained in confidence from, or in relation to, a foreign entity... or [or *whether it relates to*] national defence or national security..."[342] So long as the information "relates to" *any* of the

---

[335] Ibid. §§38.01(1) and (2).

[336] Ibid. §38.02(1).

[337] Ibid. §38.06(2).

[338] Stewart, *Public Interest Immunity, supra* note 328, at 255.

[339] *See*, e.g., their contributions to Daniels & Macklem, The Security of Freedom, *supra* note 328.

[340] Kent Roach, *Better Late Than Never: the Canadian Parliamentary Review of the Anti-Terrorism Act*, 13:5 Inst. for Research on Pub. Pol'y: Choices (2007), at 7.

[341] CEA, *supra* note 159, §38.131. Forcese, *Assessing the Secrecy Rules, supra* note 141, at 12.

[342] CEA, ibid. §38.131(8)–(10).

permitted grounds for issuing the certificate, the court must uphold it—and the decision is final.[343] For Stewart,

> Sections 38.13 and 38.131 as enacted represent an improvement over the earlier version. But the right of appeal is still extremely limited, both institutionally and in the scope of the grounds. It is not the person presiding over the proceeding who makes the decision either to issue the certificate or to vary or cancel the certificate; indeed these sections apply only after the person presiding *and* a judge of the Federal Court, Trial Division have done whatever they can do. Furthermore, the new provisions still provide no mechanism for correcting any error by the Attorney General in assessing the balance between the interests in non-disclosure. In short, under ss. 38.13 and 38.131 the Attorney General is permitted to second-guess the outcome of a proceeding to which he was a party.[344]

In practical terms, therefore, this power gives the state something close to the last word on what will be kept secret in any matter relating to national security. The power has yet to be used, but clearly marks a significant expansion in the scope for the assertion of public interest privilege.

Concerns have also been raised about the scope and powers of Canadian intelligence agencies in the post-9/11 period. Canada's two primary agencies, CSIS and the CSE, play distinct roles. The Canadian Security Intelligence Service is a civilian agency tasked with gathering intelligence pertaining to terrorism, espionage, and other threats to national security. The Communications Security Establishment collects foreign signals intelligence.

Turning to the first of these, notably, Parliament did not add to CSIS's powers or its investigative scope with the Anti-terrorism Act. Earlier legislation had already mandated CSIS to collect "to the extent that is strictly necessary" and analyze and retain information relating to activity that "may on reasonable grounds be suspected of constituting threats to the security of Canada."[345] CSIS could also apply to a federal court judge to obtain a 60-day warrant to intercept communications of a person other than a Canadian citizen or permanent resident, or carry out other forms of search or seizure, where there are reasonable grounds to believe it necessary for CSIS to "investigate a threat to the security of Canada."[346] However, Michael Geist and Milano Homsi have argued that Section 21 allows for forms of mass secret surveillance analogous to what is permitted in U.S. law, by allowing "almost any type of communication interception, surveillance or disclosure

---

343 Ibid. §38.131(11).

344 Stewart, *Public Interest Immunity, supra* note 328, at 255.

345 Canadian Security Intelligence Service Act, S.C. 1984, ch. 21, §12 (CSIS Act).

346 Ibid. §21.

of records for the purpose of national security."[347] The warrants in this case would be limited to surveillance of communications with foreigners, but as with Section 215 of the PATRIOT Act, Section 21 of the CSIA does not require probable cause or a suspicion related to a specific subject of the warrant. The target need not even be the subject of a national security investigation.[348]

Canada's second main agency, the Communications Security Establishment, had been collecting foreign signals intelligence prior to 2001, but the Anti-terrorism Act removed a key limitation—the CSE's inability to intercept communications that either originated or terminated in Canada.[349] With the ATA's amendments to the National Defence Act, the CSE can now intercept conversations with persons in Canada so long as the interceptions are "directed at foreign entities located outside Canada."[350] But while the comparable provision in U.S. law, Section 702 of the FISA Amendment Act, requires the NSA to obtain approval from the FISA Court, under Canada's National Defence Act, an order authorizing foreign surveillance is issued by the Minister of National Defence. A measure of oversight is exercised by a Commissioner of the CSE who reports annually to Parliament on ministerial orders and other CSE activity. The act also contains safeguards that include the requirement that before issuing an order for interception, the Minister must confirm that "satisfactory measures are in place to protect the privacy of Canadians and to ensure that private communications will only be used or retained if they are essential to international affairs, defence or security."[351] As Kent Roach has suggested, this latter qualification would pose an obstacle to the use of such intelligence as evidence in a criminal trial.[352] Yet, as with Section 702 of the FISA Amendment Act, the National Defence Act also contemplates a ministerial order for the secret surveillance of a general class of persons—for example, a group of foreign users of a website with servers situated in Canada—with the effect of allowing CSE to incidentally surveil large numbers of Canadians who might also happen to be users of that site. In the wake of the revelations of the NSA's Prism program, Geist has queried whether the CSE is, at present, exercising analogous powers in relation to large Internet companies or other electronic communication service providers pursuant to the powers set out under the NDA.[353]

Attempting to quell such concerns, CSE Commissioner Robert Decary issued a press release on June 13, 2013 (the week after the initial Snowden disclosures), asserting that

---

347 Michael Geist & Milana Homsi, *Outsourcing Our Privacy?: Privacy and Security in a Borderless Commercial World*, 54 U. NEW BRUNSWICK L. J 272 (2005), at 296.

348 Ibid. at 297.

349 Martin Friedland, *Police Powers under Bill C-36*, in Daniels et al., THE SECURITY OF FREEDOM: ESSAYS ON CANADA'S ANTI-TERRORISM BILL (Toronto: University of Toronto Press, 2001) 269, at 275.

350 National Defence Act, RSC, 1985, ch. N-5 (*NDA*), §273.65.

351 Ibid. §273.65(2)(d).

352 Roach, THE 9/11 EFFECT, *supra* note 24, at 389.

353 Michael Geist, *Why Canadians Should Be Demanding Answers About Secret Surveillance Programs*, MICHAEL GEIST (blog), June 8, 2013, at http://www.michaelgeist.ca/content/view/6869/125/.

the CSE "does not direct its foreign signals intelligence collection and IT security activities at Canadians" but conceded that the CSE "may... unintentionally intercept a [private] communication that originates or terminates in Canada."[354] These amounted to a "small" but unspecified number. He also conceded that metadata was being collected but could "verify that it is collected and used by [the CSE] only for purposes of providing intelligence on foreign entities located outside Canada and to protect information infrastructures of importance to the government." A civil liberties group has brought a Charter challenge to the NDA provisions at issue, citing evidence of numerous ministerial authorizations for the collection of metadata from non-suspected persons in Canada from 2002 to the present.[355]

### III. JUDICIAL DEFERENCE TO EXECUTIVE DISCRETION IN NATIONAL SECURITY

Traditionally, courts have been deferential to the executive in matters of national security and foreign policy. In an authoritarian legal framework, courts show an even greater deference through a willingness to suspend various core liberal legal principles on the explicit or implied basis that current threats make this necessary. Courts have thus come to condone a more limited use of habeas corpus, or a modified procedure that places those in administrative detention at a significant disadvantage. Courts have also been considerably deferential to state assertions of the need to maintain privilege. They have done so where much of the information at issue has either already entered the public domain or is likely too old for its disclosure to compromise public safety—*and* where the result of maintaining secrecy is to shield government from accountability for its involvement in some of the most serious rights violations, including kidnapping and torture.

It is important to note, however, that the judiciary has not been deferential in every case on national security, or even in most of the jurisprudence in this area, in the post-9/11 period. In many cases, judges have sought to craft jurisprudence in accordance with liberal legal assumptions.[356] Yet, in ways to be explored briefly in this section, a number of critical decisions have demonstrated deference to the executive in ways that entrench

---

354 *Statement by CSE Commissioner, the Honourable Robert Décary*, Office of the Communication Security Establishment Commissioner, June 13, 2013, at http://www.ocsec-bccst.gc.ca/media/pr/2013-06-14_e.php.

355 *See* British Columbia Civil Liberties Ass'n, Notice of Civil Claim, at http://bccla.org/wp-content/uploads/2013/10/2013-10-22-Notice-of-Civil-Claim.pdf; *see also* Colin Freeze, *Data-collection Program Got Green Light from MacKay in 2011*, GLOBE & MAIL (Toronto), June 10, 2013, on Minister Peter MacKay's 2011 order reviving an earlier metadata collection program revealed by the GLOBE. As Freeze notes, "[t]here is little public information about the program, which is the subject of Access to Information requests that have returned hundreds of pages of records, with many passages blacked out on grounds of national security."

356 A notable decision in this respect is *Hamdan v. Rumsfeld*, *supra* note 104, holding that the Geneva Conventions do apply to Guantanamo detainees and striking down the validity of the existing military tribunal scheme.

important legal rules that cannot be easily reconciled with liberal notions of legality, suggesting instead a clear attempt to legalize authoritarian values.

### Judicial Deference in the U.S. Context: *Hamdi, Boumediene*, and Habeas Corpus

The reader will recall the *Hamdi* decision, discussed above, concerning a U.S. citizen detained in Afghanistan and held without charge in a navel brig in Virginia. Justice O'Connor's decision in the case, on behalf of a plurality of the court, marked an important instance of judicial deference to the executive in two respects—a decision with broad implications for detainees subject to indefinite detention.

First, while O'Connor conceded that "the national security underpinnings of the 'war on terror' although crucially important, are broad and malleable,"[357] she agreed that both the conflict and Hamdi's detention could carry on indefinitely; possibly for the "rest of his life."[358] She also accepted the government's argument that the AUMF served as sufficient authority, in itself—i.e., without further reliance on U.S. legislation, the Geneva Conventions, or any other instrument—to indefinitely detain, without charge, U.S. citizens apprehended abroad for as long as hostilities lasted. This impliedly affirmed the broader proposition that the AUMF allowed for the indefinite detention of all non-citizen combatants captured abroad in the same conflict.

The second point pertains to due process. The Fifth Amendment guarantees against citizens being deprived of their liberty "without due process of law." Justice O'Connor held that while President Bush was authorized to detain citizen combatants, the Constitution required that the citizen be given notice of the "factual basis" for his detention and a "fair opportunity to rebut the Government's factual assertions before a neutral decision-maker."[359] However, she was deferential to the executive in finding that a military commission, employing hearsay evidence, or only a summary of the evidence, could be sufficient. In her words, "the exigencies of the circumstances may demand that, aside from these core elements [notice and a neutral decision-maker], enemy combatant proceedings may be tailored to alleviate their uncommon potential to burden the Executive at a time of ongoing military conflict."[360] Hearsay was permissible, and "the Constitution would not be offended by a presumption in favor of the Government's evidence, so long as that presumption remained a rebuttable one and fair opportunity for rebuttal were provided."[361] Thus, after the government had advanced a credible case, relying in whole or in part on secret evidence, the onus could shift to the petitioner for rebuttal.[362]

---

357 *Hamdi, supra* note 105, at 12.

358 Ibid. at 12.

359 Ibid. at 26.

360 Ibid. at 26–27.

361 Ibid. at 27.

362 Ibid. at 26–27.

The U.S. Supreme Court had occasion to revisit the question of combatant detention reviews in *Boumediene v. Bush*.[363] The case marked a high-profile victory for the non-citizen detainees at Guantanamo because the majority found that detainees possessed a right under the Constitution to challenge the validity of their detention by seeking habeas corpus review in federal court. However, the decision also extended the deferential logic of the plurality in *Hamdi* by conceding that the procedure in habeas corpus cases involving Guantanamo detainees could involve a less onerous process and set of standards for the government to meet. Justice Kennedy, for the majority, was vague on the specifics, stating only that the process "need not resemble a criminal trial,"[364] and that "certain accommodations [had to] be made to reduce the burden habeas corpus proceedings will place on the military."[365] The dissenting opinion of Justice Roberts (signed by all three other justices in dissent) was yet more deferential to the government's position. Justice Roberts held that the Constitution did not apply to alien detainees held outside the United States, and that the government's scheme for review of detainee detentions through CSRTs, and the limited route of appeal (in the Military Commissions Act of 2006) to the District of Columbia Circuit Court, had satisfied Justice O'Connor's requirements in *Hamdi*.

### Post-*Boumediene* Habeas Challenges

In the wake of *Boumediene*, a number of Guantanamo detainees brought habeas challenges in federal court. Thirty-eight of the petitioners were successful at the district court or trial level. However, as the *Washington Post* noted in July of 2011, the U.S. Court of Appeals "has not affirmed a single decision ordering the release of a detainee, nor has it reversed any decision that favored government lawyers."[366] This is due partly to appellate courts taking a different view of the evidence, but also in part to a view of the applicable law that is deferential to the government's position.

In *Al-Bihani v. Obama*,[367] a leading decision among these appellate cases, the court sought to clarify the precise procedural elements and standards to apply in habeas cases by detainees, given the holdings in *Hamdi* and *Boumediene*—decisions in which the Supreme Court explicitly called for "creativity" in the court's approach. Having been denied his release at the court below, al-Bihani argued that the process at the district court was flawed because it had applied the civil standard of a preponderance of the

---

363 *Supra* note 118.

364 Ibid. at 2269.

365 Ibid. at 2276.

366 Peter Finn & Del Quentin Wilber, *Guantanamo Detainees See Legal Process Reversed*, WASH. POST, July 5, 2011. To be clear, not all of the favourable habeas decisions at the lower level were appealed. However, as Linda Greenberg of the *New York Times* notes, of the dozens of detainees that have been released in relation to this process, "[a]ll releases, even those preceded by court orders, have been exercises of executive branch discretion." Linda Greenberg, *Gitmo Fatigue at the Supreme Court*, N.Y. TIMES, Apr. 6, 2011).

367 Al-Bihani v. Obama, 590 F.3d 866 (D.C. Cir. 2010).

evidence rather than the criminal standard of evidence beyond a reasonable doubt; it shifted the burden to him to prove the unlawfulness of his detention; and it admitted hearsay. The court dismissed all three grounds. A survey of the history of habeas corpus in the United States, the court noted, shows how malleable the process can be, and how different approaches have been deemed suitable in different circumstances. Citing the majority's decision in *Boumediene*, the court held that the criminal standard of evidence was too onerous for the state to meet and thus inappropriate in this context. It also suggested that the plurality in *Hamdi* had "indirectly endorsed a preponderance standard when it suggested that due process requirements may have been satisfied by a military tribunal, the regulations of which adopt a preponderance standard."[368] Finally, it also held that hearsay had always been admissible in habeas applications, with doubts about the reliability of the evidence going to the weight to be accorded to the evidence rather than to its admissibility.[369] In April of 2011, the Supreme Court declined an appeal of *Al-Bihani v. Obama* and two other appeal decisions relating to the proper process in Guantanamo habeas cases.[370]

The collective effect of *Hamdi, Boumediene,* and *Al-Bihani* is thus to weaken the protections of habeas corpus in this context, largely as a consequence of the degree to which U.S. appellate courts have been prepared to defer to the government's concerns about secrecy, military efficiency, or security.

### Executive Privilege in Tort Actions

A further facet of authoritarian legality involves the government's reliance on the "state secrets" doctrine in tort litigation by victims of rendition. The outcome in these cases is determined, in large part, by the broad scope of the doctrine in U.S. law, and the low threshold for its application. In this sense, courts are not necessarily being unduly deferential to the executive in applying the doctrine to dismiss cases. The important contribution these cases make to authoritarian legality consists, rather, in a combination of the government's frequent reliance upon the doctrine, together with the court's ready acceptance of it *in the context of tort claims for kidnapping and torture*. Having successfully invoked it in three high-profile cases involving victims of rendition, the government has not only protected state secrets but also shielded itself from transparency or accountability for egregious conduct. Precedents of this kind play a critical role in normalizing and making permanent the expanded scope of state secrecy, and thus the exercise of unchecked executive discretion.

Briefly, the state secrets doctrine holds that in exceptional cases, the courts must place a priority on the importance of protecting national security secrets, even if doing so will

368 Ibid. at 19.

369 Ibid. at 22.

370 Warren Richey, *Supreme Court Rejects Guantanamo Detainees' Appeals for Better Protections*, Christian Sci. Monitor, Apr. 4, 2011.

result in the dismissal of an otherwise legitimate tort claim. The doctrine evolved in a series of cases in which plaintiffs sought to adduce evidence pertaining to military secrets, such as the development of the B-29 bomber,[371] the location of a nuclear warhead,[372] and a contract for espionage services.[373] In each of these earlier cases, the subject matter the government sought to keep secret was not in itself controversial or of questionable legality, unlike the case here.

The doctrine can be applied in two ways, with the threshold of applicability, in both cases, being relatively low. The court can bar a claim, from the outset, on the basis that its further litigation "would inevitably lead to the disclosure of matters which the law itself regards as confidential" (the "Totten bar").[374] In 1953, the Supreme Court held that the Totten bar could apply "where the very subject matter of the action... [is] a matter of state secret."[375] Alternatively, the court can grant an evidentiary privilege over critical evidence in a case, possibly resulting in the dismissal of that case (the "Reynolds privilege").[376] The Reynolds privilege applies to, among other things, any evidence that would reveal the "means, sources and methods of intelligence gathering."[377] The Court of Appeals has emphasized the importance of the court's role in "critically examining" the government's assertion of privilege,[378] and has held that the government cannot obtain privilege by merely asserting that information is classified.[379] Recent decisions belie this.

In *El-Masri v. the United States*,[380] *Mohamed v. Jeppesen Dataplan*,[381] and *Arar v. Ashcroft*,[382] victims of rendition sought damages for kidnapping or detention, torture, and other forms of abuse involving the CIA, other U.S. government agencies, or private corporations facilitating the flight and transfer of detainees on their behalf. In two of the cases, plaintiffs were detained—El Masri in a case of mistaken identity—and were transported to a secret CIA prison in a third country, where they were tortured and imprisoned at length. El-Masri argued that the state secrets doctrine should not apply in his case on the basis that no substantive secrecy issues remained. By the time the case had reached the U.S. Court of Appeals, the Council of Europe had published the findings of a detailed investigation of the events at issue, and President Bush had publicly confirmed the existence of the rendition program. Despite this, the Court of Appeals affirmed the dismissal of El-Masri's action on the basis of the Totten bar, on the view that the litigation

371 United States v. Reynolds, 345 U.S. 1 (1953).
372 Weinberger v. Catholic Action of Hawaii/Peace Educ. Project, 454 U.S. 139 (1981).
373 Doe v. Tenet, 329 F.3d 1135 (9th Cir. 2003).
374 Totten v. United States, 92 U.S. 105 (1876), at 107.
375 *Reynolds, supra* note 371, at 11.
376 Ibid.
377 Al-Haramain Islamic Found. v. Bush, 507 F.3d 1190 (9th Cir. 2007), at 1203.
378 Ellsberg v. Mitchell, 709 F.2d 51 (1982) at 58.
379 Ibid. at 57.
380 479 F.3d 296 (4th Cir. 2007).
381 No. 08-15693 (9th Cir. 2010).
382 No. 06-4216 (2d Cir, 2009).

would likely disclose operational details, identities and roles of the various defendants, along with details of confidential CIA agreements. In *Mohamed v. Jeppesen Dataplan*, the Court of Appeals applied the Reynolds privilege to uphold a dismissal of the action, on the basis that there was "no feasible way to litigate Jeppesen's alleged liability without creating an unjustifiable risk of divulging state secrets."[383] The state secrets doctrine was also invoked in *Arar v. Ashcroft*, but the case was dismissed on other grounds, enabling the court to forgo ruling on the issue.

In May, 2011, leave to appeal *Jeppesen* to the U.S. Supreme Court was dismissed without reasons. An editorial in the *New York Times* asserted: "The court's choice is a major stain on American justice. By slamming its door on these victims without explanation, it removed the essential judicial block against the executive branch's use of claims of secrecy to cover up misconduct that shocks the conscience."[384] The plaintiff in *El-Masri* had advanced a similar argument at the Court of Appeals. Applying the state secrets doctrine in his case was, he argued, tantamount to shielding "egregious executive misconduct"[385] from any accountability. In response, the court held that El-Masri's position "fundamentally misunderstands the nature of our relationship to the executive branch."[386] The courts are meant to decide cases, not to provide a "roving writ to ferret out and strike down executive excess."[387] To attempt to deal with the merits of the government's conduct would make the court "guilty of excess in our own right... especially when the challenged action pertains to military or foreign policy."[388] Overlooked here is the more fundamental point that the court's reluctance in this context creates a wide ambit for unchecked executive power, amounting, in essence, to a kind of common law immunity from tort liability for rendition and other acts of cruelty.

## Judicial Deference in the Canadian Context

Among the most notable examples of judicial deference to the executive in areas of national security are the Supreme Court of Canada's decisions in *Suresh*,[389] *Charkaoui*,[390] and *Canada v. Khadr*.[391] In one sense, each of these cases represents a significant defeat for the government, or an important judicial limit on executive power. Each case affirms the constitutional rights of the claimant before the Court. Yet, in another sense, each of

383 Mohamed v. Jeppesen Dataplan, No. 08-15693 (9th Cir, 2010), at 13548.
384 *Malign Neglect*, N.Y. TIMES, May 21, 2011.
385 El-Masri v. United States, 479 F.3d 296 (4th Cir. 2007), at 312.
386 Ibid.
387 Ibid.
388 Ibid.
389 *Supra* note 187.
390 *Supra* note 147.
391 Canada (Prime Minister) v. Khadr, [2010] S.C.C. 3, [2010] 1 S.C.R. 44. Other examples include the court's decision in Re: Application under s. 83.28 of the Criminal Code, [2004] 2 S.C.R. 248 (upholding the judicial investigation provisions of the Anti-terrorism Act), and R. v. Ahmad, [2011] S.C.C. 6 (upholding the constitutionality of aspects of state secrecy provisions of the Canada Evidence Act).

the cases represents a crucial limitation on rights by inscribing in law significant scope for executive discretion to violate core human rights without impunity.

The Court was strikingly deferential in *Suresh* by seeking to preserve a measure of executive discretion to carry out deportations in the face of a risk of torture—holding that the discretion to do so was consistent with Section 7 of the Charter. In *Charkaoui*, the Court demonstrated a considerable degree of deference in two ways. One was to agree with the government that sensitive information could be relied upon to justify detention, yet still remain confidential. The Court thus paired indefinite detention without charge with something less than a full and fair hearing. The Court was also deferential in agreeing that the use of special advocates could amount to a "substantial substitute" for non-disclosure.[392] In the penultimate paragraph of the decision, the Court hints at a rationale for this deference, but fails to make it clear:

> In the context of national security, non-disclosure, which may be extensive, coupled with the grave intrusions on liberty imposed on a detainee, makes it difficult, if not impossible, to find substitute procedures that will satisfy s. 7. Fundamental justice requires substantial compliance with the venerated principle that a person whose liberty is in jeopardy must be given an opportunity to know the case to meet, and an opportunity to meet the case. Yet the imperative of the protection of society may preclude this. Information may be obtained from other countries or from informers on condition that it not be disclosed. Or it may simply be so critical that it cannot be disclosed without risking public security. This is a reality of our modern world.[393]

Why evidence may be "so critical" in a given case that it cannot be disclosed without unduly risking public security—or why the risk to public security should outweigh the right to a fair hearing—is not made clear. The Court simply accepts the government's claim that the need to "protect society" may in some cases make it necessary to conceal evidence from a detainee *even if that entails something less than a fair trial.* Clearly a deeper fear about public safety animates this passage, and the Court accepts this fear without critical interrogation.

*Khadr* concerned an unusual set of facts. In 2003 and 2004, Canadian intelligence agents visited Omar Khadr, a Canadian citizen who was a minor at the time, in custody at Guantanamo. They interrogated Khadr knowing that he had been deprived of sleep and that the fruits of the interrogation would be shared with U.S. prosecutors in a war crimes matter before a military tribunal. Canada's Supreme Court held that information gathered from the interrogation contributed to his continuing detention and violated international human rights obligations and Section 7 of the Charter. As a remedy for these

---

[392] *Charkaoui, supra* note 147, ¶61.
[393] Ibid.

breaches, Khadr had sought an order compelling the government to seek his repatriation. The Court opted instead to declare that Khadr's Charter rights had been violated and to leave it to the government to "decide how best to respond to this judgment in light of current information, its responsibility for foreign affairs, and in conformity with the Charter."[394] To go further and order the executive to seek Khadr's repatriation would fail to provide due deference to the "constitutional responsibility of the executive to make decisions on matters of foreign affairs in the context of complex and ever-changing circumstances."[395]

### IV. RESISTING ACCOUNTABILITY OR REDRESS FOR HUMAN RIGHTS VIOLATIONS

A fourth element in authoritarian legality is a tendency on the part of the executive to resist accountability for serious violations of human rights. This takes the form of both a reluctance to compensate victims of torture, rendition, or other abuses, and a reluctance to expose state involvement in these events to greater transparency. This may be done by passing law limiting liability for involvement in rights violations, by refusing to hold inquiries or commissions of investigation, or by asserting broad claims of privilege to keep secret much of the evidence at inquiries or commissions or tort cases brought by victims of torture.

The best example of this tendency in the United States can be seen in the vigorous opposition that both the Bush and Obama administrations have exercised in all tort claims by victims of rendition, abuse at Guantanamo, and the secret NSA wiretapping program.[396] Both have also refused to settle cases, or to pursue other avenues of redress. For example, either administration might have sought passage of law providing for compensation, or an exception to the "state secrets" doctrine in a given case. Either government might have ordered an inquiry or an investigation.[397] Each government has instead sought to avoid accountability by shielding its actions through the use of the state privilege, as discussed

---

394 Ibid, at para 39.

395 Ibid.

396 In addition to the cases of El-Masri v the United States, 479 F.3d 296 (4th Cir. 2007), Mohamed v Jeppesen Dataplan, No. 08-15693 (9th Cir, 2010), and Arar v Ashcroft, No. 06-4216 (2d Cir, 2009), U.S. appellate courts have dismissed tort claims by former Guantanamo detainees Shafiq Rasul, Asif Iqbal, Rhuhel Ahmed, and Jamal Al-Harith, and an action for damages for wiretapping (Al-Haramain).

397 Although Congress has conducted investigative hearings into the NSA wiretapping program, the conduct of U.S. officials at Guantanamo and at CIA sites abroad, no congressional or other official U.S. investigation has been ordered to address the treatment of individual victims of torture. Human Rights Watch contends that the failure to do provide redress to victims contravenes the United States' obligations under Article 14 of the Convention Against Torture, which requires signatories to the treaty to provide redress and compensation to victims of torture, or their dependents where the victim is deceased. See *Getting Away with Torture, supra*, note 171, at 70.

above. The Obama administration has also actively hindered investigations by foreign states and jurists.[398]

Both administrations have also been reluctant to hold individuals criminally responsible for well-documented acts of torture or cruelty. A 2006 report by Human Rights Watch alleged that at least 600 U.S. personnel were implicated in the abuse of 460 detainees in Guantanamo, Iraq, and Afghanistan.[399] Looking back on the progress of these cases in 2011, the organization reported that "[d]espite numerous and systematic abuses, few military personnel had been punished and not a single CIA official held accountable. The highest-ranking officer prosecuted for the abuse of prisoners was a lieutenant colonel, Steven Jordan, court-martialed in 2006 for his role in the Abu Ghraib scandal, but acquitted in 2007."[400]

The 2011 Human Rights Watch report concluded that responsibility for abusive practices against detainees lies with officials at the highest levels of the Bush administration, given their direct knowledge and authorization of such practices. The report urged the Obama administration to initiate criminal investigations into the role of President Bush, Vice President Cheney, Secretary of Defense Rumsfeld, and CIA director George Tenet, along with the lawyers who rendered opinions on the legality of torture, including David Addington, John Yoo, and Jay Bybee. However, several factors make this unlikely—and some are key aspects of an authoritarian legal framework.

Certain obstacles to accountability are primarily practical or political. In many cases, evidence surrounding the interrogations has been destroyed. The CIA, for example, has admitted to destroying videotapes of the interrogation of 'high-value" Guantanamo detainee Abu Zubaydah, among others.[401] Although a criminal probe into the destruction of video evidence eventually followed, the Justice Department confirmed in 2010 that no charges would be laid.[402] Another factor is that days before his inauguration, President Obama indicated his reluctance to investigate illegal practices by officials in the Bush administration, preferring to "look forward as opposed to looking backwards."[403]

---

398 Human Rights Watch cites evidence of efforts by U.S. officials to hinder progress of the prosecution of high-level Bush administration officials presided over by Judge Garzón in 2007. The report states that "[r]ecently released diplomatic cables reveal that US officials privately and repeatedly attempted to influence Spanish prosecutors and government officials to curtail the investigations and to have them taken away from Judge Garzón." *Getting Away with Torture, supra* note 171, at 100.

399 Human Rights Watch, *By the Numbers, supra* note 171, at 2.

400 Ibid. at 6.

401 Ibid. at 27.

402 Ibid.

403 David Johnston & Charlie Savage, *Obama Reluctant to Look Into Bush Programs*, N.Y. TIMES, Jan. 11 2009. The administration signaled a slight shift when it announced in June of 2011 that it would launch criminal investigations into the deaths of two prisoners in CIA custody during the Bush years, including one who died in U.S. custody in Iraq. However, at the same time, the Justice Department announced that it was closing its inquiries into the abuse of approximately 100 other detainees in CIA custody over the course of the past decade. Eric Lichtblau & Eric Schmitt, *U.S. Widens Inquires Into 2 Jail Deaths*, N.Y. TIMES, June 30, 2011.

A further critical obstacle to accountability can be found in legislation. A provision of the Detainee Treatment Act of 2005 provides a defense to involvement in abuse on the basis that an official "did not know that the practices were unlawful and a person of ordinary sense and understanding would not know the practices were unlawful."[404] The section also states that "Good faith reliance on advice of counsel should be an important factor, among others, to consider in assessing whether a person of ordinary sense and understanding would have known the practices to be unlawful." The Justice Department signaled its reliance on this section in August 2009, when Attorney General Eric Holder announced the administration's intention to investigate abuses at CIA sites abroad, in response to a "heavily redacted" report published earlier in the year by the CIA's Inspector General.[405] Holder stated that although incidents noted in the report would be investigated, the department "will not prosecute anyone who acted in good faith and within the scope of the legal guidance given by the Office of Legal Counsel (OLC) regarding the interrogation of detainees."[406]

The Canadian government, by contrast, has ordered two inquiries to examine its involvement in cases concerning the torture of its citizens abroad. The Arar Inquiry cleared Arar of wrongdoing and confirmed the RCMP's direct responsibility for providing U.S. officials with faulty information that formed the basis of Arar's rendition to Syria. With litigation and a substantial damage award likely to follow, the Canadian government reached a settlement with Arar for $10.5 million. This was an admirable gesture of accountability, but it also helped to avoid a larger measure of transparency. Almost all of the RCMP and CSIS testimony at the Arar Inquiry was censored under Section 38 of the Canada Evidence Act, as were significant portions relating to this evidence in the Arar Inquiry's final report. The Federal Court ordered the release of parts of the redacted text in the final report, and also outlined a more demanding test for the government to meet in its assertion of public interest privilege under the CEA. This included a requirement to establish evidence to support the claim that disclosure of a given piece of information would be injurious to national security.[407] Yet the censorship of much of the Inquiry testimony, along with the damage award and the avoidance of future litigation, helped the government to reduce its exposure to public scrutiny.

Following the Arar Inquiry, a further inquiry, headed by former Supreme Court Justice Frank Iacobucci, was tasked with examining the involvement of Canadian officials in the cases of Canadian citizens Abdullah Almalki, Ahmad Abou-Elmaati and Muyyed Nureddin. The three were traveling independently through Syria in 2002 when they were arrested, detained, and tortured by Syrian officials. Justice Iacobucci found that while information that CSIS gave to Syria did not directly result in their imprisonment and

404 Detainee Treatment Act of 2005, *supra* note 110, §1004(a).

405 Human Rights Watch, *Getting Away with Torture*, *supra* note 171, at 7.

406 Ibid. at 7.

407 Canada (Att'y Gen.) v. Commission of Inquiry into the Action of Canadian Officials in Relation to Maher Arar, [2007] F.C. 766.

torture, in two of the cases, it clearly contributed to it. Consular officials and intelligence agents in all three of the cases acted in ways that Justice Iacobucci found seriously "deficient."[408] In one of the cases, as was done with Maher Arar, and would later occur with Abousfian Abdelrazik, CSIS provided questions be put to a Canadian citizen in foreign custody. The Iacobucci Inquiry lasted some 22 months, with *all but four days of it* held *in camera*, and those four days dealt mostly with issues of standing.[409] In response to a Parliamentary subcommittee's recommendations, a majority of the House of Commons voted to issue the three men an official apology and provide compensation. But the minority Conservative government at the time declined to do so.[410]

Prior to the Iacobucci Inquiry, Almalki, Abou-Elmaati, and Nureddin had filed a civil suit against Canada, which had been suspended pending the outcome of the inquiry. Following the Inquiry, the plaintiffs sought disclosure of material referred to in the final report of the inquiry. The Attorney General of Canada opposed the motion in reliance on the "national security" privilege in Section 38 of the Canada Evidence Act. The Federal Court allowed the disclosure or summaries of some of the material, but ordered much of it to remain privileged.[411] The order for some of what was disclosed was made on the basis that the state had failed to establish that disclosure would cause injury. The government appealed this ruling, and the Federal Court of Appeal overturned it.[412] In the view of the appeal court, the lower court had given "undue weight to the public interest in disclosure of the information."[413] The plaintiffs' appeal to the Supreme Court of Canada was refused. The status of the civil action remains to be determined, but is much less likely to succeed without access to critical evidence in the government's possession.[414]

A final case worth noting involves the ordeal of Sudanese Canadian Abousfian Abdelrazik.[415] Having come to Canada in the mid-1990s as a political refugee from Sudan, Abdelrazik chose to return there in 2003 to visit his ailing mother. At this time, CSIS was investigating him for suspected ties to terrorism, given his acquaintance with Ahmad Rassam and Adil Charkaoui. A later Federal Court decision would find that CSIS agents provided the Sudanese government with information leading to Abdelrazik's arrest, and that the agents then traveled to Sudan to interrogate him in Sudanese custody.[416]

---

408 The Honorable Frank Iacobucci, Commissioner, *Internal Inquiry into the Actions of Canadian Officials in Relation to Abdullah Almalki, Ahmad Abou-Elmaati and Muayyed Nureddin: Final Report* (Ottawa: Ministry of Public Works, 2008).

409 Jasminka Kalajdzic, *Outsiders: The Sources and Impact of Secrecy at the Iacobucci Inquiry*, 36 QUEEN'S L.J. 160 (2010), at 163.

410 Ibid. at 170.

411 Canada v. Almalki, [2010] F.C. 1106.

412 Canada v. Almalki, [2011] F.C.A. 199.

413 Ibid. at ¶37.

414 For an exploration of the impact of §38 of the Canada Evidence Act in this case, and other obstacles the plaintiffs face, see Jasminka Kalajdzic, *Access to Justice for the Wrongfully Accused in National Security Investigations*, 27 WINDSOR Y.B. ACCESS JUST. 171 (2009), at 197–203.

415 The following narrative draws on the factual summary in Abdelrazik v. Canada, [2009] F.C. 580.

416 Ibid.

Abdelrazik alleges that, following these events, he was tortured, detained without charge for several months, and eventually released—only to be detained for another nine months partly due to the involvement of Canadian officials. By the time of his release, Abdelrazik's passport had expired, yet he was also added (at the behest of the United States) to a UN no-fly list. Canada refused to renew his passport, which stranded him in Sudan for a further 18 months. The court held that the decision to refuse him a new passport was contrary to his Charter right to return to Canada, and compelled the government to arrange his immediate return.[417] Abdelrazik is now suing the Canadian government for damages for its complicity in his torture and detention in Sudan, and for mental anguish suffered for the delay in receiving the passport (i.e., the breach of Sections 6 and 7 of the Charter).[418]

The lawsuit rests partly on the argument that Canadian courts ought to recognize a new cause of action—torture as a tort—and should apply it here on the basis of Canada's complicity in torture. The grounds for recognizing the new tort rest, in Abdelrazik's view, on the basis that Canada has a duty, under both international and domestic law, to uphold the prohibition against torture, and that it violates this duty where it fails to take preventive measures.[419] In pretrial motions still unfolding, the government has resisted these claims vigorously. Its resistance is certainly a reflection of a conventional defense strategy in tort actions to deny the applicability of a given tort or to question whether all the elements of a tort have been made out. But it is also consistent with an authoritarian legal framework in which the state seeks to preserve the widest possible space for counterterrorism measures that function without accountability or transparency.

Indeed, in a broader sense, two inferences about the conduct of the Canadian and American governments in this context seem unavoidable. Each seeks to preserve the secrecy of its operational methods so as to continue making use of them. Each also seeks to preserve the widest possible ambit of discretion to employ techniques for gathering and concealing information—on the assumption that the current "threat environment" continues to warrant this.

## Conclusion

The law surveyed in this chapter has been the subject of considerable attention on the part of scholars and journalists. The thrust of these efforts, for the most part, has been to highlight ways in which laws and policies brought about in response to 9/11 have marked a

---

417 Ibid.

418 *See* Aug. 30, 2010 decision of Madam Prothonotary Aronovitch in Abdelrazik v. Attorney Gen. of Canada & Lawrence Cannon, Federal Court of Canada (T-1580-09), peoplescommision.org, at http://www.peoplescommission.org/files/abousfianMedia/Aug30Judgement.pdf. *See also* Paul Koring, *Abdelrazik Sues Ottawa for $27-million*, GLOBE & MAIL (Toronto), Sept. 24, 2009.

419 Abdelrazik v. Attorney Gen., *ibid.* at 13.

departure from constitutionalism or the rule of law. Yet many commentators have tended to overlook a deeper thread in many of the crucial policy positions, cases and statutes on point—an insistence on the *legality* of extraordinary measures that include torture or cruelty, targeted killing, indefinite detention without charge on secret evidence, and a vastly expanded scope for state secrecy and surveillance. This chapter has thus attempted to demonstrate the degree to which law-makers and courts have sought to do more than lend a veneer of legality to a diverse range of extraordinary measures. They have consistently sought instead to *reconcile* these measures with new assumptions about security and the proper limits of the state's use of force—thereby reflecting a deeper embrace of a new concept of legality based on values distinct from those belonging to an older liberal framework.

The purpose of tracing the contours of this new conception of legality was to attempt to understand the fundamental nature of the change that has taken place in North American law in the post-9/11 period. If many of the more extreme and controversial measures deployed in this period mark, not a temporary departure from an older framework of legality, but the emergence of a new conception of legality, the measures are not likely to be reformed until the values and assumptions that underlie authoritarian legality are challenged or evolve over time.

The next chapter examines the role that the harbinger theory—or the fear of the imminent prospect of mass terror—has played in a wider cultural and political embrace of authoritarian legality.

# 3

## The Harbinger Theory in Politics, Culture, and Public Opinion

AFTER EXPLORING A series of laws and policies that mark a shift in cultural conceptions of legality, this chapter proceeds to explore a prominent and singular rationale for the shift—one that can be consistently traced through political discourse and public opinion from 2001 to the present.

Since 2001, politics and public opinion about national security in both Canada and the United States have been shaped by a wide range of beliefs and assumptions. Some are surely racist or xenophobic, while others reflect a rising culture of fear and risk management. But as numerous cases in this chapter will show, the tendency on the part of government officials has been to defend many of the more contentious measures used after 9/11 by relying on a more discrete and distinct set of claims. These involve a form of argument that builds upon an earlier trend toward greater security, or a culture of control, while in many respects marking a qualitative break from it. And while racist or imperialist assumptions may play a part in the politics of security, they are notably absent from the logic with which public officials have consistently sought to rationalize extraordinary measures. The argument at the core of this logic is one that high-profile officials continue to make in defense of illiberal measures—and one that polls confirm a large portion of the public continues to embrace.

The introduction to this book has described that argument in terms of what can be called the harbinger theory. This is a belief that 9/11 was the harbinger of a new order of terror, one in which further attacks in North America are likely to occur at some point in the near future, on a similar or greater scale as 9/11, possibly, but not necessarily, involving weapons of mass destruction (WMDs). In either case, the *extent* of the damage that terrorists can now inflict is expected to be much greater, given what the events of 2001 have proved possible. And on this basis, earlier assumptions about the absolute limits of state force against individuals have come to seem untenable or imprudent.

In the wake of 9/11, politicians and members of the public might have resisted this logic. They might have taken the view, as many experts have since, that in terms of its scale, 9/11 was an anomaly in the history of terrorism. It was unprecedented and highly improbable. An attack on that scale may have occurred once, but does not indicate what terrorists are *likely* to do in the future.[1] Yet, for reasons to be canvassed momentarily, neither the government nor the larger public of either nation chose to adopt this view.

Instead, officials in both nations embraced—and sizable portions of the public have become receptive to—either strong or mild versions of the harbinger theory: the strong version holding that terrorists are likely to act again soon, this time with weapons of mass destruction, causing casualties that could run well into the hundreds of thousands if not millions; the mild version holding that terrorists will soon act without WMDs but may inflict casualties in the high hundreds or thousands. Either event would be contrary to the historical record in which, 9/11 apart, no terror attacks anywhere in the world have ever resulted in casualties exceeding the low hundreds, with the vast majority of attacks leading to casualties in the low double digits.[2]

Yet, instead of attempting to place 9/11 in some kind of historical context, throughout the post-9/11 period, in prominent speeches, policy statements, and other rhetoric, officials have relied to a considerable degree on assertions of either the strong or mild forms of the harbinger theory. Frequent and consistent references to the theory have thus helped reinforce the general plausibility of the notion that a range of extraordinary measures were both proportionate and reasonable. A further significant dimension of this practice to be examined in this chapter is that on many if not most of the occasions on which officials have asserted the theory, they did so without grounding it in evidence or expert opinion. They also often invoked the theory with such assurance that it became less a matter of speculation than conventional wisdom. For much of the period, the official position—more so in the United States than in Canada—was that it was not a matter of if but *when* another 9/11 would be attempted.

Public opinion data throughout the period shows that a large portion of the U.S. public has feared the prospect of a further act of terror on the order of 9/11, and the concern has remained remarkably consistent over time. Canadian poll data suggests the consistency of a fear of what appears to be a lesser order of terror, though concerns about terror have remained current there too. Large portions of the public in both nations have also remained supportive of a range of counterterrorism measures that include indefinite detention, mass surveillance, and in the United States, targeted killing. These two facets of public opinion may be both a consequence and a reflection of a culture that has remained

[1] Experts inclined to view 9/11 as anomalous and highly improbable are considered in Chapter 6.

[2] National Consortium for the Study of Terrorism and Responses to Terrorism (START, 2013), *available at* http://www.start.umd.edu/gtd; discussed further in Chapter 6.

fascinated with images of catastrophic terror in movies, television, and books—and with depictions in those works that validate the use of torture and other extreme measures in the national defense. A survey of both cultural production and public opinion since 9/11 suggests that the harbinger theory has taken deep root in the social imagination, shaping firmly held assumptions about rights and security.

In light of these developments, it may be argued that much of the support for the harbinger theory on the part of politicians or government officials, in at least the early years after 9/11, was a function of the risk entailed in making threat assessments. As James Fallows has observed in the context of airport security measures, "the political incentives here work only one way. A politician who supports more open-ended, more thorough, more intrusive, more expensive inspections can never be proven 'wrong.'"[3] The absence of further attacks prove the measures worked, yet new attacks would show that "inspections must go further still." Conversely, "[a] politician who wants to limit the inspections can never be proven 'right.' An absence of attacks means that nothing has gone wrong—yet."[4] Or, as Michael Sheehan has argued, "[n]o terrorism expert or government leader wants to appear soft on terrorism. It's always safer to predict the worst; if nothing happens, the exaggerators are rarely held accountable for their nightmare scenarios."[5] And at higher levels of political debate, as John Mueller and Mark Stewart have noted, the cost of appearing soft on terror become greater still. In the lead-up to the 2004 election, President Bush speculated in passing that the war on terror may not be winnable, but that conditions could be rendered less favorable for harboring terrorists in many parts of the world.[6] Democrats immediately questioned whether Bush was as serious about fighting terror as Reagan was about fighting Communism. Similarly, at one point in his campaign, John Kerry told an interviewer that he could foresee arriving at a point where Americans could "feel safe again," when "terrorists are not the focus of our lives," and where terrorism reaches "a level where it isn't on the rise."[7] Both Vice President Cheney and President Bush were quick to assert that Kerry was "unfit to lead." Kerry was immediately forced to assume a more hawkish position, claiming "I do not fault George Bush for doing too much in the War on Terror, I believe he's done too little."[8]

The political risk entailed in being soft on terrorism is thus an important force shaping the discourse on security after 2001, and points to earlier trends in the politics of crime control and security that encouraged politicians to assume the posture of the stern

---

3 James Fallows, *If the TSA Were Running New York*, The Atlantic, May 3, 2010; cited in John Mueller & Mark Stewart, Terror, Security, and Money: Balancing the Risks, Benefits, and Costs of Homeland Security (New York: Oxford University Press: 2011), Kindle edition, location 3274.

4 James Fallows, ibid.

5 Michael Sheehan, Crush the Cell: How to Defeat Terrorism Without Defeating Ourselves (New York: Random House, 2008), cited in Mueller & Stewart, *supra* note 3, at location 3274.

6 Mueller & Stewart, *supra* note 3, at location 3280.

7 Ibid.

8 Ibid.

defender of law and order, and the alignment of electoral concerns with those of the victims of crime.[9] But this chapter seeks to move beyond the observation that politicians have been reluctant to call inflated threat assessments into question, or have tended to support vague and unsubstantiated fears about the growing threat of terror, so as to tap into powerful currents of emotion. It will attempt instead to probe the politics of security with more nuance, beginning with the following distinction.

In much of the rhetoric involving threat assessments since 2001, many North American politicians and security officials may have sought primarily to play it safe by supporting unsubstantiated fears or avoiding skeptical lines of inquiry. Thus, many endorsements of the harbinger theory may have been little more than a reflection of the lack of incentive to call it into question. But a more crucial aspect of political discussion in the post-9/11 period has been the use of the harbinger theory as part of a more aggressive posture—serving as an indispensable tool to rationalize or justify the need to suspend rights and adopt more invasive measures. It is this latter use that serves as the focus of the political rhetoric explored in this chapter.

By tracing the common use of the theory as a tool of persuasion and justification, certain patterns in its use over time become apparent. Chief among them is the self-evident character with which aspects of the harbinger theory are consistently presented; including, for example, the claim that WMD terror is more likely because the weapons are becoming more accessible or harder to track, or that a 9/11-scale attack is likelier by virtue of the greater skill or ambition of today's terrorists—claims that are seldom supported by evidence or expert knowledge. The analysis set out in this chapter and the next will demonstrate that greater measures have been supported not in response to a general tendency to threat inflation, or vague fears of future terror attacks on a significant scale—but a specific set of claims and assumptions about the form that future attacks will take. The analysis will also suggest that a recurring presentation of the harbinger theory as self-evident—and the lack of engagement with evidence or authority—has been crucial to forestalling or dissuading scepticism of the theory in public debate.

The chapter will begin in Part 1 with a look at the role of the harbinger theory in US political discourse and public opinion, and move in Part 2 to explore parallels in the Canadian context. It will conclude that given the continued currency of the theory in political rhetoric on both sides of the border and in public opinion and popular culture, the harbinger theory has become too pervasive to assume it will be easily or quickly abandoned.

---

9 David Garland, The Culture of Control: Crime and Social Order in Contemporary Society (Chicago: University of Chicago Press, 2001), and Jonathan Simon, Governing Through Crime: How the War on Crime Transformed American Democracy and Created a Culture of Fear (Oxford: Oxford University Press, 2007).

## Part 1. The United States

### I. THE RECURRING PROSPECT OF ANOTHER 9/11 IN U.S. POLITICAL RHETORIC

Bush administration officials began to invoke the harbinger theory in support of a new approach to security immediately after 9/11. An important early example is Tim Russert's interview with Vice President Cheney on NBC's *Meet the Press* on September 16, 2001. Henceforth, Cheney asserted, the United States would need to operate by a new set of rules:

> We also have to work, though, sort of the dark side, if you will. We've got to spend time in the shadows in the intelligence world. A lot of what needs to be done here will have to be done quietly, without any discussion, using sources and methods that are available to our intelligence agencies, if we're going to be successful. That's the world these folks operate in, and so it's going to be vital for us to use any means at our disposal, basically, to achieve our objective.[10]

Moments later, Cheney invoked the prospect of nuclear terror:

> A ballistic missile equipped with a weapon of mass destruction, a nuke, for example, a nuclear weapon would be far more devastating than what we just went through. If one of those was to hit one of our cities or to hit a major base overseas where U.S. forces are deployed, the casualty list would be higher. The consequences would be even greater than the terrible tragedy we've just been through.

On September 25, Attorney General John Ashcroft appeared before a Senate committee to defend the administration's call for an expansion of state powers in the USA PATRIOT Act, including wider surveillance and administrative detention power, among others.[11] He began by warning that FBI intelligence had indicated "a potential for additional terrorist incidents," including the "possibility of attacks using crop dusting aircraft."[12]

On many occasions, President Bush drew an explicit link between al Qaeda and WMDs as a basis for more invasive measures. The January 2002 State of the Union Address, better remembered for its claims about Saddam Hussein's nuclear ambitions, made this link a prominent theme:

> ... we must prevent the terrorists and regimes who seek chemical, biological or nuclear weapons from threatening the United States and the world.

---

10 Vice President Dick Cheney, interview by Tim Russert, *Meet the Press*, NBC News, Sept. 16, 2001, at http://emperors-clothes.com/9-11backups/nbcmp.htm.

11 *See Hearing of the Senate Committee on the Judiciary*, 107th Cong., 1st Sess. (Sept. 25, 2001) No. J-107-40, at 8–11.

12 Ibid. at 9.

> By seeking weapons of mass destruction, these regimes pose a grave and growing danger. They could provide these arms to terrorists, giving them the means to match their hatred. They could attack our allies or attempt to blackmail the United States. In any of these cases, the price of indifference would be catastrophic.[13]

In his 2002 "National Security Strategy,"[14] Bush stated: "The gravest danger our Nation faces lies at the crossroads of radicalism and technology. Our enemies have openly declared that they are seeking weapons of mass destruction, and evidence indicates that they are doing so with determination."[15] The document suggests that an older criminological approach is no longer tenable:

> Given the goals of rogue states and terrorists, the United States can no longer solely rely on a reactive posture as we have in the past. The inability to deter a potential attacker, the immediacy of today's threats, and the magnitude of potential harm that could be caused by our adversaries' choice of weapons, do not permit that option. We cannot let our enemies strike first.[16]

Nor, however, could the United States be constrained by existing law-of-war doctrine requiring an imminent threat before using deadly force or acting in self-defense: "We must adapt the concept of imminent threat to the capabilities and objectives of today's adversaries."[17] These include "the use of weapons of mass destruction—weapons that can be easily concealed, delivered covertly, and used without warning."

References to WMDs reappear in the 2002 *National Strategy for Homeland Security.*[18] "Unless we act to prevent it, a new wave of terrorism, potentially involving the world's most destructive weapons, looms in America's future."[19] The enemies are "working to obtain chemical, biological, radiological, and nuclear weapons for the purpose of wreaking unprecedented damage on America."[20] The department lauds the passage of the USA PATRIOT Act, but calls for additional powers to make information sharing among agencies and governments easier, and to "review authority for military assistance in domestic security."[21]

---

13 *Text of President Bush's 2002 State of the Union Address*, WASH. POST, Jan. 29, 2002, at http://www.washingtonpost.com/wp-srv/onpolitics/transcripts/sou012902.htm.

14 The White House, *The National Security Strategy of the United States of America* (September 2002).

15 Preface, ibid. Evidence is referred to but none is cited.

16 Ibid. at 15. A similar caution about the imminent prospect of WMD terror is set out in the President's *National Strategy to Combat Weapons of Mass Destruction* (December 2002), at 1: "... terrorist groups are seeking to acquire WMD with the stated purpose of killing large numbers of our people and those of friends and allies—without compunction and without warning."

17 Ibid.

18 Office of Homeland Security, *The National Strategy for Homeland Security* (July 2002).

19 Ibid. at vii.

20 Ibid.

21 Ibid. at 47–49.

Throughout these early years, other members of the administration offered similar assessments about the nature of the threat. In 2003, CIA Director George Tenet told Congress that "bin Laden has a sophisticated biological weapons capability,"[22] while Secretary of Homeland Security Tom Ridge wrote that "extremists abroad are anticipating near-term attacks that they believe will either rival, or exceed" those of September 11.[23] In February of 2005, CIA Director Porter Goss, testifying before the Senate Intelligence Committee, asserted that "it may be only a matter of time before Al Qaeda or another group attempts to use chemical, biological, radiological and nuclear weapons."[24]

At this stage, however, the case for extreme measures was often understated because many of the measures—warrantless wiretapping, waterboarding, black sites, targeted killing—had not yet come to light. By 2006, when some of them had been reported, concerns about WMDs or large-scale terror would serve as a primary justification. In January of that year, Bush urged Congress to renew the sun-setting provisions of the USA PATRIOT Act and defended the NSA's recently revealed secret wiretapping program in light of the threat posed by "terrorists like bin Laden" who seek to "arm themselves with weapons of mass murder."[25] In September of that year, Bush was compelled to respond growing concerns about the use of waterboarding, CIA black sites, and military commissions for Guantanamo detainees.[26] The measures, he argued, were used in large part due to a concern in the months after 9/11 that a second attack would soon follow involving WMDs. The United States had indeed carried out secret detentions and interrogations, involving high-level al Qaeda figures such as Abu Zubaydah. The United States, he said, had no choice but to employ "an alternative set of procedures" which were "tough [yet] safe and lawful and necessary." The information gleaned "saved innocent lives by helping us stop new attacks"—attacks involving cells in east Asia, Britain, and the United States. From one detainee, interrogators learned about the group's "efforts to obtain biological weapons," and gleaned the admission that he had "met three individuals involved in al Qaeda's effort to produce anthrax." More broadly, Bush asserted that there had been no further attacks in the United States since 9/11 because "our government has changed its policies and given our military, intelligence and law enforcement personnel the tools they need to fight this enemy and protect our people and preserve our freedoms."[27]

---

22 Testimony, *Hearing: Current and Future Worldwide Threats to the National Security of the United States before the Senate Committee on the Armed Services*, 108th Cong. (Feb. 12, 2003).

23 Press Release, Dep't of Homeland Security, Thomas Ridge, *Threat Level Raised* (Dec. 21, 2003).

24 Prepared Statement of Porter J. Goss, Director of Central Intelligence. *Current and Projected National Security Threats to the United States*, Senate Select Committee on Intelligence (Feb. 16, 2005) at 2, *available at* Federation of American Scientists, at http://www.fas.org/irp/congress/2005_hr/021605goss.pdf.

25 Text of the President's 2006 State of the Union, *We Strive To Be A Compassionate, Decent, Hopeful, Society*, N.Y. Times, Jan. 31, 2006, *available at* http://www.nytimes.com/2006/01/31/politics/text-bush.html?pagewanted = all.

26 Ibid.

27 The question of whether CIA interrogation yielded intelligence that helped avoid future attacks is explored in Part 2 of Chapter 6.

The administration would continue to make similar claims about terrorism and necessary measures in its closing years. Its "National Security Strategy" of 2006 asserted that terrorists "continue to pursue WMD."[28] "The hard core of the terrorists cannot be deterred or reformed; they must be tracked down, killed, or captured [...] using a broad range of tools."[29] Speaking to Congress in June 2007, FBI Director, Robert Mueller argued that the "economics of supply and demand dictate that someone, somewhere, will provide nuclear material to the highest bidder, and that material will end up in the hands of terrorists."[30] The 2007 "National Strategy for Homeland Security" invoked the prospect of WMD use and called for various expanded powers, including greater surveillance under the Foreign Intelligence Surveillance Act.[31]

Following President Obama's inauguration in 2009, former Vice President Cheney retained a measure of public attention while defending a hawkish approach to national security. Speaking with editors of Politico.com in February of that year, Cheney warned of the "high probability" of a "9/11-type event where the terrorists are armed with something much more dangerous than an airline ticket and a box cutter—a nuclear weapon or a biological agent of some kind."[32] Likely to take place in a large American city, the attack would involve "the deaths of perhaps hundreds of thousands of people." With a view to responding to Obama's progressive supporters, Cheney asserted: "If it hadn't been for what we did—with respect to the terrorist surveillance program, or enhanced interrogation techniques for high-value detainees, the Patriot Act, and so forth—then we would have been attacked again. [...] Those policies we put in place, in my opinion, were absolutely crucial to getting us through the last seven-plus years without a major-casualty attack on the U.S." Speaking in May of 2009 on the same day that President Obama gave a speech about national security, Cheney expanded upon his position in an address given at the American Enterprise Institute. "Nine-eleven made necessary a shift of policy aimed at a clear strategic threat—what the Congress called 'an unusual and extraordinary threat to the national security and foreign policy of the United States.'"[33] With follow-up attacks involving anthrax, the knowledge that al Qaeda was pursuing nuclear weapons, and the discovery of Pakistani physicist Abdul Qadeer (A.Q.) Khan's illicit trade in materials for nuclear bomb–building,

---

[28] The White House, *The National Security Strategy of the United States of America* (September 2006), at http://georgewbush-whitehouse.archives.gov/nsc/nss/2006/, at Part V.

[29] Ibid. pt. III.

[30] A transcript of Mueller's remarks is contained in Susan Cornwell, *FBI's Mueller: Al-Qaida Has Intent to Use Nuclear Weapons*, PRISON PLANET.COM, June 11, 2007, at http://www.prisonplanet.com/articles/june2007/110607_b_Mueller.htm.

[31] Homeland Security Council, *The National Strategy for Homeland Security* (October 2007) at 7.

[32] John Harris, Mike Allen & Jim Vandehei, *Cheney Warns of New Attacks*, POLITICO.COM, Feb 4, 2009, at http://www.politico.com/news/stories/0209/18390.html.

[33] Richard Cheney, *Vice President Cheney's Remarks at the American Enterprise Institute*, COUNCIL ON FOREIGN RELATIONS, May 21, 2009, at http://www.cfr.org/defense-strategy/vice-president-cheneys-remarks-american-enterprise-institute/p19470.

the threat, Cheney asserted, was unprecedented: "foremost on our minds was the prospect of the very worst coming to pass—a 9/11 with nuclear weapons."[34]

President Obama's speech on national security that same day sought to convey a contrary spirit. The Bush administration, "faced with an uncertain threat" had made "a series of hasty decisions."[35] The Obama administration would begin by banning "so-called enhanced interrogation techniques," and "categorically rejecting" the argument that "brutal methods like waterboarding were necessary to keep us safe."[36] Torture would be prohibited, and the detention and interrogation of suspects would hereafter be subjected to the rule of law.

But in ways explored in the previous chapter, many of Obama's policies were consistent with those of his predecessor. Although some detainees could be transferred to other countries, tried or released, 48 would need to be detained indefinitely due to the danger they posed coupled with the lack of admissible evidence against them (they still remain in this category as of this writing). Obama would also soon confirm his intention to maintain the practice of extraordinary rendition, and dramatically increase the use of targeted killing.[37] And he too would rationalize the use of these measures in light of the harbinger theory.

For example, in the President's "National Security Strategy" of 2010, WMDs are a prominent concern. "The American people face no greater or more urgent danger than a terrorist attack with a nuclear weapon..."[38] The usual reasons are cited: excessive stockpiles remain; a black market trade in material and know-how continues; and "terrorists are determined to buy, build, or steal a nuclear weapon."[39] Additional threats are still posed by biological and radiological weapons.[40] To counter this, the administration will prosecute where possible, but reserves the right to indefinitely detain those who "pose a danger to the American people" and who cannot be prosecuted for lack of evidence.[41] It will seek to exhaust all reasonable alternatives before employing military force, but reserves the right to "act unilaterally if necessary to defend our nation and our interests."[42]

Similarly, in his 2011 "National Strategy for Counterterrorism,"[43] published after bin-Laden's death, the President writes "[i]n the past two and a half years, we have eliminated more key al-Qa'ida leaders in rapid succession than at any time since September 11,

---

34 Ibid.

35 *Text: Obama's Speech on National Security*, N.Y. Times, May 21, 2009, at http://www.nytimes.com/2009/05/21/us/politics/21obama.text.html?pagewanted = all.

36 Ibid.

37 *See* discussion in Chapter 2.

38 The White House, *The National Security Strategy of the United States of America* (May 2010), at 23.

39 Ibid.

40 Ibid. at 20.

41 Ibid. at 36.

42 Ibid. at 22.

43 The White House, *National Strategy for Counterterrorism* (June 2011).

2001."[44] Yet despite this, "we continue to face a significant terrorist threat from al-Qa'ida." Without any attempt to substantiate the assertion, the administration continues to insist that the "danger of nuclear terrorism is the greatest threat to national security. Terrorist organizations, including al-Qa'ida, have engaged in efforts to develop and acquire weapons of mass destruction (WMD)—and if successful, they are likely to use them."[45]

After bin Laden's death in May of 2011, administration officials have continued to describe the threat in terms consistent with both the mild and strong versions of the harbinger theory. While the locus of the threat had shifted from the core al Qaeda group in Afghanistan and Pakistan to its affiliates—primarily al Qaeda in the Arab Peninsula—the new groups were said to pose a "serious threat to the homeland,"[46] a "direct and significant threat,"[47] or an "urgent and undeniable" danger.[48] Speaking in October of 2012, Secretary of Defense Leon Panetta warned of the prospect of a "cyber-Pearl Harbor":

> An aggressor nation or extremist group could use these kinds of cyber tools to gain control of critical switches… They could derail passenger trains, or even more dangerous, derail passenger trains loaded with lethal chemicals. They could contaminate the water supply in major cities, or shut down the power grid across large parts of the country.[49]

If terrorists were to launch "several attacks on our critical infrastructure at once, in combination with a physical attack on our country," the result could "paralyze and shock the nation and create a profound new sense of vulnerability."

However, in a speech in May of 2013, President Obama marked a significant shift in assessments of the outstanding threat. While the nation is "still threatened by terrorists," as confirmed by events "from Benghazi to Boston… [W]e have to recognize" he asserted, "that the threat has shifted and evolved from the one that came to our shores on 9/11."[50] The core al Qaeda movement in Afghanistan and Pakistan is "on the path to defeat" and has had no part in attacks on the United States since 9/11. The focus has

---

44 Ibid., Preface.

45 Ibid. at 8.

46 Matthew Olsen, Director of the National Counterterrorism Center, in submission to House Permanent Select Committee on Intelligence, cited in Jason Ryan, *After Awlaki's Death, al Qaeda Still a Major Threat*, ABC News, Oct. 6, 2011. *See also* FBI Director, Robert Mueller's comments on the same occasion.

47 John O. Brennan, Assistant to the President for Homeland Security and Counterterrorism, on Ensuring al-Qa'ida's Demise, text of remarks at Paul H. Nitze School of Advanced International Studies, Washington, D.C., June 2011.

48 Hillary Rodham Clinton, Secretary of State, *Opening Remarks at the Global Counterterrorism Forum*, Istanbul, Turkey, June 7, 2012, *at* U.S. Dep't of State, at http://www.state.gov/secretary/20092013clinton/rm/2012/06/191912.htm.

49 Elisabeth Bumiller & Thom Shanker, *Panetta Warns of Dire Threat of Cyberattack on US*, N.Y. Times, Oct. 11, 2012.

50 *Obama's Speech on Drone Policy*, N.Y. Times, May 23, 2013.

begun to shift to "various al Qaeda affiliates," and from "Yemen to Iraq, from Somalia to North Africa, the threat today is more diffuse, with Al Qaeda's affiliates in the Arabian Peninsula—AQAP—the most active in plotting against our homeland." More crucially, "while none of AQAP's efforts approach the scale of 9/11," Obama said, many continue to plot attacks such as the attempt to set off a bomb on a flight at Christmas 2009. What remains, then, are smaller offshoots, or regions where extremists have gained a foothold, such as Libya, Iraq, or Syria; though even here, the threats are often more "localized." A critical threat is now posed by home-grown extremists who are capable of significant harm; "[b]ut as we shape our response," Obama asserted, "we have to recognize that the scale of this threat closely resembles the types of attacks we faced before 9/11... [And] if dealt with smartly and proportionally, these threats need not rise to the level that we saw on the eve of 9/11." In light of this, Obama outlined a plan for winding down the war on terror. The administration would "finish the work of defeating al Qaeda and its associated forces." It would attempt to submit the practice of targeted killing to greater transparency and oversight. It would seek to "refine and ultimately repeal" the Authorization to Use Military Force passed in September of 2001—the source of authority of many of the more controversial measures, including targeted killing and indefinite detention. The President would also continue efforts to close Guantanamo and transfer the remaining detainees to U.S. prisons.

The speech marked an important attempt to repudiate the harbinger theory, and to break with over a decade of presidential endorsements of it. But in hindsight, the break has proven to be temporary, with Obama soon reaffirming the indispensible use of the theory in defense of invasive measures in light of later events that include the Snowden revelations. Even before this retreat, however, in the May 2013 speech itself, Obama's forward vision for national security still appeared committed to many of the tenets of authoritarian legality, suggesting the harbinger theory might soon have proven impossible to resist in any event. Thus, although targeted killing might become subject to a form of review, possibly judicial or independent, Obama did not say it would stop.[51] Decisions about whom to target would likely continue to be shielded by secrecy, afforded significant judicial deference, and be subject to limited accountability. Nor did Obama suggest that many or most of the remaining Guantanamo detainees would be released, since even with the repeal of the AUMF, the detainees might still be held under other authority. Obama was also careful not to rule out the possibility that the AUMF might be refined rather than repealed, which seems a far likelier outcome in the present congressional climate. And finally, although mass surveillance was addressed only indirectly, it too would

---

[51] On the day of the speech, the White House published a "Fact Sheet" setting out standards for the use of lethal force in counter-terror investigations. It sets out criteria for the president's decision-making but does not contemplate subjecting the decision to independent oversight prior to targeted killings. *Fact Sheet: U.S. Policy Standards and Procedures for the Use of Force in Counterterrorism Operations Outside the United States and Areas of Active Hostilities*, May 23, 2013, at http://www.whitehouse.gov/the-press-office/2013/05/23/fact-sheet-us-policy-standards-and-procedures-use-force-counterterrorism.

seem likely to remain, given Obama's reluctance to commit to significant reform on that front. In short, Obama's vision for the future of U.S. counterterrorism policy might entail an end to the war on terror, but not to much of the essential apparatus of authoritarian legality.

Within weeks of making this speech, the administration's position on the nature of outstanding threats would shift in response to the revelations of Edward Snowden in June of 2013. As a broad public debate about surveillance unfolded, prominent officials in the administration were pressured to justify the vast scope for NSA surveillance. Within days of the Snowden leaks, James Clapper, Director of National Intelligence, issued a press release, asserting the surveillance had "yielded intelligence regarding proliferation networks and [has] directly and significantly contributed to successful operations to impede the proliferation of weapons of mass destruction and related technologies."[52] Appearing with Clapper before the Senate Intelligence Committee in September of 2013, the Director of the NSA, General Keith Alexander, defended the programs by invoking the prospect of mass terror.[53] Alexander noted that in a single seven-day period that month, 972 people had been killed in terrorist attacks in Kenya, Pakistan, Afghanistan, Syria, Yemen and Iraq. "We need these programs," he asserted, "to ensure that we don't have those same statistics here."

President Obama would then speak at some length about surveillance powers in January of 2013, ostensibly in response to the final report of the President's Review Group on Intelligence and Communications Technologies. The speech marked a significant regression in his rhetoric on the nature of outstanding threats relative to his May 2013 speech. Defending the need to retain the NSA secret surveillance programs, Obama invoked the prospect of terror involving WMDs, along with the possibility of attacks on the scale of 9/11, several times throughout the speech, asserting, for example, that "...emerging threats from terror groups and the proliferation of weapons of mass destruction place new, and in some ways, more complicated demands on our intelligence agencies," and "...[t]he men and women at the NSA know that if another 9/11 or massive cyberattack occurs, they will be asked by Congress and the media why they failed to connect the dots..."[54]

The fear of 9/11-scale terror has continued to serve as a basis for supporting authoritarian measures among other prominent government officials. In December of 2013, as surveillance reform legislation was debated in Congress, the *New Yorker* published an interview with Democratic Senator Diane Feinstein, Chair of the Select Committee on

---

[52] James Clapper, *Facts on the Collection of Intelligence Pursuant to Section 702 of the Foreign Intelligence Surveillance Act*, June 8, 2013, at http://www.dni.gov/index.php/newsroom/press-releases/191-press-releases-2013/872-dni-statement-on-the-collection-of-intelligence-pursuant-to-section-702-of-the-foreign-intelligence-surveillance-act.

[53] Paul Lewis & Dan Roberts, *US Intelligence Chiefs Urge Congress to Preserve Surveillance Programs*, The Guardian, Sept. 26, 2013.

[54] Department of Justice, *Remarks by the President on Review of Signals Intelligence*, (Jan. 17, 2014), at http://www.whitehouse.gov/the-press-office/2014/01/17/remarks-president-review-signals-intelligence.

Intelligence, in which Feinstein invoked the memory of 9/11—and thus the possibility of another 9/11—to defend mass surveillance. "Nothing is dimmed in my mind," she said of a visit to Ground Zero, "I saw the part of the steel structure that the planes went through. I saw the white roses on the names etched in bronze in the fountain. [...] They will come after us again, if they can."[55]

Another example concerns a pair of challenges to the constitutionality of the NSA bulk phone metadata collection program in federal district court in Washington, D.C. and New York following the Snowden revelations. In each case, the claimants were seeking a preliminary injunction to stop the surveillance from being carried out, which required the court to arrive at a conclusion as to whether the program was likely to be found constitutional at the end of a longer judicial process. Both courts ruled on the applications in December of 2013, but came to opposite conclusions. In the Washington D.C. case, Judge Richard J. Leon held that the program was likely unconstitutional, describing aspects of it as "almost Orwellian."[56] In the New York case, Judge William H. Pauley III had found the program likely constitutional, but, significantly, his analysis was framed at the outset of the case by invoking obstacles the NSA had confronted in the lead-up to 9/11 without similar powers in place—suggesting that the validity of the program today hinged in large part on the possibility of another 9/11. As Judge Pauley noted, the NSA had intercepted the calls that hijacker Khalid al-Mihdhar had made in San Diego to Yemen in the months prior to 9/11, but could not ascertain that al-Mihdhar was in the United States because they were using "overseas signals intelligence capabilities that could not capture al-Mihdhar's telephone number identifier." "Telephone metatadata," the judge asserted, "would have furnished the missing information" and may have enabled the NSA to notify the FBI of al-Mihdhar's presence in the United States.[57] The bulk metadata program may "vacuum up information about virtually every telephone call to, from, or within the United States," but only a program of such scale could "detect relationships so attenuated and ephemeral that they would otherwise escape notice."[58] This does not render it constitutional; the program was upheld for, among other reasons, a lack of evidence that metadata would be used for a purpose other than preventing terrorism. But the analysis is clearly colored by the narrative with which the case is framed—preventing another 9/11. In the closing paragraphs, Judge Pauley asserts more broadly that bulk data collection is necessary because, "[a]s the September 11th attacks demonstrate, the cost of missing such a thread can be horrific."[59]

---

55 Ryan Lizza, *State of Deception*, New Yorker (Dec. 16, 2013).

56 Klayman v. Obama, 13 Civ. 0851 (D.C.C. 2013), at 49.

57 American Civil Liberties Union v. Clapper, 13 Civ. 3994 (S.D.N.Y. 2013), at 1–2.

58 Ibid. at 52. This claim, and the question of whether bulk data collection and other invasive measures have helped prevent another 9/11, is explored in Part 2 of Chapter 6.

59 Ibid.

## II. THE IMAGE OF MASS TERROR IN POPULAR CULTURE AND PUBLIC OPINION

In a 2006 study on the politics of counterterrorism, U.S. political scientist Ian Lustick noted that in the years following 9/11, the catastrophic threat of terrorism loomed large in the public imagination—as evidenced by its pervasiveness in popular culture. A number of films appeared with plots involving dramatic attempts to stop acts of nuclear or radiological terror, including *The Sum of All Fears,* in which a nuclear bomb is set to explode over Baltimore; *Antibody*, involving a terrorist who carries an implanted nuclear detonator; and *Blast!*, with a plot to deploy an electromagnetic bomb over the United States.[60] Similar themes pervaded made-for-TV movies in the United States, including *Winds of Terror* (2002), involving a bioweapon attack; *The President's Man 2* (2002), about a plot to construct a nuclear bomb; *Smallpox* (2002), involving a bioterror plot; *Operation Wolverine: Seconds to Spare* (2003), about terrorists hijacking a train for the purpose of carrying out a large-scale gas attack on a U.S. city; *Counterstrike* (2003), in which nuclear-armed terrorists hijack an ocean liner; *Critical Assembly* (2003), where students construct a nuclear bomb stolen by terrorists; and *Dirty War* (2004), involving the detonation of a radioactive bomb in London (produced by the BBC but aired in the United States by HBO).[61] The prospect of WMD terror was also common in popular literature—in, among other books, Tom Clancy's *Splinter Cell*, James Patterson's *London Bridges*, and Robert Ludlum's *The Lazarus Vendetta*.[62]

The fear of large-scale terror has continued to occupy a prominent place in public consciousness through various popular productions. Perhaps the most notorious example of this was the Fox Network television series *24*, which aired from November 2001 to May 2010, with a brief reprise in 2014. Over the course of its eight-year run, the series dramatized several nuclear ticking-bomb scenarios and valorized the use of torture as a necessary and proportionate means to prevent terror. In fact, every season aside from the first (produced before 9/11) and the brief 2014 revival has concerned efforts to thwart an imminent act of nuclear, biological or radiological terror.[63] Following on the heels of *24*, in 2011 HBO launched its immensely popular series *Homeland* (in its third season as of this writing) which features a plot involving an American solder, Brody, who has returned from several years of captivity at the hands of al Qaeda and has now secretly turned against the United States. The threat in each season has been less clearly defined, with Brody plotting at certain points to kill the Vice President of the United States but at

---

60 Ian S. Lustick, Trapped in the War on Terror (Philadelphia: University of Pennsylvania Press, 2006), at 25.

61 Ibid.

62 Ibid.

63 *See* the plot summaries for each season at http://en.wikipedia.org/wiki/24_(TV_series).

other times intimating a desire to assist an Iraqi terror group in carrying out a large-scale attack, possibly radiological, targeting Washington or Congress.

Other films, books, and television shows have continued to invoke possibilities of large-scale terror, or to suggest the efficacy of torture, including *Zero Dark Thirty*. Filmed in a faux-documentary style, it implied that information gleaned through torture at CIA black sites was integral to locating bin Laden in 2011. Cumulatively, these works have helped to maintain the plausibility of the harbinger theory as a way of understanding the nature of the *possible* threat of terror. Confronted with so many seemingly realistic depictions of hypothetical large-scale attacks, a wider public has been consistently encouraged to envision a further major attack in the near future on the same or greater scale as 9/11. Questions about torture, surveillance, and indefinite detention are, in turn, assessed in light of these assumptions, generating a large measure of support for the proposition that such measures have become reasonable and necessary in the current threat environment. Public opinion polling provides evidence of the currency and *persistence* of both the fear of mass terror and a belief in the need for greater security.

Turning to the question of public opinion, it should be noted that a detailed exploration of public perceptions about terror and security in the post-9/11 period is beyond the scope of this chapter. The purpose of the brief survey of polls that follows is to support three general propositions. For much of the post-9/11 period, large portions of the U.S. public have held a belief in the *imminent* possibility of a large-scale terror attack. A large portion has also held—and still holds—the belief that another attack on the scale of 9/11 at some point in the future is inevitable. And finally, concurring with these beliefs is a large degree of enduring support for authoritarian legal measures.

In relation to the first point, polls conducted in the early years after 9/11 indicated a broad public fear of the possibility of terror involving WMDs in particular.[64] A Hart-Teeter poll in 2004 asked Americans to "consider ways in which terrorists might attack the United States and say which one or two worry them most."[65] Forty-eight percent named bioterrorism as their primary concern; 37 percent most feared an attack involving chemical weapons; and 23 percent feared a nuclear attack. A 2005 poll conduct by Daniel Yankelovich and Public Agenda, a non-profit organization interested in opinions on U.S. foreign policy, asked 1,004 Americans whether they were concerned that "terrorists may obtain biological, chemical, or nuclear weapons."[66] Yankelovich found that "an overwhelming 88% of the population is afraid this could happen." A 2006 Gallup poll asked more specifically: "Do you think it is likely—or not likely—that terrorists will

---

64 For pointing me to two of these polls, I am indebted to Dan Gardner's chapter on terrorism in RISK: WHY WE FEAR THE THINGS WE SHOULDN'T—AND PUT OURSELVES IN GREATER DANGERS (Toronto: McLelland and Stewart, 2008).

65 Hart-Teeter, *From the Home Front to the Front Lines: America Speaks Out About Homeland Security*, Council for Excellence in Government (March 2004), at 3.

66 Daniel Yankelovich, *Poll Positions: What Americans Really Think About U.S. Foreign Policy*, 84:5 FOREIGN AFF. 2 (Sept./Oct. 2005), at 15.

set off a bomb that contains nuclear or biological material in the US *within the next five years*?"[67] Forty-seven percent believed that it was.

Throughout the same period, polls suggest that support for security policy was strong. The 2004 Hart-Teeter poll found that 56 percent of respondents expressed support for the USA PATRIOT Act and agreed that it is "a necessary and effective tool in preventing terrorist attacks."[68] Two-thirds (65 percent) of Americans said they were "very or somewhat satisfied with the government's job of protecting their civil liberties."[69] As many as 75 percent of Americans said they were "very or somewhat satisfied with the government's performance on preventing terrorist attacks."[70]

A series of Gallup polls since 2005 have explored the public's response to the use of more specific measures. In 2005, Gallup found that 65 percent of Americans supported the U.S. government's assassination of known terrorists—down from 77 percent who held this view in October of 2001.[71] Thirty-nine percent supported the U.S. government's use of torture against known terrorists "if the terrorists know details about planned attacks on the US."[72] (A majority, 59 percent, were opposed.)

A Gallup poll in May of 2009 found that while a majority approved of Obama's ban on coercive interrogation,[73] substantial support for other Bush administration tactics continued: 65 percent of Americans believed that the United States should not close Guantanamo and move some prisoners to U.S. prisons;[74] 59 percent believed that Khalid Sheikh Mohammed should be tried in a military rather than civilian court;[75] 77 percent believed he should get the death penalty if convicted; 40 percent believed the prison at Guantanamo had "strengthened US national security," as opposed to 37 percent that said it had not had much effect, and 18 percent that believe it had weakened it.[76] In response to the release of the torture memos in April of 2009, respondents were asked whether they thought "the use of harsh interrogation techniques for terrorism suspects was justified or not justified?"[77] Fifty-five percent believed they were; only 36 percent believed they were not. In an August 2009 poll, respondents were asked: "As you may know, Attorney

---

67 *Terrorism in the United States*, (2006) Gallup, at http://www.gallup.com/poll/4909/Terrorism-United-States.aspx (emphasis added).

68 Hart-Teeter, *supra* note 65, at 7; by contrast, only 33% of Americans believe "the Patriot Act is bad for America, agreeing with those who say that it goes too far and could violate average Americans' civil liberties."

69 Ibid.

70 Ibid.

71 Darren K. Carlson, *Would Americans Fight Terrorism By Any Means Necessary?* Gallup (Mar. 1, 2005) at http://www.gallup.com/poll/15073/Would-Americans-Fight-Terrorism-Any-Means-Necessary.aspx.

72 Ibid.

73 *War on Terror* Gallup (May 2009) at http://www.gallup.com/poll/5257/War-Terrorism.aspx. Seventy-four percent were in favor of limiting interrogations to the U.S. Military's Field Manual.

74 Ibid.

75 Ibid.

76 Ibid.

77 Jeffrey M. Jones, *Slim Majority Wants Bush-Era Interrogations Investigated*, Gallup (Apr. 27, 2009), at http://www.gallup.com/poll/118006/Slim-Majority-Wants-Bush-Era-Interrogations-Investigated.aspx.

General Eric Holder has appointed a special prosecutor to investigate the U.S. government's use of harsh interrogation techniques against terrorism suspects during the Bush administration. From what you know or have read, do you approve or disapprove of this investigation?" While 47 percent approved, 49 percent disapproved.[78]

More recent poll data confirms the persistence of similar opinions. A CNN poll in 2010 found that 60% of respondents believed that "terrorists will always find a way to launch major attacks no matter what government does."[79] In April of 2013, the *Washington Post* asked: "How concerned are you about the possibility there will be more major terrorist attacks in the United States—is that something that worries you a great deal, somewhat, not too much or not at all?"[80] Sixty-nine percent were concerned a great deal or somewhat, with 30% concerned not too much or not at all.[81] The *Post* noted that when the question was asked in late September 2001, 83 percent were concerned a great deal or somewhat, versus 17 percent who not concerned much or at all.[82]

Few polls have probed beliefs about the harbinger theory directly, though a national survey conducted by Angus Reid Public Opinion in September 2011 did essentially this. It asked roughly 1,800 Americans across the country: "All things considered, do you think a terrorist attack similar in scope and magnitude to 9/11 will take place in the United States again in your lifetime?"[83] Fifty-eight percent believed it either "definitely will or probably will" (the responses were not distinguished), with 23 percent agreeing that it "probably will not or definitely will not."[84] Similarly, in September of 2012, Rasmussen Reports conducted a survey of 1,000 Americans that asked "how likely is it that another 9/11 will take place in America in the next 10 years?"[85] Sixty-five percent believed that it was likely (including 29 percent who believed it to be "very likely"), with 27 percent who believed it to be "unlikely," and only 2 percent who thought it "not at all likely."

---

78 Gallup, *War on Terror, supra* note 73.

79 CNN/Opinion Research Corporation Poll (January 2011), at http://i2.cdn.turner.com/cnn/2010/images/01/11/rel1aa.pdf.

80 WASH. POST poll April 2013: <http://www.washingtonpost.com/wp-srv/politics/polls/postpoll_20130418.html>.

81 Ibid.; 32% were concerned "a great deal," and 37% were concerned "somewhat."

82 Ibid.; in 2001, 43% were concerned "a great deal," and 39% percent were concerned "somewhat." Thirty-two percent were concerned "a great deal," and 37% were concerned "somewhat."

83 Angus Reid Public Opinion, *Americans Expect New Attack Similar to 9/11 in Their Lifetimes* (2011), at 5. The survey also indicated the gender of the respondents and their political affiliation (Republican, Democratic, Independent), but not their ages. Men and women were roughly the same (57% and 58%, respectively, believing an attack likely); while Republicans were more inclined to believe in the inevitability of another 9/11-scale attack than Democrats (66% and 52%, respectively, replying that such an event "definitely will or probably will" occur), at http://www.angusreidglobal.com/polls/44020/americans-expect-new-attack-similar-to-911-in-their-lifetimes/.

84 Ibid.

85 Rassmussen Reports, *65% See Another 9/11 As Possible in Next 10 Years*, at http://www.rasmussenreports.com/public_content/lifestyle/general_lifestyle/september_2012/65_see_another_9_11_as_possible_in_next_10_years.

Just as fears of the prospect of large-scale terror continue in significant numbers, so too does support for authoritarian measures. A *Washington Post*–ABC poll of February 2012 found that 70 percent of respondents approved of the President's decision to keep the prison at Guantanamo Bay open.[86] Eighty-three percent of those polled approved of his drone policy, including 77 percent of Democrats.[87] An NBC News and *Wall Street Journal* poll in June of 2013 asked whether targeted killing should be carried out against American citizens abroad who become "suspected members of terrorist groups."[88] Forty-three percent believed that they should, while 25 percent disagreed. (Twenty-nine percent believed they "don't know enough.") A Gallup poll that year asking about the use of drone strikes against U.S. citizens abroad "who are suspect terrorists" reported similar results.[89]

In the wake of the June 2013 Snowden revelations about NSA mass surveillance of phone and Internet data, a CBS News Poll a month later asked "Do you think the government's collection of Americans' phone call records is a necessary tool to help find terrorists, or do you think it is not necessary?"[90] Fifty-two percent believed it is, while 43 percent disagreed. A Quinnipiac University poll that month asked whether respondents "support [or] oppose the federal government program in which all phone calls are scanned to see if any calls are going to a phone number linked to terrorism?"[91] Fifty percent were in support and 44 percent were opposed. Other polls reported similar findings.[92]

When asked about counterterrorism policy in a more general sense, a majority of Americans continue to be supportive. A poll for CBS News and the *New York Times* in April of 2013 asked whether respondents "approve or disapprove of the way Barack Obama is handling the threat of terrorism."[93] Fifty-six percent approved, versus 35 percent who did not. Similarly, a CNN poll of June 2013 asked whether respondents think "the Obama administration has gone too far, has been about right, or has not gone far enough in restricting people's civil liberties in order to fight terrorism." While 43 percent

---

86 Scott Wilson & Jon Cohen, *Poll Finds Broad Support for Obama's Counterterrorism Policies*, WASH. POST, Feb. 7, 2012.

87 Ibid.

88 NBC News & Wall Street Journal poll (conducted by the polling organizations of Peter Hart (D) and Bill McInturff (R), May 30–June 2, 2013), at http://www.pollingreport.com/terror.htm. N = 1,000 adults nationwide; margin of error ± 3.1.

89 Gallup Poll, Mar. 20–21, 2013, at http://www.pollingreport.com/terror.htm. N = 1,020 adults nationwide; margin of error ± 4.

90 CBS News Poll, July 18-22, 2013; N = 1,036 adults nationwide; margin of error ± 3: <http://www.pollingreport.com/terror.htm>.

91 Quinnipiac University, June 28–July 8, 2013, at http://www.pollingreport.com/terror.htm. N = 2,014 registered voters nationwide; margin of error ± 2.2.

92 *See, e.g.*, the ABC News–*Washington Post* poll, June 12–16, 2013, at http://www.pollingreport.com/terror.htm.

93 CBS News–*New York Times* poll, May 31–June 4, 2013, at http://www.pollingreport.com/terror.htm. N = 1,022 adults nationwide; margin of error ± 3.

believed the administration had gone too far, 38 percent believed it had been "about right" and 17 percent believed it "has not gone far enough."[94]

Throughout the post-9/11 period, then, the possibility of mass terror has been a pervasive motif in popular culture, along with depictions that suggest torture and other extreme measures to be necessary and effective means of countering the threat. During the same period, a sizable portion of the U.S. public affirmed a belief in the imminent possibility of large-scale terror and often expressed support for the use of extraordinary measures in light of it.

## Part 2. Canada

The analysis set out above cannot be mapped on to the Canadian context in a simple way. There are, however, some notable similarities. During the fall of 2001, Canada's Parliament passed the Anti-terrorism Act, which at the time was understood to be a law of profound significance with far-reaching political and legal consequences. As with the USA PATRIOT Act, the Anti-terrorism Act does not contain all the measures associated with authoritarian legality (for example, the security certificate regime was already in place in the Immigration Act). Yet parliamentary debates and committee hearings surrounding the passage of the Act, and later parliamentary reviews of it, furnish a primary setting for statements by government and security officials that tie counterterrorism policy to fears of large-scale terror. Government statements made in other contexts, along with public opinion on terror threats and responses, also pertain more closely to the Anti-terrorism Act, given its centrality in Canada's counterterrorism law and policy.

### I. THE SPECTER OF LARGE-SCALE TERROR IN CANADIAN POLITICAL DISCOURSE

In the period following 9/11, the government's two primary spokespersons on counterterrorism were Anne McLellan and Irwin Cotler. Both acted for a time as Minister of Justice, and McLellan also served as Minister of Public Safety and Emergency Preparedness. Of the two, Cotler played a role more analogous to that played by U.S. officials such as Cheney or Bush in making frequent reference to the prospect of mass terror. But both McLellan and Cotler invoked fears of large-scale terror to justify the need for new, more invasive measures.

McLellan's rhetoric, upon the introduction of the Anti-terrorism Act, and its defence before House and Senate committees in the fall of 2001, was subtle. References to the prospect of mass terror were few, and more subdued, but she clearly contemplated a

---

94 CNN/ORC Poll, June 11–13, 2013, at http://www.pollingreport.com/terror.htm. N = 1,014 adults nationwide; margin of error ± 3.

threat on the order of 9/11 itself. Soon after the bill was first tabled, for example, she told a parliamentary committee: "We must be able to disable organizations before they are able to put hijackers on planes or threaten our sense of security, as we have seen in recent days with the scare of anthrax."[95] Three ideas were clear in her discourse: 9/11 represented a significant shift in the security landscape; it did so because it raised the prospect of terror on a much larger scale; and this required and justified a shift from a reactive to a preemptive approach.

Thus, on October 15, introducing the bill on first reading, she asserted that 9/11 constituted a "substantial threat to domestic and international stability";[96] on second reading, she stated that "[o]ur world changed dramatically on September 11;" and before committee on October 18, she explained:

> One of the fundamental questions posed this week is: why do we need Bill C-36? Why do we need new tools to fight terrorism? Yes, we have hijackings, sabotage, and murder offences already in the Criminal Code. They do remain available to us. But terrorism, ladies and gentlemen, is a special threat to our way of life. When dealing with groups that are willing to commit suicidal acts of mass destruction against innocent civilians, it is necessary to consider whether existing legislative tools are adequate to the challenge.[97]

---

95 House of Commons, Standing Committee on Justice and Human Rights, *Evidence* (Meeting No. 29, Oct. 18, 2001) 37th Parliament, 1st Sess., at http://www.parl.gc.ca/HousePublications/Publication.aspx?DocId=652657&Language=E&Mode=1&Parl=37&Ses=1.

The reference to anthrax was not simply a dramatic gesture, but an allusion to a concern about bio-terror raised in question period on October 15, following first reading of the anti-terror bill. Canadian Alliance Member Diane Ablonczy asked: "Mr. Speaker, the sergeant-at-arms has just informed us that an envelope opened by a staff member in the journals branch in this building contained some type of substance that caused a rash on her arms. We know that in the U.S. there has been one death from anthrax and 11 others have tested positive. The U.S. government says that it has enough medicine to treat up to two million people but here in Canada, health and rescue professionals say that there is not enough medicine to save more than about 2,000 people from an attack. Is this the health minister's idea of doing a good job for Canadians?" Moments later, Ablonczy asked "Mr. Speaker, I know the Minister [of Health, Art Eggleton] is intending to do his best but the fact of the matter is that our own professionals in health and rescue are sounding the alarm and have been for some time. They are saying that we really do not have the resources to treat a serious biochemical attack. We all hope there will not be one and maybe there will not but we have to be prepared. If we only have enough preparation to treat 2,000 people that is not enough. What will the minister be doing about it?" House of Commons, *Debates*, 37th Parliament, 1st Sess., 094, Oct. 15, at http://openparliament.ca/debates/2001/10/15/james-moore-2/.

96 House Hansard, Oct. 15, ibid. McLellan employs both a phrase and a sentiment that would appear in the preamble to the Anti-terrorism Act: "Whereas acts of terrorism constitute a substantial threat to both domestic and international peace and security; Whereas acts of terrorism threaten Canada's political institutions, the stability of the economy and the general welfare of the nation."

97 House Standing Committee, Oct. 18, *supra* note 95.

Given the stakes at issue, the tools would have to be preventive in nature: "The insidious nature of terrorism has dictated the need for new measures. These measures must have a preventative focus, because punishing terrorist crimes after they occur is not enough. Ladies and gentlemen, the way I very simply explain this is, if we don't stop the terrorists getting on the plane, it's too late."[98]

Irwin Cotler was more explicit about the prospect of mass terror. In November of 2001, while Parliament debated the Anti-terrorism Act, the University of Toronto held a conference that brought together numerous academics, security experts, and officials to consider the bill. Cotler presented a paper in which he spoke of 9/11 triggering the passage of a "juridical watershed."[99] From here on in, he said, counter-terror law "must be appreciated and assessed in the context of the existential threat of this terrorism, including the lethal face of terrorism as in the deliberate mass murder of civilians in public places [and...] the potential use of weapons of mass destruction."[100] Cotler would reiterate a concern about mass terror in several venues over the coming years. For example, he told the *Ottawa Citizen* in 2004: "we're not talking here about your ordinary domestic criminal. We're talking about your transnational super-terrorist. We're not talking about domestic crime, as serious as that is, we're talking about a transnational, existential threat of the character that 9/11 was."[101]

Cotler also raised the prospect of mass terror repeatedly before a Senate committee at its belated three-year review of the Anti-terrorism Act in 2005. In February of that year, he urged that counterterrorism law and policy should take account of contextual factors including "the potential access to, if not prospective use, of weapons of mass destruction."[102] In November, he sought to justify the Act as a means of "denying terrorists the capacity to carry out their attacks or to, above all, access weapons of mass destruction."[103] In each iteration of his argument, the prospect of mass terror was invoked to justify a

---

98 Ibid.

99 Irwin Cotler, *Thinking Outside the Box: Foundational Principles for a Counter-Terror Law and Policy*, in Ronald Daniels, Patrick Macklem & Kent Roach, eds., THE SECURITY OF FREEDOM: CANADA'S ANTI-TERRORISM BILL (Toronto: University of Toronto Press, 2001), at 114.

100 Ibid.

101 Ian Macleod & Andrew Duffy, *A Question of Balance: Canada's Justice Minister Says New Anti-terror Laws Protect Human Rights. Critics Beg to Differ*, OTTAWA CITIZEN, Dec. 11, 2004. Substantially the same statement was made on February 21, 2005, in a submission to the Special Committee of the Senate on the Anti-terrorism Act at http://www.parl.gc.ca/Content/SEN/Committee/381/anti/02eva-e.htm. *See also* Irwin Cotler, Address to the Fifth Meeting of Ministers of Justice or of Ministers or Attorneys General of the Americas (Apr. 28, 2004), at http://www.oas.org/juridico/english/moj_v_can.pdf.

102 Special Senate Committee on the Anti-terrorism Act, *Evidence* (Meeting of Feb 21, 2005) 38th Parliament, 1st Sess., at: http://www.parl.gc.ca/Content/SEN/Committee/381/anti/02eva-e.htm.

103 House of Commons, Subcommittee on Public Safety and National Security of the Standing Committee on Justice, Human Rights, Public Safety and Emergency Preparedness, *Evidence* (Meeting No. 28, Nov. 16, 2005) 38th Parliament, 1st Sess., at http://www.parl.gc.ca/HousePublications/Publication.aspx?DocId=2115848&Mode=1&Language=E.

range of measures including new terrorism offenses, the expansion of state privilege, and the use of administrative detention.

One further statement worth noting in this category is a 2004 policy paper published by the Privy Council Office that serves as a parallel to the American "National Security Strategy" noted above. Titled "Securing an Open Society: Canada's National Security Policy,"[104] the document identifies a series of threats to national security.[105] Among them are the "proliferation of weapons of mass destruction," which is an issue "whether or not Canada [is] the primary target of such an attack, [since] the impact on our security could be immense." A primary concern within this category is bioterrorism and the prospect of a "pandemic...if groups seek to spread disease deliberately."[106] The document advocates a range of measures, including new terrorism offenses, expanded privilege, and greater sharing of information among foreign and domestic agencies.

The prospect of large-scale terror has also been an important motif in the rhetoric of security experts and officials. It was often invoked in the course of important policy discussions, including parliamentary committees in the lead up to, and later reviews of, the Anti-terrorism Act. While these appearances may not have garnered significant media attention, they helped shape perspectives on the nature of the threat at issue and supported the government's case for the urgency of new and radical policy.

In October of 2001, for example, Joseph Magnet, a constitutional law scholar from the University of Ottawa, told the House Standing Committee on Justice and Human Rights that the evolution of terrorism was following "three long-term trends."[107] Before 2001, there had been fewer annual incidents of terror, but they were becoming more lethal. They were also now beginning to embrace a "war paradigm." This entailed "asymmetric warfare against states by non-state networks," a paradigm in which no demands are made, no negotiation takes place, and non-combatants are targeted. Although Magnet did not invoke the prospect of WMD terror, his overview suggested that terror was only becoming more destructive and ambitious in its aims. By virtue of these developments, preemptive measures had become more critical. RCMP Chief Giuliano Zaccardelli emphasized the limitless nature of terrorists' ambitions, and the danger posed by their willingness to "commit suicidal acts of mass destruction against innocent civilians."[108] Terrorism, in his view, "poses an extraordinary threat to society," calling for "extraordinary action."

---

104 Privy Council Office, 2004.

105 Ibid, at 8.

106 Ibid.

107 House of Commons, Standing Committee on Justice and Human Rights, *Evidence* (Meeting No. 38, Oct. 31, 2001) 37th Parliament, 1st Sess., at http://www.parl.gc.ca/HousePublications/Publication.aspx?DocId=1041091&Language=E&Mode=1&Parl=37&Ses=1.

108 House of Commons, Standing Committee on Justice and Human Rights, *Evidence* (Meeting No. 30, Oct. 23, 2001) 37th Parliament, 1st Sess., at http://www.parl.gc.ca/HousePublications/Publication.aspx?DocId=1041045&Language=E&Mode=1&Parl=37&Ses=1.

Perhaps the most prominent expert on terrorism in committee hearings that fall was Professor Paul Wilkinson of the Centre for the Study of Terrorism and Political Violence at the University of Saint Andrews, in Scotland. Speaking to the House Committee on Justice on October 24, he asserted that "[w]e have crossed the threshold [...] into the era of mass terrorism, and we see a group that is actually hell-bent upon killing large numbers of people."[109] The first stages of this might have been in the process of unfolding at present:

> What I think we have seen in the case of the American atrocities is a group that really does have no compunction about massive lethality, and so we are a major step closer to the use of weapons of mass destruction by a terrorist group. We do not yet know enough about the anthrax that is being used in the United States and has turned up in some other countries, for example, in Argentina. We don't yet know whether [this] is part of the al-Qaeda network's efforts or whether it is something being done by some other group or groups or by a rogue state. There is a great debate about that. However, in the information we already have about the acts carried out by the bin Laden al-Qaeda network we can certainly see that if they had access to a means of dispersing chemical, nuclear, or biological weapons, there is no reason to think they would be in any way deterred from doing it by moral constraints.[110]

Before a Senate committee the same day, he emphasized that the 9/11 attacks were "the worst cases of mass terrorism we have experienced in modern history," but possibly less severe than they might have been. As he explained: "[m]any of the specialists involved in the investigation of the suicide hijackings in the United States are of the opinion that there was a plan to fly one of the airliners at 500 miles an hour into a civilian nuclear reactor. If that had happened, and the action had caused a major disaster at that plant, the consequences would have been experienced by many of the urban areas on the Canadian side of the border as well as within the United States."[111]

Later committee hearings, held in 2005 and 2010, featured further expert opinion on the prospect of WMDs. In 2005, Dr. Boaz Gainer of the International Policy Institute for Counter-terrorism mused about the prospects of nuclear and biological terrorism,[112]

---

109 House of Commons, Standing Committee on Justice and Human Rights, *Evidence* (Meeting No. 32, Oct. 24, 2001) 37th Parliament, 1st Sess., at http://www.parl.gc.ca/HousePublications/Publication.aspx?DocId=1041055&Language=E&Mode=1&Parl=37&Ses=1.

110 Ibid.

111 Senate, Special Senate Committee on the Subject Matter of Bill C-36, *Evidence* (Meeting No. 31, Oct. 24, 2001) 37th Parliament, 1st Sess., iss. 3, at http://www.parl.gc.ca/Content/SEN/Committee/371/sm36/pdf/03issue.pdf.

112 *See* House of Commons, Subcommittee on Public Safety and National Security of the Standing Committee on Justice, Human Rights, Public Safety and Emergency Preparedness, *Evidence* (Nov. 2, 2005) 38th Parliament, 1st Sess., at http://www.parl.gc.ca/HousePublications/Publication.aspx?DocId=2090678&Language=E&Mode=1.

while Professor Gavin Cameron of the University of Calgary was asked about nuclear terror in Canada.[113] Cameron conceded that "[w]e have almost no evidence of weapons-usable material, let alone a weapon itself, reaching the hands of a terrorist organization." In his view, "the bigger threat, the more likely threat anyway, particularly in the context of Canada, is things like radiological terrorism, the use of a radiological dispersal device—it is very easy to do, it uses nuclear material that's widely available—or an attack on a nuclear facility, of which obviously Canada has a number." Biological or chemical terror also posed a significant risk, he said, given the "large body of people who have the technical expertise to create those sorts of weapons" and the large membership and significant funds at the disposal of al Qaeda and other groups. In 2010, when asked by a Senate committee tasked to consider the "current status of terrorism" and its relevance to Canada, Tom Quiggin of the Canadian Centre of Intelligence and Security Studies at Carleton University asserted that "[w]hen I look five to ten years down the road, the things that keep me awake at night are chemical and biological weapons in the hands of terrorist groups driven by scientists who have an environmental or global outlook."[114]

An important further class of statements made outside of Parliamentary debates and discussions can be found in the annual reports of the Canadian Security Intelligence Service. Both their 2003 and 2004 reports list terrorism as a primary concern, noting WMD terror as both a direct and an indirect threat to Canadian security.[115] Later reports confirm that the "proliferation of chemical, biological, radiological, nuclear and explosive (CBRNE) weapons—also collectively referred to as weapons of mass destruction (WMD)—and their delivery vehicles (whether to states or non-state actors) poses a grave threat to the security of Canada, its allies, and to the international community."[116]

In 2012, the federal government published its first policy statement dealing explicitly with counterterrorism.[117] While the "proliferation of more sophisticated weaponry—including weapons of mass destruction,"[118] remains a concern, the prospect of terrorism is often

---

113 Ibid. (Oct. 5, 2005) at http://www.parl.gc.ca/HousePublications/Publication.aspx?DocId=2018796&Mode=1&Language=E.

114 Senate, Special Senate Committee on Anti-terrorism, *Evidence* (Issue 4, June 21, 2010) 40th Parliament, 3rd Sess., at http://www.parl.gc.ca/Content/SEN/Committee/403/anti/04ev-e.htm?comm_id = 597&Language = E&Parl = 40&Ses = 3.

115 The papers are no longer available online. I rely for this point on a summary of them by Livianna Tossutti, Osvaldo Croci and Amy Verdun, *National Threat Perception: Survey Results from Canada*, 18.2 Garnet Working Paper (May 2007), at 5.

116 Canadian Security and Intelligence Service, *2009–2010 Public Report* (Ottawa, 2010). See also the previous year's report, in which inexplicably, the threat appears less serious: "Chemical, biological, radiological, nuclear and explosive (CBRNE) weapons are an ongoing concern for the Service." *2008–2009 Public Report* (Ottawa, 2010).

117 Canada, *Building Resilience Against Terrorism: Canada's Counter-terrorism Strategy* (Ottawa: Ministry of Public Safety, 2012).

118 Ibid. at 9.

described in vague but ominous terms as a "serious and persistent threat to the security of Canada,"[119] "a significant threat to Canada, Canadians and Canadian interests abroad,"[120] or, in the case of the "Sunni Islamist groups affiliated with al Qaeda"—in particular AQAP and al Shabaab—"a substantial threat to Canada."[121] While AQAP has "pursued international attacks that may have affected Canada, such as their failed December bombing of Northwest Airlines Flight 253 in Canadian air space," al Shabaab poses a threat in part because "[s]everal Canadians are believed to have left Canada to join the group."[122] In light of the continuing danger posed by those groups and by "violent homegrown extremists," the document affirms a larger preemptive strategy that includes greater state secrecy and the use of security certificates under immigration law.[123]

Yet, as with administration officials in the United States, Canadian government and security officials continue to invoke the possibility of terror involving WMDs or other threats of large-scale terror. In 2013, Public Safety Canada published its "Public Report on the Terrorist Threat to Canada."[124] It warns that "[a]lthough al Qaida has not successfully conducted an international terrorist attack in years, it is still planning to do so if the opportunity arises. Canada continues to be featured on al Qaida's list of priority targets."[125] Al Qaida in the Arabian Peninsula poses a concern, given that an airliner plot was foiled in 2012; the group might stage attacks "originating elsewhere in the world [that] could affect flights to or travelling over Canada."[126] The situation in Syria is also critical. Canada is "concerned that Syria's conventional and chemical weapons could fall into the hands of terrorist groups."[127] A 2013 report of the Canadian Security and Intelligence Service also maintains a concern of the prospect of large-scale terror.[128] Asking "what could Al-Qaeda look like in 2018?," the document sets out various hypothetical possibilities.[129] One is rising "instability and weak governance in [al Qaeda's] base regions" leading to the group exercising "effective control over states holding weapons of mass

119 Ibid. at 6.

120 Ibid. at 7.

121 Ibid.

122 Ibid.

123 Ibid., Annex B.

124 Public Safety Canada, *2013 Public Report on the Terrorist Threat to Canada: Building a Safe and Resilient Canada* (Ottawa, 2013).

125 Ibid. at 11.

126 Ibid. at 19.

127 Ibid. at 20.

128 Canadian Security and Intelligence Service, *The Future of al Qaeda: Results of a Foresight Project* (Ottawa, Canada: 2013).

129 Ibid. The report consolidates papers presented at a workshop hosted by the CSIS Academic Outreach Program in January of 2013. At 5, the report indicates that the papers were written by "prominent specialists who took part in the entire project"; however, "the identity of their authors is not disclosed because the Chatham House rule was invoked throughout the exercise." At 6, the report cautions that "[t]he scenarios are not intended to predict AQ's future. They provide a range of credible alternative futures and describe contexts within which to explore the signs and implications of the evolution of AQ to the year 2018."

destruction."[130] In this case, "[a]rmed with chemical, biological, radiological and nuclear deterrents to [counter-terror] activities, [al Qaeda] poses an entirely new threat to global security."[131] A further possibility:

> the continued absence of a successful, major terrorist attack in North America since 2001 may induce a period of quiet and calm that lulls us into a state of false complacency, lowering our guard and, in turn, provoking Core Al-Qaeda or one of its allies to chance a dramatically spectacular attack.[132]

### II. WIDER PUBLIC PERCEPTIONS OF TERROR AND SECURITY POLICY

In the United States, as noted above, a widespread belief in the possibility of mass terror, and in particular terror involving WMDs, played a supporting role in a politics consistent with authoritarian legality. Canadian poll data is less clear on the extent of a belief in the prospect of mass terror or its likelihood in Canada. But in the post-9/11 period, substantial portions of the Canadian public have expressed a concern about the threat of terror and have supported increased security at the cost of civil liberties. The data is thus unclear as to the extent to which Canadians accepted the harbinger theory. But the data does suggest that a substantial number of Canadians have held beliefs that are compatible with a reliance on the harbinger theory on the part of their government and security officials.

Thus, in the early period after 9/11, few believed that an attack in Canada was likely—only 14 percent of Canadians, according to a 2002 Pollara poll.[133] But an Ekos poll of that year found that 45 percent of Canadians believed it to be very likely that "the U.S. will experience another similar scaled or worse terrorist disaster in the coming year."[134] By 2005, more Canadians were concerned about terrorism in Canada. A Strategic Council poll found that 62 percent of Canadians believed a terrorist attack in Canada was likely, with that number rising to 71 percent in a poll conducted a year later.[135] The Strategic Council also found that 62 percent strongly supported "[g]iving the U.S. any information it requests about Canadian citizens whom they suspect of being terrorists."[136] Seventy-two percent strongly supported "having video cameras in all public places." Eighty-one per cent were strongly in favour of "deporting or jailing anyone who publicly supports terrorists."

---

130 Ibid. at 5.

131 Ibid. at 18.

132 Ibid. at 40.

133 Clark Campbell, *Canadians Want Strict Security, Poll Finds*, GLOBE & MAIL (Toronto) Aug. 11, 2005.

134 *September 11th in Hindsight: Recovery and Resolve*, EKOS (Aug. 30, 2002), at http://www.ekos.com/admin/articles/9sept2002.pdf.

135 Pollara poll, cited in Tossutti, Croci, & Verdun, *supra* note 115, at 11.

136 Ibid.

Later polls suggest a consistency of opinion. An Ipsos Reid survey of 2011 found that 58 percent of Canadians affirmed "they are more concerned about a terrorist attack in Canada now than before 9/11."[137] A full 77 percent of respondents disagreed that "Canada and the U.S. can relax security measures now that there hasn't been an attack in 10 years." And 74 percent believed "the Canadian government's response has been 'appropriate.'" An Ipsos poll conducted in July of 2013, in the wake of Edward Snowden's revelations, found that although 49 percent of Canadians believed it "completely unacceptable" for "governments to monitor everyone's email and other online activities," 47 percent said it was "acceptable in some circumstances," and 4 percent thought it "completely acceptable."[138] To prevent future attacks, 64 percent found such monitoring "acceptable in some circumstances" and 13 percent "completely acceptable." An Abucus Data poll that summer similarly found that 62 percent of Canadians support an intrusion on personal privacy to enable the federal government to investigate possible terrorist threats.[139]

## Conclusion

Throughout the post-9/11 period, North American governments have continuously invoked strong or mild forms of the harbinger theory to justify the need for extraordinary measures. Large portions of the U.S. and Canadian public have been receptive to inflated threat claims, in part as a response to 9/11, but also as a response to the frequent depiction of large-scale terror in media and popular culture. Populations in both nations have also proved receptive to arguments about the need for greater security in light of the threat. The next chapter explores the wider resonance of this logic in expert literature and legal scholarship.

---

137 Amy Chung, *Canadians' Fears of Terror Rose Post 9/11*, POSTMEDIA NEWS (Sept. 7, 2011).

138 Ipsos Press Release, *Canadians Split on Whether It's Acceptable for Governments to Monitor Email and Online Activities In Some Circumstances*, (Aug. 28, 2013), at http://www.ipsos-na.com/news-polls/pressrelease.aspx?id = 6233.

139 Abacus Data, "NSA and Snowden: Canadians, Terrorism and Online Privacy" (June 2013): http://abacusinsider.com/politics-public-affairs/nsa-snowden-canadians-terrorism-online-privacy/.

# 4

# The Future of Terror in Expert Literature and the Advocacy of Extreme Measures

THE FOCUS IN this chapter shifts from the role of the harbinger theory in politics and public opinion to its role in academic and expert literature. The central claim in this chapter is that over the course of the post-9/11 period, the harbinger theory has played a crucial contextual role in the embrace of authoritarian measures by gaining legitimacy in a number of interrelated fields of study. The chapter will focus on three of them: expert opinion on the use of weapons of mass destruction (WMDs); the history and evolving nature of terrorism; and work by advocates of extreme measures.

The chapter will argue, more specifically, that the prevalence of a kind of catastrophic imagination in the first two bodies of literature served to promote its role in the third. In ways to be explored below, experts on WMDs and the history of terror have lent legitimacy and authority to the claim that an act of mass terror—on the scale of 9/11 or greater—has become more likely since 2001. In light of this work, and the salience of the views expressed in it, advocates of extreme measures have argued with greater plausibility that, on the basis of the growing threat, the limits on state power of an older, liberal legality are no longer reasonable. This view has, in turn, played a critical role in shaping public debate, law, and policy throughout the post-9/11 period.

Yet a crucial aspect of the development of the harbinger theory in all three of the literatures surveyed in this chapter pertains to the way in which the argument for the prospect of mass terror is structured. The chapter will highlight a consistent tendency on the part of a variety of authors to assert the imminent possibility of terror involving WMDs without supporting the claim with reference to evidence or authority, or without seeking to present the claim as a matter of some controversy. The chapter seeks therefore to demonstrate how the harbinger theory gained a large degree of legitimacy through a common tendency to offer assessments of the outstanding threat based on a selective or partial consideration of evidence or expert opinion. And thus, while some of the literature or threat assessments surveyed in this chapter might seem dated, they are important in illustrating how the harbinger theory was promulgated at critical junctures in the post-9/11 period. Many also contain forms of reasoning that remain current.

The argument is set out in three parts. Part one surveys recent literature dealing with the prospect of nuclear and biological terror. Focusing first on nuclear terror, the chapter will trace the outlines of a consensus among a prominent group of experts who contend that the prospect that non-state actors will use these weapons is relatively new, possibly imminent, and apocalyptic in its potential import. All three beliefs are also often held out as uncontroversial, or the subject of wide agreement about the evidence—contrary to a body of skeptical opinion to be explored in Chapter 6. Turning briefly to recent literature on biological terror, the chapter will argue that although the field lacks an analogous "consensus view" about the likelihood or magnitude of a bioterror attack, a number of experts, writing after 2001, have argued for the increasing danger that it poses. The cause for concern here stems from rapid advances in biotechnology, greater accessibility of materials, and evidence of the recent use and interest in bioweaponry on the part of various terrorist groups.

In the second part, the focus shifts to work by historians and scholars of the evolving nature of terrorism itself. The catastrophic imagination makes its appearance here in the form of a shared sense that global terror groups are becoming more ambitious and genocidal, as technologies of terror are becoming more accessible and lethal. Notable here is the confidence with which experts assert a belief in the inevitability of mass terror, together with an absence of any consideration of contrary evidence or opinion.

The third part explores the harbinger theory among three prominent American jurists—Richard Posner, Alan Dershowitz, and John Yoo—who have offered extended arguments in support of the use of extreme measures in national security. By virtue of their profile as academics or public intellectuals, all three have played a role in legitimizing the harbinger theory among a wider public, along with a set of corollary assumptions about security. Each of them views the threat of terror after 9/11 to be considerably greater and more likely to involve the use of WMDs, with potentially catastrophic consequences for the state. On this basis, each also argues that liberal legal limits on state power must be set aside in favour of various extreme or preemptive measures that include torture and targeted killing. Yet a common approach among all three is to invoke the imminent prospect of terror involving WMDs as self-evident or beyond debate, and thus not a claim in need of supporting opinion, or critical assessment in the few cases where authority is cited.

A final point to note at the outset is that the various authors surveyed here demonstrate a lack of interest in contrary opinion about the prospect of mass terror due in large part to an emphasis on *theoretical* possibilities rather than practical realities. In ways to be seen, the common thread in this chapter will be the tendency on the part of many purporting to offer insight into the near future of terrorism to assume that what could occur in theory is the same as what is likely to occur in practice. The works assessed here thus remain relevant in part because the theoretical possibilities invoked in them remain valid, and will continue to be invoked in defense of authoritarian measures for the foreseeable future.

## Part 1. Apocalyptic Fear Among Experts on Mass Terror

### I. THE IMMINENT PROSPECT OF NUCLEAR TERROR

Pervasive references to the possibility of nuclear terror in political rhetoric and works of popular culture in the period after September 11 might lead one to assume that fears in this regard were somewhat new. But in fact the prospect of nuclear terror has been a concern from the time that nuclear weapons were first tested in the 1940s.[1] Throughout the Cold War, there had been a long-standing debate about whether a non-state actor could deploy such a weapon, by obtaining fissile material and building a crude device on its own, or by stealing a bomb itself.[2] The debate was never settled, however, and many continued to doubt that a non-state actor in possession of fissile material could build and effectively deploy a nuclear device without facing enormous, possibly insurmountable challenges.[3]

Yet after 9/11, the nature of the discussion about nuclear terror had changed. Numerous experts and observers had come to view the prospect as real and immediate on the basis that certain variables had altered the situation, making this form of terror seem more plausible, more likely, and unprecedented in its possibilities. In advancing this claim, some new facts were relied upon, but much of the argument continued to rest on older claims that had remained contentious, and the contentious nature of them was often glossed over. Moreover, in keeping with an older tradition of assessing the nuclear question, experts inclined to believe in the imminent threat of nuclear terror tended to lend

---

[1] Leo Szilard, a Hungarian physicist and contributor to the Manhattan Project, wrote about nuclear bombs in 1945: "The position of the United States in the world may be adversely affected by their existence.... Clearly if such bombs are available, it will not be necessary to bomb our cities from the air in order to destroy them. All that is necessary is to place a comparatively small number in major cities and detonate them at some later time.... The long coastline, the structure of our society, and the heterogeneity of our population may make effective controls of such 'traffic' virtually impossible." Cited in Jonathan Schell, A HOLE IN THE WORLD: AN UNFOLDING STORY OF WAR, PROTEST AND THE NEW AMERICAN ORDER (New York: Nation Books, 2004), at 67.

[2] For a survey of Cold War opinion for and against the possibility of nuclear terror, see Stanley S. Jacobs, *The Nuclear Threat as a Terrorist Option*, 10: 4 TERRORISM AND POLITICAL VIOLENCE 149–163 (1998).

[3] Ibid. at 152.

emotional and often persuasive force to their fears by framing their discussion in vivid and apocalyptic imagery.

Figures representative of this new consensus view on nuclear terror include Graham Alison and Matthew Bunn of Harvard's Belfer Center for Science and International Affairs, and co-authors Charles Ferguson and William Potter of the Monterey Institute's Center for Nonproliferation Studies.[4] In a widely read, mainstream nonfiction work in 2004, *Nuclear Terrorism: The Ultimate Preventable Catastrophe*, Allison asserted, without qualification, that "a nuclear terrorist attack on America in the decade ahead is more likely than not"[5]—a claim he would repeat in 2006 without altering the time frame.[6] (Elsewhere, his concerns were extended to Canada.[7]) In 2005, writing for a more technical and scholarly audience, Ferguson and Potter concluded that the United States "has faced the threat of nuclear terrorism for many years, but this peril looms larger today than ever before."[8] In 2009, confirming the currency of a claim he had made in a number of reports, articles, and speeches, Matthew Bunn opined that "[t]here remains a very real danger that terrorists could get and use a nuclear bomb, turning the heart of a major city into a smoldering radioactive ruin."[9] In 2014,

---

4 For other contributions to this consensus view, see Frank Barnaby, How to Build a Nuclear Bomb and other Weapons of Mass Destruction (London: Granta Books, 2004), and Michael Levi, On Nuclear Terrorism (Cambridge, MA: Harvard University Press, 2007). Also worth mentioning here is the work of the U.S Congress's Commission on the Prevention of WMD Proliferation and Terrorism (which included Graham Allison, Senators Bob Graham and Jim Talent, and others), World At Risk (New York: Vintage Books, 2008). For a comprehensive survey of the literature on nuclear terror, see, e.g., Brian Jenkins, Will Terrorists Go Nuclear (New York: Prometheus Books, 2008).

5 Graham Allison, Nuclear Terrorism: the Ultimate Preventable Catastrophe (New York: Henry Holt, 2005), at 15.

6 Graham Allison, *The Ongoing Failure of Imagination*, Bull. Atomic Scientists 36–41 (Sept./Oct. 2006), cited in John Mueller, Atomic Obsession: Nuclear Alarmism from Hiroshima to Al Qaeda (Oxford: Oxford University Press, 2010) at 181. Mueller also notes that in 1995, Allison asserted that an act of nuclear terror against "American targets" would occur "before the decade is out." Mueller, citing Allison at 181; *see* Graham Allison, *Must We Wait for the Nuclear Morning After?*, Wash. Post, Apr. 30, 1995. Adopting Allison's sense of urgency, the World at Risk report, *supra* note 4, at xv, states: "The Commission believes that unless the world community acts decisively and with great urgency, it is more likely than not that a weapon of mass destruction will be used in a terrorist attack somewhere in the world by the end of 2013."

7 Graham Allison, *Is Nuclear Terrorism a Threat to Canada's National Security?*, 2005 Int' J. 713, at 714: "...nuclear terrorism is a very serious threat to Canada, as well as to the US and the world. [...] Directly, Montreal or Toronto or Vancouver could be the target of a nuclear terrorist bomb." At 717: "Given its close ties with the United States and the support it provides in the global war on terrorism, Canada is undoubtedly on al Qaeda's target list."

8 Charles D. Ferguson & William C. Potter, The Four Faces of Nuclear Terrorism (London: Routledge, 2005), at 1.

9 Matthew Bunn, "Reducing the Greatest Risks of Nuclear Theft and Terrorism" 138:4 Daedalus (Fall 2009) 112; *see also* Matthew Bunn, *Securing the Bomb 2010: Securing All Nuclear Materials in Four Years*, Project on Managing the Atom, Belfer Center for Science and International Affairs, Harvard Kennedy School and Nuclear Threat Initiative (April 2010), at www.nti.org/e_research/Securing_The_Bomb_2010.pdf. For more recent pronouncements, see, e.g., *Next Steps to Strengthen Nuclear Security and Prevent Nuclear Terrorism*, presentation notes of April, 2011, at a Vienna meeting of the Fissile Materials Working Group, available at http://belfercenter.ksg.harvard.edu/experts/368/matthew_bunn.html.

a report that Bunn co-authored with three other security experts stated that although "the world has made important progress" in reducing the risks of nuclear and radiological terrorism, they "remain real and dangerous threats."[10] "Terrorist groups continue to seek nuclear weapons and the materials and expertise needed to make them," the report warned, and "[s]ome potential nuclear weapons materials remain dangerously vulnerable."[11]

Experts who warn of the risk of nuclear terror tend to agree that the task of producing fissile material lies beyond the present scope of a non-state actor. But a number of authors also agree that nuclear terror seems viable in the short term based on four facts. The first is the prodigious supply of poorly guarded fissile materials throughout the world, in the form of both weapons and reactors, in sites where sensitive materials are often easily open to theft, sale, or (in the case of a nuclear reactor) attack by airplane or other means.[12] Frequent reports of theft, loss, or illicit transfer of material lend substance to these fears—making the prospect of material eventually falling into the hands of terrorists seem all but inevitable. A second factor in support of the terrorists is the claim that, once fissile material is obtained, building a viable nuclear weapon does not pose a significant hurdle, since the necessary knowledge is readily available in the public domain and the requisite skill is also readily attainable. A third factor is the ease with which fissile material could be concealed and delivered, or the difficulty of detecting its transit across the world's many porous and open borders. Fourth and finally, each of the authors points to the fact that Al Qaeda and other global terror groups have been known to seek WMD, including nuclear bomb technology, since at least the mid-1990s, making the threat less abstract and hypothetical.[13]

The strongest argument of the consensus school is the danger posed by copious supplies of poorly guarded fissile material. Ferguson and Potter envision a range of acquisition scenarios ranging from a state "voluntarily shar[ing] material", to a "senior official ... for ideological or mercenary motives" providing it, to the keepers of the material being "bribed or coerced", to terrorists obtaining it in a period of political unrest.[14] The frequency and number of thefts, in recent years, of weapons-grade material from Russia and

---

[10] Matthew Bunn, Martin Malin, Nickolas Roth & William H. Tobey, *Advancing Nuclear Security: Evaluating Progress and Setting Goals*, Project on Managing the Atom, Belfer Center for Science and International Affairs, Harvard Kennedy School and Nuclear Threat Initiative (March 2014), at http://belfercenter.ksg.harvard.edu/files/advancingnuclearsecurity.pdf, at i.

[11] Ibid.

[12] Allison, NUCLEAR TERROR, *supra* note 5, at 98; Ferguson & Potter, FOUR FACES, *supra* note 8, at 119; Bunn, *Securing the Bomb 2010, supra* note 9, at 6. Ferguson and Potter add, at 107, that fissile materials are easier to obtain than bombs because both "the amount of fissile material that might theoretically be accessible to terrorists is staggering," and that "fissile materials are often handled in in difficult-to-measure bulk form, introducing measurement uncertainties that can mask repeated diversions of small quantities." They also note although a number of thefts of fissile materials have been reported in the past decade, but none have involved stolen bombs.

[13] Allison, NUCLEAR TERRORISM, *supra* note 5, at 12–14; Bunn, *Securing the Bomb 2010, supra*, note 9 at 13; Ferguson & Potter, FOUR FACES, *supra* note 8, at 116–17.

[14] Ferguson & Potter, ibid. at 118.

other states of the former Soviet Union lend some of these scenarios further plausibility. After 1989, according to Allison, "there have been hundreds of confirmed cases of successful theft of nuclear materials in which the thieves were captured, sometimes in Russia, on other occasions in the Czech Republic, Germany and elsewhere."[15] Every month, reports surface of "yet another occasion in which nuclear material was stolen or a theft attempted."[16] Indeed, as Alison notes, between 1989 and 1992, German officials reported over 700 cases of "attempted nuclear sales, including sixty instances that involved seizure of nuclear materials."[17] Although none of these reported thefts have resulted in the loss of a known quantity of fissile material, he asserts (without substantiation) that "there can be no doubt about the fact that enough nuclear material to build more than twenty nuclear weapons was lost in the transition from the Soviet Union to Russia."[18]

A further concern lies with nations that have tenuous or insecure political orders, such as Pakistan, North Korea, Iran and possibly China. There remains a danger, with at least the first three countries, that officials might assist terrorists in the theft or sale of material or knowledge.[19] For many observers, the case of Pakistani nuclear scientist Abdul Qadeer Khan confirms this fear. While working with the Dutch government in the 1970s, Khan obtained designs for uranium enrichment processes, which enabled him to fast-track Pakistan's controversial nuclear program in the 1980s, and to play an instrumental role in its success in building a nuclear bomb by 1998.[20] Yet in 2003, American intelligence agents uncovered that for many years Khan had also been operating a private nuclear consulting firm "on the side"—supplying parts and blueprints for uranium enrichment to the governments of Libya, Iran, and North Korea. Many in Pakistan and abroad have speculated that a network as large and sophisticated as the one in which Khan was involved could not have existed without at least some knowledge or complicity on the part of the Pakistani government.[21] For Alison and others, an equally pressing concern to the one posed by a figure such as Khan is the prospect that, at some point soon, Islamic radicals may succeed in toppling the West-friendly regime in Pakistan, thus placing nuclear weapons and materials directly into the hands of a regime sympathetic to al Qaeda.[22] Pakistan

---

[15] Allison, NUCLEAR TERRORISM, *supra* note 5, at 9; *see also* 68–74. Ferguson and Potter set out a similar series of concerns in FOUR FACES, *supra* note 8, at 54–61, 107–10, and 126–31.

[16] Allison, NUCLEAR TERRORISM, *supra* note 5, at 9.

[17] Allison, ibid. at 71.

[18] Allison, ibid. at 10. Bunn, *Securing the Bomb 2010, supra* note 9, at v., provides an updated (but somewhat vague) tally of such activity: "There have been over 18 documented cases of theft or loss of plutonium or highly enriched uranium (HEU), the essential ingredients of nuclear weapons. Peace activists have broken into a Belgian base where U.S. nuclear weapons are reportedly stored; two teams of armed men attacked a site in South Africa where hundreds of kilograms of HEU are stored; and Russian officials have confirmed that terrorist teams have carried out reconnaissance at Russian nuclear weapon storage facilities."

[19] Allison, NUCLEAR TERRORISM, *supra* note 5, at 76–81.

[20] For an account of Khan's involvement in nuclear affairs from the 1970s onward, see William Langewiesche, THE ATOMIC BAZAAR (New York: Farrar, Straus and Giroux, 2008).

[21] Allison, NUCLEAR TERRORISM, *supra* note 5, at 63.

[22] Allison, ibid. at 78; Bunn, *Securing the Bomb 2010, supra* note 9, at vi.

is understood to have some 50 nuclear bombs and enough highly enriched uranium for 50 more.[23]

Another compelling claim from this school of experts is the ease with which a bomb or fissile material could be transited, given the difficulty of detecting its movement. Allison and Bunn believe that, as Bunn puts it, the "small size and weak radiation signal" of the material, together with the "myriad potential pathways" into a country—through a shipping container, an open port, an open border—make detection all but impossible.[24] Ferguson and Potter are only slightly more cautious on this point. If theft of material came to light, a "massive hunt" would follow, along with "greatly intensified security over transportation links and points of entry."[25] But many conceivable scenarios would remain in which material could easily avoid detection.

The more contentious, but critical, claim from this school is that once fissile material is obtained, building and effectively deploying a crude nuclear weapon would not be difficult. I will defer until Chapter 6 the question of how and why this is a contentious claim, and seek here to establish two more basic points. First, members of the consensus school believe that nuclear bomb building is readily within reach of non-state actors in possession of fissile material because of its technical, theoretical simplicity. Second, members of this school present the simplicity claim as "widely acknowledged" and beyond debate, when in fact there is a vigorous debate about the issue (to be explored in Chapter 6).

Taking up these points in reverse, Allison begins his discussion of the issue by positing that "in the popular imagination, the belief persists that building a nuclear weapon requires Manhattan Project–style science. Those who work with nuclear weapons have always known better."[26] Citing David Lilienthal, chairman of the Atomic Energy Commission in the late 1940s, and Theodore Taylor, a nuclear physicist credited with designing "the smallest and largest" U.S. atomic arsenals, Allison suggests that in the view of those intimately involved in U.S. nuclear bomb–building programs, the process involves basic knowledge that is widely available, and is commonly understood to be, as Taylor puts it, "very easy. Double underline. Very easy."[27] Ferguson and Potter make a more sweeping claim: "Most physicists and nuclear weapons analysts have concluded that construction of a gun-type device would pose few technological barriers to technically competent terrorists."[28] In support, they cite a series of government reports and expert opinions,[29] including passages from a 2002 U.S. National Research Council report stating that "Crude HEU [highly enriched uranium] weapons could be fabricated without

---

23 Allison, NUCLEAR TERRORISM, *supra* note 5, at 75.

24 Bunn, *Securing the Bomb 2010, supra* note 9, at v; Allison, ibid. at 107.

25 Ferguson & Potter, FOUR FACES, *supra* note 8, at 138–39.

26 Allison, NUCLEAR TERRORISM, *supra*, note 5, at 93.

27 Allison, ibid. Allison's source for Taylor's statement is Dan Stober, *No Experience Necessary*, BULL. ATOMIC SCIENTISTS 57 (March/April 2003), at 62.

28 Ferguson & Potter, FOUR FACES, *supra* note 8, at 132.

29 *See* the sources cited in endnote 52 in Ferguson & Potter, ibid.

state assistance";[30] a 2003 open letter by the Union of Concerned Scientists stating that HEU is "the easiest material in the world for terrorist to use to make a nuclear bomb";[31] and Frank von Hippel, a physicist in the employ of the Bush administration's Office of Science and Technology Policy, who stated in 2001, "It is generally agreed, however, that educated terrorists could turn weapon-grade uranium...into a gun type nuclear explosive."[32] Writing in 2010, Mathew Bunn characterizes the literature on this point in similar terms: "Repeated assessments by the U.S. government and other governments have concluded that it is plausible that a sophisticated terrorist group could make a crude nuclear explosive—capable of destroying the heart of a major city—if they got enough plutonium or HEU."[33]

Ferguson and Potter's case for the simplicity of building a crude nuclear device may be taken as representative, given the concurrence of Allison, Bunn and Wier, and others, on its essential points.[34] They begin by noting that the most likely method that terrorists would employ for building a bomb is a "gun-type" device, which involves the firing, within a tubular shell, of one piece of HEU into another, causing the chain-reaction of subatomic particles that sets off a nuclear explosion.[35] A viable weapon would require only 40 to 50 kilograms of HEU, an amount small enough to envision being easily transported.[36] Designs for a gun-type weapon are widely available online.[37] A small group would likely need to be assembled that had knowledge of explosives, metalworking and chemistry, and the group would need between several weeks and several months to test and refine the parts of the bomb.[38] Ferguson and Potter conclude that:

> Because of the inherent simplicity of a gun-type device, designing and constructing it would be relatively straightforward. Testing the non-nuclear parts of the device would likely be required, and an appropriate testing area would be needed (such

---

30 Committee on Science and Technology for Countering Terrorism, *Making the Nation Safer* (Washington: National Academies Press, 2002) at 45, cited in Ferguson & Potter, FOUR FACES, *supra* note 8, at 132.

31 Union of Concerned Scientists, Scientists' Letter on Exploiting Nuclear Material, to W.J. "Billy" Tauzin, Sept. 25, 2003, cited in Ferguson & Potter, FOUR FACES, *supra* note 8, at 132.

32 Frank von Hippel, *Recommendations for Preventing Nuclear Terrorism*, Federation of American Scientists Public Interest Report, Nov. /Dec. 2001, cited in Ferguson & Potter, FOUR FACES, *supra* note 8, at 132.

33 Bunn, *Securing the Bomb 2010, supra* note 9, at 16.

34 *See, e.g.*, Frank Barnaby, HOW TO BUILD, *supra* note 4, at 78–83; Matthew Bunn & Anthony Wier, *Terrorist Nuclear Weapon Construction: How Difficult?*, 607: ANNALS AM. ACAD. POL. & SOC. SCI. 133, (2006) at 144; Michael Levi, ON NUCLEAR TERRORISM, *supra* note 4, at 35–45. Although Levi agrees that the technical steps in bomb building are theoretically straightforward, he raises various potential practical issues that may be encountered at each stage (discussed in Chapter 6).

35 Ferguson & Potter, FOUR FACES, *supra* note 8, at 131. Allison, NUCLEAR TERRORISM, *supra* note 5, at 96; Bunn, *Securing the Bomb 2010, supra* note 9, at 16.

36 Ferguson & Potter, ibid. at 132; Allison, ibid. at 95–96; Bunn, ibid. at 16.

37 Ferguson & Potter, ibid. at 133; Allison, ibid. at 94–95; Bunn, ibid. at 16.

38 Ferguson & Potter, ibid. at 133.

> as a terrorist training camp...) to avoid arousing suspicion. Assuming such tests could be accomplished and a sufficient amount of HEU obtained in the appropriate form, terrorists could have a moderate degree of confidence that their IND would result in a substantial nuclear yield.[39]

To corroborate the plausibility of this scenario, Ferguson and Potter, along with Alison, Bunn and Wier, cite the use of the gun-type design by the United States at Hiroshima and by the South African government in the construction of a small arsenal of nuclear weapons in the late 1980s.[40]

Finally, members of the consensus school are often intent on conveying the prospect of imminent nuclear terror in vividly catastrophic terms—which is to say, in ways that are sure to stir the emotions. Allison is particularly effective at this by spelling out for his mostly non-specialist readers the impact that the epicenter of the blast would have on specific cities, from New York to Houston to Washington and Los Angeles. He writes, for example, that

> [i]f Al Qaeda was to rent a van to carry the ten-kiloton Russian weapon into the heart of Times Square and detonate it adjacent to the Morgan Stanley headquarters at 1585 Broadway, Times Square would vanish in the twinkling of an eye. [... The] fireball and blast wave would destroy instantaneously the theatre district, the New York Times building, Grand Central Terminal, and every other structure within a third of a mile of the point of detonation. [...] On a normal workday, more than half a million people crowd the area within a half-mile radius of Times Square. A noon detonation in midtown Manhattan could kill them all. Hundreds of thousands of others would die from collapsing building, fire, and fallout in the ensuing hours....[41]

Bunn envisions the consequences of an attack on a world historical scale, in language that exemplifies the catastrophic imagination:

> It is important to understand the full history-changing scope of the catastrophe that even a single terrorist nuclear bomb could cause. The heart of a major city could be reduced to a smoldering radioactive ruin, leaving tens or hundreds of thousands of people dead. Terrorists—either those who committed the attack or others—would probably claim they had more bombs already hidden in other cities (whether they

---

39 Ibid. at 134.

40 Ferguson & Potter, ibid. at 134; Bunn & Wier, *Terrorist Nuclear Weapon Construction, supra*, note 34, at 139–40; Allison, NUCLEAR TERRORISM, *supra* note 5, at 96.

41 Allison, ibid. at 4.

did or not), and the fear that this might be true could lead to panicked evacuations, creating widespread havoc and economic disruption.[42]

Potter and Ferguson cast the impact in broader political terms:

Consequences stemming from a terrorist-detonated nuclear weapon in an American city would emanate beyond the immediate tens or hundreds of thousands of fatalities and the massive property and financial damage. Americans who were not killed or injured by the explosion would live in fear that they could die from future nuclear terrorist attacks. Such fear would erode public confidence in the government and could spark the downfall of the administration in power.[43]

In short, the threat is conceived of in extreme terms. As Allison puts it: "Nuclear terrorism is not only an existential threat to the idea of America, it is also a threat to civilization as we know it."[44]

## II. THE IMMINENCE OF BIOLOGICAL TERROR

By contrast to the recent literature on nuclear terror, there is no clear consensus view among recent opinion on bioterror as to the likelihood and magnitude of an attack in the near future.[45] However, many experts have emphasized the growing nature of the threat, based on the evolving state of biotechnology, the relatively greater accessibility of materials in contrast to nuclear and other forms of WMDs, and evidence of interest in bioweaponry among terror groups.

Discussions of bioterror range across a wide spectrum of possible uses of airborne pathogens, viruses, bacteria, and synthetic chemicals meant to cause widespread harm or death to humans and other life forms. Experts are divided over the level of difficulty involved in making and discharging bioweaponry, but they agree on the basic stages in production. An effective act of bioterror would first entail cultivating the substance in

---

42 Bunn, *Securing the Bomb 2010*, *supra* note 9, at 3.

43 From Ferguson & Potter, FOUR FACES, *supra* note 8, at 3. Imagining Ottawa as a potential target of nuclear terror, Allison, in *Is Nuclear Terrorism a Threat*, *supra* note 7, at 717, writes: "A nuclear bomb going off on Parliament Hill in Ottawa would cause everything from the supreme court to the Ottawa Congress Centre to disappear; everything for several blocks past the National Archives and the Canadian War Museum would be left in rubble; and fires would consume the Canadian Museum of Nature. Tens of thousands of people would die immediately and the seriously injured would number in the hundreds of thousands. Fallout from the blast would be carried by winds across Canada, contaminating farmland and cities alike and creating thousands of additional casualties."

44 Allison, NUCLEAR TERRORISM, *supra* note 5, at 212.

45 On the scope and divided nature of opinion on the question, see Andreas Wenger & Reto Wollenmann, *Bioterrorism: A Complex Threat*, in Wenger & Wollenmann, eds., BIOTERRORISM: CONFRONTING A COMPLEX THREAT (London: Lynne Reinner Publishers, 2007).

question from natural sources or obtaining it from an existing laboratory, and preserving it in its lethal state or growing it, pending its transportation to its target destination.[46] This would involve, at the least, the use of a laboratory, and a team of skilled biochemists and other experts. In order to effectively spread a pathogen by airborne means, for example, a terror group would require expertise in meteorology and techniques of airborne dispersal.[47] Finally, the deployment of the weapon would require specific weather conditions and would initially have limited geographic scope—raising the possibility of containment or failure.

Despite these constraints, however, some have argued that because it is less complex, expensive, and elaborate for non-state actors with genocidal ambitions to make and use biological weapons—at least relative to nuclear weapons—bioterror poses a real and pending threat. Barry Kellman, a special advisor to Interpol on biocrime and a member of a U.S. National Academy of Science committee on destructive uses of biotechnology, advances this view in *Bioviolence: Preventing Biological Terror and Crime* (2007). For Kellman, "making a lethal bioweapon is well within many people's capability."[48] While it bears similarities with the process of making a dirty bomb (with radioactive material), "a bioweapon can kill many more people than a dirty bomb."[49] Kelman also notes that "[p]reparing and effectively weaponizing pathogens might require sophisticated equipment and scientific expertise but far less than what would be required to produce even a rudimentary nuclear weapon. Pathogens are naturally available, and refined seed stocks of potentially weaponizeable agents are found widely in laboratories around the world. Getting weapons-grade nuclear material is, by contrast, extraordinarily difficult and far more expensive."[50]

Frank Barnaby, member of an Oxford Research Group on the terrorist use of weapons of mass destruction, concurs.[51] Making biological weapons, he argues, involves fewer "facilities and resources" than what is required for building a nuclear bomb; moreover, "the organisms used in the weapons reproduce themselves so that only a small quantity of them are needed to start the production process."[52] Many of the necessary tools and

---

46 See William R. Clark's discussion of the technical steps involved in the Aum Shinrikyo attack of 1995 and the anthrax attacks in November 2001 in the United States, BRACING FOR ARMAGEDDON? THE SCIENCE AND POLITICS OF BIOTERRORISM IN AMERICA (Oxford: Oxford University Press, 2008), ch. 10.

47 Ibid. at 166.

48 Barry Kellman, BIOVIOLENCE: PREVENTING BIOLOGICAL TERROR AND CRIME (Cambridge: Cambridge University Press, 2007), at 16.

49 Ibid.

50 Ibid. The authors of WORLD AT RISK (the report of a 2008 U.S. congressional committee on the proliferation of WMDs, *supra* note 4) make a similar point, at 11: "We accept the validity of intelligence estimates about the current rudimentary nature of terrorist capabilities in the area of biological weapons but caution that the terrorists are trying to upgrade their capabilities and could do so by recruiting skilled scientists. In this respect the biological threat is greater than the nuclear; the acquisition of deadly pathogens, and their weaponization and dissemination in aerosol form, would entail fewer technical hurdles than the theft or production of weapons-grade uranium or plutonium and its assembly into an improvised nuclear device."

51 Barnaby, HOW TO BUILD, *supra* note 4, at 78–83.

52 Ibid. at 48.

equipment for making biological weapons are "dual purpose, very similar to that used in, for example, a brewery for making beer. [They] can therefore be bought from commercial suppliers without raising suspicions."[53] Both medical research laboratories and nature itself offer ready sources of material for the would-be terrorist, including, in the latter case, anthrax, brucellosis, and plague.[54] In Barnaby's view: "A reasonably sophisticated terrorist group with access to financial and technical resources able to employ people adequately trained in biology and in handling biological material will be able to acquire a biological-warfare agent and establish a programme to produce an effective biological weapon using it."[55] This serves to ground his conclusion that "[t]here is a serious risk that terrorist groups will acquire and use WMDs."[56]

For other commentators, the danger is imminent. Jim Davis, a director of the U.S. Air Force's Counterproliferation Center, asserts that the "likelihood that biological weapons will be used against our nation continues to rise."[57] His view is based in part on the claim that bioweapons are becoming easier to make, with the necessary knowledge more accessible and necessary skills more common. There are, he fears, "many thousands of highly educated microbiologists or other health science professionals worldwide that are capable of growing, weaponizing, and employing a [bioweapon] agent. Much of the technical information is now readily available on the Internet, in libraries, and through mail-order channels that provide 'how-to' manuals."[58] Noting al Qaeda's interest in using bioweaponry, and citing the anthrax attacks on U.S. Senate and government offices in the fall of 2001 as a precedent, Davis sets out two scenarios as the "most likely [bioweaponry] scenarios that the United States and its allies might face in the future."[59] One involves the deployment of a host of bioweapon agents over a span of years, targeting the U.S. agriculture industry, causing significant economic disruption and widespread panic. Another involves the use of anthrax, or an analogous substance, to carry out airborne bioterror attacks on U.S. cities:

> Five 100-pound bags of anthrax could easily be smuggled in grain sacks on one of many shipments that arrive in U.S. ports everyday. These bags could be lined with plastic so no powder was prematurely released. Three to five major cities, on the order of Houston or Los Angeles, would be targeted, each requiring only a

---

53 Ibid. at 51.

54 Ibid. at 53.

55 Ibid. at 124.

56 Ibid. at 136.

57 Jim A. Davis, *A Biological Warfare Wake-Up Call: Prevalent Myths and Likely Scenarios*, in Jim A. Davis and Barry R. Schneider, eds., The Gathering Biological Warfare Storm (Westport, CT: Praeger, 2004), at 187.

58 Ibid. at 190.

59 Ibid. at 192.

> 100-pound bag. Appropriate aerosolizing devices could be easily procured in the United States to mount on an automobile, airplane, or boat.[60]

This would lead to the infection and death of "hundreds of thousands" of people, which would "overwhelm the U.S. medical system," causing a "human, economic, and political catastrophe" of the first order.[61]

Colonel Michael Ainscough, a physician with the U.S. Air Force and Surgeon General Chair at Air University, argues that it is "increasingly likely that non-state terrorists will use biological attacks."[62] Of particular concern for Ainscough is the possibility of "genetically engineered agents that may resist known therapies."[63] Advances in genetics have enabled the creation of substances with "new pathogenic characteristics," including "increased survivability, infectivity, virulence, [and] drug resistance," giving rise to "one of the gravest threats we will face."[64] Whereas previous bioterror attacks, including those attempted by the Aum Shinrikyo group in Japan in the 1990s, had been modest in their effects, Ainscough suggests that "with the capabilities of biological engineering and a new generation of weapons, this may change."[65] Indeed, in his view, the threat posed "can only increase as technology develops."[66] Among various possible "paths to enhance biothreats," Ainscough notes that the genome sequences for a number of viruses, plasmids, and bacteria have now been published; thus, "it seems only a matter of time until microbiologists develop synthetic genes, synthetic viruses, or even complete new organisms. Some of them could be specifically produced for biological warfare or terrorism purposes."[67]

Bioweaponry also presents a unique set of challenges to existing defenses. Kellman argues that in "the vast majority of cities in the world, detection capabilities are essentially

---

60 Ibid. at 200.

61 Ibid. For similarly cautious assessments in the period from 2001 to 2005, see Marie Isabelle Chevrier, *Why Do Conclusions from the Experts Vary?*, in Andreas Wenger & Reto Wollenmann, eds., BIOTERRORISM: CONFRONTING A COMPLEX THREAT (London: Lynne Rienner Publishers, 2007), at 140–43. Among the sources cited are Jonathan B. Tucker's *Biosecurity: Limiting Terrorist Access to Deadly Pathogens*, Peaceworks, No. 52, U.S.Institute of Peace (2003). At 11, Tucker writes: "Recent evidence suggests that the threat of bioterrorism is real and growing. Documents and computer hard drives seized during the March 1, 2003, capture of Khalid Sheikh Mohammed, a key operational planner for Al Qaeda, revealed that the organization had recruited a Pakistani microbiologist, acquired materials to manufacture botulinum toxin, and developed a workable plan for anthrax production."

62 Michael Ainscough, *Next Generation Bioweapons: Genetic Engineering and Biological Warfare*, in Davis & Schneider, THE GATHERING BIOLOGICAL WARFARE STORM, *supra* note 57, at 176.

63 Ibid. at 165.

64 Ibid. Tucker, *supra*, note 61, at 11, expresses a similar concern: "Rapid advances in biological science and technology are also changing the nature of the bioterrorism threat. Genetic engineering has made it theoretically possible to render natural disease agents more lethal, contagious, or environmentally persistent, evade detection and diagnosis, and defeat existing drugs and vaccines."

65 Ibid. at 176.

66 Ibid. at 185.

67 Ibid. at 178.

nonexistent, and available medical response capacities are already overburdened with a host of natural epidemics."[68] While an attack involving multiple or complex forms of weaponry in the United States, or a similarly developed nation, "might be devastating," he suggests that it could be "many orders of magnitude more catastrophic where populations are crowded and public health capabilities are already strained and ineffective."[69] A 2003 report by the CIA entitled "The Darker Bioweapons Future" supports this view.[70] Summarizing research provided to the CIA by the National Academy of Science, the report states that "[a]ccording to experts, the biotechnology underlying the development of advanced biological agents is likely to advance very rapidly, causing a diverse and elusive threat spectrum. The resulting diversity of new [bioweapon] agents could enable such a broad range of attack scenarios that it would be virtually impossible to anticipate and defend against."[71] Ainscough adds to these concerns the difficulty of responding to new and unknown forms of bioweaponry. "A terrorist attack with a biologically engineered agent," he writes, "may unfold unlike any previous event. The pathogen may be released clandestinely so there will be a delay between exposure and onset of symptoms. Days to weeks later, when people do develop symptoms, they could immediately start spreading contagious diseases."[72] Many of the infected would by then have travelled around the country or the world, vastly expanding the scope of the affected populations, and "public anxiety" in response.

The potential consequences of bioterror also place this category of weapon in a class of its own. Kellman suggests that bioweapons may exceed both chemical and atomic weapons in their potential for lethal harm:

> A well-planned attack using chemicals or explosives could be devastating, but it is hard to conceive an attack with casualties exceeding ten thousand victims. By contrast, it has been estimated that release of 250 pounds of highly refined anthrax spores over a major American city could infect up to three million people. In truth, the potential number of victims is unknowable—it depends on where it happens, the type of pathogen, and the sophistication of the weapon maker. Yet, there is a widespread consensus among experts that a high end bioattack would inflict casualties exponentially greater than any chemical or conventional attack.[73]

Bioweapons are also distinguished by their capacity to be spread through contagion: "no other type of weapon can replicate itself and spread."[74] They are also likely sources of

---

68 Kellman, *supra* note 48, at 14.

69 Ibid.

70 CIA Directorate of Intelligence, *The Darker Bioweapons Future*, Federation of American Scientists (2003), http://www.fas.org/irp/cia/product/bw1103.pdf.

71 Ibid.

72 Ainscough, *supra* note 62, at 176.

73 Kellman, *supra* note 48, at 15–16.

74 Ibid. at 17.

"mass panic," given the potentially slow and drawn-out period of time in which they might take effect.[75]

I return in Chapter 6 to the question of bioterror and the contentious nature of the claims canvassed here. At this stage, I have sought only to emphasize the presence of a school of opinion, in the period after 2001, which conflates fears about Al Qaeda and other terror groups with concerns about advances in biotechnology, and lends authority to a belief in the imminent threat of bioterror in ways that are analogous to recent work on nuclear terror—i.e., by emphasizing theoretical possibilities over practical realities that might make the actual use of such weapons more problematic.

## Part 2. Theories of the Evolving Nature of Terrorism

Many of the scholars who grappled with the evolving nature of terrorism in the wake of 9/11 were inclined to argue that the threat it posed had now become much greater than ever before. A crucial part of what made it a larger threat was the greater likelihood that terrorists would resort to the use of WMDs, or that such a possibility was in fact imminent. In setting out this position, however, many of the experts at issue demonstrated the same tendency explored above to present the likely prospect of terror involving WMDs as a self-evident or uncontroversial claim. The logic in much of this literature—as in the literature by experts on nuclear or biological terror—is that because it is theoretically straightforward to build and deploy a weapon of this nature, in practical terms it is inevitable. Yet, as with many of the experts explored above, historians of terror have tended to advance theories about the likely use of WMDs without either acknowledging or engaging to a significant degree a considerable body of skeptical opinion on point.

Consider, for example, the role of WMDs in the work of Walter Laqueur, a long-standing and prominent contributor to the field of terrorism studies, beginning with *Terrorism* (1974), through a series of more recent studies, including *The New Terrorism: Fanaticism and the Arms of Mass Destruction* (1999) and *No End to War: Terrorism in the Twenty-first Century* (2004).[76] For Lacqueur, the prospect of WMD terror is more likely now due in part to the changing nature of terrorism itself. From roughly the mid-1960s, when terrorism began to emerge as a common tactic for advancing political grievances, to the early 1990s, most groups employing terror had more limited aims and objectives. Across the political spectrum, groups resorting to terror tended to be regional and internal in their focus, with the use of terror as a tool for advancing separatist or sectarian politics

---

[75] Ibid.

[76] Walter Laqueur, TERRORISM (New York: Little, Brown, 1977); *Postmodern Terrorism: New Rules for an Old Game*, FOREIGN AFFAIRS (Sept./Oct. 1996); THE NEW TERRORISM: FANATICISM AND THE ARMS OF MASS DESTRUCTION (Oxford: Oxford University Press, 1998); NO END TO WAR: TERRORISM IN THE TWENTY-FIRST CENTURY (New York: Continuum, 2004); *The Terrorism to Come*, POL'Y REV. 126 (Aug. 2004).

appearing to peak in the 1970s and beginning to wane globally by the late 1980s.[77] In the 1990s, Lacqueur suggests, the internal or regional focus gave way to broader, non-regional movements of Islamic extremists, which drew upon a much wider pool of recruits and made use of more sophisticated tools for communication and dissemination. The aim of this newer form of terror was "no longer to conduct propaganda but to effect maximum destruction."[78]

And while the scope and ambition of global terror were expanding, so too were the technologies of terror. In 1999, Laqueur wrote: "[T]here has been a radical transformation, if not a revolution, in the character of terrorism… [f]or the first time in history, weapons of enormous destructive power are both readily acquired and harder to track."[79] The technical knowledge and skills required for building weapons of mass terror were becoming less complex and "not that rare or expensive."[80] Revisiting the issue in 2004, Laqueur asserted with greater certainty:

> [i]t is only a question of time until radiological, chemical, or biological weapons will be used more or less systematically by terrorist groups. [...] There is much reason to believe that if such attacks should be carried out in the near future, many, perhaps the great majority, will fail, or will have a smaller effect than anticipated. But it should also be clear that if only one out of ten, one out of a hundred such attempts succeeds, the damage caused, the number of victims will be infinitely higher than at any time in the past.[81]

To his credit, Lacqueur demonstrates a degree of skepticism as to the likely success of most terrorist attempts to use WMDs, suggesting the low probability of its use or effectiveness at any given point in time. However, his analysis of the prospect of its use is premised largely on the basis of generalizations (weapons of "enormous power" now becoming "readily acquired"). Absent from the discussion is a consideration of the *evidence* of how such weapons might be more readily acquired and used—or skeptical perspectives on point. Terror involving WMDs seems more plausible in Lacqueur's recent work in large part due to facts relating to the shifting *politics* of terrorism. Thus, as he writes, while "[m]ost of the terrorist groups of the past would not have used such weapons," given moral or political constraints to the notion of killing hundreds of thousands or even millions of people, for the newer, more fanatical groups, these restraints "have become weaker or are no longer existent."[82]

---

77 Laqueur, No End to War, ibid. at 28.

78 Ibid, at 9.

79 Laqueur, The New Terrorism, *supra* note 76, at 4.

80 Ibid. at 5.

81 Laqueur, No End to War, *supra*, note 76, at 226–27.

82 Ibid. at 227.

Philip Bobbitt offers a similar but more intricate theory of the evolving nature of global terror. He also demonstrates a similar tendency to warn of the greater likelihood of WMD terror without grounding this opinion in an exploration of the evidence for and against such a claim. The result is a persuasive—and given his background, an authoritative—but not necessarily balanced or accurate assessment of the outstanding threat.

Bobbitt's credibility rests in part on having acted as counsel to President Jimmy Carter and the State Department, his past membership in the National Security Council, and his expertise as a historian of warfare. In a widely read work of general nonfiction published in 2008, *Terror and Consent: the Wars for the Twenty-First Century*, Bobbitt approaches the contemporary threat in terms of a larger transition from an older geo-political order defined by sovereign nation states and conventional protectionist economies to a globalized, post-sovereign order based on what he calls the "market state."[83] The goal of the market state is to maximize the economic welfare and opportunity of its citizens, and thus it embraces, at all levels of its legal and social make-up, technologies and regulatory mechanisms that expand access to the world market. The transition is changing the nature of terrorism because "[d]ifferent constitutional orders spawn different terrorisms."[84] The rise of the market state, in Bobbitt's view, will "radically redistribute the availability of [WMD] owing to the development of clandestine markets."[85] Bobbitt asserts that "nuclear weapons will become commodified... while biological weapons will be easily and cheaply created owing to the Internet-assisted dispersal of knowledge, which will allow developers to bypass the difficult initial stages of recombinant DNA techniques, and even the need to culture viruses and bacteria."[86] Without grounding any of these claims in evidence or expert opinion, the line here between high-order political speculation and science fiction becomes hard to draw.

As with Laqueur, shifting modes of operation of global terrorism serve as a basis for Bobbitt's argument that the *weapons* of terrorism are also likely to evolve. We are likely to see a shift, he suggests, from "market state terrorism" to "nation state terrorism," giving rise to a number of differences, including the fact that the latter will be far more lethal.[87] Whereas nation-state terror was marked by a desire for a large audience but typically involved relatively few casualties, Bobbitt notes that the annual number of casualties in international terrorism has steadily risen since the early 1990s.[88] Drawing on a wider range of sources for funding, market state terrorists are better financed.[89] They

---

83 Philip Bobbitt, Terror and Consent: The Wars for the Twenty First-Century (New York: Knopf, 2008), at 9.

84 Ibid.

85 Ibid.

86 Ibid.

87 Ibid. at 46.

88 Ibid. at 46. In support of this claim, Bobbitt cites Anna Pluta and Peter Zimmerman, *Nuclear Terror: A Disheartening Dissent, Survival* 48, No. 2 (2006) at 55, and Brent Ellis, *Countering Complexity: An Analytical Framework to Guide Counter-terrorism Policy-Making*, 6:1 J. Mil. & Strategic Stud. (2003) at 3.

89 Ibid. at 49.

also "outsource" portions of their operation to local groups—in the way that al Qaeda works with operatives in places ranging from Bali, Morocco, Egypt, Turkey, Spain, Iraq, and Britain.[90] Bobbitt also suggests that "market state terrorist structures more greatly resemble VISA or Mastercard organization charts than they do centralized, hierarchical structures of nation state governmental organizations, including nation state terror groups."[91] Thus, in distinction to groups such as the Irish Republican Army (IRA) or Basque Homeland and Freedom (Euskadi Ta Askatasuna, or ETA), newer forms of terror involve associations among wider networks of smaller groups, over larger expanses of space, with more tenuous social, ideological or economic links.

Bobbitt also asserts that market state terrorists are more likely to seek and use WMDs than their predecessors, on the basis of their greater ambitions.[92] Neither the Palestine Liberation Organization (PLO) nor the IRA was interested in such a weapon because they feared international opinion or a negative reaction against or within their own membership. By contrast, weapons of mass terror suit the tendency on the part of market state terrorists to be "more theatrical, producing vivid dramas and tableaux" for a world connected by network technology.[93] "Market state terrorists want a lot of people dead *and* a lot of people watching."[94] The target is also no longer a single nation-state or leadership, but something more expansive: "anti-globalization," "anti-Americanism," "anti-liberalism"—rendering civilian populations in both the United States and Europe more vulnerable to indiscriminate attack. Finally, Bobbitt describes the new terrorism as distinct because it is "no longer simply a technique but is also an end in itself."[95] The goal is not to seize control of a national government, or to gain sovereignty or independence over a certain territory, but instead to promote a "constant state of terror."[96]

Yet, the fact of these ambitions, or changing modes of organization, does not in itself make WMD use more likely. While Bobbitt makes a clear case for why today's global terrorists would likely *want* to obtain WMDs, and how certain geopolitical factors might make a market for such weapons theoretically viable, there is no evidence in Bobbitt's work for the fact that such a market has indeed emerged for nuclear, biological, chemical, or radiological weapons or materials.

Richard Falk advances a similar assessment of the growing threat posed by global terrorists, premised in part on a break in the history of terrorism represented by the events of September 11 in particular.[97] But, interestingly, Falk's argument for the increasing

---

90 Ibid. at 50.
91 Ibid. at 51.
92 Ibid. at 58.
93 Ibid. at 60.
94 Ibid.
95 Ibid. at 62.
96 Ibid.
97 Richard Falk, THE GREAT TERROR WAR (New York: Olive Branch Press, 2003), ch. 2.

danger posed by terrorists is made without resort to generalized claims about WMD use that might readily be challenged by reference to skeptical expert opinion.

September 11 was distinguished, in Falk's view, by the "perpetrators' daring method," the choice of "prime targets of power and wealth," and the "astonishing degree of success in carrying out the deadly mission."[98] They also caused "extraordinary shock effects of the overall spectacle of death and destruction, as well as the acute sense of continuing danger and vulnerability along with a grudging acknowledgment of the ingenuity and resolve displayed by the attack."[99] In contrast to earlier acts of terror, the intent of these attacks was "genocidal."[100] They gave rise to what Falk calls "megaterrorism," which "differ[s] from earlier expressions of global terrorism, by magnitude, scope and ideology, representing a serious effort to transform world order as a whole, and not merely change the power structure of one or more states."[101] They also validated the notion that terrorism would "shift from a primary emphasis on shock and symbolic vulnerability to a new stress on the scale of harm and substantive vulnerability of the target state, thereby blurring the boundary between war and terrorism."[102]

Yet, for Falk, 9/11 had demonstrated that this shift could occur without the use, as many had predicted (including Laqueur), of WMDs.[103] "Never in the history of terrorism had an operation of such stunning proportions been pulled off," he asserts. The "technical ingenuity" and simplicity of the operation—the use of "virtually no instruments of violence" aside from box cutters, and a relatively small monetary cost (under a half million dollars, as he notes)—suggested that the threat of a catastrophic attack "required no special technological sophistication other than the rather easily acquired knowledge to pilot and navigate large commercial airliners while in the air."[104] The primary lesson of the event was that "[s]uddenly, relations of power between enemies could no longer be measured by financial capacity or shaped by the balance of capabilities."[105] A new level of vulnerability had become apparent—one that could not be addressed by the nation's conventional military arsenal, which was designed to pursue "territorial actors." Instead, it now seemed "entirely possible that future megaterrorism would produce even greater damage than the September 11 attacks simply by aiming at nuclear power plants, water supply systems, electricity grids, major tunnels and bridges, seaports, crowded sports arenas, and IT networks."[106] What is missing from Falk's analysis, however, is an informed

98 Ibid. at 38.
99 Ibid.
100 Ibid. at 43.
101 Ibid. at 39.
102 Ibid. at 53.
103 Ibid. at 53.
104 Ibid. at 52.
105 Ibid.
106 Ibid. at 53.

exploration of the likelihood of any of these later events occurring, or the likely damage to result if they did. (Chapter 6 explores a number of such assessments.)

One further thread in historical accounts of the evolution of terror is worth noting. This is the notion that what is at stake in the prospect of a terror attack involving WMDs in a developed Western nation is the very survival of the state, or its viability as a liberal democracy. If an attack involving WMDs were to be carried out, what would it mean for the state or society in a broader sense? The question plays a critical role in shaping emotional and cultural resonances of the harbinger theory, and therefore in justifications for the legal entrenchment of extreme measures. What is notable here is the sense of the "unthinkable"—the notion that the prospect of WMD terror presents a threat so grave to society and the state that it must be avoided at all costs.

Walter Laqueur gestures in this direction by asserting that the widespread panic following an attack involving WMDs could cause "as much damage as the terrorist act itself,"[107] leading to a "paralysis of normal life, epidemics, post-traumatic stress, and tremendous anxiety, especially if the nature and the extent of the danger remains unknown."[108] In this case, the "economic consequences could be disastrous and the political consequences horrible."[109]

Michael Ignatieff presents the argument more explicitly. In *The Lesser Evil* (2004), after surveying the modern history of terrorism from its roots in late 19th-century anarchism to the present, he writes: "inexorably, terrorism, like war, is moving beyond the conventional to the apocalyptic."[110] An act of nuclear terror, he suggests, would mark a break in the modern history of terror—a history in which earlier acts were unsuccessful in defeating "liberal democracy." In the nightmare scenario, indeed, "we *could* lose."[111] But defeat would assume an unprecedented form:

> It would not be like an invasion, conquest, or occupation, of course, but rather would entail the disintegration of our institutions and way of life. A succession of mass casualty attacks, using weapons of mass destruction, would leave behind zones of devastation sealed off for years and a pall of mourning, anger, and fear hanging over our public and private lives.[112]

The notion of nuclear or mass terror as an existential threat to a society or a nation resonates across the three bodies of literature under review here,[113] but also beyond. Two

---

107 Laqueur, The New Terrorism, *supra* note 76, at 271.

108 Ibid. at 272.

109 Ibid.

110 Michael Ignatieff, The Lesser Evil: Political Ethics in an Age of Terror (Princeton NJ: Princeton University Press, 2004), at 147.

111 Ibid. at 153.

112 Ibid.

113 Graham Allison, for example, in Nuclear Terrorism, *supra* note 5, at 212, writes: "Nuclear terrorism is not only an existential threat to the idea of America it is also a threat to civilization as we know it." See also

further examples are worth noting, to demonstrate the extent to which remarkably similar scenarios are feared.

U.S. Senator Sam Nunn, speaking to a journalist in the course of promoting his film, *Nuclear Tipping Point* (2010), was asked: "Is the thinking that if terrorists got their hands on a bomb they would automatically use it?" Nunn replied:

> I think they'd probably do it in a calculating way. My worst case [scenario] is, they would set off one explosion. It would be a crude weapon; it wouldn't come in on a missile. It would probably come in on the back of a truck to a city. And if one went off and killed hundreds of thousands of people, they'd basically probably announce they had six or eight more in cities around the country or around the globe. That would have huge devastating impact, certainly on the people who were the original victims, but also the whole world economy. You'd have people dumping out of cities all over the world like nothing we've ever seen.[114]

Jonathan Schell, writing in 2007, provides a second example.[115] The prodigious supply of nuclear technology throughout the world raises the "terrifying specter of a terrorist group that acquires and uses a nuclear weapon, or perhaps several of them, to lash out against a great city somewhere in the world."[116] He fears that:

> Tens of thousands or perhaps hundreds of thousands might die. The city would be rendered uninhabitable by radiation for decades. If it were a national capital, the nation's government could be destroyed. Beyond these direct consequences lie indirect ones that are no less real for being veiled in great uncertainty. For example, if that country were the United States, would the government survive? What emergency measures might it adopt, and for how long? Would the Constitution remain in effect, and, if it were suspended, would it ever be restored? Would liberty around the globe be taken away by governments straining every nerve to prevent new attacks? Would terror-stricken populations of other cities flee to the countryside? Might the global economy collapse?[117]

---

the discussion of John Yoo, below; in WAR BY OTHER MEANS: AN INSIDER'S ACCOUNT OF THE WAR ON TERROR (New York: Atlantic Monthly Press, 2006), at xii, Yoo asserts: "We (along with Israel) are the first to face a terrorist enemy intent on carrying out the catastrophic destruction of our nation." The threat is real in part due to the fact, as Yoo asserts at 62, that "[w]eapons of mass destruction have increased the potential casualties a single terrorist attack can wreak, from the hundreds or thousands of innocent lives into the hundreds of thousands or even millions. This does not even count the profound, long-term destruction to cities, contamination of the environment, and long-term death or disease for large segments of the civilian population."

114 Tom Sabulis, *Ex-Senator Nunn Warns of Nuclear Terror Threat*, ATLANTA JOURNAL-CONSTITUTION, Feb. 15, 2010.

115 Jonathan Schell, THE SEVENTH DECADE: THE NEW SHAPE OF NUCLEAR DANGER (New York: Henry Holt, 2007).

116 Ibid. at 6.

117 Ibid. 6–7.

## Part 3. The Harbinger Theory in Advocacy of Extreme Measures

Moving from the literature on WMDs and the history of terror to work by law scholars and jurists, the intention in what follows is to trace the impact of the catastrophic imagination on the formation of law and policy itself. This part of the chapter explores the work of American jurists Richard Posner, Alan Dershowitz, and John Yoo as prominent voices in a wider academic and public discussion about the use of extreme measures in national security. It should be noted, however, that although these authors are not alone in their support of extreme measures, their views run against the grain of prevailing opinion among North American law scholars.[118]

As was noted in Chapter 2, most jurists writing on counterterrorism law after 9/11 view torture, indefinite detention without charge, and targeted killing as a clear departure from constitutionalism and the rule of law. And for many, the measures are either not easily reconcilable with those principles or altogether abhorrent to them. In ways to be explored, Posner, Dershowitz, and Yoo conceive of these measures as either not contrary to core constitutional principles or justifiable exceptions to them. Yet the significance of their views, and the importance of canvassing them here, rests primarily on their position in the academy and in the larger public debate on security policy. Holding posts at the University of Chicago, Harvard, and Berkeley, respectively, and drawing on accomplishments in various fields, each has enjoyed a degree of celebrity both inside and outside the academic world, providing them with frequent access to high-profile media and other opportunities to communicate their position to a wider audience.

This part of the chapter will attempt to show how the harbinger theory has played a crucial role in their work by informing a common architecture of belief.[119] At the core of this structure are three inter-related assumptions. First, an attack involving WMDs at the hands al Qaeda or its affiliates is a real possibility in one or more large North American cities in the near future. The possibility of such an attack poses an unprecedented, catastrophic, and possibly existential threat to the state. Given the magnitude of the threat, it is reasonable and prudent to employ a series of preemptive or extreme measures. More appropriate to a military campaign than to law enforcement, the measures are justified on the

---

[118] Other figures supportive of extreme or illiberal measures to one extent or another include Oren Gross, Bruce Ackerman, Eric Posner, and Adrian Vermeule. *See,* e.g., Oren Gross, *The Prohibition on Torture and the Limits of the Law,* in Sanford Levinson, ed., TORTURE: A COLLECTION (Oxford: Oxford University Press, 2004); Bruce Ackerman, BEFORE THE NEXT ATTACK: PRESERVING CIVIL LIBERTIES IN AN AGE OF TERRORISM (New Haven CT: Yale University Press, 2006); and Eric Posner & Adrian Vermuele, TERROR IN THE BALANCE: SECURITY, LIBERTY, AND THE COURTS (New York: Oxford University Press, 2007).

[119] On the role of architectures of belief in the formation of law generally, see Paul Kahn's CULTURAL STUDY OF LAW (Chicago: University of Chicago Press, 1999); and in the context of counterterrorism law, SACRED VIOLENCE: TORTURE, TERROR, AND SOVEREIGNTY (Ann Arbor: University of Michigan Press, 2008).

assumption that the threat of mass terror entails something closer in nature to an act of war than a crime.

But here too, the framework is premised upon the uncritical acceptance of the technological claims about WMDs on which it rests, or the failure to acknowledge their controversial character.

## I. RICHARD POSNER AND THE POETICS OF CATASTROPHE

Posner is both a U.S. Federal Appeals Court judge and a legal academic. He gained prominence in academic circles as a pioneer of one of the predominant theoretical paradigms in legal scholarship, "law and economics." Much of his scholarship looks at legal issues through the lens of cost-benefit analyses, probability theory, and other conceptual tools of economics. Many of these tools are brought to bear in his discussion of the evolving threat of terror.

Among the most notable is his distinction between frequencies of events and their probabilities. In drawing this distinction, Posner offers insightful criticism of figures who are skeptical of fears about terrorism for failing to recognize that the probability of an attack may be high or low regardless of its statistical frequency. Thus, as Posner argues, when the political scientist John Mueller questions the merit of the U.S. government's multi-billion-dollar counterterrorism effort when "the lifetime chance of an American being killed by international terrorism is one in 80,000,"[120] he fails to distinguish a frequency from a probability. As Posner points out, "the 'chance' of one in 80,000 is not the odds of a terrorist attack, that is a probability; it is a frequency."[121] Frequencies tell us only about the past. They are relevant to the future only if there are "solid grounds for expecting the future to be like the past."[122] Our real concern, then, is with probabilities, but because of the many variables at play, this too is hard to measure with any certainty. Therefore, the larger challenge, in Posner's view, is that the "analysis of terrorist threats and counterterrorist responses must be framed in terms of probabilities—even when probabilities cannot be computed."[123]

However, although we lack precise statistical *knowledge* of the probability of mass terror, there are, in Posner's view, a host of reasons to believe that it is increasing. The potential supply of terrorists is "larger than it has ever been";[124] the frequency of large-scale attacks suggests that "Islamic extremists are on a roll" (he cites events in Iran, Iraq, Pakistan, Afghanistan, Lebanon, and the Toronto and Heathrow plots, among others);[125]

---

120 John Mueller, *Is There Still a Terrorist Threat?* FOREIGN AFF. 2 (Sept./Oct. 2006), at 8; cited in Richard Posner, COUNTERING TERRORISM: BLURRED FOCUS, HALTING STEPS (Lanham MD: Rowman and Littlefield, 2007), at 4.

121 Posner, COUNTERING TERRORISM, ibid, at 4.

122 Ibid.

123 Ibid. at 1.

124 Ibid. at 8.

125 Ibid. at 9.

and the "lethality and availability of highly destructive weaponry are growing."[126] The case for extreme measures is also premised upon arguments about the potential impact of mass terror. Both the likelihood and impact of an attack are subjects that Posner has explored in some detail.

His most extended treatment of them is set out in *Catastrophe* (2004),[127] where he draws on expert opinion on nuclear and biological terror. The probability of nuclear terror is growing for the same reasons offered by Allison and others, explored above: copious, poorly guarded supplies in Russia and Pakistan, ready availability of bomb designs, and ease of bomb construction.[128] Yet, just as Allison and other experts in the consensus school have done, Posner presents an impression of scientific opinion on the matter as more or less unanimous. The sources on which Posner relies lend a similar impression. For example, when first introducing the possibility of nuclear terror, Posner asserts that while building a bomb "is costly and requires considerable engineering sophistication, it may not be beyond the ability of a well-financed group if it can get its hands on plutonium or highly enriched uranium."[129] Posner supports this claim by citing three sources: a report of the National Research Council, a study by researchers at MIT, and a source he describes as "skeptical," an online FAQ posted by the Council on Foreign Relations.[130] The FAQ is no longer available, but a survey of other FAQs on related topics on the same website suggests that the source at issue was not likely a primary text containing expert opinion.[131] Apart from this single citation, mentioned in a footnote in passing, Posner gives no further consideration to contrary opinion on nuclear terror.

The positive sources he cites are, upon closer examination, not much more authoritative than Posner's own assertions. The National Council report states only that "[t]he basic technical information needed to construct a workable nuclear device is readily available in the open literature. The primary impediment that prevents countries or technically competent terrorist groups from developing nuclear weapons is the availability of [fissile material]."[132] No opinion is rendered or mention made of the practical, technical challenges posed at the bomb-making stage, or contrary views that raise questions in this respect.[133] The MIT study states only that following 9/11, a concern has grown over

---

126 Ibid.

127 Richard Posner, CATASTROPHE: RISK AND RESPONSE (Oxford: Oxford University Press, 2004).

128 Ibid. at 73–4.

129 Ibid. at 74.

130 National Research Council of the National Academies, MAKING THE NATION SAFER: THE ROLE OF SCIENCE AND TECHNOLOGY IN COUNTERING TERRORISM (Washington: National Academies Press, 2002); John Deutch, et al., THE FUTURE OF NUCLEAR POWER (Boston: MIT Press, 2003); and the skeptical source, the Council on Foreign Relations, *Terrorism: Questions and Answers: Making a Bomb*, at http://terrorismanswers.com/weapons/making2.html.

131 *See, e.g.*, the Council's backgrounder on al Qaeda, at http://www.cfr.org/terrorist-organizations/al-qaeda-k-al-qaida-al-qaida/p9126.

132 National Research Council, ibid. at 40. Posner cites pages 40–41.

133 These are explored in Chapter 6.

the possibility of a "sub-national group" acquiring "nuclear weapons capability," and that "[t]errorist or organized crime groups are not expected to be able to produce nuclear weapons material themselves; the concern is their direct acquisition of nuclear materials by theft or through a state sponsor."[134]

Further on in *Catastrophe*, Posner cites Frank Barnaby in support of a more ambitious claim: a group "as small as 'two or three people with appropriate skills could design and fabricate a crude nuclear explosive [ . . . ].'"[135] Barnaby asserts:

> It is a sobering fact that the fabrication of a primitive nuclear explosion using plutonium or suitable uranium would require no greater skill than that required for the production and use of the nerve agent produced by the AUM group and released in the Tokyo underground.[136]

Yet Barnaby presents no evidence for this claim and omits any mention of contrary opinion. Once again, I defer for the moment the issue of how and why this claim is contentious. I seek to emphasize here only the point that claims about nuclear bomb building—and thus the prospect of nuclear terror itself—are made to seem more persuasive by being repeatedly presented, in both Posner and his sources, as non-contentious.

Turning to the issue of the consequences of mass terror, Posner offers frightening scenarios about nuclear or radiological explosions and bioweaponry. A "crude nuclear explosive" crafted by a small group could "set off the energy equivalent to 100 tons of TNT, or 50 times that used in the Oklahoma City bombing of 1995."[137] If terrorists were to crash a plane into a nuclear reactor, or to use a coated conventional bomb, they could cause "extensive radioactive contamination" that might disrupt or destroy a large metropolitan center or a significant portion of the nation.[138] But in the most extreme scenario, the potential impact is almost unlimited:

> A terrorist who got hold of smallpox virus, gene spliced it . . . grew the virus in living cells, and extracted modest quantities of the virus in fluid form could place the fluid in aerosolizers that he would unobtrusively deposit in airport departure lounges, shopping malls, movie theatres, indoor stadiums, and other enclosed spaces in which people congregate. The aerosolizers would spray an invisible mist that could infect hundreds or even thousands of people within a few minutes at each location,

---

134 Deutch, THE FUTURE OF NUCLEAR POWER, *supra* note 130, at 65–66. Posner cites pages 65–66.

135 Posner, CATASTROPHE, *supra*, note 127, at 74, citing Barnaby, HOW TO BUILD, *supra* note 4, at 36.

136 Barnaby, HOW TO BUILD, ibid.

137 Posner, CATASTROPHE, *supra* note 127, at 74. Posner draws again here on Barnaby, HOW TO BUILD, *supra* note 4.

138 Posner, CATASTROPHE, ibid, at 74.

> all of whom would then be carriers. Within weeks, hundreds of millions of people around the world would be infected, and the disease would be unstoppable.[139]

At this furthest extreme, not only is the existence of the state at issue, but also a large portion of the human race itself. Yet, in formulating this scenario, Posner draws on bioterror authorities in the same selective fashion in which he drew on the literature by nuclear experts. A lengthy discussion about making bioweapons, gene splicing, and airborne dissemination is based exclusively on authorities representing one side of a larger, contentious debate.[140]

Posner's findings in *Catastrophe* would soon come to play an important role in his work on counterterrorism law and policy. At the outset of *Not a Suicide Pact: the Constitution in a Time of National Emergency* (2006),[141] Posner asserts: "[t]he research I have been conducting for the past several years on catastrophic risks, international terrorism, and national security intelligence has persuaded me that we live in a time of grave and increasing danger, comparable to what the nation faced at the outset of World War II."[142] The danger is posed by "Islamic terrorists" who are:

> numerous, fanatical, implacable, elusive, resourceful, resilient, utterly ruthless, seemingly fearless, apocalyptic in their aims, and eager to get their hands on weapons of mass destruction and use them against us. [...] [f]or all we know, we may be quite safe. But we cannot afford to act on that optimistic assumption.[143]

We cannot be complacent precisely because of the stakes at issue. Setting a tone of fear and terror that frames his entire discussion, Posner sets out a series of vivid catastrophic scenarios that demonstrate a measure of both technological sophistication and ingenuity:

> Now, in the early years of the twenty-first century, the nation faces the intertwined menaces of global terrorism and proliferation of weapons of mass destruction. A city can be destroyed by an atomic bomb the size of a melon, which if coated with

---

139 Ibid. at 79–80.

140 At 288, ibid. Posner cites the Committee on Research Standards and Practices to Prevent Destructive Application of Biotechnology and National Research Council of the National Academies, BIOTECHNOLOGY RESEARCH IN AN AGE OF TERRORISM (Washington DC: National Academies Press, 2004); Michael Ainscough's contribution to THE GATHERING BIOLOGICAL WARFARE STORM, *supra* note 57; Sidney Drell, et al., eds., THE NEW TERROR: FACING THE THREAT OF BIOLOGICAL AND CHEMICAL WEAPONS (Stanford: Hoover Institution Press, 1999); and Judith Miller, et al., GERMS: BIOLOGICAL WEAPONS AND AMERICA'S SECRET WAR (New York: Simon and Schuster, 2001).

141 Richard Posner, NOT A SUICIDE PACT: THE CONSTITUTION IN A TIME OF NATIONAL EMERGENCY (Oxford: Oxford University Press, 2006).

142 Ibid. at 3. Posner is referring here to CATASTROPHE, *supra* note 127, and PREVENTING SURPRISE ATTACKS: INTELLIGENCE REFORM IN THE WAKE OF 9/11 (Lanham MD: Rowman and Littlefield, 2005).

143 Posner, NOT A SUICIDE PACT, *supra* note 141, at 5.

> lead would be undetectable. Large stretches of a city can be rendered uninhabitable, perhaps for decades, merely by the explosion of a conventional bomb that has been coated with radioactive material. Smallpox virus bioengineered to make it even more toxic and vaccines ineffectual, then aerosolized and sprayed in a major airport, might kill millions of people.[144]

The threat of mass terror is therefore increasing, but is not precisely quantifiable. Given its potential gravity, certain measures are justified in response.

The range of measures that Posner proceeds to advocate, in this and other works, include indefinite detention without charge,[145] a broader presidential power to suspend habeas corpus,[146] the use of military tribunals,[147] increased surveillance,[148] limits on free speech, and torture.[149]

Throughout his discussion of these measures, the idea of mass terror is frequently evoked. Consider, for example, his advocacy of torture. In an essay entitled "Torture, Terrorism and Interrogation" (2004), Posner argues: "... what is required is a balance between the costs and the benefits of particular methods of interrogation... the costs can be outweighed by the benefits if torture is the only means by which to save the lives of thousands, perhaps tens or hundreds of thousands, of people. In so extreme a case, it seems to me, torture must be allowed."[150] Elsewhere, Posner asserts: "If it is dire enough and the value of the information great enough, only a die-hard civil libertarian will deny the propriety of using a high degree of coercion to elicit the information. It might be the whereabouts of a kidnapping victim, the location of a ticking time bomb, the site of a biological weapon about to be deployed, the identity of key terrorist leaders, or the details of terrorist plots."[151] But Posner is careful to distinguish between the justified use of torture and its legalization. While the practice of torture may sometimes be "absolutely vital to averting a catastrophic attack," giving rise to a "moral duty to torture,"[152] he contends that it "should not be considered *legally* justified."[153] Posner would prefer that the fate of the public officer who orders torture in an extreme scenario be left to politics and democratic accountability, rather than "codify[ing] the instances in which such conduct is allowed."[154]

---

144 Ibid. at 2.

145 Ibid. at 65.

146 Ibid. at 39.

147 Ibid. at 73.

148 Ibid. ch.4.

149 Ibid., at 12.

150 Richard Posner, *Torture, Terrorism and Interrogation*, in Sanford Levinson, ed. TORTURE: A COLLECTION, *supra* note 118, at 293.

151 Posner, NOT A SUICIDE PACT, *supra* note 141, at 81.

152 Ibid. at 38.

153 Ibid. at 12.

154 Ibid. at 86.

Posner's concerns about mass terror also frame his critique of the role of the criminal justice system in countering terrorism. While criminal justice has a role to play, the current threat requires the state to act more swiftly, in greater secrecy, and often with less information or evidence than is called for in a system committed to due process. Essential features of due process that ensure the accused a range of protections—probable cause for detention and charge, disclosure, an open trial, the opportunity to confront witnesses, the limited use of hearsay, and the higher standard for a conviction—present those who would defend us from a catastrophic attack with numerous obstacles.[155] In some cases, due process "forces the government to tip its hand and impairs its ability to extract information from a suspect." In other cases, open hearings or trials might "yield clues to the government's investigative methods and reveal classified information."[156]

But Posner's deeper contention is with the implied trade-off that criminal justice system makes between liberty and security. The requirement for proof beyond a reasonable doubt and other facets of due process, such as the excludability of improperly obtained evidence, "weights false positives (convicting innocent persons) much more heavily than false negatives (acquitting guilty persons)."[157] Anticipating Dershowitz's notion of a turn toward preemption in Western jurisprudence, Posner argues that this weighting becomes "questionable when the defendant is a terrorist determined to wreak mayhem on a large scale and likely to do so if acquitted."[158]

In response, Posner calls for a "coherent jurisprudence" and new law that is more deferential to the executive and those gathering intelligence; more expansive in its reading of the constitution; and takes into account the limited expertise of the judiciary in national security matters.[159] This new body of law would draw on a "tradition of flexible interpretation of the Constitution that permits judicial departures from, as well as judicial elaborations of, the actual language of the document, and the balancing of competing interests."[160]

Thus, in Posner's view, the Bill of Rights would not prevent the codification of a power to detain terror suspects without charge or probable cause beyond 48 hours,[161] to authorize coercive interrogation techniques,[162] to hold trials without juries (or with military commissions),[163] or to carry out *reasonable* surveillance of terror suspects without a warrant.[164] Legislation on administrative detention could fashion an initial upper limit of

---

155 Posner, COUNTERING TERRORISM, *supra* note 120, at ch. 7.
156 Ibid, at 174.
157 Ibid.
158 Ibid. at 175.
159 Ibid. at 173, 177.
160 Ibid. at 177.
161 Ibid. at 180.
162 Ibid. at 193.
163 Ibid. at 181.
164 Ibid. at 192–93.

28 days, with periodic reviews to follow, in which the government must show why the detention continues to be reasonable.[165] And rather than seeking to codify the limits on interrogation in counterterrorism investigations, a law could simply require that "methods forbidden in an ordinary criminal investigation be expressly authorized in writing by the Secretary of Defense, the Attorney General, or the President himself."[166] Accountability would, in this way, "be substituted for deniability and legal hair splitting."[167]

With respect to surveillance, Posner suggests that the National Security Agency's Terrorist Surveillance Program could be given a wide authority to conduct "initial sifting" and data mining of all domestic electronic communication without a warrant. "Human searches," or the reading of "purely domestic" communications, might also be done on a warrant obtained on lower standards than is presently permitted.[168] The Foreign Intelligence Surveillance Act of 1978[169] forbids such searches without probable cause to believe that one party is a spy or a terrorist. But Posner believes the Act could be amended to require "reasonable suspicion," or go further and adopt the test applicable to the Canadian Security Intelligence Service: "belief, on reasonable grounds, that a warrant—is required to enable the Service to investigate a threat to the security of Canada."[170] The difference here is that while the Fourth Amendment requires probable cause for the issuance of a warrant, it does not, as Posner notes, stipulate what it is that one must have cause to believe. It is therefore likely to permit a test as broad as that found in Canadian law.

Posner also offers a number of suggestions for what increased surveillance might entail. With a view to exercising greater oversight over scientific research, he proposes that laws be enacted requiring "all scientific research projects in specific areas, such as nanotechnology and experimental high-energy physics, to be reviewed by a federal catastrophic risks assessment board and forbidden if the board found that the project would create undue risk to human survival."[171] He moots the argument that "citizens of foreign countries that are hostile to the United States, and citizens of countries (mainly Muslim) in which a significant fraction of the population is deeply hostile to the United States even if the government is friendly, should not be admitted to the advanced study of dangerous technologies, such as nuclear engineering, nanotechnology, molecular biology, computer science, and artificial intelligence."[172] To assist in these approaches, the state should address an oversight in U.S. law: the lack of an equivalent to the United

---

165 Ibid, at 181.
166 Ibid, at 193.
167 Ibid.
168 Ibid. at 195–96.
169 50 U.S.C. ch. 36, §1566.
170 Canadian Security Intelligence Service Act, R.S.C., 1985, ch. C-23, §21(2)(a); cited in Posner at 196.
171 Posner, CATASTROPHE, *supra* note 127, at, 221.
172 Ibid. at 222.

Kingdom's Official Secrets Act.[173] An analogous law would allow the U.S. government to "prevent or punish the knowing publication or other dissemination of classified material concerning national security, provided that the material was classified in accordance with properly statutory criteria (which do not yet exist)."[174] It would also be prudent, in his view, to expand the scope of public surveillance in what he considers to be sensitive areas. FBI agents or informants should, for example, be encouraged to attend mosques where known radical imams preach, and to photograph or record events.[175]

Thus, for Posner, the threat of mass terror at the hands of al Qaeda, or a related group, is growing. The fact is well supported by expert opinion and has profound implications. It presents both law enforcement and national security with a new kind of problem. "I prefer to regard it as sui generis," he writes, "than to try to squeeze it into familiar preexisting categories such as 'war' or 'crime.' "[176] Lawmakers and judges can assist in countering the threat by crafting a new set of tools that would set due process to one side and the laws of war to the other.

## II. ALAN DERSHOWITZ AND THE PREEMPTIVE TURN

In contrast to Posner, Alan Dershowitz sees the threat of mass terror as similar in nature to both crime *and* war, in ways that fundamentally challenge our understanding of both. But as with Posner, the case for wartime-type powers against terrorists is premised on a set of catastrophic fears about the evolving threat of terror—and those fears in turn are grounded not so much in evidence emerging from the science at issue as in a series of hypothetical yet provocative scenarios.

The harbinger theory plays a critical role in two of his works on countering terror after 9/11.[177] The earlier book, *Why Terrorism Works*, begins with an attempt to understand how terror became legitimized before 2001, and what might have been done to avoid it. His explanation helps to contextualize his reading of the evolving threat facing the United States and Israel.

Dershowitz contends that when the PLO and other regional groups began to resort to terror in earnest in the late 1960s and 1970s, they quickly discovered that it garnered them a greater measure of recognition by European nations, the United States, and, above all, the UN than they were able to gain through years of less violent efforts. This helped to legitimize the practice of terror and only encouraged more of it. It would have been more prudent, Dershowitz suggests, if Western governments had responded

---

173 1989 ch. 6, U.K.

174 Posner, NOT A SUICIDE PACT, *supra*, note 141, at 110.

175 Ibid. at 112.

176 Posner, COUNTERING TERRORISM, *supra* note 120, at 227.

177 Alan M. Dershowitz, WHY TERRORISM WORKS: UNDERSTANDING THE THREAT, RESPONDING TO THE CHALLENGE (New Haven CT: Yale University Press, 2003); and PREEMPTION: A KNIFE THAT CUTS BOTH WAYS (New York: W.W. Norton, 2006).

to acts of terror with an overwhelming show of force and a denial of any recognition whatsoever—precisely the strategy that Israel has employed since the second Intifada, resulting in a sharp decline in attacks. As terrorism continues to evolve, however, it has become untethered to a specific national agenda and fallen largely within the domain of groups without a particular political agenda and is therefore less susceptible to reason. A number of terror groups are also more ambitious in the violence they aim to inflict, actively seeking to employ WMDs. Given this more dangerous form of terror, we are now at a point at which the struggle against it could result in "cataclysmic defeat—the nuclear, chemical, or biological destruction of the planet or large segments of it."[178]

Liberal democracies are thus left with two options. One is to seek to minimize all conceivable risk by suspending all constitutional and human rights, and then employing unlimited surveillance, torture, and other police and military measures.[179] The other option, which Dershowitz favors, is to strive to maintain a commitment to civil liberties, but with greater limits than we have been accustomed to in recent decades. One chapter defends the use of torture in a "ticking bomb" scenario and the use of "judicial torture warrants" in other, less extreme situations.[180] Another chapter promotes the use of national ID cards, military tribunals, expanded surveillance, tighter border controls, greater exchanges of information among agencies, and greater limits on free speech.[181]

As with Posner, a pending sense of apocalypse is central to Dershowitz's argument throughout. Yet his references to mass terror are often more carefully worded than either Posner's or John Yoo's (considered below). There are a few direct assertions that an attack is imminent, although his rhetoric and tone clearly suggest this. The opening sentence of the book states: "The greatest danger facing the world today comes from religiously inspired terrorist groups... that are seeking to develop weapons of mass destruction for use against civilian targets."[182] Speaking of the evolving nature of terror after September 11, he writes "their object is massive destruction and mass murder of hundreds, even thousands, of civilians. Tomorrow we may be faced with terrorist mass weapons—nuclear, chemical, and biological—capable of destroying entire cities and more."[183] Later in the book, speculating on a possible follow-up to September 11, he writes, "[t]he real problem is that a comparable catastrophic attack could be carried out in the future for even less money, with even fewer people, from almost any country in the world. If the apocalyptic terrorists seek to escalate the damage they cause to include nuclear, chemical, or biological disaster, it will probably require some state support..."[184] Assessing the merits

---

178 Dershowitz, WHY TERRORISM WORKS, ibid. at 12.

179 Ibid. ch. 3.

180 Ibid. ch. 4.

181 Ibid. ch. 5.

182 Ibid. at 1.

183 Ibid. at 9–10.

184 Ibid. at 182–83.

of various extreme measures, he wonders how acts of mass terror would change public perceptions of them: "[...] what if matters were to get considerably worse? What if bio-terrorism were to expand from sporadic outbreaks of anthrax to systematic spreading of lethal diseases? What if a nuclear or chemical explosion seemed imminent?"[185] In the book's closing pages, Dershowitz becomes more direct:

> I believe there is a small but significant possibility that Islamic radicals could succeed in killing hundreds of thousands—perhaps even more—Americans and Israelis. If they manage to secure access to weapons of mass destruction, I have little doubt there will be some who would try to use them against New York, Los Angeles, Washington, D.C., or Tel Aviv. [...] Whether they succeed or fail will depend on many factors, including our preparedness to prevent such an attack. It may also depend somewhat on dumb luck. We can do little about the latter, but we can do much about the former.[186]

None of these vivid scenarios is supported by citations to expert opinion on point. As will be seen in the work of John Yoo, Dershowitz is interested not in the technical debate about the real prospect of mass terror, but in the less contentious fact of its theoretical possibility.

By continuously invoking this possibility, the many references to mass terror play a critical role in framing Dershowitz's discussion of torture and other measures. His advocacy of judicially sanctioned torture is the most contentious of his recommendations. It rests on two arguments. The first is a claim that in extreme situations, torture has always been used and always will be; and, therefore, the pretense on the part of Western states to have abolished it is hypocritical. For this reason, contrary to our constitutional tenets, or to those who have argued that modern legal systems derive their very character from the prohibition on torture, liberal society is not in fact *committed* to abolishing torture.[187] It represents an important ideal, but one that we easily abandon when faced with the tragic choice of the ticking bomb scenario. Should we remain hypocritical or naive and continue to ignore or acquiesce in this persistent underground use of torture, turning a blind eye to much crueler and more arbitrary uses of state violence? The prudent course would be to subject its use to the rule of law by condoning "non-lethal" forms of physical

---

185 Ibid. at 195–96.

186 Ibid. at 226.

187 *See*, e.g., David Luban, *Liberalism, Torture, and the Ticking Bomb*, 91 VA. L. REV. 1425 (2005); and Jeremy Waldron, *Torture and Positive Law: Jurisprudence for the White House*, 105 COLUM. L. REV. 1681 (2005). At 1687, Waldron writes, "the rule against torture operates in our law as an *archetype*—that is, as a rule which has significance not just in and of itself, but also as the embodiment of a pervasive principle." He also notes, at 1719, "...in the heritage of Anglo-American law, there is a long tradition of rejecting torture and regarding it as alien to our jurisprudence...Actually, a case can be made that torture is now to be regarded as alien to *any* system of law."

coercion and requiring authorities to seek a warrant to carry them out. Dershowitz offers only one example of what he has in mind by non-lethal torture: a "sterilized needle being shoved under the fingernails."[188] Later, he speaks in more general terms of submitting suspects to "judicially monitored physical measures designed to cause excruciating pain without leaving any lasting damage."[189] Whatever the method, he argues that "a formal, visible, accountable, and centralized system" would lead to suspects being subjected to less violence precisely because such a system would be "somewhat easier to control than an ad hoc, off-the-books, and under-the-radar-screen nonsystem."[190]

But Dershowitz's core argument for torture is the older consequentialist claim on which Posner and others have relied.[191] For Dershowitz, "[t]he simple cost-benefit analysis for employing such non-lethal torture seems overwhelming: it is surely better to inflict non-lethal pain on one guilty terrorist who is illegally withholding information needed to prevent an act of terrorism than to permit a large number of innocent victims to die."[192] The argument becomes more persuasive in the context of mass terror. Dershowitz relates that in the weeks after September 11, U.S. intelligence received information that "a ten-kiloton nuclear weapon may have been stolen from Russia and was on its way to New York City, where it would have been detonated and kill hundreds of thousands of people."[193] The source of the information proved unreliable, but Dershowitz invites the reader to imagine that the source did appear to be credible and that it was a captured terror suspect. In such a case, it is "not absolutely certain torture will work, but it is our last, best hope for preventing a cataclysmic nuclear devastation in a city too large to evacuate in time."[194]

In *Preemption* (2006), Dershowitz develops a line of argument already present in the later chapters of his earlier book. Due to its catastrophic potential, the contemporary threat of terror has given rise to a paradigm shift in perceptions of crime and security, best encapsulated in the notion of "preemption." The emergence of the concept is tied to a larger cultural shift in which western states are "moving away from [their] traditional reliance on deterrent and reactive approaches and toward more preventive and proactive approaches."[195] These include "the use of force, power, compulsion, censorship, incarceration, and death."[196] The preemptive paradigm marks a break with an earlier

---

188 Dershowitz, Why Terrorism Works, *supra* note 177, at 148.

189 Ibid. at 159.

190 Ibid. at 158.

191 *See* Richard Posner, *Torture, Terrorism and Interrogation*, in Torture: A Collection, *supra* note 150. At 295, Posner asserts: "if the stakes are high enough torture is permissible. No one who doubts that should be in a position of responsibility." *See also* Orin Gross's contribution to the same collection, "The Prohibition on Torture and the Limits of the Law."

192 Dershowitz, Why Terrorism Works, *supra* note 177, at 144.

193 Ibid.

194 Ibid. at 145.

195 Dershowitz, Preemption, *supra* note 177, at 2.

196 Ibid. at 27.

criminological framework premised upon a rational actor who may be deterred by the prospect of punishment, and "society's ability (and willingness) to withstand the blows we seek to deter."[197] Both assumptions are, as he asserts, "now being widely questioned as the threat of weapons of mass destruction in the hands of suicide terrorists becomes more realistic and as our ability to deter such harms by classic rational cost-benefit threats and promises becomes less realistic."[198]

The shift in favour of preemption thus entails two general propositions. One is that the "calculus" of risk and harm prevalent in the criminal law is no longer appropriate. In the past, Western jurists preferred that ten guilty men go free rather than convicting one innocent person. They are now prepared to contemplate the need to detain or even kill an innocent person rather than allow "ten possibly preventable terrorist attacks to occur."[199] This implies that "preemptive decisions"—about detention, torture, or targeted killing—will be based on "uncertain predictions, which will rarely be anywhere close to 100% accurate."[200] It may also entail the need to posit "some false positives (predictions of harms that would not have occurred) in order to prevent some predicted harms from causing irreparable damage."[201]

A second proposition holds that because terrorism is no longer susceptible to deterrence, and because the stakes are so grave, the older limits on the state's use of force against individuals no longer apply. Terrorists who present a credible threat of using WMDs blur the line between combatants and criminals. The result is not that we are at war, but that we may apply both military force and the laws of war selectively. "The reality," Dershowitz asserts, "is that terrorists involved in an ongoing insurgency or campaign of terror are in a hybrid status that may well justify treating them as combatants for the purposes of targeted killings but not as prisoners of war once they are captured."[202] Other preemptive measures that are now appropriate include preventive detention, destruction of sites where WMDs are being built, and military occupation of regions known to support terror (Iraq, Afghanistan).

As in the closing chapters of *Why Terrorism Works*, Dershowitz's discussion of preemptive measures in *Preemption* is framed by frequent allusions to mass terror.[203] Yet, with only two exceptions, none of these references is substantiated by citations to authorities on the use of WMDs. The two exceptions involve newspaper articles that summarize the views of others. Dershowitz's use of these sources is worth addressing briefly, to

---

[197] Ibid. at 7.
[198] Ibid. at 8.
[199] Ibid. at 12.
[200] Ibid. at 11.
[201] Ibid. at 11.
[202] Ibid. at 126.
[203] References to WMDs or mass terror are found in PREEMPTION, *supra* note 177, at 2, 8, 10, 18, 19, 23, 140–145 (a detailed discussion of bioterrorism), and 235.

demonstrate its consistency with the selective way that Posner and other commentators on WMDs have dealt with authority.

The first is an article from *Forward* about a 2004 study published by the National Intelligence Council (an organization linked to the CIA and operating under the auspices of the U.S. government).[204] Dershowtiz cites a passage from the article summarizing the NIC's study as "predicting that America is 'likely' to be hit by bio-terrorist attacks at some point in the next 15 years."[205] The passage also suggests that a bioterrorist laboratory "could well be the size of a household kitchen, and the weapon built there could be smaller than a toaster." Drawing from the same article, Dershowitz continues: "A leading expert on bioterrorism, who serves as a consultant to the Pentagon, warned that although biological agents have 'the potential to be much more life-threatening [than nuclear weapons], we are not prepared to prevent or control this threat.' "[206] The suggestion here is that credible experts have concluded that (a) an attack is imminent; (b) because of the simplicity of creating a bioweapon and the difficulty of detecting it; and (c) that the weapon itself poses a potentially greater danger than a nuclear bomb. Yet neither Dershowitz nor the article cited indicates whether the predications in the report were qualified in any way; nor does he seek to contextualize or balance them against contrary opinion. The likelihood of a bioterror attack "in the next 15 years," and the assumptions on which this claim rests, are thus presented as a matter of settled scientific opinion despite the very limited research and evidence that Dershowitz cites.

Dershowitz's use of the second source is more questionable still. Dealing with a more extreme scenario involving the weaponization of smallpox, he cites a *New York Times* article that fails to support the claim he seeks to make. He writes: "… recent advances in synthesizing long molecules of DNA have made it more likely that 'the technique might be used to make the genome of the smallpox virus' and weaponizing it."[207] However, the cited article does not state that it is "more likely" that smallpox will be manufactured; it states only that the technique in question "puts within reach the manufacture of small genomes, such as those of viruses" including smallpox. The article also states that "[s]ome biologists fear that the technique might be used to make the genome of the smallpox virus." It does not state that the discovery of the technique makes the production by *terrorists* "more likely," or comment upon the merits of the biologists' fears. It fails to do this precisely because it does not address the question of what is involved in making a virus. The article simply suggests that the *theoretical possibility* of making smallpox virus is now

---

[204] Ori Nir & Marc Perelman, *CIA-Linked Study Warns of Bio-Terrorst Attacks During Next 15 Years*, FORWARD (Jan. 21, 2005), at http://www.forward.com/articles/4161/. The report at issue is *Mapping the Global Future: Report of the National Intelligence Council's 2020 Project*, at https://www.hsdl.org/?view&did=474931.

[205] Dershowitz, PREEMPTION, *supra* note 177, at 140, citing Nir & Marc Perelman, *CIA-Linked Study, supra* note 204.

[206] Nir & Perelman, ibid, citing an interview with Richard Danzig.

[207] Dershowitz, PREEMPTION, *supra* note 177, at 143, citing Nicholas Wade, *A DNA Success Raises Bioterror Concerns*, N.Y. TIMES, Jan. 12, 2005.

"within reach." Ignoring these distinctions, Dershowitz then writes: "What is known is that if terrorists can manage to introduce smallpox into our borders, the devastation may be catastrophic since most Americans are not currently immunized against that killer disease." Once again, this may be true, but much turns on the phrase "manage to introduce...into our borders." What would this involve? And how likely is it? Without considering better informed opinion on the matter, Dershowitz's treatment of it implies that relatively little is involved. The imminent possibility of a smallpox attack, or one involving another extremely virulent bioweapon, is once again framed here as a scientific certainty—when in fact (for reasons to be explored later in this book) the state of the question in scientific circles is much less clear.[208]

### III. JOHN YOO AND THE EXIGENCIES OF WAR

Turning next to John Yoo, we find that the role of authority in assertions of the likelihood of mass terror disappears altogether. In contrast to Posner and Dershowitz, Yoo is both more certain about the imminence of mass terror and more decisive in asserting that the threat posed by terrorists who would use WMD is best understood as a form of war rather than crime.

Yoo is a law professor at Berkeley who gained notoriety for his work as counsel in the Department of Justice from 2001 to 2003. While there, he co-authored a series of memos on the legality of certain extreme counterterrorism measures, including coercive interrogation. Since his return to Berkeley, Yoo has sought to defend the Bush administration's response to terror through a series of books, articles, and editorials. His most comprehensive treatment of the subject is set out in *War By Other Means* (2006).[209]

The central claim in this book is that the events of September 11, and the ongoing threat of attack by al Qaeda and its affiliates, are best understood as a form of war and best addressed using powers available under the laws of war. A critical part of this claim is that the groups involved pose a credible threat of obtaining WMDs and deploying them in the United States in the short term. The threat is therefore much more serious than a crime—it even bears an existential import: "We (along with Israel) are the first to face a terrorist enemy intent on carrying out the catastrophic destruction of our nation."[210] Despite the fact that this enemy is a non-state actor, it can "inflict violence at a level once only in the hands of nations."[211] Al Qaeda, acting in "small guerrilla bands, aided by the spread into the global public domain of virulent technologies—chemical, biological, and nuclear—can wreak destruction such as no small group has ever been able to before."[212]

---

208 Expert debates on bioterror are explored in Chapter 6.

209 John Yoo, War By Other Means: An Insiders Account of the War on Terror (New York: Atlantic Monthly Press, 2006).

210 Ibid. at xii.

211 Ibid. at 3.

212 Ibid. at 7.

Maintaining a strong link between al Qaeda and mass terror, Yoo alludes to the possible use of WMDs no less than nine times throughout the book.[213]

According to Yoo, the threat posed by al Qaeda is tantamount to war not only given the group's capacity to carry out a catastrophic attack, but also because if a nation-state had carried out the attacks of September 11, there would have been no debate as to whether we were at war.[214] As with a nation at war, "al Qaeda's attacks are highly organized, military in nature, and aimed at achieving ideological and political objectives."[215] Congress has also agreed to view this as a war, having passed the Authorization for Use of Military Force (AUMF) on Sept 14, 2001.[216] In Yoo's view, this was, in effect, the congressional declaration of war required by the U.S. Constitution. As Yoo notes, the text of the authorization refers explicitly to "grave acts of violence" that "pose an unusual and extraordinary threat to the national security and foreign policy of the United States."[217] The AUMF provides the only necessary legal authorization for addressing September 11 as an act of war, and thus legitimizes the use of a range of military powers and tactics.

Yoo also makes the case for taking a war-type approach on practical grounds, and his arguments here mirror those of Posner. Restricting the nation's response to the tools of law enforcement would unnecessarily burden its defenses. Police must have probable cause to arrest; they must inform suspects of their right to silence and to counsel; if detained, suspects must be charged, and if charged, they require a trial by jury, disclosure, and the chance to face their accusers in open court. "Applying criminal justice rules to al Qaeda terrorists would gravely impede the killing or capture of the enemy, as well as compromise the secrecy of the United State's military efforts."[218] When the conflict is seen as a war, the U.S. is entitled deploy a wider set of tools:

> A nation at war may kill members of the enemy's armed forces. But law enforcement personnel may use force only in defense of their lives or those of others. Once captured, an enemy combatant can be detained until the end of the conflict. Combatants have no right to a lawyer or a criminal trial to determine their guilt or innocence under the usual laws of war. They are simply being held to prevent them from returning to the fight.[219]

And since the Geneva Conventions apply only to "high contracting parties" or to those who voluntarily accept their terms, in Yoo's view, they do not apply to captured members of al Qaeda because that group is neither a signatory to the treaty nor a voluntary

---

213 Ibid. at 7, 45, 62, 172, 173, 181, 188, 199, and 232.
214 Ibid. at 4.
215 Ibid. at 9.
216 Pub. L. 107–40, 115 Stat. 224 (2001).
217 Yoo, War by Other Means, *supra*, note 209, at 11.
218 Ibid. at 16.
219 Ibid. at 16–17.

subscriber.[220] Al Qaeda is instead an "unprecedented enemy,"[221] one consisting of only a "covert network of cells with no territory to defend, no population to protect, no armed forces to attack."[222] Its only purpose and modus operandi is to launch "surprise attacks on purely civilian targets."[223] Our best defense is to gain intelligence by capturing and interrogating their leaders, or intercepting their communications.[224]

The threat is so grave that it justifies not only indefinite detention without charge, and coercive interrogation bordering on torture, but also targeted killing. As technology has improved, targeted killing has become more humane, since the targeting is more effective and the collateral damage is minimized.[225] Errors do still occur, but we can "only ask that our soldiers and policy makers make reasonable decisions under the circumstances."[226] A further justification for this practice lies in a liberal reading of the UN Charter. Article 51 of the UN Charter recognizes a state's "inherent right of individual or collective self-defence...if an armed attack occurs." Yoo reads into this passage a state's right to use force in the face of "imminent attack,"[227] but questions what "imminence" might entail in this context. He argues that the magnitude and nature of current threats call for a more expansive interpretation, and that imminence "should not be understood as a purely temporal concept."[228] The trouble lies in the fact that "[i]mminence as a concept does not address cases in which an attack is likely to happen, but we are not sure when."[229] The right to self-defense must also take into account "the degree of expected harm, [which is] a function of the probability of the attack and the estimated casualties and damage."[230] To support his reading of this key provision of international law, Yoo invokes a form of the harbinger theory:

> The speed and severity of attack possible today means that the right to preempt now should be greater than in the past. Weapons of mass destruction have increased the potential casualties a single terrorist attack can wreak, from the hundreds or thousands of innocent lives into the hundreds of thousands or even millions. This does not even count the profound, long-term destruction to cities, contamination of the environment, and long-term death or disease for large segments of the civilian population. WMDs can today be delivered with ease—a suicide bomber could detonate a "dirty bomb" using a truck or spread a biological agent with a small airplane. Detection is difficult, as no broad mobilization and deployment of regular

---

220 Ibid. at 23.
221 Ibid. at 21.
222 Ibid. at 21.
223 Ibid. at 21.
224 Ibid. at 21, 39.
225 Ibid. at 49.
226 Ibid. at 57.
227 U.N. CHARTER art. 51.
228 Yoo, WAR BY OTHER MEANS, *supra*, note 209, at 61.
229 Ibid. at 62.
230 Ibid.

> armed forces will be visible, and imminent attacks will be virtually impossible to prevent using conventional military force. Probability, magnitude, and timing must all be relevant factors in which to use force against the enemy.[231]

Notably, none of these assertions about WMDs use are supported with reference to expert opinion or other evidence. Indeed, the entire text contains no attempt to ground assertions about the technology or likelihood of WMDs in any authority or evidence. The claims are thus asserted as though they were self-evident or beyond dispute.

On the assumption, then, that this is indeed a war, involving the most serious threats, the argument for holding captured combatants at Guantanamo seems, from Yoo's perspective, uncontroversial. Nations at war have traditionally imprisoned enemy combatants, not as a form of punishment but as a means of incapacitation, which is permissible "until the end of hostilities."[232] Both American citizens, such as Jose Padilla, and alien detainees at Guantanamo are prisoners of war subject to the President's unfettered discretion to detain or imprison as Commander in Chief, for the duration of the conflict.[233] In Yoo's view, the AUMF "implicitly included the power to detain enemy combatants."[234] As prisoners of war, detainees do not have a right to counsel, except when facing charges in a military tribunal, or elsewhere, for violating the laws of war.[235]

Among the most critical of the president's powers is the use of coercive interrogation. Yoo asserts that the 2002 capture and interrogation of Abu Zubaydah, a high-ranking member of al Qaeda in Pakistan, yielded information leading to the capture of Ramzi bin al Shibh, another key al Qaeda figure, which led in turn to the capture of Khalid Sheikh Mohammed, "architect" of the 9/11 attacks.[236] Assessing the significance of these actions, Yoo writes "[n]ot only did their capture take significant parts of the al Qaeda leadership out of action, they led to the recovery of much information that prevented future terrorist attacks and helped American intelligence more fully understand the operation of the terrorist network."[237] A notorious aspect of these interrogations is that they were the subject of advice in an August 2002 memo that Yoo authored with Jay Bybee, Assistant Attorney General, for Alberto Gonzales, counsel to the President. The memo authorized conduct falling short of torture, which was defined in this way:

> ... physical pain amounting to torture must be equivalent in intensity to the pain accompanying serious physical injury, such as organ failure, impairment of bodily

[231] Ibid. at 62–63.
[232] Ibid. at 129.
[233] Ibid. at 144–45.
[234] Ibid. at 149.
[235] Ibid. at 152.
[236] Ibid. at 167.
[237] Ibid. at 167.

> function, or even death. For mental pain or suffering to amount to torture [under U.S. law ratifying the UN Convention Against Torture[238]], it must result in significant psychological harm of significant duration, e.g., lasting for months or even years."[239]

Yoo affirms that "the advice was entirely accurate."[240] Interrogators, he suggests, are not held to the same standards as those applicable to suspects held at "an American police station." The argument for interrogation bordering on torture is, once again, purely consequential: "What if, as the popular Fox television program *24* recently portrayed, a high-level terrorist leader is caught who knows the location of a nuclear weapon in an American city? Should it be illegal for the President to use harsh interrogation short of torture to elicit this information?"[241] For Yoo, the question is not academic: "Unfortunately, these are no longer hypothetical questions. We do face an enemy that is intent on carrying out surprise attacks on innocent civilians, with WMDs if possible, by using covert cells of operatives hidden within the United States."[242]

Other measures that Yoo supports—in light of the outstanding threat—include military commissions for trying combatants, expanded surveillance in the USA PATRIOT Act, and warrantless wiretapping by the National Security Agency. Military commissions are necessary for greater secrecy, but also provide for a fair trial, despite allowing for relaxed rules of evidence.[243] They also allow for closing portions of proceedings, without compromising the defendant's rights, since his attorneys remain present.[244] The USA PATRIOT Act's expanded scope for searches with warrants issued on lower standards, and the increased sharing of information obtained surreptitiously, are justified, but the act should be amended to allow the wiretapping of domestic and foreign targets with greater latitude or on lower thresholds of suspicion.[245]

## Conclusion

The three fields explored in this chapter—expert opinion on WMDs, the history of terror, and work by advocates of extreme measures—share several characteristics. Among them is a frequent expression of the harbinger theory and a tendency, in many instances,

---

[238] 18 U.S.C.A. §2340A(a); Convention against Torture and Other Cruel, Inhuman or Degrading Treatment or Punishment, G.A. res. 39/46, annex, 39 U.N. GAOR Supp. (No. 51) at 197, U.N. Doc. A/39/51 (1984); 1465 UNTS 85.

[239] Cited in Yoo, War by Other Means, *supra* note 209, at 169.

[240] Ibid. at 169.

[241] Ibid. at 172.

[242] Ibid. at 173.

[243] Ibid. at 206.

[244] Ibid. at 217.

[245] Ibid. at 116.

to ground claims about the imminent prospect of WMD terror upon a selective reading of a narrow range of authority and evidence. Yet portions of this literature are often moving and persuasive precisely because they emphasize hypothetical technological *possibilities* of mass terror that cannot be ruled out, at least in theory. Much of the literature thus retains a degree of plausibility despite the existence of a vigorous debate about the likelihood of WMD use, which will be explored in Chapter 6.

But before turning to that debate, the next chapter considers the question of how liberal jurists and scholars in the period have tended to respond to claims about the imminent prospect of mass terror.

# 5

## Opportunity Lost

## LIBERAL DEFERENCE TO THE HARBINGER THEORY

OVER THE COURSE of the post-9/11 period, liberal jurists and rights advocates have made various efforts to persuade a wider public of the need to reform counterterrorism measures. Yet, in ways to be explored throughout this chapter, they have also tended to demonstrate a curious indifference, ambivalence, or even deference to inflated threat claims, undermining the case for reform in ways that are instructive. This chapter will advance the argument that by failing to be more critical of variations on the harbinger theory, or to challenge them directly, liberal advocates have missed an important opportunity to make a stronger case for reform—a case that might still be made.

The chapter begins with the assumption that reform advocates have made several strong arguments in defense of rights in a wide variety of high-profile venues and campaigns. They have commonly argued that rights are not incompatible with security; that extraordinary measures ought to be used only where demonstrably justified; and that many if not most such measures have been ineffective or unnecessary.

But advocates for reform have also tended to be less inclined to challenge beliefs about the unprecedented gravity of outstanding threats—or the belief that such threats *compel* the state to adopt a more preemptive, extreme set of rules. Some commentators have suggested they lack the means or qualifications to assess the nature of the threat of terrorism, or have conceded the difficulty of challenging government assertions of superior knowledge of the issue based on confidential intelligence. But a number of liberal advocates have also embraced the harbinger theory as a kind of self-evident truth. Much of the scholarship and advocacy for reform includes brief concessions to the hypothetical possibilities of catastrophic terror in the near future, without relying on evidence or authority to substantiate these possibilities. As a consequence, many liberal forays into debates about rights and security after 9/11 have conceded a fundamental point that ought to have been at the heart of the debate from the outset—whether September 11 was in fact a harbinger.

There are certainly important exceptions, with some reformers calling the tendency toward threat inflation into question as a basis for new measures. But even where liberals have been critical of the practice of threat inflation, they have tended to explore this as a facet of psychological overreaction, or policy entrepreneurialism, rather than challenging the claims in a technical or literal sense: namely, that large-scale terror of one form or another is in fact imminent.[1] Instead, much of the work done in recent years to advocate reform has entailed one of two common approaches. Authors have tended to accept the validity of the fear of a pending catastrophe or have conceded the need for certain exceptions to conventional criminal or constitutional protections, or both. Yet, as this chapter will argue, either approach, or a combination of the two, has served as a less persuasive basis for reform because both entail a need to depart in some way from liberal legal values.

The broader argument of this chapter, then, is that reform advocates have been effective in exposing the misunderstandings that underlie a belief in the need to trade liberty for security or the futility of many measures used thus far. But they have tended not to unsettle a deeper belief that current threats warrant a new approach to security that often involves extreme or invasive measures.

To support this argument, the chapter examines two common approaches to advocating reform. One involves a tendency to minimize or ignore claims about (a) the gravity of current threats or (b) why this warrants a new approach to security, or both. The second approach is to pay deference to either or both claims. The goal here is to explain in part why rights advocates who have taken a deferential approach to some of the more inflated rhetoric about the threat of terrorism have inadvertently helped to condition—or have failed to hinder—a larger embrace of authoritarian legality. A further purpose is to set the context for the next chapter, which sets out an approach to reform that seeks to address this problem.

---

[1] *See* discussion below of David Cole & Jules Lobel, LESS SAFE, LESS FREE: WHY AMERICA IS LOSING THE WAR ON TERROR (New York: New Press, 2007), ch. 8; *see also* Cass Sunstein, WORST-CASE SCENARIOS (Cambridge MA: Harvard University Press, 2009), ch. 1; and Oren Gross & Fionnuala Ni Aolain, LAW IN TIMES OF CRISIS: EMERGENCY POWERS IN THEORY AND PRACTICE (Cambridge: Cambridge University Press, 2006), at 103–09, drawing on Kahneman and Tversky's notion of the "availability heuristic" to describe the impact of an early framing of a terrorist incident by policy "entrepreneurs" as an act of war rather than crime. Daniel Kahneman, *Availability: A Heuristic for Judging Frequency and Probability* 5 COGNITIVE PSYCHOL. 207 (1973).

## Part 1. A Reluctance to Engage the Harbinger Theory

This part will examine the work of non-governmental organizations (NGOs) and legal journalists, two groups that have been key contributors to public debates on security law and policy. Before proceeding, it may help to begin by noting that a good portion of the NGOs and journalists advocating liberal reform have tended to rely on one or more of four closely related arguments.

i. *The compatibility argument* holds that human rights, due process, and constitutionalism are compatible with countering terrorism because rights can be upheld without significantly hindering security;
ii. *The argument that rights cannot be "balanced" with security*: i.e., talk of rights and security being balanced or traded off often is premised on the false assumption that we gain more of one by having less of the other;
iii. *The necessity and proportionality argument* contends that we are justified in infringing rights only when, and to the extent that, the need to do so can be demonstrated and the extent of the breach is proportionate to the benefit derived; and finally,
iv. *The practical futility argument* holds that most if not all of the extreme measures used thus far have been ineffective or unnecessary—yielding no new information or further protection not available by other means.

Notably, the arguments circumvent the question of the nature of the threat of terrorism. Instead, they are crafted on the assumption that terrorism may indeed pose a greater threat, or are compatible with that assumption. What the arguments are not designed to do is to contest claims about the threat of terror itself. Yet, for reasons to be explored, side-stepping this crucial issue has marked an important concession in the debate about rights and security. In much of their work, liberal advocates can be seen to assume an essentially defensive posture, conceding that some rights or liberties may have to be curtailed and arguing primarily about where to draw the line. What is proportionate? What is excessive? What is necessary? However, without an effective critique of the often inflated claims made about terrorism, whatever response to these questions that reformers have managed to offer has often seemed secondary to the basic concession—tacit or overt—that new threats call for new measures.

### I. JURISTS AND NGOS

Over the course of the post-9/11 period, NGOs, associations of jurists, and other activist groups have produced an extensive body of material—reports, books, films, websites—advancing a case for reform of authoritarian measures. Broadly speaking, the work falls into one of two categories. One consists of investigations, exposés, or reports of violations, coupled with arguments in favour of reform. Another consists of declaratory statements or affirmations of liberal legal principles. I highlight one exemplary document from each category.

## The International Commission of Jurists

The first is the 2009 report of the Geneva-based International Commission of Jurists on human rights and counterterrorism.[2] The report stands out in terms of its scope and the scale of the investigation on which it is based. It draws on hearings held over the course of three years by a panel of Commission members in 16 regions, relating to 40 countries, representing all parts of the globe. The ICJ published its 200-page report in February of 2009, with press conferences and presentations in New York; Washington, D.C.; Toronto; London; and elsewhere, featuring prominent jurists, including former Canadian Supreme Court of Canada Justice Ian Binnie and former Irish President and UN High Commissioner for Human Rights Mary Robinson, among others. In other words, this was intended to be something more than an academic exercise. It was an earnest attempt by liberal jurists to make a public case for liberal legality to the widest possible audience.

The panel found that after 9/11, the United States and other Western nations had lost sight of, or in some cases had consciously abandoned, a postwar paradigm of international law that assumed the centrality of absolute or non-derogable rights.[3] Nations had now

---

2 International Commission of Jurists, *Assessing Damage, Urging Action: Report of the Eminent Jurists Panel on Terrorism, Counter-terrorism and Human Rights* [hereinafter "ICJ Report"] (Feb. 16, 2009), at http://www.refworld.org/docid/499e76822.html. The International Commission of Jurists is a non-governmental organization founded in 1952, consisting of 60 senior judges, counsel, and academics. Its mandate is to advance the principles of human rights and the international rule of law. In 2005, it convened an eight-member panel to study the question of counterterrorism and human rights due partly to concern that "a security-dominated agenda" following September 11 resulted in an attempt by many governments to "bypass well-established human rights and rule of law principles." Members of the Panel were Arthur Chaskalson, former Chief Justice of South Africa; Mary Robinson, former President of Ireland and former United Nations High Commissioner for Human Rights; former president of the European Commission on Human Rights, Stefan Trechsel; Robert K. Goldman, Professor of the American University's Washington College of Law; Pakistani Supreme Court counsel Hina Jilani; Georges Abi-Saab, an international law scholar and former judge of the Appeals Chamber of the International Criminal Tribunals for the former Yugoslavia and Rwanda, and of the International Court of Justice; Professor Vitit Muntarbhorn of Chulalongkorn University in Bangkok; and E. Raúl Zaffaroni of the Supreme Court of Argentina. (*See* the Executive Summary of the ICJ Report at http://www.icj.org/report-of-the-eminent-jurists-panel-on-terrorism-counter-terrorism-and-human-rights/.)

3 The primary instruments of the paradigm include the Universal Declaration of Human Rights, G.A. Res. 217A (III) 1948, U.N. Doc. A/810 at 71 [hereinafter, Universal Declaration]; Geneva Convention Relative to the Protection of Civilian Persons in Time of War, Aug. 12, 1949, 6 U.S.T. 3516; 75 U.N.T.S. 287; Geneva Convention Relative to the Treatment of Prisoners of War, Aug. 12, 1949, 6 U.S.T. 3316; 75 U.N.T.S. 135; International Covenant on Civil and Political Rights, Sept. 19, 1966, 999 U.N.T.S. 171, Can. T.S. 1976 No. 47, 6 I.L.M. 368 (entered into force 23 March 1976, accession by Canada 19 May 1976) [ICCPR]; International Covenant on Economic, Social and Cultural Rights, Dec. 16, 1966, 993 U.N.T.S. 3; S. Exec. Doc. D, 95–2 (1978); 6 I.L.M. 360 (1967); and Convention against Torture and Other Cruel, Inhuman or Degrading Treatment or Punishment, Dec. 10, 1984, United Nations Treaty Series, vol. 1465, 85.

shifted away from this framework under the assumption that recent events have made it obsolete. The phenomenon is universal. "From New York to Nairobi," the authors write, "from Brussels to Bogotá, and from Moscow to the Maghreb, the voices heard by the Panel spoke with disturbing consistency and regularity that well-established principles of international law are being ignored."[4] Encapsulating the thrust of their findings, the Panel states:

> Terrorism sows terror, and many States have fallen into a trap set by the terrorists. Ignoring lessons from the past, they have allowed themselves to be rushed into hasty responses, introducing an array of measures which undermine cherished values as well as the international legal framework carefully developed since the Second World War. These measures have resulted in human rights violations, including torture, enforced disappearances, secret and arbitrary detentions, and unfair trials. There has been little accountability for these abuses or justice for their victims.[5]

Many chose to abandon the earlier framework in the belief that "the current threat posed by terrorism was not, and could not have been, envisioned before."[6] Moreover, the threat is said to be "so unprecedented and exceptional that the world is facing a genuine emergency, and that in the face of such an emergency, the rules must change, and individuals must forego many of their liberties for the greater good."[7] The issues for the Panel were therefore whether the threat is indeed exceptional, and if so, whether the older rights framework poses an undue constraint when dealing with it.

The panel responded to the first question by drawing a historical comparison to earlier claims about terror. Current threats share "important parallels" with past terror crises.[8] In earlier historical moments (Chile, Argentina, the United Kingdom), terror threats were also believed to be unprecedented, serious, and long-lasting. And in each of those cases, the arguments served as a basis for serious rights violations that in retrospect are widely considered excessive and unnecessary.

Applying this lesson to the present, the Panel makes use of the necessity and proportionality argument. If present talk of the threat being serious and unprecedented resonates with earlier beliefs and practices, citizens and governments ought to demand stronger evidence of the claim. They should also demand proof that the rights framework is no longer adequate and that any new measures are in fact necessary. On the basis of its hearings and discussions with government and security officials in many nations, the Panel concludes that such evidence has been lacking: "Whether the [current

[4] ICJ Report, *supra* note 2, at 10.
[5] Ibid. at 2.
[6] Ibid. at 18.
[7] Ibid. at 22.
[8] Ibid. ch. 2.

terror] threat is exceptional or not, the Panel heard no persuasive evidence that the tried-and-tested framework of international law was inadequate."[9] The extreme measures surveyed in the report cannot therefore be justified. Later in the text, the Panel becomes more explicit: "counter-terrorism measures themselves must always be taken with strict regard to the principles of legality, necessity, proportionality and non-discrimination."[10]

Designed in the early postwar period, the older rights framework is still relevant precisely because it was crafted with emergencies in mind. In other words, non-derogable rights were neither designed for government in times of peace nor meant to be limited to threats in the ordinary course. They were meant as a tool for preserving liberal ideals in a way that still gave states the necessary flexibility to respond to national emergencies. In this view, the magnitude or nature of the threat could not be the basis for asserting the framework's obsolescence.

A third claim is more abstract—the compatibility of rights and security. As the authors state:

> There is no inherent contradiction between, on the one hand, upholding human rights and the rule of law and, on the other, ensuring people's safety by countering terrorism. The Panel does not accept the characterisation of "human rights" and "security from terrorism" as being somehow at opposing poles, and the duty imposed on States as one of balancing these antithetical demands.[11]

The ICJ's use of the argument is typical of a wide range of rights advocacy, from scholarship on counterterrorism policy at national and international levels;[12] declarations or reports by other associations of rights advocates;[13] and statements by non-governmental organizations.[14]

The report concludes with the Panel's call for a "stocktaking and repairing the damage" at all levels—national, regional, and international—with a view to making "a fresh start."[15] It urges that we "prevent the normalization of the exceptional" by revisiting

---

9 Ibid. at 24.

10 Ibid. at 169.

11 ICJ Report, *supra* note 2, at 21.

12 *See*, e.g., David Dyzenhaus, ed., Civil Rights and Security (Farnham, Surrey: Ashgate, 2009) and Benjamin Goold & Liora Lazarus, eds., Security and Human Rights (London: Hart Publishing, 2007), which both contain contributions with respect to counterterrorism law in the United States, Canada, and Britain.

13 *See* International Commission of Jurists, 2004 Berlin Declaration, *Upholding Human Rights and the Rule of Law in Combating Terrorism*, at http://www.refworld.org/docid/41dec1f94.html; and ICJ Report, *supra* note 2. *See also Ottawa Principles on Anti-terrorism and Human Rights*, in Craig Forcese & Nicole LaViolette, eds., The Human Rights of Anti-terrorism (Toronto: Irwin Law, 2008) and International Bar Association, 2003 report, *International Terrorism: Legal Challenges and Responses*, Task Force on International Terrorism (Ardsley, NY: Transnational Publishers, 2003).

14 See Amnesty International, *Counter Terror with Justice*, at http://www.amnestyusa.org/news/multimedia/counter-terror-with-justice.

15 ICJ Report, *supra* note 2, at 164.

post-9/11 law and policy, overhauling of much of it in accordance with the principle of necessity and proportionality, and strengthening procedural safeguards.[16]

The Persuasive Limits of the ICJ Report

Among the many strengths of the report is the Panel's recognition that a pervasive break from liberal principles is due in large part to a widespread belief in the exceptional nature of current threats. Yet instead of challenging this belief, or interrogating it in much detail, the Panel seeks to dismiss or defuse it by historicizing it. Consistent with an older pattern of threat inflation, the Panel implies that it can be safely cast aside as an overreaction.

To historicize the claim is not, however, to refute it. Indeed, in only one instance does the report address the reasons commonly cited for claiming that the current threat is exceptional. As the authors write:

> [I]t has been argued that groups like al-Qaeda are international in character; have access to more dangerous technologies of killing (e.g. "dirty" bombs etc.); utilise highly sophisticated communication technologies to carry out attacks and thwart law enforcement measures; have individuals who employ tactics, such as suicide bombing, which require different tactics on the part of law enforcement personnel; and/or have ill-defined, existential, or unrealisable demands, making negotiation difficult.[17]

The prospect of mass terror is itself touched on only obliquely. More "dangerous technologies of killing" may exist, but have no significance in and of themselves. The Panel then draws a striking conclusion: "it is irrelevant for immediate purposes to determine if there is one terrorist threat or multiple threats, or *if this threat is quantitatively or qualitatively different to past threats*. Suffice to say that in different parts of the world terrorism poses a real and substantial threat needing to be effectively countered in accordance with international law."[18]

The conclusion is striking because throughout the report, the Panel identifies a belief in the unprecedented nature of current threats as paramount. Yet not only is this belief unchallenged, it is also largely affirmed ("a real and substantial threat"). The ICJ's larger case for reform rests therefore on the following argument. The threat that terrorism poses may indeed be unprecedented, but this issue is irrelevant. What is important is whether we can establish that an older liberal framework hinders the task of national security. And we cannot. Therefore, we should remain committed to it and abandon illiberal practices. The argument thus shifts the focus from a fear of terror to a demand for evidence.

16 *See* recommendations at 155 of the ICJ Report, ibid.

17 ICJ Report, *supra* note 2, at 22 (emphasis added).

18 Ibid. ch. 24.

Without clearer proof that the old rules are ill-suited to national defense, any departures from them are suspect.

For the fearful skeptic, however, the rationale for a new set of rules lies precisely in assumptions and beliefs about the nature of the threat at issue. Due to its profound gravity, we must act preemptively. And in many instances, this will entail extreme measures—which are justified not in terms of their proven effect, but in terms of the *need to be preemptive*. In other words, we carry out targeted killing and hold detainees indefinitely without charge not because we can be certain that this will prevent a catastrophic attack, but because we believe that we cannot afford to experiment. We may lack evidence that these measures are necessary or effective, and thus we may be perpetrating a grave injustice. But we must err on the side of caution. The stakes are too grave to do otherwise.

The skeptic's logic is questionable on many fronts. The authors of the report would argue, for example, that while they remain agnostic about the magnitude and nature of current threats, they have at least unsettled the more important claim that current threats *warrant* a new set of rules. Yet the persuasive force of this argument is limited so long as other assumptions about the nature and potential impact of mass terror remain intact. For example, if one believes that an event of mass terror in some form is imminent and possibly catastrophic, the choice is clear. Preemptive measures, though extraordinary, will seem more compelling than a call to remain committed to firm limits on the state's use of force for its own sake.

But perhaps more importantly, the ICJ does not take issue with the need to embrace a larger preemptive paradigm. It only takes issue with violations of international law that this might entail. In ways to be explored below, other liberal advocates take a similar approach, advancing a case for reform by challenging the apparent incompatibility of liberal legalism and certain preemptive measures—rather than challenging deeper assumptions about the need for a wholesale shift toward "preemption" as a primary legal and political principle.

### The "Ottawa Principles"

A second category of rights advocacy among jurists, NGOs, and other groups can be found in declarations of principle and other affirmative statements. Several have been issued over the course of the past decade.[19] In some respects, one such declaration, the Ottawa Principles on Anti-terrorism and Human Rights is representative.[20] Emerging from an international colloquium held in 2006, the Ottawa Principles assume the form of a quasi-statutory set of declaratory rules or principles. A sense of the document's style can be gleaned from Section 1.1.2, which states: "All measures taken by states to fight terrorism must respect human rights and the rule of law, while excluding any form of

---

19 *See*, e.g., *supra* note 13.

20 The Ottawa Principles are included in Forcese & LaViolette, The Human Rights of Anti-terrorism, *supra* note 13.

arbitrariness as well as any discriminatory or racist treatment, and must be subject to appropriate supervision."

The introduction to the document affirms a version of the compatibility argument noted earlier. The authors:

> shared a common view that the preservation of human rights—not least the right to life—is the central motivator of anti-terrorism. They also believed that human rights constitute an elemental and immutable constraint on how anti-terrorism is conducted. The struggle for collective security must not be an assault on the individual's life, liberty and security of the person.[21]

The remainder of the document affirms that "[a]s a general rule, terrorist acts are criminal acts subject to applicable domestic, transnational and/or international criminal law enforcement measures";[22] the need to submit states of emergencies or derogations from core rights to the rule of law;[23] the absolute prohibition on torture;[24] and various limits on the gathering, exchange, and assertion of privilege over intelligence.[25] It also affirms that any deployment of force by a state acting in self-defense must be "necessary and proportionate in accordance with international law."[26]

The Ottawa Principles, and other such statements, are primarily assertive or expressive. Their purpose is less to persuade than to publicly affirm. They also serve to amplify certain rhetorical strategies in favour of reform. They seek, that is, to reframe public debates about rights and security in terms favorable to liberal legal principles.

In this case, for example, the authors propose a conceptual link between the idea of national security and the preservation of human rights: i.e., rights as a "central motivator of anti-terrorism." Not only are rights compatible with security, they are also the very object of security. By protecting rights, we are not hindering our security, but advancing it.

To be clear, these are important and worthwhile contributions to the project of reform. But while they focus on the compatibility of rights and security, the Ottawa Principles, and other such statements, marginalize or ignore other critical assumptions that motivate illiberal measures. This in turn affects how skeptical audiences respond (if they take notice of them at all). For those who believe that extreme measures are warranted by the gravity of current threats, affirmations about the compatibility of rights and security would appear to miss the point. So long as beliefs about mass terror and the need for greater preemptive measures remain unchallenged and widespread, an idea of human rights as an "immutable constraint" will seem neither self-evident nor persuasive to many.

---

21 Ibid. at 18.
22 Ibid. Principle 3.1.
23 Ibid. Principle 2.4.
24 Ibid. Principle 4.1.
25 Ibid. Principles 7 & 8.
26 Ibid. Principle 3.2.3.

## II. COLE, LOBEL, AND DANNER AND JOURNALISTIC ADVOCACY FOR REFORM

Another important part of the campaign for liberal reform involves books and essays meant for a wider public audience. These include works of nonfiction for the general reader and articles in high-profile journalistic venues. This section considers two prominent examples.

### Cole and Lobel

The first is David Cole and Jules Lobel's 2007 work, *Less Safe, Less Free: Why America is Losing the War on Terror*.[27] Both Cole and Lobel are legal academics, but as the style and format of this book suggests, they aim to address a broader audience.[28] The book also builds on Cole's national profile as a lawyer and public intellectual. Cole has acquired this profile by appearing in a number of leading U.S. Supreme Court counterterrorism cases and writing frequently in such venues as the *New York Review of Books, The Nation*, and *The New York Times*. The book thus represents an important effort to advance a public case for a return to liberal legality.

Cole and Lobel advance their case at the outset by expressing concern with the Bush administration's embrace of a "preventive paradigm" for counterterrorism. The paradigm is marked by the use of a series of "highly coercive tactics,"[29] from arbitrary detention, torture, and cruel treatment to war. The administration has "treated the most fundamental commitments of the rule of law as if they were optional protocols to be jettisoned in the face of the threat of terrorism."[30] The measures violate the rule of law's requirement for "equality, transparency, fair procedures, individual culpability, clear rules...and respect for basic human rights."[31] The measures instead impose "double standards on the most vulnerable, operate in secret, [deny] fair trials, [impose] guilt by association, [... and] assert unchecked unilateral power."[32]

The great irony, however, is that the measures are defended as necessary for the sake of our security, but have only made us "more vulnerable to attack."[33] They have "wasted" resources that might have been used more effectively, alienated allies, and "provided recruitment fodder for our enemies."[34] None of the interrogations appears to have produced any significant intelligence not already available.[35] And claims about the handful

---

[27] Cole & Lobel, LESS SAFE, LESS FREE, *supra* note 1.

[28] I credit Ben Goold with the observation that U.S. legal academics often produce work that straddles the worlds of scholarship and nonfiction for the general reader. I note that in this case, LESS SAFE, LESS FREE was published by a trade rather than university press, and was widely reviewed in electronic and print media venues.

[29] Cole & Lobel, *supra* note 1, at 1.

[30] Ibid. at 2.

[31] Ibid.

[32] Ibid. at 1.

[33] Ibid. at 2.

[34] Ibid.

[35] Ibid. at 122–28.

of attacks that were thwarted on the basis of information from interrogation are cast seriously into doubt.[36] Instead of employing such conspicuous yet counterproductive measures, the administration should have devoted more of its resources to less visible but more effective measures. These include the safeguarding of sensitive material sites and bolstering regulation of related industries. They might also have done more about nuclear disarmament, at home and abroad.

In the process of making the case against the preventive paradigm, Cole and Lobel employ all four common arguments for liberal legality noted above. They invoke the compatibility claim by asserting that a more effective counterterrorism strategy would recognize the rule of law as "an asset, not an obstacle" to security.[37] Their larger argument combines the balance, proportionality, and practicality arguments. They contend that while it is "often wrong to sacrifice liberty, freedom, and rights in the search for security, [...] trade-offs are inevitable [and] in some circumstances sacrifices in liberty may be warranted if they can promise substantial improvements in security." Yet the choice to be made is "not simply between liberty and security, but between effective security measures and counterproductive ones. The administration's coercive preventive model not only sacrifices liberty but compromises our security."[38]

Notably, Cole and Lobel are also alive to the role played by the fear of mass terror as a motivator for the use of extreme measures. "The preventive paradigm," they note, "is premised on a claim that ordinary cost-benefit calculations are not appropriate when the potential risks are catastrophic."[39] Indeed, often the most extreme measures—coercive interrogation, rendition—are "invariably defended with some version of the familiar 'ticking time bomb' hypothetical" in which the measures are necessary to thwart a mass-casualty attack.[40] The authors point out that the Bush administration's National Security Strategies argue against limits on the state's use of force based explicitly on the threat posed by "suicide terrorists and weapons of mass destruction."[41] They also note similar logic at play in public discourse. *Washington Post* editorial writer Charles Krauthammer argued for the use of torture in a widely cited 2005 article in the *Weekly Standard*, on the basis of a nuclear ticking bomb scenario. A number of commentators have argued for preventive detention on the basis of "doomsday scenarios," including Paul Rosenzweig of the Heritage Foundation, Yale Law Professor Bruce Ackerman, and Michael Chertoff, Director of Homeland Security in the Bush administration.[42] The claim in each case is, as Cole and Lobel note, that "the increased threat posed by weapons of mass destruction warrants action on less clear evidence of a future attack."[43]

---

36 Ibid.
37 Ibid. at 17.
38 Ibid.
39 Ibid. at 189.
40 Ibid. at 4.
41 Ibid. at 4.
42 Ibid. at 189.
43 Ibid. at 190.

In response to this logic, Cole and Lobel seek to characterize the fear of mass terror as a form of "overreach," or emotional overreaction. Drawing upon social science research, they suggest that "emotional factors are likely to cause us to overestimate risks based on vivid, emotionally laden events, such as terrorist attacks, and to underestimate costs and risks that are abstract, statistical, and likely to arise in the long term."[44] They devote a chapter of the book to the psychology of perception about risks relating to emotional images and events.[45] They make a clear case that both citizens and governments easily overstate risks, and acquiesce in coercive practices in response. These in turn lead to a "slippery slope" in which the practices become more widespread and coercive.

Yet the question of the likelihood of mass terror itself is not engaged in any depth. Cole and Lobel characterize it as a "low probability event," but without *establishing* this. On the contrary, when they do confront the question directly, they remain agnostic in similar terms to the ICJ:

> It may well be that the potentially catastrophic dangers posed by al-Qaeda and other terrorist groups shift the cost-benefit analysis. But the highly emotional climate created by the fear of terrorism also makes the likelihood of balancing error event greater than before.[46]

The authors are not therefore seeking to defend rights on the basis of *evidence* of the low probability of the event—and thus the absence of a growing threat to security. They defend them by arguing that when "ad hoc balancing" is left to members of government, the legislature, or the executive, they are "likely to overestimate the benefits of preventive measures and to downplay or ignore altogether the long-term costs to both liberty and security."[47]

Cole and Lobel's work thus sets out a forceful argument against extreme measures. It offers a more comprehensive case for reform than those offered in other texts under review in this chapter by inviting readers to question certain measures as impractical, excessive, or unjustified. It also goes a step further by identifying the fear of mass terror as an important factor in the embrace of those measures, and encourages readers to be critical of it. The argument might, however, have been rendered more forceful still had they gone beyond characterizing the fear of mass terror as an overreaction and offered evidence and argument as to why mass terror is neither imminent nor likely. But this is admittedly a limited criticism of what is otherwise a very valuable contribution to the case for reform.

---

[44] Ibid. at 191.

[45] Ibid. ch. 8.

[46] Ibid. at 201.

[47] Ibid.

Mark Danner

Mark Danner is a prominent U.S. journalist and author who has written frequently in defense of liberal legality for a wider public in a number of high-profile venues. One of his recent efforts to advocate for reform, set out over the course of two lengthy articles in the *New York Review of Books* in 2009, provides an important example of an argument that might have been made more persuasive by engaging the harbinger theory.[48]

In the first article, Danner sought to share with a wider audience the findings of the International Committee of the Red Cross *Report on the Treatment of Fourteen High Value Detainees in CIA Custody*.[49] It recounts in vivid detail evidence about the use of coercive measures by the CIA and U.S. military at Guantanamo and various black sites, and the frequency of their use. It notes the ICRC's position that the acts amounted torture or cruel and unusual treatment, and a violation of international law. Danner devotes much of his discussion in both articles to addressing the administration's role in orchestrating these events. He asserts that on the basis of the evidence in the report, and many other sources, "we know that the decision to [carry out torture] was taken at the highest level of the American government and carried out with full knowledge and support of its most senior officials."[50]

In Danner's view, such findings rationally compel certain responses. One would expect the U.S. government to abandon its policies around "coercive interrogation," which Obama did upon taking office. One would also expect an official repudiation of the legality and propriety of such practices, which is beginning to occur. One might also hope to see that those who ordered and carried out torture are held accountable, through some form of "societal sanction," which has not occurred. But most crucially, Danner suggests that one would expect that

> some judgment [would] be made, based on the most credible of information compiled and analyzed and weighed by the most credible of bodies, about what these policies actually accomplished: how they advanced the interests of the country, if indeed they did advance them, and how they hurt them.[51]

Until this judgment is made, questions about torture will remain. What was gained from using it? And was it really effective? At the moment, these issues remain politicized. President Obama has said that torture is neither legal nor effective. Former Vice President Cheney and other Bush administration officials deny this. They claim that waterboarding

---

48 Mark Danner, *US Torture: Voices from the Black Sites*, N.Y. REV. OF BOOKS, Apr. 9, 2009; and *The Red Cross Torture Report: What It Means*, N.Y. REV. OF BOOKS, Apr. 30, 2009 ("The Red Cross").

49 International Committee of the Red Cross, *ICRC Report on the Treatment of Fourteen "High Value Detainees" in CIA Custody*, ICRC 2009, at http://www.nybooks.com/media/doc/2010/04/22/icrc-report.pdf.

50 "The Red Cross," *supra* note 48.

51 Ibid.

and other measures were effective in preventing further attacks. Upon review of secret evidence, Obama insists the "facts don't bear [Cheney] out." Cheney and others reply that the point cannot be settled without revealing information that must remain secret. Danner cites numerous admissions by high-level officials and military personal casting doubt on the quality of the intelligence gathered. Either way, in public discourse and opinion, the question remains caught in an impasse. So long as it does, Danner fears, torture or other coercive measures will be used more readily in the future.

In Danner's view, the only way to move beyond this impasse is to settle the question of whether torture really worked by providing "authoritative and convincing information about how it was really used and what it really achieved."[52] Neither the various reports by liberally inclined NGOs nor the press are capable of producing the kind of "bipartisan, broadly credible, and politically decisive effort" that is required to "pronounce authoritatively" on the issue. In Danner's view, only the creation of a bipartisan commission on the order of the Watergate Select Committee or the 9/11 Commission could settle the question, definitively and credibly, of "whether or not torture made Americans safer."

Danner's proposal is forceful and timely. He points to a critical source of widespread misunderstanding about torture, and a potential source of support for its use in the future. But, notably, his proposal seeks to curb the future use of torture without challenging in any significant way the beliefs that made its recent use seem necessary. In other words, Danner seeks to discredit the use of torture in extreme circumstances, but not the notion that we *are* in an extreme situation. Indeed, the very urgency of his proposal arises at least in part from the sense that the United States remains in a kind of exceptional state, or could return to one in short order.

This is not to overlook the importance of his contribution, or others like it. Although he focuses on torture, Danner also challenges the larger claim that current threats warrant the use of extreme measures by showing that those measures may not actually render any practical benefit. But although Danner's approach offers a persuasive case for reform, it might have been more persuasive still if he had probed the rationale for torture a stage further. Rather than ending at the point of debating the utility of torture and other measures, or asking what we gained from torture, Danner might also have asked: why did we believe we *needed* to torture in the first place?

## Part 2. Liberal Deference to Claims About Mass Terror

While many liberals have played down or ignored the prospect of mass terror in their arguments for reform, some begin with it as a central assumption. Among this group, some have demonstrated a vivid sense of the threat at issue, but maintained a commitment to core human or constitutional rights. In other cases, the threat is cited as a need

52 Ibid.

for occasional suspensions of core rights, but subject to the rule of law. This part focuses briefly on examples in both categories: Ronald Dworkin in the first, and Michael Ignatieff and Bruce Ackerman in the second.

By paying heed to the harbinger theory, the authors in both groups can be seen to undermine their own case for reform by legitimizing fears and beliefs about the prospect of mass terror. While the arguments in each case are persuasive, the collective effect of their deference to catastrophic fears is to bolster the validity of the perception that a significant threat remains, and a new, more radical approach to security is in order.

### I. DWORKIN'S DEFENSE OF LIBERAL LEGALITY

Dworkin (who died in 2013) was a leading liberal law scholar and public intellectual whose extensive writings on counterterrorism law appeared in the *New York Review of Books* and national newspapers, as well as in works of mainstream nonfiction. Yet, in the course of setting out an eloquent and persuasive defense of civil liberties in the wake of 9/11, Dworkin concedes the apocalyptic dimension of outstanding threats to national security. The concession is initially quite nuanced. He is careful to remain agnostic about the probability or magnitude of another attack. Yet he clearly acknowledges the possibility that it may be quite serious, and for this reason liberal jurists ought to attempt to defend rights in light of this new reality.

For example, in a 2002 *New York Review of Books* essay, "The Threat to Patriotism," Dworkin surveys a number of extreme measures employed by the Bush administration in the fall of 2001.[53] Arguing along the same lines as Cole and Lobel, Dworkin insists that while the threat may be great, the necessity for such measures ought to be justified individually. But the argument is framed within a larger concession to the immensity of the threat posed by mass terror. "Do we really face such extreme danger from terrorism," he asks, "that we must act unjustly? That is a difficult question. We cannot yet accurately gauge the actual power of the linked groups of terrorist organizations and cells that apparently aim to kill as many Americans as possible." He then asserts:

> But al-Qaeda killed, by latest reckoning, approximately 3,000 people in minutes on September 11, which is a quarter of the number of murders in the entire country in 1999. If they or some other terrorist organization has or gains access to nuclear, chemical, or biological weapons and the means to use them, then the threat to us would be truly enormous. It would justify unusual and, in themselves, unfair measures if the government thought that these would substantially reduce the risk of catastrophe. Even then, however, it would be imperative to permit only the smallest curtailment of traditional rights that could reasonably be thought necessary, and to attempt to mitigate the unfairness of these measures so far as safety allows.

---

[53] Ronald Dworkin, *The Threat to Patriotism*, N.Y. REV. OF BOOKS, Feb. 28, 2002.

Dworkin concludes that the government has thus far failed on both counts, and urges reform on the proportionality and necessity test. He also appears to concede that a suspension of the rule of law may be justified in such extreme cases. The argument is thus not over whether a drastic set of measures ought to be employed, but whether their necessity can be justified.

Later, Dworkin will tend to insist more clearly on principle—on non-derogable rights as an absolute limit on how unfair or unjust the government can be.[54] But even then, he continues to pay heed to fears of mass terror. His next article in the *New York Review of Books* the following year begins:

> Two years after the September 11 catastrophe Americans remain in great danger. The danger is of two kinds, of which the first—further terrorist attacks—is obvious. Well-financed terrorists, who live and undergo training in various foreign countries, are determined to kill Americans and are willing to die in order to do so. If they gain access to nuclear weapons, they would be able to inflict even more terrible harm.[55]

(The second danger is the one posed to civil liberties.) The remainder of this lengthy piece makes no further mention of the threat. The prospect of mass terror is asserted as "obvious" at the outset, and the assumption is never revisited. Further rights violations are canvased. The Bush administration is advised to grant detainees the protection of either the laws of war or the criminal law. The entire discussion is carried out under the larger assumption that the threat posed is so great as to place it somewhere between a crime and a war. The problem calls for nothing short of a "new legal system for terror that can one day be encoded in some new set of international conventions." The system would combine the constraints of the two older models, and reflect a liberal rule of law.

The larger point is that Dworkin concedes throughout these pieces that circumstances call for new measures, and a new approach. The debate is only about which new measures can be justified and how. The issue for Dworkin, as for many other liberal jurists, is how far the state can go in employing force in this model, and what tests, rules, and principles should apply. The question is thus not whether a new, more pre-emptive approach is in order, but what it should entail.

## II. IGNATIEFF, ACKERMAN, AND LESSER EVILS

I turn now to Michael Ignatieff and Bruce Ackerman, but this category might also include authors such as Oran Gross, Mark Tushnet, and Eric Posner and Adrianne Vermuele.[56] I should note that authors in this category straddle a fine line between

---

54 Ronald Dworkin, *Terror and the Attack on Civil Liberties*, N.Y. REV. OF BOOKS, Nov. 17, 2003.

55 Ibid.

56 *See*, e.g., Oren Gross, *The Prohibition on Torture and the Limits of the Law*, in Sanford Levinson, ed., TORTURE: A COLLECTION (Oxford University Press, 2004); Mark Tushnet, *Defending Korematsu?: Reflections on*

illiberal advocates of extreme measures and defenders of liberal legality. Like Posner, Dershowitz, and others, Ignatieff and Ackerman argue for the necessity of certain measures, while insisting on the need to subject them to the rule of law and to judicial and public oversight. In contrast to Posner and Dershowitz, however, Ignatieff and Ackerman do not endorse the use of torture or cruel and unusual treatment, even if what they propose amount to this. The distinction I seek to draw among members of this group is indeed debatable. But I include the work of both Ignatieff and Ackerman because it *purports* to argue for reform in defense of liberal legality, and on the basis of a fear of catastrophic threats.

## Michael Ignatieff

Of all the writers in this category, Ignatieff offers perhaps the most vivid set of threat scenarios, and argues for the widest range of extraordinary measures. He set out his case in a widely read 2004 article in the *New York Times Magazine*, "Lesser Evils,"[57] later expanded into a best-selling book.[58] The article begins by posing the question of what it would mean for the United States to lose the war on terror:

> Consider the consequences of a second major attack on the mainland United States—the detonation of a radiological or dirty bomb, perhaps, or a low-yield nuclear device or a chemical strike in a subway. Any of these events could cause death, devastation and panic on a scale that would make 9/11 seem like a pale prelude. After such an attack, a pall of mourning, melancholy, anger and fear would hang over our public life for a generation.[59]

The possibility rests on the assumption that such an attack is technologically well within the means of terrorists. Without supporting or expanding on the assertion, Ignatieff writes: "An attack of this sort is already in the realm of possibility. The recipes for making ultimate weapons are on the Internet, and the matériel required is available for the right price."[60] The result would be the end of democracy:

> A succession of large-scale attacks would pull at the already-fragile tissue of trust that binds us to our leadership and destroy the trust we have in one another. Once the zones of devastation were cordoned off and the bodies buried, we might find ourselves, in short order, living in a national-security state on continuous alert, with

---

*Civil Liberties in Wartime*, 2003 WIS. L. REV. 273; and Eric Posner & Adrian Vermuele, TERROR IN THE BALANCE: SECURITY, LIBERTY AND THE COURTS (Oxford: Oxford University Press, 2007).

57 Michael Ignatieff, *Lesser Evils*, N.Y. TIMES MAGAZINE, May 2, 2004.

58 Michael Ignatieff, THE LESSER EVIL: POLITICAL ETHICS IN AN AGE OF TERROR (Princeton NJ: Princeton University Press, 2004).

59 Ignatieff, *Lesser Evils, supra* note 57.

60 Ibid.

> sealed borders, constant identity checks and permanent detention camps for dissidents and aliens. Our constitutional rights might disappear from our courts, while torture might reappear in our interrogation cells. The worst of it is that government would not have to impose tyranny on a cowed populace. We would demand it for our own protection.[61]

For this reason, a series of measures are necessary; indeed "[t]o defeat evil, we may have to traffic in evils: indefinite detention of suspects, coercive interrogations, targeted assassinations, even pre-emptive war."[62]

But in each case, Ignatieff suggests that we remain committed to the rule of law, seeking to "strike a balance" between being tethered by law and dispensing with it altogether. Those in preventive detention ought to receive the right to counsel and a form of review before military tribunals. Torture ought to remain prohibited, but not lesser forms of coercive interrogation: including "forms of sleep deprivation that do not result in lasting harm to mental or physical health, together with disinformation and disorientation (like keeping prisoners in hoods) that would produce stress."[63] The President's power to make war, or to carry out targeted killing ought to be subjected clear rules, including a requirement that force may be used only where "the danger that must be pre-empted is imminent."[64]

Clearly the necessity for the various measures hinges on Ignatieff's assumptions about the imminence of mass terror, and the nature of the threat it poses. His blueprint for counterterrorism policy is distinguished from authoritarian legalism only to the degree that it avoids an explicit embrace of torture and seeks to subject executive power to judicial and congressional oversight.

The larger point, however, is that Ignatieff argues for limits on the state's use of force while doing a great deal to bolster the kind of fear that is used to justify the state's use of force. Against the grain, then, of the larger liberal position he purports to maintain, the implied thrust of his argument is quite clearly that current threats warrant more extreme, illiberal measures.

### Bruce Ackerman

A professor at Yale Law School, Ackerman is a prominent figure in the U.S. legal academy. In 2004, he published a controversial article entitled "The Emergency Constitution,"[65]

---

61 Ibid.

62 Ibid.

63 Ibid.

64 Ibid.

65 Bruce Ackerman, *The Emergency Constitution*, 113 YALE L.J. 1029 (2004).

later expanded into a widely-read book, *Before the Next Attack: Preserving Civil Liberties in the Age of Terror* (2006).[66] The article began in this way:

> Terrorist attacks will be a recurring part of our future. The balance of technology has shifted, making it possible for a small band of zealots to wreak devastation where we least expect it—not on a plane next time, but with poison gas in the subway or a biotoxin in the water supply. The attack of September 11 is the prototype for many events that will litter the twenty-first century.

A few pages later, he asserts "It may only be a matter of time before a suitcase A-bomb obliterates a major American city."[67] Ackerman reiterated these fears in 2010:

> Smaller and smaller groups can obtain more lethal weapons at a lower and lower cost—creating a continuing risk of devastating attack. Even if Al Qaeda disintegrates, fringe groups from other places will rise to fill the gap. We won't need to look far to find them. If a tiny band of native extremists blasted the Federal Building in Oklahoma City, others will detonate suitcase A-bombs as they become available....[68]

In both his earlier book, *Before the Next Attack*, and his more recent *Decline of the American Republic*, Ackerman has argued that without a clearer, more effective framework for emergency government in place, civil liberties in the United States and other Western nations will suffer a permanent erosion as leaders respond to each attack by instituting excessive but permanent measures that ought to be temporary. He proposes that to be better prepared for the inevitability of more catastrophic attacks in the future, Congress should pass legislation that would function as a kind of "emergency constitution." It would authorize the use of a range of extraordinary measures that Ackerman only sketches in outline, including the power to arrest and detain without reasonable grounds and without charge. He contemplates a situation in which hundreds or even thousands may be detained on mere suspicion, but in which compensation would be provided for the many innocent people likely to be affected. Ackerman is, however, categorical in ruling out the use of torture or cruelty. The scheme would serve several purposes. It would provide a genuine security function (preventing a follow-up attack). It would reassure the public of the continuing power and control of the government. And it would ensure that emergency powers remain subject to the rule of law and avoid becoming permanent.

To do this, the emergency constitution would be subject to what Ackerman calls the "super-majoritarian escalator." An initial set of emergency powers would be limited to a

---

66 Bruce Ackerman, Before the Next Attack: Preserving Civil Liberties in the Age of Terror (New Haven CT: Yale University Press, 2006).

67 Ackerman, *The Emergency Constitution, supra* note 65, at 1036.

68 Bruce Ackerman, The Decline and Fall of the American Republic (Cambridge MA: Harvard University Press, 2010), at 167.

week or two, and then require escalating majorities in Congress or Parliament to extend the emergency in two-month intervals—to the point where an 80 or 90 percent majority would be required to extend it. This would make a permanent emergency unlikely; compel prosecutors to justify ongoing detentions; and defray pressure on the judiciary in attempting to oversee executive power in a time of emergency.

Ackerman's argument emphasizes the need for "temporary reassurance" in the face of "episodic terror."[69] His primary concern is with emergency or extreme measures becoming permanent. Yet, in a fundamental sense, his argument for emergency law is premised on the assumption that further mass terror on the scale of 9/11 or greater is *inevitable*. As with Ignatieff, then, Ackerman makes a plausible case for liberal limits on executive action in extreme circumstances; but in the process, both authors also promote a sense of permanent emergency that is ultimately not conducive to the cause of liberal reform.

## Conclusion

Over the course of the past decade, reform advocates have set out a sophisticated and often persuasive set of arguments in defense of liberal legality in several venues. Yet across the board, arguments for reform have tended not to challenge two key assumptions. One is a belief in the possible imminence of mass terror. The other is a belief that the nature and magnitude of the threat warrants a shift to a more preemptive approach, entailing the use of a new, more elaborate set of security measures.

The failure to challenge these assumptions has kept the debate about rights and security centered on the question of appropriate measures and focused the discussion on the proportionality and efficacy of those measures rather than questioning their necessity. This chapter has sought to demonstrate the limitations of such an approach as a means of persuasion. It laid the groundwork for a larger claim that liberals might have made a stronger argument in favor of rights by challenging beliefs about mass terror more directly. The next chapter explores this alternative approach.

[69] Ibid. at 1045.

# 6

## An Alternative Case for Reform

THIS CHAPTER PROPOSES a different case for reform of extreme or invasive counter-terrorism measures from the common approaches surveyed in the last chapter. The case it sets out is based on a challenge to three propositions:

i. 9/11 marked a new order of terror, one in which an attack on a large urban center in North America is likely to occur at some point soon on the same scale or greater;
ii. given the gravity of the threat, more invasive measures are necessary; and
iii. even if larger attacks are not likely, such measures are still justified on the basis that terrorism presents a special kind of threat, warranting a lower tolerance for the risk it presents.

To challenge these claims, the chapter unfolds in three parts.

The first part canvasses argument and evidence as to why *mass* terror (involving several hundred or thousands of casualties) through the use of nuclear or biological weapons is highly unlikely in the foreseeable future. It also demonstrates that acts involving chemical or radiological terror, while somewhat less improbable than nuclear or biological terror, are likely to be far more limited in scale than is often feared. This part of the chapter explores a diverse body of literature, offering a synthesis of arguments that have not often been explored outside of the scientific or expert literature.

The second part explores the nature of the threat posed by terrorism not involving WMDs. Drawing primarily on the work of John Mueller and Mark Stewart, it canvasses a number of reasons why non-state actors since 9/11 have been limited in their capacities to carry out attacks much smaller in scale than 9/11 and therefore pose a threat more consistent with terrorism prior to 2001. It also addresses the potential counterclaim that large-scale attacks since 9/11 have been avoided at least in part by the use of invasive measures such as torture, targeted killing, and mass secret surveillance. Shifting focus somewhat, this part then concludes by considering the prospect of cyberterror and its possible use as a tool to inflict mass casualties. Conceding that cyberterror can be used to cause serious economic damage, the discussion points to a consensus among experts as to the implausibility of this form of terror as a means of killing and injuring large numbers of people, if it is in fact capable of inflicting any casualties directly.

Finally, the third part will argue that in the absence of the harbinger theory, and in light of evidence that future acts of terror in North America are likely to be no more serious or frequent than events prior to 9/11, the case for authoritarian measures becomes more difficult to sustain. Advocates for reform may still, however, face a further obstacle in a form of reasoning that may become pervasive as the harbinger theory loses salience. Some might argue that authoritarian measures are still justified on the basis that terrorism represents a special kind of threat, regardless of the number of casualties involved. Thus, even if the impact of an attack were to be low compared to 9/11, it might still seem significant (striking, horrible, tragic) in a way that distinguishes it from any other form of criminal activity. On this view, we might justifiably perceive an act of terror such as the Boston bombing, or the bombing of a plane killing two hundred or three hundred passengers, as something greater than crime but less than war. We are justified in lowering our tolerance for this risk, and curtailing certain liberties in an effort to avoid it.

The chapter offers two responses to this line of reasoning. One is to suggest that we ought to resist lowering our tolerance of terrorism on the basis that the risk it presents is comparable to risks we accept in other facets of modern life. The other is that we ought to resist treating terrorism as a special kind of threat because it is *essentially* criminal in nature and not significantly greater than the threat posed by other serious forms of criminal conduct. As a consequence of both arguments, the chapter concludes that terrorism should be addressed as a form of crime rather than as war or a hybrid of the two. A more sensible and effective way to respond to terrorism is through the conventional protections and limits of the criminal law and, as Kent Roach and others have suggested, through the regulation of sensitive sites and materials.[1]

---

[1] Kent Roach, SEPTEMBER 11: CONSEQUENCES FOR CANADA (Montreal: McGill-Queens University Press, 2003); David Cole & Jules Lobel, LESS SAFE, LESS FREE: WHY AMERICA IS LOSING THE WAR ON TERROR (New York: New Press, 2007).

## Part 1. Challenging Assumptions About the Imminence of WMD Terror

### I. WHY NUCLEAR TERROR IS MUCH LESS LIKELY THAN MANY SUGGEST

Chapter 4 surveyed the work of a school of experts who argue for the imminent prospect of nuclear terror. As noted in that chapter, a number of the authors have tended to ignore a long-standing tradition of credible, contrary opinion. The chapter also noted that a belief in the rising likelihood of nuclear terror commonly rests on four assumptions:

1. the prodigious supply of poorly guarded fissile material;
2. the availability of information about how to build a nuclear bomb;
3. the ease with which a bomb could be built, delivered, and reliably exploded (especially a crude "gun-type" bomb using highly enriched uranium (HEU)); and
4. the fact that al Qaeda and other groups have been known to seek one.

The discussion that follows draws briefly on a body of work that offers a contrary perspective. Key contributors to this corpus of skeptical of opinion include John Mueller, a political scientist and historian of the nuclear bomb;[2] Michael Levi, a recent Fellow for Science and Technology at the U.S. Counsel for Foreign Relations;[3] Steven Younger, a nuclear weapons designer for the U.S. government;[4] and Swiss nuclear scientists Christoph Wirz and Emmanuel Egger.[5] Often cited documents among this group include the first volume of the U.S. congressional Gilmore Commission (1999),[6] and a 1987 collection of papers by nuclear scientists and other experts, *Preventing Nuclear Terrorism*,[7] which contains one of the most exhaustive pre-9/11 studies on the obstacles facing a non-state actor in building a nuclear bomb.[8]

---

[2] Mueller addresses the challenges confronting the would-be nuclear terrorist in OVERBLOWN: HOW POLITICIANS AND THE TERRORISM INDUSTRY INFLATE NATIONAL SECURITY THREATS, AND WHY WE BELIEVE THEM (New York: Free Press, 2006) and ATOMIC OBSESSION: NUCLEAR ALARMISM FROM HIROSHIMA TO AL QAEDA (London: Oxford University Press, 2009), and further explores the probability and risk of nuclear terror in a book co-authored with Mark Stewart, TERROR, SECURITY AND MONEY: BALANCING THE RISKS, BENEFITS, AND COSTS OF HOMELAND SECURITY (London: Oxford University Press, 2011, Kindle edition).

[3] Michael Levi, ON NUCLEAR TERRORISM (Cambridge MA: Harvard University Press, 2007).

[4] Steven Younger, ENDANGERED SPECIES: HOW WE CAN AVOID MASS DESTRUCTION AND BUILD A LASTING PEACE (New York: Harper Perennial, 2008).

[5] Christoph Wirz and Emmanuel Egger, *Use of Nuclear and Radiological Weapons by Terrorists?*, 87:859 INT'L REV. RED CROSS 497 (2005).

[6] Gilmore Commission (Advisory Panel to Assess Domestic Response Capabilities for Terrorism Involving Weapons of Mass Destruction), *First Annual Report: Assessing the Threat*, Dec. 15, 1999, at www.rand.org/nsrd/terrpanel.

[7] Paul Leventhal & Yonah Alexander, eds., PREVENTING NUCLEAR TERRORISM: THE REPORT AND PAPERS OF THE INTERNATIONAL TASK FORCE ON PREVENTION OF NUCLEAR TERRORISM (New York: Lexington Books, 1987).

[8] J. Carson Mark, Theodore Taylor, Eugene Eyster, William Maraman & Jacob Wechsler, *Can Terrorists Build Nuclear Weapons?*, in PREVENTING NUCLEAR TERRORISM, ibid.

Perhaps the single overriding observation among members of the skeptical school is that although the prospect of nuclear terror seems simple and plausible in theory, it entails so many significant obstacles in practice that it is extremely unlikely to occur in the foreseeable future. Levi and Mueller, for example, have catalogued up to 20 separate stages involved in the process, and have suggested separate odds for overcoming potential obstacles at each stage.[9] As Mueller notes, many nuclear terror alarmists acknowledge the obstacles but note that in theory each is "not impossible" to surmount. In response, he suggests that "while it may be 'not impossible' to surmount each individual step, the likelihood that a group could surmount a series of them quickly becomes vanishingly small."[10]

A further common observation among this group relates to a point on which authors on both sides of the debate agree. The production of either HEU or weapons-grade plutonium is essentially beyond the capacity of a non-state actor.[11] (Either is essential for a bomb.) Both sides thus agree that if a terror group is to obtain a nuclear bomb, it must obtain either the bomb itself or the fissile material to make one from another source.

## Why the Supply of Fissile Material Poses Less of a Risk Than Is Often Alleged

Writing in 1998, Stanley Jacobs cast doubt on the danger posed by terrorists stealing an intact nuclear weapon. "A diverted device," he writes, "could be used directly only if the terrorists had access to the appropriate resources for arming and firing or otherwise delivering the device."[12] This usually involves a "coded sequence of events, possibly involving two or more trained persons." Some weapons require certain conditions—a certain number of rotations of given parts, correct temperatures, locations, and other such variables. A common feature from the 1960s onward is the use of "permissive action links," or protective systems, which require coded signals for detonation. As Graham Allison and others have noted, the obstacles posed by these codes and systems can be overcome (e.g., bribing officials at the source). Yet, this gives rise to further risks, including detection and betrayal.[13] Terrorists might also seek to remove the fissile material within these devices, but for Jacobs, "this seems only marginally credible" given the challenges entailed

---

[9] *See* Levi, ON NUCLEAR TERRORISM, *supra* note 3, ch. 3, and Mueller, *The Atomic Terrorist: Assessing the Likelihood*,(International Commission on Nuclear Non-Proliferation and Disarmament, 2009), at 13.

[10] Mueller, ibid. at 12. *See also* Levi, *supra* note 3 at 7; Younger, *supra* note 4, at 87, and the Gilmore Commission, *supra* note 6, at 21 & 29.

[11] *See* the discussion of Allison, Bunn, and Ferguson and Potter in Chapter 4.

[12] Stanley Jacobs, *The Nuclear Threat as a Terrorist Option*, 10: 4 TERRORISM & POL. VIOLENCE 149 (1998), at 151.

[13] *See also* Mueller, an earlier version of *The Atomic Terrorist: Assessing the Likelihood* (2008) at 7, at http://polisci.osu.edu/faculty/jmueller/APSACHGO.PDF; and William Langewiesche, THE ATOMIC BAZAAR: THE RISE OF THE NUCLEAR POOR (New York: Farrar Straus and Giroux, 2007), at 33–48, cited in Mueller.

in building a nuclear bomb, which is "highly sophisticated in terms of construction geometries"—a point explored further below.

The first report of the U.S. congressional Gilmore Commission in 1999 addressed concerns with respect to Russian stockpiles, which at the time were thought to be the most likely source of stolen weapons or material. The Commission found that "Russian strategic and tactical weapons are perhaps more secure than had been initially feared."[14] Despite the fact that protocols around the transfer and maintenance of Russian weapons had raised concerns, the authors cited the same obstacles noted by Jacobs and others as to the use of stolen weapons—locks, coded systems, and other protective mechanisms.[15] The Commission also sought to qualify concerns about the status of some 250 tons of HEU and 50 tons of weapons-grade plutonium known to be in Russia's possession. The black market for such materials was "less worrying" given the fact that "[b]etween 1992 and 1996, more than 1,000 claims were made involving the illicit sale and smuggling of nuclear material; however, only six instances were substantiated, and none of those involved the quantities needed to construct an effective 'homemade' device that could cause mass casualties—thereby suggesting that the black market, if it exists at all, is limited in size and grossly exaggerated in impact."[16]

More recent assessments corroborate these findings. They also address concerns about Pakistan, and the fear that a sizable black market might exist, given the discovery of the A.Q. Khan network in 2003.

With respect to Russia, Muller, Langewiesche, Younger, and others have questioned the continuing threat posed by its stockpiles of older or smaller weapons. Mueller cites frequent and adamant denials on the part of Russian military officials as to the possibility that terror groups may have obtained some of the known KGB "suitcase nukes," which have fewer security mechanisms. Citing a 2002 study by the Center for Nonproliferation Studies, Mueller asserts that it is "unlikely that any of these devices have actually been lost and that, regardless, their effectiveness would be very low or even non-existent because they require continual maintenance."[17] Most of the smaller bombs, which are more likely to be stolen, use plutonium, which emits enough radiation to be easily detected "by passive sensors at ports and other points of transmission."[18] Moreover, as Mueller points

---

14 Gilmore Commission, *supra* note 6, at 29. The Commission also cites Karl-Heinz Kamp, *Nuclear Terrorism Is Not the Core Problem*, 40:4 *Survival* 168 (Winter 1998–99), at 170.

15 The Commission relies for this point on Peter deLeon et al., THE THREAT OF NUCLEAR TERRORISM: A REEXAMINATION, N-2706 (Santa Monica CA.: RAND, 1988).

16 Gilmore Commission, *supra* note 6, at 30.

17 Mueller, *The Atomic Terrorist* (2008), *supra* note 13, at 6. Mueller also cites Langewiesche, THE ATOMIC BAZAAR, *supra* note 13, at 19; Center for Nonproliferation Studies, *Suitcase Nukes: A Reassessment* (Monterey, CA: Monterey Institute of International Studies, Sept. 22, 2002), at 4 and 12; and Jeffrey Smith & David Hoffman, *No Support Found for Report of Lost Russian Suitcase-Sized Nuclear Weapons*, WASH. POST, Sept. 5, 1997.

18 Mueller, *The Atomic Terrorist* (2008), *supra* note 13, at 6. *See also* Richard Rhodes, TWILIGHT OF THE BOMBS: RECENT CHALLENGES, NEW DANGERS, AND THE PROSPECTS FOR A WORLD WITHOUT NUCLEAR WEAPONS (New York: Vintage Books, 2010). Rhodes also notes, at 288, that plutonium is "far more susceptible to predetonation during assembly" than HEU.

out, the issue of bribery is more complex upon closer examination.[19] In both Russia and Pakistan, potential officials risking the prospect of taking a bribe in these cases would face certain death if caught. Mueller speculates that the sums required to secure cooperation of even a small group of people would likely be quite large. And as noted, with more people involved, the probability of detection or disruption rises.

Younger concedes the potential for theft or illicit transfer of weapons or materials in nuclear states, but asserts that "regardless of what is reported in the news, all nuclear nations take the security of their weapons very seriously."[20] One example he provides is the Russian nuclear weapons laboratory at Arzamas. It is protected by "a tripled array of fences nearly 20 feet tall that are regularly patrolled by guards and dogs and monitored by radar and other sensors."[21] Bribery is a possibility, but "there would still be the problem of getting the weapon out of the country, a complex operation requiring planning and a knowledge of who needs to be bribed and when."[22] Even if a weapon were obtained, the locks would require special know-how, information, or equipment and "*very few* people have access to that."[23]

Nuclear physicists Christoph Wirz and Emmanuel Egger concur. Existing nuclear states keep material and weaponry "well protected and guarded," such that "a theft would involve many risks and great efforts in terms of personnel, finances and organization."[24] In the case of stolen weapons, they note a series of protective mechanisms cited by others, but with one notable addition. Both Russian and U.S. nuclear weapons possess systems that will "destroy critical components or render them useless if someone handles the weapon improperly or tries to open it." If a group of terrorists managed to open a nuclear weapon without destroying it and removed the fissile material, there would arise a further possibility that "the quantity will not be sufficient for a primitive design; to obtain enough, several weapons would have to be stolen."[25]

As for other weapons or material in either Pakistan or Russia, Mueller and others have pointed out that each nation has "an intense interest in controlling any weapons on its territory since is likely to be a prime target of any illicit use by terrorist groups."[26] Russia has Chechen rebels to contend with. Pakistan's government has any number of extremist groups to guard against. In 2008, summing up the recent history of lost material, Mueller writes: "in the last ten years or so, there have been 10 known thefts of highly enriched

[19] Mueller, *The Atomic Terrorist* (2008), *supra* note 13, at 12.
[20] Younger, ENDANGERED SPECIES, *supra* note 4, at 93.
[21] Ibid.
[22] Ibid.
[23] Ibid.
[24] Wirz & Egger, *Use of Nuclear and Radiological Weapons, supra* note 5, at 502.
[25] Ibid.
[26] Mueller, *The Atomic Terrorist* (2008), *supra* note 13, at 6. *See also* Gavin Cameron, *Weapons of Mass Destruction Terrorism Research: Past and Future*, in Andres Silke, ed., TERRORISM: TRENDS, ACHIEVEMENTS AND FAILURES (London: Frank Cass, 2004) at 8, and Langewiesche, THE ATOMC BAZAAR, *supra* note 13, at 19 (both cited in Mueller).

uranium—in total less than 16 pounds or so, far less than required for an atomic explosion."[27] Dafna Linzer adds to this: "the thieves—none of whom was connected to al Qaeda—had no buyers lined up, and nearly all were caught while trying to peddle their acquisitions."[28] Langewiesche notes that if terrorists were to succeed in obtaining fissile material in Pakistan, Russia, or elsewhere in Asia, they would face the challenge of transporting it over hundreds if not thousands of miles of hostile terrain, and likely while being pursued by security officials.[29] More recent attempts to tally the total amount of HEU stolen or missing remain low, noting only one or two further events since 2008, with one author concluding, "none of the incidents involved enough material to fabricate a nuclear weapon."[30]

In separate works, John Mueller and William Langewiesche have argued against the likelihood that Pakistan, North Korea, or any future nuclear power would provide bombs or nuclear material to terrorists. It would be too risky for that nation to be discovered as the source of the bomb, given that an extreme reaction by the United States or Israel would be all but certain.[31] Mueller suggests "there is a very considerable danger the bomb and its donor would be discovered even before delivery or that it would be exploded in a manner and on a target the donor would not approve (including on the donor itself)."[32] More crucially, as Mueller notes, in the history of the bomb (nearly 70 years as of this writing), "no state has ever given another state—even a close ally, much less a terrorist group—a nuclear weapon (or chemical, biological, or radiological one either, for that matter) that the recipient could use independently."[33]

A further source of concern among nuclear alarmists relates to the uncovering in 2002 of the underground trade in nuclear materials involving the Pakistani nuclear scientist A.Q. Khan. As noted in Chapter 4, many commentators cite the Khan case as confirmation of the danger that a market may exist. On this view, Khan was only the tip of the iceberg. Mueller and Langewiesche draw the opposite conclusion. In their view, the discovery of the Khan network was evidence of the ease of detection rather than the potential size of the market. As Mueller argues, the network was "rather easily penetrated by intelligence agencies (the CIA, it is very likely, had agents within the network), and the operation was abruptly closed down when it seemed to be the right time."[34]

---

27 Mueller, *The Atomic Terrorist* (2008), *supra* note 13, at 8. Mueller concedes that there may have been unreported thefts.

28 Dafna Linzer, *Nuclear Capabilities May Elude Terrorists, Experts Say*, WASH. POST, Dec. 29, 2004 (cited in Mueller).

29 Langewiesche, THE ATOMIC BAZAAR, *supra*, note 13, at 48–50 (cited in Mueller).

30 William H. Tobey, Belfer Center for Science and International Affairs, Harvard, *We Are Failing at Nuclear Security*, European Leadership Network (Mar. 3, 2014). *See also* Marina Koren, *Top Ten Cases of Nuclear Thefts Gone Wrong*, SMITHSONIAN.COM, Feb. 4, 2013.

31 Mueller 2008, *supra*, note 13, at 5; Langewiesche, *supra*, note 13, at 20 (cited in Mueller).

32 Ibid.

33 Ibid.

34 Ibid. at 5; *see also* Langewiesche, THE ATOMIC BAZAAR, *supra* note 13, at 169–72 (cited in Mueller).

In summary, if a bomb were stolen, the protective system would pose a further obstacle. Transportation, betrayal, and discovery would pose further potential obstacles. The quality and amount of material obtained would be a further issue. Yet if terrorists succeeded in overcoming each of these obstacles, they would encounter still more at the next stage.

## Why Building a Nuclear Bomb is Much Harder That It Seems

From at least the 1960s onward, a literature has emerged around the question of what challenges are entailed in building a reliably functional nuclear or atomic weapon. Among the most frequently cited narratives in this literature is one that relates to a project known as the "Nth Country Experiment."[35] At the time the project was conducted by the U.S. military in 1964, the world's only nuclear powers were Russia, the United Kingdom, and the United States. The United States wanted to know how easily, if at all, another nation seeking to build a nuclear bomb could do so, working without the classified information in possession of the nuclear powers. It commissioned two recent Ph.D. graduates in physics and provided them with a laboratory and ample time to work. Three years later, the two young scientists impressed their military sponsors by producing a blueprint for a bomb that was more powerful and sophisticated than the one they were asked to create. The question seemed to be settled: it could be done quite readily, with a very small team, and no classified information. For this reason, the story is frequently cited by figures in the "imminent danger" school as proof of the simplicity of the task.[36] Yet each time it is cited by members of this group, a critical fact is either ignored or mentioned only in passing. *The bomb was never built.*

The Nth Country Experiment goes to the heart of a critical issue in the debate. In theory, say the alarmists, it is easy to build a bomb, given the relative simplicity of the physics at issue. In practice, say the skeptics, it is not.[37] The skeptics' arguments for why bomb building is harder in practice than it sounds are key. They offer some of the most

---

[35] Dan Stober, *No Experience Necessary*, BULL. ATOMIC SCIENTISTS (May–June 2003).

[36] *See, e.g.*, Graham Allison, NUCLEAR TERRORISM: THE ULTIMATE PREVENTABLE CATASTROPHE (New York: Henry Holt, 2004) at 94: "In the end, they produced a document with such precise details on how to build the bomb, and what materials would be required, that Seldon remarked that it 'could have been made by Joe's Machine Shop downtown.'"

Ferguson and Potter, in THE FOUR FACES OF NUCLEAR TERRORISM (New York: Routledge, 2005) at 137, begin a paragraph addressing the experiment by asking: "Could a reasonably technically competent small terrorist group design *and build* an implosion device?" (emphasis added). The paragraph describes how the two novices at the Livermore Laboratory triumphantly succeeded in producing a design for a more powerful bomb than the one requested, but it makes no mention of the fact that the bomb was never built.

*See also* Matthew Bunn & Anthony Wier, *Terrorist Nuclear Weapon Construction: How Difficult?*, 607:1 ANNALS AM. ACAD. POL. & SOC. SCI. 133 (2006), at 145: "They quickly decided that designing a workable gun-type bomb would be too easy to show off their technical skills in a way that would improve their subsequent job prospects; instead, they successfully designed a workable implosion bomb…" What the authors mean here by "successfully designed" is not explored.

[37] *See, e.g.*, Levi's analysis of the Nth Country Experiment in Chapter 3 of ON NUCLEAR TERRORISM, *supra* note 3.

persuasive reasons to believe that nuclear terror is a highly unlikely event. The challenges occur at several stages, including:

i. the acquisition of an adequate amount of appropriate fissile material from one or more sources;
ii. building the device;
iii. testing it without being detected (a useful though not essential step);
iv. transporting it undetected;
v. reliably exploding the device; and
vi. effecting an explosion of the intended magnitude.

In considering these points, one might recall (from Chapter 4) the strongest argument set forth by the alarmist school. This is the claim that, at the very least, with a sufficient sample of fissile material, a non-state actor could easily build at least a crude "gun-type" nuclear weapon that would be somewhat reliable. This would only have to involve creating a device that would slam together two pieces of HEU.

To lend a sense of the force of this argument, Richard Rhodes invokes the authority of nuclear physicist and Nobel laureate Luis Alvarez, who was involved in creating the first atomic bomb. Alvarez suggested to Rhodes that "[y]ou can make a fairly high-level nuclear explosion just by dropping one piece [of HEU] onto another *by hand*."[38] Why, then, would it be hard to build a crude, gun-type nuclear weapon?

In short, it would not be hard in the sense of theoretically difficult. It would be hard in the practical sense—at least if you wanted to be reasonably sure it would work. (I will return momentarily to the question of whether one might wish to settle for a bomb that was unpredictable and to simply save the testing for its actual use in Manhattan or Toronto.) It is harder to build a bomb than Alvarez's comment would suggest because in order to cause a significant explosion—one or more kilotons—it would be necessary to use two samples of HEU of a sufficient size, purity or quality, *and* an appropriate shape. And although experts debate the necessary size of a sample to cause an explosion in the kilotons, many agree that the tasks of acquiring material of the right kind and shape would present a host of challenges that have proved daunting or insurmountable to many states, and would be especially difficult for a small group of non-state actors.

On the basis of these facts, a number of experts contend that a wide gap exists between the theory or physics of a nuclear bomb and its accomplishment in practice—regardless of the bomb's design. The simple explosion that Alverez contemplates would require

---

[38] Richard Rhodes, TWILIGHT OF THE BOMBS, *supra* note 18, at 289. See also Luis W. Alvarez, ADVENTURES OF A PHYSICIST (New York: Basic Books, 1988), at 125: "with modern weapons-grade uranium, the background neutron rate is so low that terrorists, if they have such material, would have a good chance of setting off a high-yield explosion simply by dropping one half of the material onto the other half." (Cited in Levi, ON NUCLEAR TERRORISM, *supra* note 3.)

sufficient amounts of HEU, in a certain shape and consistency; and it may also involve a weapon carefully calibrated to perform as intended. The calibration of such a weapon would require significant expertise with metals and substances, crafting and machining; time and material to work with; and possibly the opportunity to test some if not all of the components. The work would be dangerous, difficult to conceal, and time consuming—all raising the risk of failure or discovery.[39] To explore these issues, I deal first with the prospect of building a weapon, then consider the possibly of setting off a bomb without first testing it.

Writing in 1998, Stanley Jacobs asserted that "[w]hile the design of a workable device may be *approximated* based on readily accessible, unclassified information, the conversion of that information into a functioning device is a task of a far different magnitude."[40] The reason for this relates to the scale of the undertaking: "Although a functional nuclear weapon requires only a small amount of plutonium…, obtaining the requisite amount of weapons-grade material, assembling the technical personnel to create the device, equipping a laboratory-ship to build the device, obtaining all the other materials needed, funding the operation and keeping the entire enterprise secret appear to be a series of steps that have effectively prevented any successful attempt."[41] Despite claims by experts and physicists to the effect that "a small group of dedicated individuals with appropriate backgrounds in physics and nuclear chemistry, resources, security, etc., could fabricate a nuclear device, it has not been accomplished in over half a century."[42] Iraq failed to accomplish the goal "after spending more than 20 years and over a billion dollars."[43]

An important source of corroboration for this view is a commonly cited study published in 1987 by a team of U.S. nuclear weapons experts, commissioned by the International Task Force on the Prevention of Nuclear Terrorism.[44] The authors sought to assess what would be involved in creating either a crude gun-type device or a more sophisticated design. They found that while a crude gun-type weapon could conceivably be manufactured by a non-state actor, "substantially more than a critical mass of uranium is needed, and plutonium cannot be used" (given issues with "predetonation" unique to plutonium).[45] Other types of design would require either greater amounts of fissile material or material of a higher quality.[46] Speaking generally, they assert: "The amounts of fissile material necessary would tend to be large—certainly several, and possibly ten times,

[39] Jacobs, *Nuclear Threat as a Terrorist Option, supra* note 12, at 152–53.
[40] Ibid. at 152.
[41] Ibid.
[42] Ibid.
[43] Ibid.
[44] J. Carson Mark, Theodore Taylor, Eugene Eyster, William Maraman & Jacob Wechsler, *Can Terrorists Build Nuclear Weapons?*, in PREVENTING NUCLEAR TERRORISM, *supra* note 7.
[45] Ibid. at 55. At 62, the authors explain why predetonation complicates or precludes the use of plutonium in a gun-type design.
[46] Ibid. at 56.

the so-called formula quantities."[47] The weight of any complete device would also likely be large, "probably more than a ton."[48] They also found that:

> [s]chematic drawings of fission explosive devices of the earliest types [i.e., including the gun-type] showing in a qualitative way the principles used in achieving the first fission explosions are widely available. However, the detailed design drawings and specifications that are essential before it is possible to plan the fabrication of actual parts are not available. The preparation of these drawings requires a large number of man-hours and the direct participation of individuals thoroughly informed in several quite distinct areas: the physical, chemical, and metallurgical properties of the various materials to be used, as well as the characteristics affecting their fabrication[...].[49]

On this basis, the authors conclude that at an absolute minimum the team involved "could scarcely be fewer than three or four and might well have to be more."[50] The preparation involved would be "a number of weeks (or, more probably, months)."[51]

The authors note in the event the theft of material was detected, a search would soon follow involving significant tools and resources: "In addition to all the usual intelligence methods, the most sensitive technical detection equipment available would be at [the searcher's] disposal. As long as thirty-five years ago, airborne radiation detectors proved effective in prospecting for uranium ore. Great improvements in such equipment have been realized since."[52] There are also "a number of obvious potential hazards" to confront in the process of building, including "the possibility of inadvertently inducing a critical configuration of the fissile material at some stage in the procedure," and being exposed to high levels of toxicity and radiation.[53] Finally, the device itself would function unpredictably: "Terrorists would not be in a position to know even the nominal yield of their device with any precision."[54]

Writing more recently, Levi, Younger, and Wirz and Eggers present a similar set of challenges with even the most basic, gun-type design. Levi sets out several. Noting that a crude gun-type weapon could be fashioned by modifying a purchased artillery piece, he explains that a group would have to test it "at least once using natural or depleted uranium, introducing at least a small probability of detection."[55] The impact of such testing

---

[47] Ibid. at 60: "Formula quantities" refers to regulated amounts of material that may be safely stored or transported in and among U.S. military nuclear installations. The authors cite as an example 5kg of U-235 (HEU) or 2 kg of plutonium.

[48] Ibid. at 60.

[49] Ibid. at 58.

[50] Ibid.

[51] Ibid. at 59.

[52] Ibid. at 60.

[53] Ibid. at 62–63.

[54] Ibid. at 63.

[55] Levi, *supra* note 3, at 38–39.

and the preparation facility involved could attract attention. Without the requisite knowledge of how to use such an artillery piece, further tests would be necessary. A terror group would also face additional challenges around the precise design and function of the initiator mechanism in the gun (which would set off the nuclear chain reaction). Without this, they would have to create an effectively functioning uranium "bullet and target" mechanism.[56] Levi sets out a number of potential pitfalls at this particular stage, involving a detailed discussion of the physics of nuclear fission (more on this below).[57] Without building this correctly and precisely, the device could cause the material to pre-detonate or to yield a much smaller explosion.[58]

All of these scenarios contemplate a set of tests before use. But an important issue to address before proceeding is whether a group of terrorists might simply forego the testing stage and attempt to carry out the attack itself—taking their chances as they treat Manhattan or Toronto as their testing ground. They would thus circumvent at least some of the hurdles mentioned above—but how likely are they to succeed in setting off a nuclear explosion? The answer depends in large part on the validity of Luis Alvarez's claim that merely slamming two pieces of HEU together would suffice to create high-powered nuclear explosion. Michael Levi offers a critical reading of this assertion. The reading depends, however, on an understanding of the process of nuclear fission itself. When examined in closer detail, this process makes clear that the likelihood and size of an explosion is closely dependent on the quality, size and shape of the material. Alvarez's theory of a simple explosion is premised on having not only two pieces of a certain size but also an optimum quality and shape.

The reason for this relates the physics of nuclear fission. As Levi explains, a nuclear explosion is a consequence of the process of nuclear fission. Fission occurs on an atomic level. It begins when a subatomic particle known as a neutron strikes the nucleus of another atom—for example, a uranium atom—causing that atom to split and release both energy and more neutrons. The release of energy and neutrons can cause other atoms to split, leading to a further release of energy and more neutrons, and further atom splitting. Eventually, this chain reaction within a mass of uranium will cause it to explode due to the release of greater amounts of energy. The force of the resulting explosion will depend on how many atomic splits, or "fissions," have occurred by that point in time.

It is important to note, however, that not every neutron that strikes an atom will cause the atom to split. Also, where fission does occur, the nature of the fissile material will affect the likelihood of a chain reaction occurring or continuing. Certain forms of uranium, for example, are more conducive to the formation of a chain reaction than others. As Levi notes, neutrons striking a piece of Uranium 238 are less likely to result in either fission or a chain reaction than those hitting a piece of Uranium 235, given the greater

---

56 Ibid. at 43.

57 *See* discussion 43–46, ibid.

58 Ibid. at 43.

likelihood that escaping neutrons in an atomic split of Uranium 238 will be "captured" or will "disappear and be unable to cause additional fissions."[59] The uranium samples used in a nuclear weapon will therefore usually contain a blend of both Uranium 235 and 238, but will consist of at least 90 percent Uranium 235 (i.e., "weapons-grade" uranium).

In addition to the quality or make-up of a given mass, two other vital factors for the fission process are the size and shape of the sample. In a sample that is too small, the neutrons would escape "through the surface of the uranium."[60] In a sample that is too large, the neutrons may never escape, which would allow the energy created by early reactions to dissipate, and for the chain reaction to die out. As Levi explains, "[a]t some size and shape in between, the material is barely able to sustain a chain reaction—just enough neutrons leak to balance their production through fission. That configuration is referred to as a critical mass."[61] A sample might therefore lack the right balance of size and shape, rendering it either "sub-critical" or "super-critical." A critical or super-critical mass is required to trigger and sustain the fission process for some period. But in short order, the chain reaction will cause the uranium mass to expand and either become sub-critical or explode—in each case, bringing the chain reaction to an end.

Levi further explains that the size of the resulting explosion will depend on how many fissions occur before the sample explodes, and that this number depends on how soon the chain reaction begins. When two critical or sub-critical masses are slammed together, they become super-critical—due, that is, to a greater density of atoms and neutrons. If the chain reaction starts early, it will cause the mass to expand earlier in time. However, even a small amount of expansion will cause the material to become sub-critical quickly, leading to fewer fissions and either a smaller explosion, or no explosion at all. Yet if the reaction starts a sufficient period after two the masses are brought together into a super-critical mass, the material will have time to become *denser* than in the earlier case. A greater density of neutrons and atoms will allow for more fission—for two reasons. More density leads to a higher rate of collisions between atoms and neutrons; and, given the greater density of material, it will take longer for the material to expand to become sub-critical once again. More fission makes a more forceful explosion more likely.

These details are important because although a chain reaction can be triggered by any neutron striking a uranium atom, the likelihood of setting off a chain reaction early turns on how many neutrons are emitted by either of two masses when striking one another. The more neutrons that are emitted by either piece, the more likely it is that the chain reaction will be triggered early, when the material is less critical (or dense)—yielding a smaller explosion. Conversely, the fewer neutrons emitted and the faster two pieces come together, the more dense the material will be, and the more fission that may occur. Thus,

---

59 Levi, On Nuclear Terrorism, *supra* note 3, at 36.

60 Ibid.

61 Ibid. at 37.

the size, shape, and quality of the material—and how they come together—are key factors in assessing the resulting yield.[62]

To return, then, to Levi's critique of Alvarez, Levi begins by noting that Alvarez's claim is often cited in scenarios of terrorists breaking into a nuclear installation and setting off an explosion on site, without resort to a gun-type apparatus. In one variation, Matthew Wald asserts that "a 100-pound mass [of weapons-grade] uranium dropped on a second 100-pound mass, from a height of about 6 feet, could produce a blast of 5 to 10 kilotons."[63] Levi suggests:

> These assertions are correct, but they can easily be misinterpreted. Making a nuclear weapon is harder than they suggest.
>
> How can they be misinterpreted? The experts making these claims assume the two pieces of uranium are in ideal shapes for creating an explosion. Take the last example, where the final mass of uranium is about one hundred kilograms (or about two hundred pounds). This weight would provide about two critical masses for a spherical piece of uranium, which leads to a blast of five to ten kilotons, as claimed. Yet for other shapes, one hundred kilograms of material may not even form a critical mass, in which case no explosion will occur; alternatively, the two shapes may form more than a critical mass but not the two critical masses that would lead to a five- to ten-kiloton explosion. Depending on the shapes and sizes of nuclear material a terrorist group acquires, then, the group may have to reshape the material, or, in some cases, decide between reshaping the material and accepting a reduced yield.[64]

Put otherwise, *unless* a terror group obtains material of the right kind, shape, and size, it will *have* to reshape the material or accept a lower yield. Merely obtaining a sample or two of HEU will not likely place a terror group in the position to create the simple explosion that Alvarez contemplates—at least, not without overcoming further obstacles.

As Levi points out, reshaping material would entail "more challenges and create new vulnerabilities."[65] He doubts whether "standard machine shop tools are adequate for manipulating uranium."[66] Moreover, "having equipment and tools with sufficient capabilities is different from having individuals skilled enough to use them successfully."[67] This introduces further opportunities for failure. Chief among them is the high probability of accidents occurring while working with the material itself: "Uranium metal is

---

62 Ibid.

63 Matthew Wald, *Suicidal Nuclear Threat Is Seen at Weapons Plants*, N.Y. Times, Jan. 23, 2003, cited in Levi, On Nuclear Terrorism, *supra* note 3, at 39–40.

64 Levi, *supra* note 3, at 39–40.

65 Ibid. at 40.

66 Ibid.

67 Ibid.

vulnerable to spontaneous ignition when finely divided, creating the risk of fire during processing, and of ensuing detection."[68]

As an example of the degree of challenge involved in shaping material, Levi cites a report of the Iraq Survey Group (investigating in 2003), which found "no evidence that Iraq had acquired or developed the technology of dealing with casting and machining issues of highly enriched uranium."[69] The report also noted various difficulties Iraqi scientists encountered in using casting furnaces to melt uranium, for the purpose of pouring it into molds. While the Iraqis were able to create spherical and cylindrical pieces for an implosion device, the pieces were "of relatively poor quality as pertaining to void and impurity incursions."[70] Terrorists seeking to build a gun-type device would encounter different problems, yet in Levi's view, the "impurity problem the ISG refers to could still be significant." If a terrorist group encountered the same issue, "it might only obtain a yield of roughly ten tons, still devastating but a thousand times smaller than a typical crude nuclear weapon."[71]

Younger's analysis is consistent with Levi's. Drawing on his work building nuclear bombs for the U.S. government, he emphasizes the importance of three specific hurdles. Although one can obtain a general idea of how to build a bomb from public sources, he asserts, "none of these sources has enough detail to enable the confident assembly of a real nuclear explosive."[72] It would take more than having the right tools, it would also require a "working knowledge of how the parts fit together, what tolerances are permitted or required, the compatibility of materials [. . .], and many other details."[73] Uranium is also "exceptionally difficult to machine."[74] Plutonium, "one of the most complex metals ever discovered," is an extremely sensitive material. Tolerances create further issues:

> "Just put a slug of uranium into a gun barrel and shoot it into another slug of uranium" is one description of how easy it is to make a nuclear explosive. However, if the gap between the barrel and the slug is too tight, then the slug may stick as it is accelerated down the barrel. If the gap is too big, then other, more complex, issues may arise. All of these problems can be solved by experimentation, but this experimentation requires a level of technical resources that, until recently, few countries had. How do you measure the progress of an explosive detonation without destroying the equipment doing the measurements? How do you perform precision measurements on something that only lasts a fraction of a millionth of a second?[75]

---

68 Ibid.
69 Cited at 42 in Levi, ibid.
70 Citing the report, ibid.
71 Ibid. at 42.
72 Ibid. at 88.
73 Ibid.
74 Ibid.
75 Ibid. at 89.

For these reasons, Younger is also skeptical of the likelihood that terrorists could create a small, easily transportable nuclear device. Even if the designs for "suitcase bombs" are readily available, in his view only the United States and Russia have the engineering capability and material "to turn the blueprints into hardware."[76]

Wirz and Eggers, writing in 2010, corroborate these arguments.[77] Mueller cites several others who draw similar conclusions.[78] A sizeable body of experts thus agree that what can be accomplished in theory becomes much less feasible when attempted in practice.

## On Recent Terrorist Efforts to Obtain a Nuclear Weapon

In 2002, the Gilmore Commission issued a fourth report that addressed the available evidence surrounding al Qaida's efforts to obtain a nuclear weapon.[79] It cited numerous statements by Bush administration officials to the effect that the group was actively seeking to acquire nuclear and other weapons of mass destruction. Yet, upon examining the evidence in some detail, authors of the report concluded that very limited steps had been taken beyond that point beyond verbal expressions of interest and a collection of disparate notes and articles.[80]

Over the course of the decade, further inquiries have been made into al Qaeda's interest in and attempts to acquire WMDs.[81] John Mueller has attempted periodic overviews of this evidence, and he maintains a similarly skeptical position. In 2009, he argued that apart from occasional expressions of interest by senior al Qaida figures, the evidence points to only two serious attempts to pursue an interest in nuclear terror.[82] The first relates to a claim made by a defector from al Qaida in 1996, Jamal al-Fadl. Fadl is alleged to have told the CIA of an attempt he made in 1993 to obtain uranium from Sudan on behalf of bin Laden, and of the uranium turning out to be counterfeit.[83] Mueller questions the veracity of the incident partly on the basis of Fadl's credibility. The second involves conversations that bin Laden and other members of al Qaida had with two Pakistani nuclear scientists in August of 2001. Pakistani intelligence officers have described these as "academic" in nature.[84] Others, including Graham Allison, claim that the scientists provided bin Laden with "blueprints" for a bomb; Mueller asserts they were little more than "a hand-drawn

---

76 Ibid. at 91.

77 Wirz & Eggers, *supra* note 5.

78 *See* Mueller's most recent and extended discussion of the challenges faced by the would-be nuclear terrorist in Chapter 12 of ATOMIC OBSESSION, *supra* note 2.

79 Gilmore Commission, *Fourth Annual Report to the President and the Congress of the Advisory Panel to Assess Domestic Response Capabilities for Terrorism Involving Weapons of Mass Destruction* (Dec. 15, 2002).

80 Ibid. at 20.

81 For a comprehensive summary, see Rolf Mowatt-Larssen, Belfer Center for Science and International Affairs, Harvard, *Al Qaeda Weapons of Mass Destruction Threat: Hype or Reality?* (Jan. 2010).

82 Mueller, *The Atomic Terrorist* (2009), *supra* note 9, at 16.

83 Ibid. at 16.

84 Ibid.

rough bomb design."[85] The scientists would also have been of limited use to the group, in Mueller's view, given that their specialty was not bomb design but the production of fissile material—a task that is well beyond a non-state actor, as many have noted.[86] Mueller also cites al Qaida documents seized by the U.S. government in Afghanistan in 2001, which reveal that the group's budget for work on WMD acquisition was only some two to four thousand dollars.[87]

Mueller had occasion to revisit the issue in 2011, in the wake of bin Laden's killing and the seizure of computers at his compound. They contained extensive notes and information on the group's activities over the course of the decade. Muller writes:

> A multi-agency task force has completed its assessment, and according to first reports, it has found that al Qaeda members have primarily been engaged in dodging drone strikes and complaining about how cash-strapped they are. [ . . . ] The full story is not out yet, but it seems breathtakingly unlikely that the miserable little group has had the time or inclination, let alone the money, to set up and staff a uranium-seizing operation, as well as a fancy, super-high-tech facility to fabricate a bomb.[88]

This speaks only to the group's interest in nuclear terror. In the next section, I briefly address al Qaida's efforts to obtain biological weapons.

In any case, whether or not al Qaida's efforts were cause for concern, the group may not have been alone in seeking to deploy a nuclear weapon. Other groups may have been interested, and others might be in the future. Reports also still surface from time to time of stolen quantities of HEU, giving rise to serious concerns.[89] In response, the argument of this chapter is to counsel caution and skepticism. Where a non-state actor obtains HEU, this is cause for concern. But it does not mean that nuclear terror is likely or imminent. Many obstacles remain.

This is because—to summarize—in addition to the task of acquiring fissile material, the task of building, transporting, and deploying a nuclear bomb are much more complex and challenging than is often assumed. Future developments and events may change this analysis. But in this case, rights advocates will be in a position to evaluate them with a spirit of scientifically informed skepticism, and to set out a more cautious, sober assessment.

---

[85] Mueller, ibid., cites Allison's NUCLEAR TERRORISM, *supra* note 36, at 24 on this point. For the point that what was shown was only a rough sketch, he cites George Tenet (with Bill Harlow), AT THE CENTER OF THE STORM: THE CIA DURING AMERICA'S TIME OF CRISIS (New York: Harper Collins, 2007), at 268.

[86] Mueller, *The Atomic Terrorist* (2009), *supra* note 9, at 16.

[87] John Mueller, *The Truth About al Qaeda: Bin Laden's Files Revealed the Terrorists in Dramatic Decline*, FOREIGN AFF. (Aug. 2, 2011).

[88] Ibid.

[89] *See, e.g.*, Peter Goodspeed, *Ongoing Nuclear Threat Looms Over Seoul Summit*, NAT'L POST (Toronto), Mar. 24, 2012, citing the June 2011 arrest of a group in Moldavia for smuggling 4.4 grams of weapons-grade uranium as part of a sale that may have involved up to 9 kilograms.

## II. WHY BIOTERRORISM IS HARDER THAN IT MAY SEEM

Chapter 4 surveyed common arguments in support of the view that a major bioterrorism attack was likely in the near future. They include the claims that:

1. certain biological substances are among the most lethal potential weapons in existence;
2. many can be manufactured with limited knowledge or equipment, and with natural or readily obtainable material; and
3. such weapons can be easily dispersed to cause mass casualties.

A number of experts have cast these arguments into doubt. What follows is a brief overview of skeptical perspectives on bio-terrorism.

William Clark, an emeritus professor of immunology at the University of California, lends a general sense of these perspectives in his 2008 book *Bracing for Armageddon*:

> Those who think deeply about America's response to bioterrorism should be very clear about one thing. It is almost inconceivable that any terrorist organization we know of in the world today, foreign or domestic, could on their own develop, from scratch, a bioweapon capable of causing mass casualties on American soil. It just isn't going to happen. The isolation and purification of the requisite pathogens from nature, although theoretically possible is far beyond the ability of all but a handful of advanced scientific laboratories in the world. So is the development of a mass-scale delivery system for most pathogens.[90]

Clark contemplates challenges at both the production and dissemination stage. A more detailed exploration of these challenges is set out in the 1999 Gilmore Commission report, noted above, and in Clark's assessment of the bioterror episode involving the Japanese Aum cult in the mid 1990s.

The Gilmore Commission's first report assessed the prospect of bioterror in addition to nuclear terror. It noted that would be bioterrorists would face significant obstacles at several stages. A group might acquire lethal substances from four sources: a germ bank, a research laboratory or hospital, a natural source, or a rogue state.[91] But a "principal obstacle" is to produce "a genuinely lethal strain of the agent in sufficient quantities to cause mass casualties."[92] (The Aum group, for example, failed to do precisely this, despite

---

90 William R. Clark, Bracing for Armageddon: The Science and Politics of Bioterrorism in America (Oxford: Oxford University Press, 2008) at 170–71.

91 At 162, ibid., Clark notes that in the United States, as a result of the 2002 Bioterrorism Act, it has become "much, much harder" to obtain pathogens from a lab, bank or hospital. The Act regulates the transfer and production of listed pathogens through an elaborate licensing and reporting scheme, with strict penalties.

92 Gilmore Commission, *Assessing the Threat, supra* note 6, at 22.

attempting it with the benefit of both considerable expertise and facilities.) One way the obstacle might be overcome is to produce a strain of a poisonous substance—e.g., anthrax spores—from natural sources and to cultivate it into large quantities. While conceivable, the Commission asserts that the task is "difficult in practice and doubtless well beyond the capabilities of most terrorist groups."[93] The reasons for this relate to the challenges of working with such substances.

Once a lethal strain is obtained, one key challenge is to make it stable. The Commission cites Russian bioweapon scientist Ken Alibek on this point: "the most virulent culture in a test tube is useless as an offense weapon unless it has been put through a process that gives it stability and predictability. The manufacturing technique is, in a sense, the real weapon, and it is harder to develop than individual agents."[94] Producing airborne viral agents becomes an even greater challenge, the Commission notes, given that they are "extraordinarily difficult to work with."[95] The production, packaging and storing of viruses entails a further set of opportunities for failure, and risk to those involved.[96] Some agents, such as botulinum toxins, become unstable once purified, requiring further testing and special knowledge of how to maintain toxicity for storage and dissemination.[97] U.S. military researchers have also found that maintaining a high enough level of purity to use toxic agents as a weapon reduces 70 to 80 percent of the sample supply.[98]

Other potential obstacles the Commission considers relate to acquiring necessary "training, advanced techniques, and specialized equipment."[99] While some of the testing could be conducted in small laboratories, larger tests "will likely invite the attention of law enforcement or intelligence agencies."[100] Testing is of course not strictly necessary, but if a group were to continuously try to carry out a bioterror attack until it worked—testing in the field—they would likely face a growing risk of detection.

In addition to issues about equipment and testing, the Commission concedes the existence of debate on the question of how much expertise is necessary to develop certain lethal substances. Yet it also notes that most experts agree that at a minimum, a team would require the involvement of a microbiologist, a pathologist, and an aerosol physicist and meteorologist (if airborne dissemination were the chosen route).[101] Assembling such a team, in the Commission's view, poses the greatest hurdle. The fear and paranoia that would surround their work would only add to the difficulties.

---

93 Ibid.
94 Ibid. at 22–23.
95 Ibid. at 23.
96 Ibid.
97 Ibid.
98 Ibid.
99 Ibid.
100 Ibid.
101 Ibid.

The final stage, dissemination, presents a further set of obstacles. If a group's aim were to inflict tens or hundreds of thousands of casualties, it would have to create an "aerosol cloud" as a vehicle. This can be created from a liquid or powder form, but both are difficult to produce and control. Samples of the virus must be dried, which in the process "tends to kill inordinate amounts of the organisms."[102] Portions also cling to surfaces, making it hard to handle and increase the chance of infection.[103] In a "slurry" liquid form, the substance must be kept refrigerated, causing it to settle at the bottom of its container and to clog the dissemination device. (The Commission notes that this is precisely what occurred when the Japanese group Aum Shinrikyo attempted to spray anthrax from the roof of a Tokyo building.[104]) The disseminating particles must also be the proper size—between 1 and 5 microns. But building a tool to disseminate particles of this size would pose "a major technical hurdle for any prospective biological terrorist."[105]

Even if all of these hurdles were overcome, one further opportunity for failure remains: "As bioagents are aerosolized and become airborne, they decay rapidly. It is estimated that 90% of the microorganisms in a slurry are likely to die during the process of aerosolization."[106] Temperature changes, humidity, wind, smog, and other environmental factors will further impede the effect.

William Clark's assessment of Aum Shinrikyo sheds further light on the magnitude of these challenges. Aum had carried out seven attacks, four with anthrax and three with botulinum toxin.[107] The group's overt aim was to inflict as many casualties as possible. Had it succeeded, Clark believes, the casualties would have been in the thousands or tens of thousands. Yet its failure was instructive in many respects.

Aum was led by Seiichi Endo, who possessed a doctorate in molecular biology. The team had other trained experts and access to labs and equipment. As Clark suggests, however, the group's critical shortcoming was its failure to gather the necessary expertise. As he notes, "none were experienced in microbiology or other biological sciences directly impinging on bioweapons development. None had the biotechnology background for large-scale pathogen production. None had the engineering skills to produce an efficient weapons delivery system."[108]

The group began by producing botulinum from natural sources. But there are, as Clark explains, various strains of botulinum toxin in nature, and only a few of them are harmful to humans. Greater expertise would have been critical at an early stage in selection and production.[109] The team also faced challenges in purifying and producing a high enough

---

102 Ibid. at 24.
103 Ibid.
104 Ibid. at 25.
105 Ibid.
106 Ibid.
107 Clark, Bracing for Armageddon, *supra* note 90, at 164.
108 Ibid. at 169.
109 Ibid. at 165.

quantity of the organism. It encountered further trouble stabilizing the quantity in storage, and settling upon effective methods of delivery.

Clark believes that Endo probably obtained anthrax samples by stealing them from a local university. But he failed to produce further quantities of it, lacking sufficient expertise and knowledge.[110] "This usually come from years of experience, judging when cultures must be subdivided and recognizing from the appearance of the cells themselves what more may be needed."[111] Even more expertise is required to "encourage a high degree of spore formation without killing off huge amounts of bacteria."[112] The drying, storing, and dissemination of anthrax spores presented further issues. The method Endo chose—spraying a liquid slurry from the top of an eight-story building—was "almost certainly doomed to failure."[113] This was due in part to the poor quality of what was disseminated. Samples collected from the incident were later analyzed in a U.S. university. They were found to contain "a low level of anthrax spores" and a specific strain "used to vaccinate farm animals against anthrax. It is essentially completely harmless in humans."[114] Even if Endo had worked with a lethal strain, the group had also failed to engage experts in weather conditions and aerosolized dissemination. Without this expertise, Clark believes "the amount of damage done to humans even in the immediate vicinity of the building would have been minimal at best."[115]

Other experts have corroborated the skeptical position set out by Clark and the Gilmore Commission.[116] I conclude this part by drawing on one final authority, Milton Leitenberg, a senior research scholar at the Centre for International Security Studies at the University of Maryland.[117] For Leitenberg, bioterror on a significant scale is highly improbable, and claims about al Qaida's interest it have been grossly inflated.

Writing in 2007, Leitenberg relates the findings of a survey he conducted of a series of databases that have tracked "bioweapons-related events" throughout the twentieth century, including hoaxes, expressions of interest, and actual attempts to procure, produce or use a biological agent.[118] He notes that:

> events that were actual examples of use were overwhelmingly chemical, and even these involved the use of easily available off-the-shelf, nonsynthesized industrial products. Many of these events were instances of individual murder and not

---

110 Ibid.

111 Ibid. at 167.

112 Ibid.

113 Ibid. at 168.

114 Ibid.

115 Ibid.

116 *See*, e.g., Andreas Wenger & Reto Wollenmann, eds., BIOTERRORISM: CONFRONTING A COMPLEX THREAT (Boulder CO: Lynne Rienner Publishers, 2007), and in particular, the contributions by Milton Leitenberg, Peter Lavoy, Marie Isabell Chevrier, and Andreas Wenger.

117 Ibid. at 39–76.

118 Milton Leitenberg, *Evolution of the Current Threat*, in Wenger & Wollenmann, ibid. at 49.

> attempts to cause mass casualties. [... T]here are only a few recorded instances in the years from 1900 to 2000 of the preparation of biological pathogens in a private laboratory by a nonstate actor.[119]

The three most serious events on record involve the Rajneesh cult in Oregon in 1984; Aum Shinrikyo in Japan in 1995; and use of anthrax in the U.S. congressional incident in the fall of 2001. The question raised in each of these cases is whether the group could produce a biotoxin and how much damage it could accomplish.

The Rajneesh group is notable for having successfully cultured a biological agent—a form of salmonella that members dispersed by hand in salad bars of restaurants throughout a small Oregon city. Over 700 people suffered from food poisoning, but there were no casualties.[120] Although Leitenberg does not explore this case in much detail, Clark makes two notable points about the event. One is that the group obtained the original salmonella cultures from an industrial supplier in Seattle more easily than would be the case today, given the passage of stricter regulation around the storage, sale, and transfer of dangerous pathogens.[121] He notes that "[f]ailure to account fully for every organism under a laboratory's control could result in suspension of that laboratory's license. While a determined individual might still find a way to get at a lab's stock of Select List pathogens, it is much, much harder today than it was in 1984, or even 2001."[122] Another critical point is that the group was able to order the sample and cultivate it without detection due in part to the fact that the cultivation of salmonella, "an ordinary bacterium," is technically and practically simple; and also due to the fact that the Rajneesh compound contained "a clinic, pharmacy, and a state-licensed medical laboratory,"[123] along with a trained nurse. Moreover, the group in this case began with an original sample of the bioagent, and it was not a lethal agent.

Leitenberg notes that Aum Shinrikyo had "unsuccessfully attempted to procure, produce, and disperse anthrax and botulinum toxin."[124] It obtained only a strain of anthrax that was "nonpathogenic under any conditions"—and the group was also "unsuccessful in working with even that properly."[125]

This leaves the U.S. congressional anthrax episode of 2001. Leitenberg describes this as the single most significant bioweapon event on record, given the quality and nature of the weapon at issue. The question for him and other bioweapon experts is what it portends about bioterror in a larger sense. In this case, samples of less than a gram of a deadly strain of anthrax

---

119 Ibid.

120 Clark, BRACING FOR ARMAGEDDON, *supra* note 90, at 89.

121 Ibid. at 162; Clark cites the Public Health Security and Bioterrorism Preparedness and Response Act of 2002 (Bioterrorism Act), 107th Cong., H.R. 3448 ENR.

122 Clark, ibid. at 162.

123 Ibid. at 163.

124 Leitenberg, *Evolution of the Current Threat, supra* note 118, at 49.

125 Ibid.

were found in letters sent to U.S. Senators Tom Daschle and Patrick Leahy, killing five people and injuring several more. Given the high purity of the samples, Leitenberg conjectures that the pathogen might have been derived from a U.S. military source, or expertise arising from it.[126] His view corroborates with Clark's analysis.

Clark explains that the samples used in the 2001 attack were "if not of the very highest level of purity and potency, certainly good enough to cause very serious problems."[127] They were not the work of "an amateur microbiologist or a survival chemist"; rather, they were "likely made in a government or possibly university research facility highly specialized in producing anthrax spores."[128] In addition to the purity of the samples, the group or individual responsible used a highly efficient distribution method—i.e., placing less than a gram of the sample in various letters. This helped evade detection yet could still result in the death of "dozens of people under the right conditions, and maybe more."[129] Clark concludes:

> In the end, the most unsettling aspect of Amerithrax is that it was not likely carried out by a foreign terrorist. At present, all evidence suggests that it was most likely an American scientist, who was either working or had worked in an American laboratory—possibly even a government laboratory—who carried out these attacks. The failure of the FBI to identify the individual involved suggests this was a highly sophisticated person who knew exactly what it would take to cover his or her tracks.[130]

Both Clark and Leitenberg are cautious about the event's larger significance.[131] Their assessments also predate the findings of an extensive FBI investigation that concluded in 2010. It found that the likely source of the sample in this case was a senior bioweapons researcher in the U.S. military by the name of Bruce Edwards Ivans.[132] This finding has been disputed by later inquiries, but considerable evidence still suggests that the ultimate source of the sample was a U.S. military research facility.[133]

Setting this issue aside, as Leitenberg points out, the Amerithrax episode is an outlier. "Without this event, and except for the Rajneesh salmonella incident," he writes, "there would still be no evidence of the capability of a nonstate actor to produce a biological

126 Ibid. at 66.

127 Clark, BRACING FOR ARMAGEDDON, *supra* note 90, at 170.

128 Ibid.

129 Ibid.

130 Ibid.

131 Ibid. at 170–71.

132 U.S. Department of Justice, *Amerithrax Investigative Summary* (Feb. 19, 2010), at http://www.justice.gov/archive/amerithrax/docs/amx-investigative-summary.pdf.

133 *See*, e.g., National Research Council, Board on Life Sciences; Committee on Science, Technology, and Law, *Review of the Scientific Approaches Used During the FBI's Investigation of the 2001 Anthrax Letters* (2011), at http://dels.nas.edu/resources/static-assets/materials-based-on-reports/reports-in-brief/Anthrax-Report-Brief-Final.pdf.

agent. There has also been no evidence uncovered to date of state assistance to a nonstate actor to produce biological agents."[134]

Leitenberg concludes his survey of bioweapon events over the course of the century by stating:

> Scenarios of national bioweapons exercises that place various bioweapons agents in advanced states of preparation into the hands of terrorist groups simply disregard the knowledge and experience that such groups would need to have in order to work with pathogens. [...] If and when a nonstate terrorist group does successfully reach the stage of working with pathogens, there is every reason to believe that such action will involve classical agents, without any molecular genetic modifications.[135]

He conjectures that common misperceptions about bioterrorism result from the fact that "since the mid-1990s, the risk and imminence of the use of biological agents by nonstate actors and terrorist organizations—or bioterrorism—have been systematically and deliberately exaggerated."[136] The culprits, in his view, are a "small group of vociferous proponents of 'the bioterroism threat' [who have] obtained allies at the most senior levels of the executive branch and in Congress."[137] While the proponents of the bioterror threat seek to encourage greater security around biomaterials, he suggests that state resources would be better used to prepare for more likely scenarios, such as a flu pandemic or other natural viruses.

One further notable aspect of Leitenberg's analysis is his treatment of al Qaida's efforts to obtain biological weapons, and the threat posed by the group's interest in bioterror.[138] The evidence suggests that two significant attempts were made. The first came to light in December of 2001, through a cache of papers discovered in an al Qaeda training camp near Kandahar. It contained copies of journal articles on bioweaponry, and a set of letters and notes authored by a Pakistani microbiologist in the mid-1990s to Ayman al-Zawahiri (formerly bin Laden's closest associate, and purported leader of al Qaeda at present). The letters document a failed attempt to obtain samples of anthrax and other pathogens from the UK's Society for Applied Microbiology.

The second attempt involved the efforts of a Malaysian man, Yazid Sufaat. Working at a laboratory near Kandahar, Sufaat is alleged to have attempted to create anthrax for al Qaeda, in the period preceding his arrest in Malaysia in December 2001.[139] His expertise was limited, however, given that he possessed only a Bachelor of Science degree and had

134 Leitenberg, *Evolution of the Current Threat, supra* note 118, at 65.
135 Ibid. at 66.
136 Ibid. at 67.
137 Ibid. at 67.
138 Ibid. at 54–58.
139 For details of this episode, Leitenberg draws on the National Commission on Terrorist Attacks upon the United States, THE 9/11 COMMISSION REPORT (New York: Norton, 2004).

been a lab technician for a brief period in the Malaysian military. He might have worked periodically with one other Indonesian member of al Qaeda, but otherwise appears to have worked alone. He failed to procure an effective strain of anthrax.

Leitenberg explains that aside from these two episodes, the only other evidence of al Qaeda's efforts to obtain biological or chemical weapons were in fragmentary notes from a disk believed to belong to al-Zawahiri, covering a period in the late 1990s. They indicate an interest acquiring nerve gas, and in finding people to assist with this, but suggest that no further steps were taken.[140]

## III. SKEPTICAL PERSPECTIVES ON RADIOLOGICAL AND CHEMICAL TERROR

The argument against the likelihood or imminence of mass terror must also address the possible use of radiological and chemical weapons. For reasons to be explored, both weapons are more easily deployed than nuclear or biological weapons, but are much less lethal in comparison. Also, on closer examination, the likelihood of causing "mass disruption" through the use of radiological weapons is much lower than many would suggest.

Recent work by John Mueller and Mark Stewart offers a basis for assessing the threat posed by chemical and radiological weapons.[141] In their view, both are often mistakenly conceived as "weapons of mass destruction" and commonly assumed to pose a comparable danger to a nuclear weapon. But although these weapons can "cause problems, kill people and inflict damage, they can scarcely do so on a large scale."[142] Chemical weapons in particular "may have the potential, under the appropriate circumstances, for panicking people; killing masses of them in open areas, however, is beyond their modest capabilities."[143] An attack involving nerve, mustard, or sarin gas would require massive quantities (i.e., tons rather than gallons) to pose a danger that extended beyond a square kilometer or a small urban space. Weather conditions would also easily diminish the effect.[144]

Radiological weapons do, however, present a special case. While they may be less likely to cause mass casualties (for reasons to be explored), they have the power to cause a great

---

140 Leitenberg, *Evolution of the Current Threat, supra* note 118, at 60. In August of 2011, the *New York Times* reported that an al Qaeda-linked group in Yemen was found by U.S. officials to be seeking to develop ricin "to be packed around small explosives for attacks against the United States." The report describes the group's efforts to create ricin from large quantities of castor beans. It also notes that "Senior American officials say there is no indication that a ricin attack is imminent, and some experts say the Qaeda affiliate is still struggling with how to deploy ricin as an effective weapon." It then proceeds to detail some of the many obstacles to deploying the poison on a large scale in various environments. *See* Eric Schmitt & Thom Shanker, *Qaeda Trying to Harness Toxin, Ricin, for Bombs, U.S. Says*, N.Y. TIMES, Aug. 12, 2011.

141 Mueller & Stewart, TERROR, SECURITY AND MONEY, *supra* note 2.

142 Ibid. Kindle edition, location 1,301.

143 Ibid. location 1,312.

144 Mueller and Stewart cite biologist Mathew Meselson and the first Gilmore Commission report on this point. *See* Mathew Meselson, *The Myth of Chemical Superweapons*, 47:3 BULL. ATOMIC SCIENTISTS 12 (April 1991), and the Gilmore Commission, *Assessing the Threat, supra* note 6, at 28.

deal of fear, panic, and long-term disruption to land use, with very serious economic consequences. They are also much less complicated to build and deploy than a nuclear weapon. Yet, a closer examination of the science involved suggests that there are *varying degrees* of probability involved in accomplishing varying degrees of destruction. Thus, although a terror group can cause a great deal of disruption with a radiological weapon more readily than it can with a nuclear or biological weapon, it is still challenging to do—and becomes more challenging still, and thus less likely, to impose greater degrees of disruption.

Wirz and Egger define a radiological weapon as "any device that is designed to spread radioactive material into the environment, either to kill, or to deny the use of an area."[145] Experts assume that terrorists would most likely attempt a radiological attack through the use of a "dirty bomb," or a "crude device comprising conventional explosives such as TNT or a fuel oil/fertilizer mix laced with highly radioactive materials."[146] The heat from the explosion would cause the radioactive materials to vaporize or aerosolize, and to spread easily and quickly over a potentially large space. Other methods of attack include dissemination through an "enclosed radiation source" left hidden somewhere in a large public building, or aerosolized or put into powdered form and placed within an air or water source.[147]

Experts agree that apart from casualties caused by the explosive device, all but the largest radiological weapons would be unlikely to cause mass casualties. Mueller and Stewart go as far as to assert that radiological weapons "are incapable of inflicting much immediate damage at all."[148] This is because the material cannot be dispersed in a way that forces victims to imbibe a lethal dose before leaving an affected area. It is therefore likely that "few, if any, in the target area would be killed directly, become ill, or even have a measurably increased risk of cancer."[149]

Wirz and Egger suggest that where an explosive device is used in a radiological attack, the extent of the damage, and the size of the affected area, would depend on a number of variables, including "the means used to disperse the radioactive material, the quantity of radioactive material, the weather conditions and much more."[150] The level of contamination "decreases with distance from ground zero [and also] decreases with time. [In addition,] weather conditions continuously remove radioactivity from the contaminated

---

145 Wirz & Egger, *Nuclear and Radiological Weapons, supra* note 5, at 502.

146 Michael Levi & Henry Kelly, *Weapons of Mass Disruption*, Scientific Am. 77 (November 2002), at 78; *see also* Peter Zimmerman & Cheryl Loeb, *Dirty Bombs: the Threat Revisited*, Def. Horizons 1 (January 2004), at 5.

147 Wirz & Egger, *Nuclear and Radiological Weapons, supra* note 5, at 504.

148 Mueller & Stewart, Terror, Security and Money, *supra*, note 2, at location 1,329.

149 Ibid. See also Wirz & Egger, *Nuclear and Radiological Weapons, supra* note 5, at 504; and Zimmerman & Loeb, *Dirty Bombs, supra* note 146, at 10.

150 Wirz & Egger, *Nuclear and Radiological Weapons, supra* note 5, at 505–06.

area, and [...] there is also the natural decay of the radionuclides."[151] Speculating on the possible effects of a moderate to small sized dirty bomb Wirz and Egger write:

> Mathematical models have shown that in the event of a dirty bomb attack we could expect a maximum dose rate of about 10 mSv/h at the explosion site.[152] This value depends, of course, on the hypothetical parameters, such as activity, meteorological conditions and the amount of explosives. A person would have to spend one hundred hours in this course area to have a 5% likelihood of developing symptoms of acute radiation sickness. The radioactivity emitted by a radiological weapon is therefore unlikely to present a serious or acute health hazard.[153]

Unfortunately, Wirz and Egger do not cite the models they refer to, or specify the quantity of radioactive material involved in these calculations. Other experts suggest that the potential damage could be considerable if the bomb were large enough.

Levi and Kelly have considered the possible damage of an explosive device containing 3,500 curies of cesium 137—a very large sample, but one involving an amount that known to be "orphaned" in the former Soviet Union.[154] A bomb of this size could contaminate some 800 square kilometers:

> The disaster would not be of Chernobyl's magnitude; it would release less radiation overall, and none in the form of potent short-lived isotopes such as iodine 131. But its strategic placement would wreak havoc. Over an area of about 20 city blocks, there would be a one-in-10 increased risk of death from cancer for residents living in the area (without decontamination) for 30 years, a 50 percent increase over the background rate. A broader area of 15 square kilometers—varying from four to 20 square kilometers, depending on the weather—would be contaminated above the relocation threshold recommended by the International Commission on Radiological Protection and accepted by the NRC. If these standards were relaxed and the relocation threshold were the same as that used around Chernobyl, the area affected would still be roughly 100 city blocks. The property value of this area is estimated in the hundreds of billions of dollars.[155]

---

151 Ibid.

152 Ibid. Radiation dosages are measured in "sieverts" ("Sv"), after the Swedish physicist Rolf Sievert. "10 mSv/h" denotes a quantity of 10 milli-sieverts ("mSv") per hour. To put this into context, a brain CT scan would yield 0.8 to 5 mSv, a chest CT scan 6 to 18 mSv. A fatal dose would involve between 4500–6000 mSv. *See* J.G. Van Unnik, J.J. Broerse, J. Geleijns, J.T. Jansen, J. Zoetelief, & D. Zweers, *Survey of CT Techniques and Absorbed Dose in Various Dutch Hospitals*, 70:832 British J. Radiol. (1997) at 367–71.

153 Ibid.

154 Levi & Kelly, *Weapons of Mass Disruption*, *supra* note 146, at 80.

155 Ibid.

This is, however, an extreme scenario.[156] Is it any more or less likely than scenarios involving smaller amounts of material or a smaller explosive charge? The answer turns on a series of variables. In addition to the device used, weather, access to materials, and so forth, a key issue is how easy it is to *build* a radiological device.

Mueller and Stewart contend that radiological weapons are "easier to assemble than a nuclear weapon," but that the "construction and deployment of one is difficult and requires considerable skill."[157] Experts often point out the ready availability of radioactive materials—either among supplies or equipment stored in hospitals, universities, and industrial sites—and the difficulty of securing them. But as Wirz and Egger point out, "not all of these sources would be suitable for use in an RDD [radioactive dispersion device]. Most are far too weak to cause extensive damage. Furthermore, many radioactive sources are in metallic form and would not be dispersed very effectively by high explosives."[158] Samples can certainly be obtained more readily than HEU or other fissile materials for a nuclear bomb, but for Wirz and Egger, building a radiological weapon "requires advanced know-how and planning, a very targeted approach and considerable expenditure."[159] Levi and Kelly support this cautionary view:

> Although they are relatively simple in principle, constructing and deploying one of these mechanisms is difficult to do. It is more complicated than wrapping stolen materials around a stick of dynamite. Such a clumsy weapon might only scatter large chunks of material, limiting the area affected and making cleanup easy. An effective dirty bomb is, however, much easier to assemble than a nuclear weapon, although it would still require considerable skill.[160]

Once again, this does not mean that radiological terror is not likely. It suggests, rather, that it may be more complicated and thus *less likely* the further up the scale of complexity and destructive capacity one seeks to go. In short, scenarios that envision large swaths of New York or London rendered uninhabitable by a radiological weapon are possible, but much less plausible or likely than a smaller scale attack that renders a few square kilometers unusable.

It may be worth mentioning briefly that experts also agree that a number of "low cost, practical steps" can be taken to considerably reduce the threat posed by radiological terror, and to "minimize the effects if an attack should occur."[161] These include stricter regulation and licensing of the trade and possession of such material, and tighter security standards for storage.

---

156 Zimmerman & Loeb, *Dirty Bombs, supra* note 146, at 10, offer similar speculation at the higher end: "It is unlikely that anything but a super-RDD will kill more than a few hundred Americans, but the task of cleaning up to currently acceptable levels of residual radiation will be enormous. There is not yet any technical solution other than razing structures and carting them away."

157 Mueller & Stewart, Terror, Security and Money, *supra*, note 2, at location 1,329. Mueller & Stewart cite Levi & Kelly's *Weapons of Mass Disruption, supra* note 146.

158 Wirz & Egger, *Use of Nuclear and Radiological Weapons, supra* note 5, at 503.

159 Ibid. at 503–04.

160 Levi & Kelly, *Weapons of Mass Disruption, supra* note 146, at 78.

161 Ibid. at 81. *See also* the recommendations of Zimmerman & Loeb, *Dirty Bombs, supra* note 146.

Governments might also mandate that inspections be carried out with increased frequency and thoroughness; and that more investments be made in detection mechanisms for tracing stolen material.[162] Levi and Kelly also propose "an extensive array of radiation-detection systems at key points such as airports, harbours, rail stations, tunnels, highways and borders." By 2002, the United States had begun to undertake initiatives of this kind in Boston, New York, and Washington. Finally, they suggest, "routine checks of scrap-metal yards and landfill sites would also protect against illegal or accidental disposal of dangerous materials."[163] In short, the danger posed by radiological weapons may be managed by a more aggressive campaign to secure the possession, movement, and disposal of radioactive materials.

### Conclusion to Part 1

Nuclear and biological terror may appear simple in theory, but ample evidence suggests that both are very difficult to carry out in practice. Future attempts are likely to be fraught with obstacles, rendering their success unlikely. This is not to say that safeguarding such materials and carefully regulating their storage and movement is not critical. The point, rather, is that claims about the *inevitability* of large-scale nuclear or biological terror are implausible. Similar conclusions can be drawn about mass terror involving radiological and chemical weapons. Although more readily deployed than biological or nuclear weaponry, these forms of attack are also fraught with a host of challenges rendering the likely damage from such events to be much less severe than is often feared.

## Part 2. Large-Scale Terror Not Involving WMDs

How likely is a large-scale terror attack in a North American city in the foreseeable future not involving WMDs? The broader argument in this chapter is that a stronger case for reform can be made not by summarily dismissing the harbinger theory as implausible, but by demonstrating its implausibility through evidence and analysis. Once again, the theory posits the short-term likelihood of mass terror through either WMDs or conventional weaponry. This part will argue that terror not involving WMDs is likely to be no greater in scale or scope than acts prior to 9/11. The reasons are due primarily to the nature of the actors and the means at their disposal.

To be clear, however, the goal in this part, as with part one, is not to set out the definitive case for this claim. The goal, rather, is to sketch a *form* of argument that may be used in advocating for liberal reform. For this purpose, the discussion will draw primarily on John Mueller and Mark Stewart's more extensive 2011 study *Terror, Security, and Money* and their more recent work.[164] Mueller and Stewart's primary purpose has been to

162 Ibid. at 81.

163 Ibid.

164 Mueller & Stewart, Terror, Security and Money, *supra*, note 2; Mueller & Stewart, *Secret without Reason and Costly without Accomplishment: Questioning the National Security Agency's Metadata Program*,

assess U.S. counterterrorism expenditures in light of the "likelihood and potential consequences of terrorist acts in the United States and in other Western countries."[165] They offer numerous arguments to support the view that the prospect of mass terror involving either WMDs or conventional means has been grossly overstated. They conclude that in light of the limited risk that terrorism poses, security expenditures since 9/11 have been vastly disproportionate to their practical benefits. A similar argument can be made here for reforming security law and policy itself. In light of the limited risk of terror—a risk far lower than is often assumed—many security measures are either unnecessary or grossly disproportionate to their actual benefits.

Assessing the risk of terror in North America by international groups not involving WMDs, Mueller and Stewart begin by documenting the opposition to al Qaida on the part of populations and governments in predominantly Muslim countries of Asia and the Middle East in the post-9/11 period.[166] Regimes across the Islamic world, from Pakistan to Egypt to Yemen, have resisted the incursion of al Qaeda and related groups as potential challenges to prevailing order, or as provocations to sectarian violence.[167] Motivation to police these groups has been further spurred by acts of terror in these nations, including the Bali bombing of 2002 and the Mumbai bombing of 2008.

Citing the work of Fawaz Gerges, Mueller and Stewart note that the focus of violence among non-state actors in the Islamic world in recent years has become more local and sectarian in nature.[168] Attacks involving groups associated with al Qaida from Bali to Morocco to Jordan exhibit a similar tendency to involve local groups whose primary grievance is with regional governments and events.[169] Detention centers in Afghanistan are a reflection of this, containing very few foreigners, mostly from Pakistan.[170] In 2010, CIA Director Leon Panetta stated a belief that there may be only 60 to 100 members of al Qaida remaining in Afghanistan.[171] Yet, as Mueller and Stewart note, the group has been alienated by the Taliban, along with every government in Africa and Asia, and likely has very limited funds. Citing an assessment by Mark Sageman, a former U.S. intelligence agent in Afghanistan, Mueller and Stewart argue that what remains of al Qaida is likely "a few dozen individuals," joined by "perhaps a hundred fighters left over from al-Qaeda's

I/S: J.L. & POL'Y FOR INFORMATION SOC'Y, forthcoming (2015); Mueller & Stewart, *Aviation Security, Risk Assessment, and Risk Aversion for Public Decisionmaking*, 32:3 J. POL' ANALYSIS & MGMT. 615–33 (Summer 2013); Mueller & Stewart, *America Is Spending Too Much on Defense: To bring budgets into line, we need to move past irrational threats*, SLATE.COM, Oct. 3, 2013; and Mueller & Stewart, *The Terrorism Delusion: America's Overwrought Response to September 11*, 37:1 INT'L SECURITY 81 (2012).

165 TERROR, SECURITY AND MONEY, *supra* note 2, at location 578.

166 Ibid. at location 599.

167 Ibid.

168 Ibid. at location 588. Mueller and Stewart draw here from Fawaz Gerges, THE RISE AND FALL OF AL-QAEDA (New York: Oxford University Press, 2011) and Peter Bergen & Paul Cruickshank, *The Unraveling: The Jihadist Revolt against bin Laden*, NEW REPUBLIC, June 11, 2008.

169 TERROR, SECURITY AND MONEY, *supra*, note 2, at location 617.

170 Ibid. at location 648.

171 Ibid. at location 650.

golden days in Afghanistan in the 1990s."[172] They may continue to hold training camps, but these are likely, in their view, to be "quite minor affairs."[173] They contend that every terror attack linked to al Qaeda since 2001 appears to have been carried out by a group only tenuously related to the core group in the Afghanistan–Pakistan region.[174]

This assessment might now appear dated in light of the emergence of the Islamic State of Iraq and Syria in 2014 from "al Qaida in Iraq" and other Sunni militant groups. But at present, ISIS remains regional in focus, is attracting considerable resistance on the part of the United States in the form of air strikes, and has also likely invited greater surveillance on the part of Western nations including Canada and the United States of citizens known to be involved in ISIS as they return from the region. This is not meant to preemptively dismiss the possible threat that ISIS or Western nationals involved in it may soon come to pose. It is to suggest, rather, that at present and for the foreseeable future, the seizure of territory and the acquisition by ISIS members of military skills and conventional weaponry does not pose a qualitatively different threat from those encountered in the past—including by other U.S. and Canadian nationals known to have attended terrorist training camps in Afghanistan or Pakistan.

Aside from the core al Qaida group itself, or other larger groups such as ISIS or AQAP, what remains of international terrorism has dwindled to "thousands of sympathizers and would-be jihadists spread around the globe who mainly connect in Internet chat rooms, engage in radicalizing conversations, and variously dare each other to actually do something."[175] As Mueller and Stewart have noted, in the decade following 9/11, not a single al Qaeda "sleeper cell" had been found in the United States, nor had the group managed to recruit a single individual in North America, or carry out a single attack on U.S. soil.[176] This has continued to be the case. The primary threat has therefore shifted to smaller groups of homegrown terrorists, influenced or possibly trained by groups abroad.

Yet an examination of recent plots suggests that future attacks by these smaller groups are likely to involve, as Brian Jenkins has put it, "tiny conspiracies, lone gunman, one-off attacks rather than sustained terrorist campaigns."[177] Future attacks will likely continue to be carried out by less sophisticated, well-funded, or ambitious individuals or groups than a transnational terrorist group in the nature of al Qaeda. CIA Director Leon Panetta lent official recognition of this view when he asserted in 2010 that the "lone wolf" terrorist has become America's "main threat."[178]

---

172 Ibid.

173 Ibid.

174 Ibid.

175 Ibid. at location 698.

176 Ibid. at location 702.

177 Brian Jenkins, Would-be Warriors: Incidents of Jihadist Terrorist Radicalization in the United States Since September 11, 2001 (Santa Monica CA: RAND, 2010), at 4; cited by Mueller and Stewart, ibid., at location 768.

178 Terror, Security and Money, *supra* note 2, at location 763.

Mueller and Stewart concede that individuals or small groups may indeed be capable of carrying out significant acts of terror, but question the probability of such an event in light of the skill and capacity demonstrated in a number of recent plots. The authors point to the 2009 plot involving Najibullah Zazi as instructive in this regard. The *New York Times* cited an Obama administration official to the effect that this was the "most serious" plot in the United States since 9/11, marked an attempt by al Qaida to "carry out another mass-casualty attack in the United States," and confirmed that the group continued to pose an "existential" threat.[179] As Mueller and Stewart explain, Zazi was a high school dropout, working in a doughnut shop in Manhattan. Having decided to set off a bomb in New York, he traveled to Pakistan and received training on bomb building from members of al Qaida. He then spent a year in New York trying to build the bomb. He was naïve enough to use stolen credit cards to buy material, setting off various security and surveillance traps that assisted authorities in foiling the plot. Notably, however, he never succeeded in building the bomb, despite several "frantic" attempts to communicate (on a tapped line) with sources in Pakistan.[180]

To further assess the nature of the threat posed by these small groups and individuals, John Mueller has assembled a collection of case studies on 54 domestic terror plots in the United States since 9/11.[181] As Mueller notes, the authors of the studies "with remarkably few exceptions, describe their subjects with words like incompetent, ineffective, unintelligent, idiotic, ignorant, inadequate, unorganized, misguided, muddled, amateurish, dopey, unrealistic, moronic, irrational, and foolish."[182] Some of the cases involved ambitious plots, including plans to topple the Sears Tower in Chicago, to bomb the Brooklyn Bridge, or to use radiological weapons. But, in each of these cases, the studies suggest that the plots at issue proved well beyond the capacity of those involved, for a host of reasons ranging from a lack of expertise with explosives, a lack of access to material, weaponry, or funding, and poor planning.[183]

The Boston bombing of April 2013 is consistent with Mueller and Stewart's analysis. It involved a small domestic group not affiliated with a larger, transnational group. They used conventional explosives and caused 3 deaths and 230 injuries—certainly serious and tragic, but a small fraction of the harm inflicted by 9/11. The attack is also consistent with Mueller and Stewart's broader conclusions. Terrorism in North America will continue to involve smaller, domestic groups or individuals. There may be further attempts to carry out significant acts of terror, but the more ambitious plots will meet with obstacles. In terms of their probability, frequency, and magnitude, the danger that domestic terrorists

---

179 David Johnston & Scott Shane, *Terror Case is Called One of the Most Serious in Years*, N.Y. TIMES, Sept. 25, 2009, cited by Mueller and Stewart, ibid., at location at 785.

180 TERROR, SECURITY AND MONEY, *supra* note 2, at location 785.

181 John Mueller, ed., TERROR SINCE 9/11: THE AMERICAN CASES (Columbus OH:, Mershon Centre, Ohio State University, 2013), at http://politicalscience.osu.edu/faculty/jmueller/SINCE.pdf.

182 *The Terrorism Delusion, supra* note 164, at 88.

183 Ibid.

present is low enough to constitute a comparable risk to those we tolerate in other facets of life. But before proceeding to explore arguments in support of this claim in Part 3 of this chapter, I will briefly address an important counter-argument to the analysis set out thus far and also the case of cyberterror.

### I. DID EXTRAORDINARY MEASURES HELP PREVENT ANOTHER 9/11?

A number of factors may point to a diminished threat of terror in North America in the period after 2001, but one might argue that a further major attack, possibly on the scale of 9/11, may have been averted precisely because one or another extraordinary measure has played an instrumental if not essential role in preventing it. Without the use of mass secret surveillance, torture, or targeted killing in recent years, another 9/11 might well have occurred. Some say 9/11 itself might have been avoided had the United States made earlier use of some of these measures. And without them, the prospect of another 9/11 looms.

A response to this argument might begin with a careful assessment of the logic underpinning it. If torture or other measures are justified because they were necessary to "prevent another 9/11," then this claim is valid only if each of its main premises are true: (i) the measures were in fact necessary rather than merely helpful or even "instrumental" to prevent an attack; and (ii) the attack they helped to prevent would likely have been comparable to 9/11 in scale. To be sure, for some, an argument might be made that torture or other extreme measures are justified where they help to prevent attacks on a much smaller scale. But this is not the claim that security officials often make. Consistent with the harbinger theory, the claim is often more ambitious: the measures *prevented* another *9/11*. General Keith Alexander, director of the NSA, implied this in an appearance before Congress in June of 2013: "I would much rather be here today debating [bulk surveillance] than trying to explain how we failed to prevent another 9/11."[184] Former Vice President Cheney put it more directly in 2009: "enhanced interrogations ... prevented the violent death of thousands, if not hundreds of thousands of innocent people."[185]

But while members of the security establishment often make this more ambitious claim, they have yet to cite a single instance in which the use of one or more extreme measures was necessary to prevent a major attack in North America. The evidence points instead to a more modest role for these measures, with intelligence from torture or surveillance in many cases yielding either redundant or corollary evidence, or information obtainable through other avenues. Cases of targeted killing have yet to involve a clear instance of a terror plot in the United States that was close to being carried out. And thus,

---

184 Tom McCarthy, *NSA Chief Says Exposure of Surveillance Programs Has "Irreversible" Impact*, GUARDIAN (U.K.), June 18, 2013.

185 Richard Cheney, Vice President Cheney's Remarks at the American Enterprise Institute, *Council on Foreign Relations* (May 21, 2009), at http://www.cfr.org/defense-strategy/vice-president-cheneys-remarks-american-enterprise-institute/p19470.

not only is there no clear evidence that mass secret surveillance, torture, or targeted killing have been *essential* to preventing *any* terror attacks—let alone a major attack—there are also reasons to doubt that not using them before September 11 was a major factor in the failure to prevent that event.

To focus first on mass secret surveillance, a number of impartial observers have highlighted the lack of evidence that extraordinary powers under either Section 215 of the USA PATRIOT Act or Section 702 of the FISA Amendments Act have been necessary to prevent a single attack.[186] Some of these assessments are based on a review of confidential information, including the report of the President's Review Group on surveillance. Convened in response to the Snowden revelations and reporting in December of 2013, the Group found that "the information contributed to terrorist investigations by the use of section 215 telephony meta-data was not essential to preventing attacks and could readily have been obtained in a timely manner using conventional section 215 orders."[187] The Group took a more favorable view of the utility of the programs authorized under Section 702 (for surveillance of U.S. communications with foreigners suspected of involvement in terror). Reviewing information pertaining to 54 cases from 2007 resulting in "the prevention of terrorist attacks in diverse nations and the United States," the Group concluded that "[i]n all but one of these cases, information obtained under section 702 contributed in some degree to the success of the investigation."[188] Yet the Group was cautious about the extent of this contribution, noting that while it is "difficult to assess precisely how many of these investigations would have turned out differently without the information learned through section 702," it was satisfied that "section 702 does in fact play an important role in the nation's effort to prevent terrorist attacks across the globe."[189] An important role in preventing an attack is not, however, the same as an essential or necessary role. Given the more ambitious claim on which mass surveillance is often justified ("preventing another 9/11"), the question is not whether Section 702 was *useful* in preventing an attack—which it may well have been—but whether an attack could not have been prevented without it.

Members of the Senate Intelligence Committee have also had access to confidential information relating to the NSA's use of Section 215 and 702 programs have expressed similarly critical views. In the summer of 2013, Senators Mark Udall and Ron Wyden of the committee sought to caution the public against the NSA's conflation of the two sets

---

186 USA PATRIOT Act, Pub. L. 107–56, 115 Stat. 272 (2001), and the Foreign Surveillance Act of 1978 Amendments Act of 2008, H.R. 6304.

187 The President's Review Group on Intelligence and Communications Technologies, *Liberty and Security in a Changing World: Report and Recommendations of The President's Review Group on Intelligence and Communications Technologies*, (Dec. 12, 2013), at http://www.whitehouse.gov/sites/default/files/docs/2013-12-12_rg_final_report.pdf (Review Group Report), at 104.

188 Ibid. at 145.

189 Ibid.

of programs in its promotional rhetoric ("these programs... [have disrupted] dozens of potential terrorist plots"). Seeking to present a more nuanced assessment, they asserted:

> Based on the evidence that we have seen, it appears that multiple terrorist plots have been disrupted at least in part because of information obtained under section 702 of FISA. However, it appears that the bulk phone records collection program under section 215 of the USA Patriot Act played little or no role in most of these disruptions.[190]

The Senators supported the usefulness of 702 programs but did not state that they were essential or specifically necessary to foil attacks. And while 702 programs may have contributed to disrupting multiple plots, neither the Senators nor the Review Group have claimed the program's utility in foiling *major* attacks, or attacks on the scale of 9/11 or greater.

In public defenses of the 215 and 702 programs, government officials have tended to advance two kinds of arguments. The first is to claim that either set of programs has been useful—not essential—in foiling plots, but when pressed to give examples, none involves plots on the potential scale of 9/11. And in response to those that involve relatively serious plots, commentators have raised doubts about whether the surveillance from either program was in fact helpful or instrumental in foiling the plot.

For example, in June of 2013, within days of the first Snowden leaks, NSA Director Keith Alexander testified before the House Intelligence Committee that

> [i]n recent years, the information gather from these programs [215 and 702] provided the US government with critical leads to help prevent over 50 potential terrorist events in more than 20 countries around the world. [*FISA Amendment Act*] 702 contributed to over 90% of these cases. At least 10 of these events included homeland-based threats and [in] the vast majority business records, FISA reporting [under 215] contributed as well.

The claim, once again, is that the powers of mass secret surveillance have been helpful but not essential, with the General avoiding the assertion that a specific event could not have been prevented without either program. Of the 50 plots that NSA surveillance had helped to disrupt, the NSA and FBI could disclose details about only four of them, citing the need to maintain secrecy.[191] John Mueller and Mark Stewart have assessed the role of NSA intelligence in these four plots in light of information gathered through a series of

---

190 Senators Ron Wyden & Mark Udall, *Statement on Effectiveness of Declassified NSA Programs*, (June 19, 2013), at http://www.wyden.senate.gov/news/press-releases/wyden-udall-issue-statement-on-effectiveness-of-declassified-nsa-programs.

191 *See* testimony of Sean M. Joyce, Deputy FBI Director, cited by Tom McCarthy, *supra* note 184.

media reports on each of the cases.[192] They show that without exception, neither 215 nor 702 programs were essential or necessary to disrupting the plots, nor were any remotely comparable in scale to 9/11.

One case involves a Somali cab driver in San Diego, Basaaly Moalin, whom the FBI, following a tip, had surveilled in 2003. Concluding after a brief period that Moalin was not involved in terrorism, the FBI terminated the investigation.[193] In 2007, NSA obtained a number in Somalia believed to be linked to al Shabaab and drew a connection to Moalin when it ran the number through the 215 database. Passing this information to the FBI, the Bureau then obtained a court order to wiretap Moalin and intercepted some 2,000 calls, revealing plans to send $8,500 to members of al Shabaab to fight an invading Ethiopian group. But, as Senator Wyden would later argue, the role of the database in making the connection to Moalin was not essential: "the government had all the information it needed to go to the phone company and get an individual court order."[194] There was no urgency, Wyden noted, since Moalin was only arrested "months" after he was first identified using the 215 program. If time was of the essence, a warrant could have been obtained on an expedited basis.[195]

A second case involves a Pakistani-American, David Headley, who carried out surveillance of targets on behalf of the group that killed 166 people in Mumbai in 2008.[196] Headley was arrested in the course of preparing to carry out a later plot to bomb a Danish newspaper that had published cartoons depicting the Prophet Muhammad, though the plot was still in its early stages and "beset by many planning and financial difficulties."[197] Moreover, as the investigative journalist Sebastian Rotella has noted, British intelligence had been surveilling Headley for a period well before his arrest, raising doubt as to whether the plot would have been allowed to advance very far.[198] The FBI made the arrest not using 702 information but through a tip from the British. NSA intercepts may thus have been useful in prosecuting Headley, but not essential to apprehending him or preventing an attack.

The third plot made public in defense of the NSA programs involves three Muslim immigrants to the United States, one living in Kansas and two in New York.[199] In 2003 in response to the invasion of Iraq, the three agreed to become involved in some form of militant action against the United States. Four years later, one of the men connected with two members of al Qaeda in Yemen. With the intention of joining them in fighting

---

[192] Mueller & Stewart, *Secret without Reason, supra* note 164.

[193] Ellen Nakashima, *NSA Cites Case as Success of Phone Data-Collection Program*, WASH. POST, Aug. 8, 2013.

[194] Ibid.

[195] Ibid.

[196] Mueller & Stewart, *Secret without Reason, supra* note 164, at 15.

[197] Ibid. at 15.

[198] Sebastian Rotella, *Did NSA Surveillance Help Thwart Plotter of Mumbai Attack*, PBS.ORG, June 12, 2013, cited in Mueller & Stewart, ibid.

[199] Mueller & Stewart, *Secret without Reason, supra* note 164, at 14.

against the United States in Afghanistan or Somalia, the Americans began sending money and equipment to the contacts in Yemen. This included $23,000, GPS units, and a remote-controlled toy car. Instead of using the money to carry out attacks, the recipients dispersed it among families of deceased militants ('Islamic martyrs'). The Yeminis then persuaded the Americans to carry out a plot in the United States, proposing the New York Stock Exchange as a possible target. At the prompting of their al Qaeda contacts, one of the U.S. conspirators visited the Stock Exchange, producing, as Mueller and Stewart note, a "one-page report of his adventure consisting of information that could have been gotten from Google maps and from tourist brochures" which was "summarily trashed in disgust by his handlers."[200] The co-conspirators may not have been tracked without using the 702 program, but given how little had been done to plan, let alone carry out, the attack, it hardly serves to demonstrate the use of 702 to prevent a major attack.

The fourth and final case offered in defense of the "critical" role of NSA surveillance involves the plot by Najibullah Zazi to set off a bomb in Times Square (described above). Yet as Mueller and Stewart have noted, a link between Zazi and his overseas contacts was not discovered through NSA surveillance but through a tip the British had provided U.S. officials as a consequence of Zazi's e-mail traffic to an overseas address the British had long been tracking.[201] The case against Zazi was corroborated by 702 data, but consisted largely of evidence gathered through conventional means. More to the point, as noted earlier, given Zazi's lack of sophistication and ineptitude (failing to build a bomb after a year of trying), this was not a case involving the imminent risk of a major attack.

Notably, in a later opportunity to make its case for the utility of the 215 program in particular, the government failed to offer further proof of its effectiveness. In the first of two constitutional challenges to the program under the USA PATRIOT Act decided in late 2013 (detailed in Chapter 3), Judge Richard Leon of the U.S. District Court for the District of Columbia noted that "the Government does *not* cite a single instance in which analysis of the NSA's bulk metadata collection actually stopped an imminent attack, or otherwise aided the Government in achieving any objective that was time sensitive in nature."[202] By contrast, in the second case decided weeks later, Judge William H. Pauley III, of the District Court for the Southern District of New York, concluded that "[t]he effectiveness of bulk telephony metadata collection cannot be seriously disputed."[203] But this assertion rested in large part on the government having "acknowledged several successes in Congressional testimony."[204]

---

200 Ibid. at 15.

201 Ibid.

202 Klayman v. Obama, 13 Civ. 0851 (D.D.C. 2013), at 61.

203 American Civil Liberties Union v. Clapper, 13 Civ. 3994 (S.D.N.Y. 2013), at 48.

204 Ibid.

Another frequent defense of the utility of the NSA programs is that they could have helped prevent 9/11 itself by addressing a gap in the law that became apparent in later investigations. Such defenders often cite the case of one of the 9/11 hijackers, Khalid al-Mihdhar, as did FBI Director Robert Mueller in his appearance before the House Judiciary Committee in June of 2013, following the first Snowden disclosures.[205] As Mueller noted, U.S. intelligence agencies had been tracking al-Mihdhar prior to 2000, but had lost sight of him from January of that year onward. At roughly the same time, they became aware of an al Qaida safe house in Yemen. Yet as Mueller explained,

> [The NSA] understood that that Al Qaida safe house had a telephone number but they could not know who was calling into that particular safe house. We came to find out afterwards that the person who had called into that safe house was al Mihdhar, who was in the United States in San Diego. If we had had this [metadata] program in place at the time we would have been able to identify that particular telephone number in San Diego.[206]

The following week, before the Senate, General Alexander told the same story in defense of the NSA programs, and did so on further occasions.[207] But others, including former FBI agent and ACLU policy counsel Michael German and investigative journalist Justin Elliott, have argued that neither the 702 nor 215 programs would have been necessary to obtain the numbers of the calls made to the safe house since U.S. intelligence had access to those numbers—and the authority and the ability to trace their origins.[208] As German notes, the 9/11 Commission has documented the fact that the NSA was intercepting calls to the Yemen safe house from 1999 onward, and both the CIA and NSA knew that al-Mihdhar was a member of al Qaida well before 2001.[209] The CIA had also known early in 2000 that al-Mihdhar had obtained a multiple-entry visa to the United States but failed to place him on a watch list or advise the FBI of the fact.[210] Moreover, the 9/11 Commission found that the FBI became aware of the visa by July of 2001 and knew of al-Mihdhar's presence in the United States by August 22, 2001.[211] Yet, as German

---

205 Justin Elliott, *Judge on NSA Case Cites 9/11 Report, But It Doesn't Actually Support His Ruling*, ProPublica, Dec. 28, 2013.

206 Ibid.

207 Tom McCarthy, *supra* note 184; *see also* Peter Finn, *NSA Chief Says Surveillance Program Helped Thwart Dozens of Plots*, Wash. Post, June 27, 2013.

208 Michael German, *No NSA Poster Child: The Real Story of 9/11 Hijacker Khalid al-Mihdhar*, DefenceOne, Oct. 16, 2013, and Justin Elliot, *supra* note 205, both cited in Mueller & Stewart, *Secret without Reason, supra* note 164.

209 German, *No NSA Poster Child,* ibid.

210 Ibid.

211 Ibid.; National Commission on Terrorist Attacks upon the United States, The 9/11 Commission Report (New York: Norton, 2004), at 269–70.

observes, U.S. intelligence failed to draw a connection between al-Mihdhar and Yemen because neither the FBI nor the NSA sought to trace the calls coming into the al Qaida safe house until after 9/11, when records revealed that al-Mihdhar's calls were among them.[212] As Richard A. Clarke, former National Coordinator for Counterterrorism under Presidents Bush and Obama, told Elliot:

> Justice could have asked the FISA Court for a warrant to all phone companies to show all calls from the U.S. which went to the Yemen number. As far as I know, they did not do so. They could have [...] My understanding is that they did not need the current All Calls Data Base FISA warrant to get the information they needed. Since they had one end of the calls (the Yemen number), all they had to do was ask for any call connecting to it.[213]

Thus, German writes: "the problem was not that the government lacked the right tools to do its job (it had ample authority to trace Mihdhar's calls). The problem was that the government apparently failed to use them."[214]

Turning to the question of torture, a similar body of skeptical opinion has called into question the facts on which supporters of torture as an effective security measure have based their claims.[215] Secrecy, however, has played a greater role in this context, with much of the information that might help settle many conflicting interpretations of events still held confidential. In 2013, a task force convened by the Constitution Project, a Washington-based NGO, offered a detailed examination of available evidence on the use of torture in an effort to assess its effectiveness in preventing terror.[216] The Project describes the task force as an "independent, non-partisan" group consisting of various distinguished jurists, security experts, and academics, including former FBI Director and District Court judge, William Sessions, three-star General Claudia Kennedy, New York University law Professor Richard Epstein, and former American Bar Association President Talbot D'Alemberte.[217] In a chapter devoted to the efficacy of torture, the authors note

---

212 German, *supra* note 208.

213 Elliott, *supra* note 205.

214 German, *supra* note 208; he notes that the this conclusion was also arrived at by a joint inquiry into the events held by the House and Senate Intelligence Committees in 2002: *Report of the Joint Inquiry into the Terrorist Attacks of September 11, 2001—By the House Permanent Select Committee on Intelligence and the Senate Select Committee on Intelligence* (December 2002), at 12: http://fas.org/irp/congress/2002_rpt/911rept.pdf.

215 *See*, e.g., Jane Mayer, *Counterfactual: A Curious History of the CIA's Secret Interrogation Program*, New Yorker, Mar. 29, 2010; Peter Bergen, Manhunt: the Ten-Year Search for Osama Bin Laden from 9/11 to Abbottabad (New York: Crown, 2012); and Ali Soufan, The Black Banners: The Inside Story of 9/11 and the War Against al-Qaeda (New York: Norton, 2011).

216 The Constitution Project, *Report of the Constitution Project's Task Force on Detainee Treatment* (Washington D.C., 2013) (Task Force Report), at http://www.constitutionproject.org/publications-resources/detainee-task-force/.

217 Ibid.

that officials who authorized the CIA's enhanced interrogation program have consistently defended its effectiveness. Speaking to *Politico* in 2009, Dick Cheney asserted that

> If it hadn't been for what we did—with respect to the terrorist surveillance program, or enhanced interrogation techniques for high-value detainees, the Patriot Act, and so forth—then we would have been attacked again [. . .] Those policies we put in place, in my opinion, were absolutely crucial to getting us through the last seven-plus years without a major-casualty attack on the U.S.[218]

In his memoirs, former President Bush asserts that "[t]he CIA interrogation program saved lives," and "helped break up plots to attack military and diplomatic facilities abroad, Heathrow Airport and Canary Wharf in London, and multiple targets in the United States."[219] But many others with "personal knowledge of the CIA program" have been "extremely skeptical" of such claims, including President Obama's former National Director of Intelligence, Dennis Blair, who has stated that "[t]he information gained from these techniques was valuable in some instances, but there is no way of knowing whether the same information could have been obtained through other means."[220]

The report offers a critical perspective on claims made about the utility of information gathered from the "enhanced interrogation" of two high-profile Guantanamo detainees, Khalid Sheikh Mohammed (KSM), and Abu Zubaydah. The Report also questions whether the information was crucial in the search for Osama bin Laden and foiling a "second wave" of attacks in the United States soon after 9/11, including the alleged Los Angeles Library Tower plot (discussed below). As the Report indicates, claims in relation to KSM's importance in finding bin Laden tend to rest on the assertion that KSM was an early source in the identification of bin Laden's personal courier, Abu Ahmed al-Kuwaiti.[221] But the Task Force cites a number of sources suggesting that al-Kuwaiti had been identified by other detainees, prior to KSM's interrogation, including at least one detainee (Hassan Gul) who had divulged al-Kuwaiti's name prior to being subject to enhanced interrogation.[222] The authors of the report also point out that bin Laden was captured some eight years after the interrogations were carried out, with the trail running "cold" at several stages. As Tommy Vietor, a spokesman for the National Security Council, stated: "[i]f we had some kind of smoking-gun intelligence from waterboarding in 2003, we would have taken out Osama bin Laden in 2003."[223] As Vietor added, "[i]t

218 John Harris, Mike Allen & Jim Vandehei, *Cheney Warns of New Attacks*, POLITICO.COM, Feb. 2, 2009.
219 George W. Bush, DECISION POINTS (New York: Random House, 2010), at 171; cited in Task Force Report, *supra* note 216, at 244.
220 Cited in Task Force Report, *supra* note 216, at 244.
221 Ibid. at 246.
222 Ibid.
223 Scott Shane & Charlie Savage, *Bin Laden Raid Revives Debate on Value of Torture*, N.Y. TIMES, May 3, 2011, cited in Task Force Report, *supra* note 216, at 247.

took years of collection and analysis from many different sources to develop the case that enabled us to identify this compound, and reach a judgment that bin Laden was likely to living there."[224] In a public statement on the issue, Senators Dianne Feinstein and Carl Levin of the Senate Intelligence Committee were more emphatic in their position. Based on the Committee's investigation of the CIA program, information leading to al-Kuwaiti "had no connection to CIA detainees." The CIA had "significant intelligence... collected from a variety of classified sources." But the enhanced interrogation of KSM and another Guantanamo detainee "provided false and misleading information during their time in CIA custody."[225]

President Bush described the Library Tower in a speech of February 2006. KSM, the "mastermind" of the 9/11 attacks had "set in motion" a plot to have "terrorist operatives hijack a plan using shoe bombs to breach the cockpit door, and fly the plane into the tallest building on the West Coast."[226] Rather than Arabs to partake in the plot, KSM had recruited young Southeast Asian men, to avoid suspicion. KSM had tasked an al Qaida leader, Hambali, who was affiliated with the Southeast Asian group Jemaah Islamiyah to coordinate the group and see to their training in Afghanistan. Once recruited, the group met with bin Laden and began preparing for the attack. It was disrupted in early 2002, Bush explained, when "a Southeast Asian nation arrested a key al Qaeda operative... This critical intelligence helped other allies capture the ringleaders and other known operatives who had been recruited for this plot."[227] But, as the Task Force observes, Bush and other administration officials would repeatedly assert that the CIA's interrogation of KSM had been crucial to foiling the plot.[228] (In his memoirs, Bush states that KSM had "provided information that led to the capture of Hambali... [and] further details that led agents to Hambali's brother, who had been grooming operatives to carry out another attack on the United Statess, possibly a West Coast version of 9/11..."[229]) The Task Force concedes that names provided by KSM and others in U.S. custody offered assistance to Indonesian intelligence investigating members of the Jemaah Islamiyah group, though it remains unclear whether arrests of the "al-Ghuraba" cell linked to the Los Angeles plot depended on that information.[230] Regardless, as former CIA interrogator Ali Soufan told the Task Force, "the cell had not yet committed any attacks and weren't plotting anything; they were training and studying. In November [2003] the eighteen students were

---

224 Ibid. Shane & Savage.

225 Joint Statement of Senator Dianne Feinstein, Chairwoman, Senate Intelligence Committee, and Senator Carl Levin, Chairman, Senate Armed Services Committee (Apr. 27, 2012), at https://www.feinstein.senate.gov/public/index.cfm/files/serve?File_id=026a329b-d4c0-4ab3-9f7e-fad5671917cc; cited in Task Force Report, *supra*, note 216, at 247.

226 George W. Bush, *Status of the War on Terror: Address to the National Guard*, (Feb. 9, 2006), at http://www.presidentialrhetoric.com/speeches/02.09.06.html; cited in Task Force Report, *supra* note 216, at 253–54.

227 Ibid. at 254.

228 Ibid.

229 Bush, *supra* note 219, at 170–71, cited in Task Force Report, *supra* note 216, at 254.

230 Task Force Report, ibid. at 254–56.

repatriated to their home countries." Soufan dismissed the notion that they posed much of a danger of eventually carrying out a plot: "[t]his 'eventually' and 'possibly' was the best analysts could conclude, despite 183 sessions of waterboarding...The reality is that the al-Ghuraba cell wasn't involved, which is why the U.S. didn't request the arrest of its members and they were sent to their home countries."[231] Media reports confirm that the students making up the al-Ghuraba cell were returned to their home countries, and many were released soon after returning.[232] None have been charged for their involvement in a plot against the United States.[233]

The Task Force concluded that "the available public record, limited as it is, simply does not support a claim that waterboarding prevented the Library Tower from being reduced to rubble."[234] The role of information extracted through CIA interrogations in the arrest of members of Jemaah Islamiyah has also remained unclear, though any danger posed by those arrested was concentrated in Southeast Asia. In August of 2005, a suicide bombing exploded a bomb outside the lobby of the Jakarta Marriott Hotel, claiming 11 lives and injuring 81. The Task Force queries the possible involvement in the bombing of Hambali and other persons named by KSM and others in U.S. custody. Yet it concludes that it is "impossible to be certain whether other interrogation methods would have stopped these attacks." It is also "equally impossible to be certain that the information that captives revealed after being tortured could not have been obtained by any other means."[235]

Mark Danner argued in 2009 that until an impartial, "authoritative and convincing" assessment of America's use of torture can be presented, "its lingering mystique, owing mostly to secrecy" would remain.[236] Perhaps the most definitive official statement on the efficacy of post-9/11 torture will come from the as yet unreleased Senate Intelligence Committee report on torture. The Committee's chair, Senator Feinstein, has indicated that its members chose to investigate the CIA's use of torture in part as a response to the 2007 revelation that CIA official, Jose Rodriquez, had destroyed some 100 videotaped interrogations.[237] She and other Committee members were concerned that the CIA may have sought to conceal illegal or immoral activity. The Committee has since produced a report of some 6,600 pages, which remains confidential. But in April of 2014, it voted to make public the report's factual findings, recommendations, and executive summary—totaling some 700 pages.[238] At the time of this writing, the Committee and the White House are negotiating which portions of this shorter document should be

231 Ibid. at 256.
232 Ibid.
233 Ibid.
234 Ibid. at 257.
235 Ibid. at 258.
236 Mark Danner *The Red Cross Torture Report: What It Means*, N.Y. Rev. of Books, Apr. 30, 2009.
237 Spencer Ackerman, *Top Senator Rejects CIA Torture Report Redactions Ahead of Public Release*, Guardian (U.K.), Aug. 5, 2014.
238 Ibid.

redacted before public release. But over the past year, in various media reports, Committee members have "made clear that [the full report] has concluded the CIA materially misrepresented the scope, efficacy and intensity of its torture regime to both its legislative overseers and the Bush-era Justice Department."[239] As an earlier *Washington Post* report notes, the Committee's investigation "makes a detailed case that subjecting prisoners to 'enhanced' interrogation techniques did not help the CIA find Osama bin Laden and often were counterproductive in the broader campaign against al-Qaeda."[240]

A final measure to consider is targeting killing. As with mass secret surveillance and torture, the U.S. government has yet to provide clear evidence of a case in which targeted killing was necessary to prevent a major attack. One reason this may be the case relates to the Obama administration's understanding of when targeted killing is lawful, and the practice that has flowed from this interpretation. As the administration's leaked White Paper from February of 2013 indicates, targeted killing is carried out where (a) a person is believed to be a senior operational leader of al Qaida or an associated force; (b) he poses "an imminent threat of violent attack against the United States"; and (c) his capture is "not feasible."[241] A critical part of the test is the definition of imminence. "In this context," the memo states, "imminence must incorporate considerations of the relevant window of opportunity, the possibility of reducing collateral damage to civilians, and the likelihood of heading off future disastrous attacks on Americans."[242] In other words, imminence functions here more in the sense of "possibility" than "immediacy." It suggests, therefore, that in many if not most instances, targeted killing is carried out in cases other than where a plot is about to occur, and has not been necessary to *prevent* an attack in a direct sense.

This understanding of the use of targeted killing is consistent with what is known of the cases involving prominent targets such as bin Laden and Anwar al Awlaki, and other allegedly senior al Qaida officials. When confirming the killings of both bin Laden and Awlaki, the administration did not attempt to rely on the assertion that either was involved in a plot that was likely to be carried out in short order, or that carrying out the mission prevented a specific attack.[243] Nor has it offered such evidence in relation to any other use of targeted killing.

When pressed to justify the *unique* necessity of targeted killing as a tool of national defense, the Obama administration relies on a more conventional concept of imminence. It thus tacitly concedes that targeted killing is justified only in a true emergency, where it would directly prevent an attack in the process of unfolding. Attorney General Eric

---

239 Ibid.

240 Greg Miller, *Report Finds Harsh CIA Interrogations Ineffective*, WASH. POST, Dec. 13, 2012.

241 Department of Justice, *Lawfulness of a Lethal Operation Directed Against a U.S. Citizen Who is a Senior Operational Leader of Al-Qa'ida or an Associated Force*, made available by MSNBC Media, at http://msnbcmedia.msn.com/i/msnbc/sections/news/020413_DOJ_White_Paper.pdf.

242 Ibid. at 7.

243 *See* Chapter 2 for discussion of the President's public statements following both events.

Holder implied this in a March 2013 exchange with Senator Rand Paul, where he sought to justify the administration's view that it possessed the power to use targeted killing against U.S. citizens on U.S. soil. Holder was careful to assert that such authority applied only "in the circumstances of a catastrophic attack like the ones suffered on December 7, 1941, and September 11, 2001"—a situation of absolute urgency.[244] Holder also agreed with Feinstein's suggestion that it might be necessary to shoot down a plane hijacked by terrorists who may be American.[245] The broader point, however, is that while the government appears to concede that targeted killing of U.S. citizens in the United States can be justified only in terms of hypothetical situations of great urgency, in practical terms, government and other supporters of targeted killing have yet to produce evidence that the numerous killings outside the United States have entailed situations of immediate urgency. It is therefore at least doubtful that the measure has been necessary to prevent even a single terror attack, much less a major attack.

## II. CYBERTERROR AS A MEANS OF MASS TERROR

In recent years, many debates in national security have focused on the possibility of an attack in cyberspace. Many of the more elaborate threat scenarios have been premised on the prospect of cyberwar, or the use of cybernetic tools by *state* actors—China, Iran, Israel—as a novel means of military aggression.[246] In contrast to this, some scenarios have involved cyberterror in particular, or the use of computer networks by non-state actors to effect significant economic disruption,[247] or even attacks on critical infrastructure that result in mass casualties. In October 2012, Secretary of Defense Leon Panetta offered a notable example of the latter. Warning of a possible "cyber-Pearl Harbor," Panetta expressed the fear that

> [a]n aggressor nation or extremist group could use [various new] kinds of cyber tools to gain control of critical switches... They could derail passenger trains, or even more dangerous, derail passenger trains loaded with lethal chemicals. They could contaminate the water supply in major cities, or shut down the power grid across large parts of the country.[248]

---

244 Letter of March 4, 2013, from Attorney General Eric Holder to Senator Rand Paul, at http://www.paul.senate.gov/files/documents/BrennanHolderResponse.pdf.

245 Charlie Savage, *Senators Press Holder on Use of Military Force on U.S. Soil*, N.Y. TIMES, Mar. 6, 2013.

246 *See*, e.g., Richard A. Clarke & Robert K. Knake, CYBER WAR: THE NEXT THREAT TO NATIONAL SECURITY AND WHAT TO DO ABOUT IT (New York: Harper Collins, 2012).

247 *See*, e.g., Max Fisher, *Fmr. Intelligence Director: New Cyberattack May Be Worse Than 9/11*, THE ATLANTIC, Sept. 30, 2010.

248 Elisabeth Bumiller & Thom Shanker, *Panetta Warns of Dire Threat of Cyberattack on US*, N.Y. TIMES, Oct. 11, 2012.

He also feared that terrorists might launch "several attacks on our critical infrastructure at once, in combination with a physical attack on our country," which would "paralyze and shock the nation and create a profound new sense of vulnerability." In either case, Panetta's vision of cyberterror is a variation on the harbinger theory. Suggesting that America is becoming more vulnerable in light of new or evolving capabilities on the part terrorists, and raising the specter of bioterror ("trains loaded with lethal chemicals"), he was clearly asserting that cyberterror raised the short-term prospect of a 9/11-scale attack.

Panetta is not alone in this view. Scholars and experts on the threat posed by cyberterror have entertained similar scenarios. Sam Powers, for example, argued in 2013 that terror groups "regardless of historical precedent or their current capacity, represent the greatest threat to security, rather than states such as China and Russia."[249] As Powers writes,

> [t] hankfully, a catastrophic attack on critical infrastructure like that portrayed by Mr. Panetta and others has yet to occur. However [...] terrorist organizations and "lone wolves" have expressed interest in conducting such attacks and have demonstrated their proficiency on a smaller scale at quite an alarming level. If left unprotected, the critical infrastructure of nations may face an attack at a much larger scale, resulting in mass casualties and degradation of vital systems that are necessary to maintain national security.[250]

To support this latter claim, Powers cites a test conducted by the Department of Homeland Security in 2007 to cause the turbine of an electricity generator at the Idaho National Laboratory to "burst into smoke" through a cyberattack. Engineers had demonstrated that "by changing the operating cycle of a power generator remotely via computer, the turbines could set fire, eventually destroying the machine."[251] This has broader implications for Powers because, increasingly, vital infrastructure in North America and elsewhere have been designed around what are termed "Industrial Control Systems," or systems with a single, centralized control component, connected to a network of computers in remote locations. But whereas in the past, those networks were closed, and thus relatively secure, more of them are now linked to the Internet, with various security protocols designed to control access, but more vulnerable by virtue of being connected to the net itself.[252] As a consequence, the control systems of many federal agencies tasked with management of vital infrastructure have become constantly subject to a high volume of

---

249 Sam Powers, *The Threat of Cyberterrorism to Critical Infrastructure*, E-International Relations (September 2013), at http://www.e-ir.info/2013/09/02/the-threat-of-cyberterrorism-to-critical-infrastructure/. *See also* Marie-Helen Maras, COMPUTER FORENSICS: CYBERCRIMINALS, LAWS, AND EVIDENCE (Sudbury MA: Jones and Bartlett, 2012) at 179–80.

250 Powers, ibid. at 2.

251 Ibid. at 3.

252 Ibid.

attacks. And while "none of these attacks have crippled infrastructure and caused terror through physical damage and loss of life," Powers asserts that,"the possibility of such an attack is not without reason."[253]

A number of cybersecurity experts disagree. Peter W. Singer contends that it is one thing to hack into a computer system, but another to make things explode. The issue for Singer is that "[t]aking down hydroelectric generators, or designing malware like Stuxnet that causes nuclear centrifuges to spin out of sequence doesn't just require the skills and means to get into a computer system. It's also knowing what to do once you are in."[254] Causing serious damage "requires an understanding of the devices themselves and how they run, the engineering and physics behind the target."[255] Israel's use of the Stuxnet virus, Singer notes, involved not only computer experts "but also experts in areas that ranged from intelligence and surveillance to nuclear physics to the engineering of a specific kind of Siemens-brand industrial equipment."[256] It also involved "expensive tests, not only of the software, but on working versions of the target hardware as well."[257] By contrast, thus far, terrorists have been able to carry off very little in terms of attacks online. As Singer notes, "[t]he only publicly documented case of an actual al-Qaida attempt at a cyber attack wouldn't have even met the FBI definition. Under questioning at Guantanamo Bay, Mohamedou Ould Slahi confessed to trying to knock offline the Israeli prime minister's public website."[258] Similarly, in September of 2012, an Islamic group, Izz ad-Din al-Qassam, claimed responsibility for a "denial-of-service" attack on five U.S banks that "prevented customers from accessing the sites for a few hours."[259] This was the equivalent, in Singer's view, of "a crowd standing in your lobby blocking access or a gang of neighborhood kids constantly doing 'ring and runs' at your front doorbell… It is certainly not in the vein of a 'cyber 9/11' or 'digital Pearl Harbor.'" Instead, as he notes, terrorists are more often content to use the Internet in conventional ways—as a tool for social networking or dissemination.[260]

Other experts support Singer's analysis. As George R. Lucas has argued, "the threat of cyberterrorism […] has been vastly overblown."[261] Part of the reason has to do with the fact that "genuine cyber warfare turns out to be a very expensive, labor intensive, and therefore remains a highly state-centric enterprise."[262] While terrorists can use the net "to

---

253 Ibid.

254 Peter W. Singer, *The Cyber Terror Bogeyman*, Brookings Institute (November 2012); *see also* Peter W. Singer & Allan Friedman, CYBERSECURITY AND CYBERWAR: WHAT EVERYONE NEEDS TO KNOW (Oxford: Oxford University Press, 2014), at 96–99.

255 Ibid. *Cyber Terror Bogeyman*.

256 Ibid.

257 Ibid.

258 Ibid.

259 Ibid.

260 Ibid.

261 George R. Lucas, *Permissible Preventive Cyberwar: Restricting Cyber Conflict to Justified Military Targets*, in Luciano Floridi & Mariarosaria Taddeo, eds., THE ETHICS OF INFORMATION WARFARE (London: Springer, 2014), at 75.

262 Ibid.

great advantage for the purposes of conventional propaganda and disinformation [...] they cannot easily develop true cyber weapons, or engage in acts of cyber warfare—nor have they yet been detected as doing so, or even trying to do so." He concludes: "[t]o be blunt: neither the 14-year old hacker in the next door neighbor's upstairs bedroom, nor the two- or three-person al Qaeda cell plotting from a tiny flat in Hamburg, are going to bring down the Glen Canyon and Hoover Dams."[263] Writing in *Foreign Affairs* in 2013, Martin Libicki concurs:

> Although the risk of a debilitating cyberattack is real, the perception of that risk is far greater than it actually is. No person has ever died from a cyberattack, and only one alleged cyberattack has ever crippled a piece of critical infrastructure, causing a series of local power outages in Brazil. In fact, a major cyberattack of the kind intelligence officials fear has not taken place in the 21 years since the Internet became accessible to the public.[264]

Libicki concedes that a cyberattack could in theory "disable infrastructure or endanger civilian lives," but even in the case of a "major cyberattack on the United States," "direct casualties would most likely be limited, and indirect casualties would depend on a variety of factors such as whether the attack disabled emergency 911 dispatch services."[265] But even then, as he notes, there would have to be "no alternative means of reaching first responders for such an attack to cause casualties."[266] Cyberterror attacks are thus theoretically possible, and may do significant damage. But the evidence is lacking for claims that cyberspace may soon become the means for another attack on the scale of 9/11.

## Part 3. Terrorism as a Special Risk

Can authoritarian measures be justified without the harbinger theory? In this part, I anticipate a form of argument that may become more prevalent if the harbinger theory were to lose its salience in public discourse in the future. It is also a form of argument that may pose an obstacle to reform among portions of the electorate that currently support harsh counter-terror measures without relying on the harbinger theory or a fear of large-scale terror.

More invasive measures might be justified on the basis that terrorism represents a special kind of threat to public safety. The special nature of the threat derives not from the number of casualties or injuries, or the scale of the damage, in any single attack, but the shocking and horrific nature of terrorism itself. Acts such as the Boston bombing of 2013,

---

263 Ibid.

264 Martin C. Libicki, *Don't Buy the CyberHype*, FOREIGN AFF., Aug. 14, 2013.

265 Ibid.

266 Ibid.

or a possible bombing of a commercial airliner resulting in two hundred to three hundred deaths, may be small relative to 9/11 and consistent with the scale of terrorism prior to 9/11. But they are sufficiently horrific to justify the perception of them as something greater than crime, though less than war. We are therefore justified in lowering our tolerance for terrorism and permanently curtailing liberties in an effort—which may not always succeed—to address this special risk.

Two arguments might be made against this forceful but largely emotion-driven form of reasoning. One is that is it irrational to craft policy on the basis of a lower tolerance for terrorism given that the risk it presents is comparable to risks we accept in other facets of modern life. What we sacrifice to address this risk—in liberty and in financial and other costs—does not result in comparable benefits. We will not be significantly safer at least in part because we are not collectively at great danger to begin with.

A second argument is that we ought to resist treating terrorism as a special kind of threat because it is *essentially* criminal in nature and not significantly greater than the threat posed by other serious forms of criminal conduct. If so, terrorism is best addressed as a form of crime and dealt with under the limits of the criminal law. The limited risk posed by terrorism is best managed using a combination of law enforcement and better regulation of sensitive sites and materials.

## The Comparable Risks Theory

I draw once again on the work of Mueller and Stewart to set out briefly the argument that terrorism should not be seen as a special risk because it is comparable to many other risks we have chosen to live with.

One of the primary questions Muller and Stewart seek to address in *Terror, Security, and Money* is whether "the likelihood of being killed by terrorists [is] unacceptably high, or is it something that is negligible and that we in society are willing to accept?" Put otherwise, "just how safe is safe enough? When does a risk become acceptable?"[267] They suggest that across various fields in recent decades, after much study and debate on the question of risk tolerance, "a substantial consensus has been reached, resulting in a fair degree of agreement about risk acceptability."[268] Intolerable risks are those that present "obvious or evident" concerns or dangers—a risk "so high that no reasonable person would deem it acceptable."[269] Citing case law and studies of the US Occupational Safety and Health Administration, they find that "risks considered unacceptable are those found likely to kill more than 1 in 100,000 per year or sometimes 1 in 10,000."[270] Other studies point to a threshold for acceptable risks. The U.S. Nuclear Regulatory Commission found the acceptable annual fatality risk to be 1 in 2 million for risks from

---

[267] Terror, Security and Money, *supra* note 2, at Kindle location 890.

[268] Ibid. at location 943.

[269] Ibid.

[270] Ibid. at location 955.

accidents, and 1 in 500,000 for risks for nuclear power plant operations.[271] For the United Kingdom's nuclear sites, Britain's Health and Safety Executive has indicated that a risk of death to persons offsite should not exceed 1 in 1 to 10 million per year; institutions in Japan and Australia have made similar findings.[272] Summing up, Mueller and Stewart write: "Established regulatory practices in several developed countries suggest... that risks are deemed unacceptable if the annual fatality risk is higher than 1 in 10,000 or perhaps higher than 1 in 100,000. Risks are deemed acceptable if the annual fatality risk is lower than 1 in 700,000 or perhaps 1 in 1 million or one in 2 million. Between these two ranges is an area that might be considered tolerable risk." [273]

To quantify the risk that terrorism poses, Mueller and Stewart draw on a range of statistical data about transnational and domestic terror worldwide. They note that "the total number of people killed in the years after 9/11 by Muslim extremists outside of war zones comes to some 200 to 300 per year."[274] This includes high-profile attacks in Bali (2002); Saudi Arabia, Morocco and Turkey (2003); the Philippines, Madrid, and Egypt (2004); and in London (2005).[275] Drawing on a set of assessments of the global total of causalities from transnational terrorism, extending from 1968 to 2006, Mueller and Stewart arrive at the figure of some 420 deaths per year, for a yearly probability of being killed in an international terror strike of 1 in 14 million—based on a division of 420 by the world's population of 6.8 billion at the time they were writing.[276] To quantify the risk of domestic terror in Canada and the United States, Mueller and Stewart divide the total number of fatalities in each nation from 1970 to 2007 by the country's population. In the United States, 3,292 people were killed in terror attacks during this period (the vast majority in 9/11), and in Canada the figure is 336 (all but 7 in the Air India bombing).[277] Terrorism in the United States resulted in 1 death in 3.5 million and in Canada 1 in 3.8 million.[278]

Mueller and Stewart then compare the risk that terrorism poses with other conventional hazards we tolerate. The annual fatality rate for traffic accidents in 2008 was 1 in 8,200 in the United States, 1 in 13,500 in Canada; homicide that year resulted in 1 death per 22,000 in the United States, 1 in 55,000 in Canada. In the United States, death by accidents involving home appliances averaged from 1970 to 2007 was 1 in 1.5 million; and citing a study from 2003, the authors note that the fatality rate in the United States that year for drowning in a bathtub was 1 in 700,000.[279] Mueller and Stewart conclude their overview by asserting that it "abundantly clear... that the hazard presented to human life

271 Ibid.
272 Ibid. at location 967.
273 Ibid. at location 967.
274 Ibid. at location 844.
275 Ibid.
276 Ibid.at location 827.
277 Ibid. at location 883.
278 Ibid.
279 Ibid. at location 1015.

by terrorism outside of war zones under present conditions is very low—at least half the risk of being killed in a natural disaster and nearly a thousand times less than being killed in an accident."[280]

If terrorism does not pose a greater risk than other common risks we have come to accept as a part of modern life, it should no longer be seen as a *special* risk—a risk that flows from a special quality about terrorism per se. The case for this last point is difficult to make primarily due to the emotional resonance of terrorism. But the irony of the disproportionate attention we devote to terrorism in relation to other risks might help demonstrate the irrational nature of the belief in terror's special character.

For example, as Peter Ludlow has noted in an essay on the fear of terror and public priorities, two days after the Boston bombing in which 3 people were killed and 230 were injured, an explosion at a Texas fertilizer plan killed 14 people and injured over 160.[281] It was briefly a matter of national news so long as terrorism was a possible cause. After this was quickly ruled out, the story disappeared while the media maintained its focus on Boston. In West Virginia, less than a year later, some 300,000 residents were deprived of safe drinking water after a chemical leak into the Elk River due to a spill by a commercial firm. The story was not national news, but certainly would have been if it were terrorists who had poisoned the water. Meanwhile, as Ludlow notes, the United States spends over $7 billion annually on the Transportation Safety Administration's national security program, "to make sure we are not carrying too much toothpaste or shampoo onto airplanes" while the budget of the Occupational Safety and Health Administration is less than $600 million per year.[282]

## Terrorism as a Form of Criminal Conduct

A further argument against terrorism as a special threat or risk rests on its character as crime. Earlier chapters have made the case that the harbinger theory was essential to framing the threat of terror at the hands of al Qaeda and other transnational groups as

---

280 Ibid. at location 1016. As the discussion of Richard Posner's work on probability in Chapter 4 has indicated, Posner would take issue with the attempt to draw an inference about how many people are likely to die from terrorism in the future based on the frequency and number of people who died from it in the past. As Posner points out, the number of casualties in the past tells us nothing absolute about the *probability* of future terror events; it tells us only about the frequency of past events. And statistics about the frequency of past events can only be equated with the *risk* of those events occurring in the future if we have reason to assume that conditions will be such that events are likely to continue to occur with the same frequency. We might reasonably assume, for example, that the rates of motor vehicle accidents or deaths by lightening are likely to remain similar to those in the recent past given the continuity in the surrounding conditions at issue. For Posner the same could not be said of terrorism in light of his own beliefs about the greater likelihood of mass terror after 9/11 (evolving technology, greater ambition on the part of terrorists, etc.). For Mueller and Stewart, and for the present author, terrorism ought to be understood in terms of a similar continuity of conditions at issue in the case of car accidents or lightening strikes. Terror in North America is likely to be no more frequent or larger in scale than it was before 2001 because the conditions of the possibility of terrorism have not changed significantly in the period since.

281 Peter Ludlow, *Fifty States of Fear*, N.Y.Times, Jan. 19, 2014.

282 Ibid.

tantamount to war. If we can assume that future acts of terror are likely to be no greater in scale than events prior to 9/11, the war framework becomes more difficult to sustain. And so too does the argument against treating terrorism as something other than crime, or as a special kind of risk distinct from those presented by other forms of criminal conduct. Two lines of argument can be offered in support of this claim.

The first is that in terms of numbers, terrorism presents us with conduct that is not altogether incomparable to forms of crime we have encountered in the past. The criminal law has long been familiar with conduct that inflicts harm or damage on a large scale, including serial murder or sexual assault, financial crimes with large numbers of victims, or, more recently, cybercrime. In each of these cases, the harm imposed goes beyond the many individual victims affected, often impinging on a larger sense of public safety or trust in institutions, persons, and places. The sudden infliction of so many deaths and the often spectacular nature of terrorism certainly make it a unique form of crime, but still a crime in essence.

The second argument is that past experience has demonstrated that the criminal law is an appropriate framework within which to respond to terrorism. Since 9/11, law enforcement in Canada and the United States, working independently or with the assistance of state intelligence, have foiled a significant number of plots, including the Toronto 18 plot in 2004 and the Christmas plane bombing plot of 2009, explored above. As Kent Roach has suggested, successful attacks are not failures of the criminal law but of law enforcement.[283] Even where these occur, in cases such as Oklahoma City and the Boston bombing, conventional law enforcement methods can be used to investigate the crime, apprehend those involved, and bring an end to the threat that the individual or group had posed. Once charged with an offence, normal criminal protections can be applied to bring the accused to justice in a reasonable time.

In short, acts of terror on a scale much smaller than 9/11 have been and should be approached within the framework of the criminal law precisely because they do not pose an existential threat to the state, or to the legal, social, or political fabric of society. They are properly perceived as rare and isolated events, involving small, anomalous groups that pose a danger well within the capacity of law enforcement to address employing conventional methods.

## Conclusion

This chapter set out to provide a blueprint for an alternative approach to advocating reform of invasive or extreme counterterrorism measures. It is premised on a challenge to three assumptions: that 9/11 marked the harbinger of a new order of terror, with more events on a similar scale to be expected; the need for more invasive, preventive measures

---

283 Kent Roach, SEPTEMBER 11: CONSEQUENCES FOR CANADA (Montreal: McGill-Queens University Press, 2003).

to counter this threat; and the belief that even if terror does not pose a greater threat in terms of scale or scope than it did before 9/11, it has come to assume the character of a special threat, justifying a lower tolerance of the risk it presents.

The objective of part one was to demonstrate that forms of terror involving nuclear or biological weapons are unlikely given the multitude of obstacles to overcome. It also set out to show how a similar argument can be made against the claim that terrorists using chemical or radiological weapons can easily inflict serious harm or damage, thus rendering such an attack likely. The second part of the chapter surveyed evidence to suggest that terror not involving WMDs will likely continue to be much smaller in scale than 9/11 and similar in nature to events prior to 2001.

The final part proposed two arguments against a line of reasoning that suggests that authoritarian measures may still be justified on the basis that terrorism continues to pose a special risk in the minds of Canadians and Americans. This theory can be challenged on the ground that the risk posed by terrorism is quantitatively no greater than many other risks we accept as a part of modern life in order to enjoy benefits we perceive to be collectively of greater value. The theory could also be challenged on the grounds that it misconceives an act of terrorism as something more or other than a criminal offence. But past experience with terrorism and with other more serious crimes calls this into question. Terrorism can be dealt with appropriately and effectively within the limits of the criminal law and the regulation of sensitive sites and materials.

# 7

## Outstanding Questions and Recommendations for Reform

THIS BOOK HAS sought to make three contributions to the debate on counterterrorism law in North America. The first relates to the concept of legality. Chapter 2 argued that much of the political and juridical acceptance of controversial measures after 9/11 can be understood as part of a shift in the cultural currency, from a liberal form of legality to what might be called authoritarian legality. The remainder of the book has considered how this new form of legality arose and became entrenched, and how it might be reformed.

The central argument of this book is that for much of the post-9/11 period, support for authoritarian measures has been premised on the harbinger theory—the belief that 9/11 marked a new order of terror, with further acts likely to occur on the same scale in the near future. The book has also explored a general tendency on the part of reform advocates to avoid challenging or unsettling this belief, and argued that this failure marked a lost opportunity that liberal jurists and rights advocates might still pursue. Chapter 6 modeled possible lines of argument for this purpose.

A number of issues remain to be addressed. Is large-scale terror not still possible using simple weaponry, by unsophisticated actors—and if so, can we really rule out the *likelihood* of large-scale terror in the near future? Is it correct to assume that during the decade after 9/11, fear of mass terror was indeed a primary or determining factor in the embrace of extraordinary measures? And if the fear of mass terror did play a key role in the period, but mass terror itself is unlikely, what reforms to counterterrorism law should be made on this basis? Finally, how might jurists, lawmakers and activists make use of the form of argument modeled in this text in future moments of perceived crisis?

## Part 1. Possible Counter-Arguments

### I. CAN MASS TERROR NOT BE CAUSED BY SIMPLE METHODS?

Chapter 6 offered an overview of skeptical opinion on the likelihood of terror involving both WMDs and conventional means. It offered evidence on which to conclude that attacks of the first form are highly improbable given the number and complexity of the obstacles that a non-state actor would confront. The chapter also surveyed evidence to demonstrate that all of the conventional bomb plots foiled in Canada and the US in the post-911 period would likely have been, at most, on the order of the Oklahoma City bombing or less (10s or low 100s rather than 1000s of casualties)—and, as noted, the Boston bombing itself was consistent with this. Two possible counter-arguments remain:

*There May Be Less Sophisticated Ways of Causing Mass Casualties or Mass Disruption*

A large-scale attack might still be accomplished in one of two ways. One would involve the use of very simple methods such as a number of Molotov cocktails set off in a large subway station at rush hour, or a suicide bomber entering a crowded shopping mall cafeteria. Casualties in either case could conceivably run into the thousands. A second possibility would involve two or more such attacks carried out simultaneously, causing additional casualties, along with widespread panic and disruption. Entire cities might be voluntarily deserted, with catastrophic effects for the nation as a whole.

In short, a counter-argument to the model set out in Chapter 6 is that neither mass terror nor mass disruption depends on the use of sophisticated materials, equipment, or methods. As 9/11 itself proved, an enormous amount of damage can be caused with just a set of box-cutters and a dozen or so willing individuals. Given this fact, one might wonder: How can we be certain that future attacks are likely to remain on the smaller scale encountered in pre-9/11 attacks—especially given the larger ambitions of some contemporary terror groups? What is the point of advocating a form of critique that focuses primarily on technologically challenging forms of mass terror?

The response to be inferred from the model set out in Chapter 6 is threefold.

First, the form of critique set out here need not be restricted to technologically advanced forms of mass terror. Indeed, the thrust of the critique is not technological but *critical*. The primary aim is to encourage a broader critical spirit when confronted with claims about pending threats, regardless of their nature. The critique neither begins nor ends with an assertion that all forms of mass terror are equally unlikely or altogether impossible. It loses none of its force by conceding that some forms of terror are more likely than others, and that anything is possible. Yet it cannot anticipate every hypothetical. Instead, the aim of this form of critique is to encourage a skeptical approach to all hypotheticals, and perhaps especially *the simpler ones*.

For any given scenario that purports to establish the possibility of inflicting catastrophic damage (human or otherwise) from seemingly simple technical scenarios, the larger lesson from the literature explored in Chapter 6 is that a skeptical second look will almost always result in a more modest assessment of the actual damage *likely* to be imposed in practice. Put otherwise, the approach here takes as its point of departure the common sense view that if it were so easy to carry out many of these seemingly more dangerous yet simple scenarios, why are they not happening more often?

To be clear, then, it is not possible to anticipate the myriad hypotheticals that might make terror on the scale of 9/11 seem just as plausible today as it was surprising to us then. The point, however, is not to refute every such possibility, but to gain a *critical perspective* on them. The analysis set out here seeks to emphasize that in most cases, regardless of how simple a scenario may appear, the apparent danger it poses may begin to diminish upon a closer examination of the science and technology involved.

Thus, having raised the possibly of a relatively simple form of mass attack (Molotov cocktails in the subway, or multiple and simultaneous low-level attacks in crowded spaces), it may be worthwhile to take a final opportunity to exemplify the critical approach advocated in Chapter 6. Would it be *easy* for a lone terrorist or a group of them to cause large-scale casualties (i.e., several hundred or thousands) by deploying a simple or moderate-size bomb in a busy urban space? Set aside for the moment the fact that *it has never occurred anywhere in the world*, despite a history of some 80,000 terrorist incidents globally from 1970 to 2007.[1] In theory, it certainly sounds plausible that by tossing two or three Molotov cocktails into a busy New York or Toronto subway station at rush hour, over a thousand people might die. The question, however, is not whether it is possible, but whether it is *likely*. On this view, we can readily see that while there would certainly be tens or even hundreds of casualties, it is impossible to be reasonably certain that an attack of this kind would *likely* result in something greater. This is because a host of contingencies would come into play—for example, the size of the explosion, the architecture of the station, the scale and duration of any resulting fire, the number of exits, the quality of the emergency response, and so forth.

Perhaps a more effective way to respond to this hypothetical is to consider the real-world case of the London bombings of both July 7, 2005 and the failed attempt to carry out additional bombings on July 21. These were attempts to do precisely what the earlier hypothetical contemplates: to cause mass casualties and disruption using conventional explosives, in multiple attacks. Three key lessons can be gleaned. First,

---

[1] *See* Mueller and Stewart's use of the Global Terrorism Database maintained by the U.S. National Consortium for the Study of Terrorism and Responses to Terrorism, cited in TERROR SECURITY AND MONEY: BALANCING THE RISKS, BENEFITS AND COSTS OF HOMELAND SECURITY (Oxford: Oxford University Press, 2011), at Kindle location 877. The database records statistics relating to some 80,000 terror incidents around the world between 1970 and 2007. In terms of casualties the four most serious attacks in this period were 9/11 (2,975, excluding relief workers); Air India (329); the Lockerbie bombing in 1988 (270); and Oklahoma City (165).

although four explosions were set off in busy urban spaces (three packed subway cars and a double-decker bus on a downtown street at rush hour), the number of casualties (56 people including the four bombers) was serious though moderate in relation to the scale of 9/11.[2] Second, although this was a multiple attack, which did cause a great deal of panic and disruption, it did not amount to a lasting, significant, or "existential" threat to the British state or to English society. It certainly instilled a great deal of fear and terror. But, as with the Oklahoma City and Air India bombings, the events were soon seen as anomalous and isolated. They were followed by a number of parliamentary inquiries and administrative assessments of investigative techniques, emergency response measures, and other preventive tools.[3] Several reforms have been proposed with a view to improving security and diminishing the odds of another event of this scale, or an attack on a larger scale in the near future.[4]

A third point to draw is that the failed bombings of July 21, 2005, were an important illustration of how even plots involving simple methods can easily unravel in practice. The goal, once again, was to set off a series of explosions almost simultaneously—three on subway trains and a fourth on a bus. But in each case, only the detonator caps fired.[5] Some have speculated that this was due to the low quality of the hydrogen peroxide used in the bombs.[6] A fifth bomber claims to have had a change of heart, aborting mission moments before he was about to enter the subway.[7] A massive manhunt followed, resulting in the apprehension, within eight days, of all four main suspects, in addition to a number of others involved.[8]

One can speculate about how much more destructive or disruptive this attack might have been if it had succeeded. Two rounds of large, coordinated attacks, so close in time, certainly would have been unprecedented in the Anglo-American world, and the fear and terror to follow would have been considerable. Understandably, even the failed attacks of July 21 continue to haunt our imagination. And the fact that they failed does not prove that they were unlikely to begin with. Yet, their failure does demonstrate that

---

2 U.K. House of Commons, *Report of the Official Account of the Bombings in London on 7th July 2005* (H.C. 1087; Stationary Office, 2006).

3 *See, e.g.*, Intelligence and Security Committee, U.K. Parliament, *Report of the Official Account of the Bombings; Report into the London Terrorist Attacks on 7 July 2005* (Cm 6785; Stationary Office, 2006); H.M. Coroner (U.K.), *Coroner's Inquests into the London Bombings of 7 July 2005* (Office of H.M. Coroner, May 2011); Department for Communities and Local Government, *Improving Opportunity, Strengthening Society: One Year On—A progress report on the Government's Strategy for race equality and community cohesion* (West Yorkshire: DCLG Publications:, 2006).

4 *See* recommendations in the final chapters of both the Intelligence and Security Committee report, ibid., and the report of the Coroner's Inquests, ibid., at 17–61.

5 A single death was caused by an asthma attack triggered by smoke from one of the explosions.

6 U.S. Department of Homeland Security, *Mass Transit System Threat Assessment* (Transportation Security Administration Office of Intelligence, February 2008), at 5.

7 Duncan Gardham, *July 21 'Fifth Bomber' Jailed For 33 Years*, TELEGRAPH (U.K.), Nov. 20, 2007.

8 *Police Hold Four 21 July Suspects*, BBC NEWS, July 30, 2005.

even a technically simple form of attack is subject to a host of contingencies, which affect the likelihood of carrying out the attack as planned.

The London bombings can therefore be read in one of two ways: as an example of how technically easy it was to have caused a great deal of damage, and possibly a lot more; or as proof of how even a relatively simple plan can be foiled by one of many possible practical impediments one might encounter. Regardless of which reading one prefers, one fact remains. Bombings of this kind, and the history of terrorism generally, suggest that the goal of inflicting *casualties* on the order of 9/11, or greater, is much more challenging and much less likely than many hypothetical scenarios would suggest. This is confirmed by the examples of the Madrid bombings of 2004 and the Mumbai attacks of 2008. In March of 2004, Islamic militants inspired by al Qaeda set off 10 bombs on four trains in metropolitan Madrid, killing 191 people.[9] The Mumbai attacks involved 11 coordinated shootings and bombings by Pakistani militants that left 174 people dead.[10] These events lend a sense of how truly anomalous 9/11 was in terms of casualties.

*Even if Casualties in Post-9/11 Attacks Have Been Much Lower, Injuries Have Not*

However, these events give rise to a second concern: casualties in three of the most notorious major attacks in the post-9/11 period may only have been in the tens or hundreds, but the injuries were much greater: roughly 300 in Mumbai, 700 in London, and 1,800 in Madrid. Taking these facts into account suggests that, in a global context, attacks on the scale of 9/11 over the course of the decade that followed were not quite so improbable. It suggests instead that if terrorists could inflict close to two thousand injuries so soon after 9/11, using entirely conventional means, the danger of mass terror remains plausible to this day—and without reliance on complex technology or practical means. Other foiled bomb plots in this period involving the Toronto 18, New York's Times Square, and airports in Los Angeles in New York, among other places, add further support for this.[11]

Put another way, the argument against the imminence of mass terror in this book has been premised in large part on a distinction between the likelihood of causing mass *casualties* and mass *injuries*. But clearly, mass terror involves both. Even if only 54 people died in the London bombing, or 191 in Madrid, there were still an enormously large number of people injured—rendering the social impact of the events quite comparable in nature to what Americans experienced on 9/11. In this view, mass terror has not seemed anomalous over the past decade, nor tied in any overt way to sophisticated weaponry.

How, then, could advocates of liberal reform have plausibly argued, earlier in the decade, for reform of extraordinary measures on the basis that mass terror, by this broader definition, was implausible? Indeed, it was occurring in Western nations every two to

---

9 Paul Hamilos, *The Worst Islamic Attack in European History*, GUARDIAN (U.K.), Oct. 31, 2007.

10 Delnaaz Irani, *Surviving Mumbai Gunman Convicted Over Attacks*, BBC NEWS, May 3, 2010.

11 *See* discussion of these plots in Chapter 6.

three years, until 2008. And how can they still make this argument if it remains entirely plausible that homegrown terrorists in Canada or the United States could inflict over a thousand injuries in a conventional bombing at any point in the near future? In short, what makes an event of this nature *unlikely*?

This is indeed a powerful argument—one that rights advocates need to confront if they seek to offer a critical view of the harbinger theory. What follows are three possible responses.

First, a relatively low-casualty but high-injury attack in North America in the near future remains entirely plausible in the hypothetical. But once again, the question is whether in practical terms, an attack of this nature is *likely* at some point soon in a given place. Within the decade following 9/11, there was certainly a pattern of terror in a global context, which included major plots in Canada and the United States. But this does not equate to a high likelihood that the individual plots would succeed on the scale intended. On the contrary, the high ratio of successful plots to foiled plots suggests otherwise. For the reasons discussed in Chapter 6 and in the discussion above of the foiled London bombing of July 21, 2005, conspiracies to carry out large-scale attacks will always be subject to a host of contingencies that cast their probability into doubt.

A second point is that for various reasons—cultural, political, and economic—terror plots are more or less likely to succeed in different places and times. For example, suicide attacks have become less likely in Israel in the wake of the Second Intifada (2005) following a series of measures Israel has employed. A similar argument might be made about how expenditures and measures involving the RCMP and CSIS helped to foil the Toronto 18 plot, or render it less likely to succeed. It would also seem likely that at least some of the success that U.S. investigators have enjoyed in foiling recent plots at early stages has been the result of greater expenditures and resources devoted to counterterrorism since 9/11. In other words, large-scale terror attacks are not uniformly probable in every context. The failure to carry out another attack in North America in the past decade is due to several factors (canvassed in Part 2 of Chapter 6), but also at least in part to the increasing effectiveness of domestic counterterrorism efforts.

A third point is a qualification to this last point. Counterterrorism efforts might have become more effective with time, but this does not mean that all expanded powers for countering terrorism are necessary, effective, or justified. As the discussion in Chapter 6 has noted, a number of commentators have questioned the effectiveness of torture and other extreme measures, and pointed to a lack of evidence that any one of these measures has been necessary in preventing an attack, let alone a major attack. Moreover, the investigations of all the recent U.S. and Canadian plots canvassed in Chapter 6 are understood to have relied on conventional methods, such as warranted surveillance, informers, and non-coerced interrogations (a point explored further below). One can therefore argue that improved counter-terror efforts have contributed in some measure to lowering the probability of large-scale terror—without having to endorse extreme measures.

To summarize, multiple attacks on a lower scale, or attacks involving simple methods, may certainly cause a great deal of fear, disruption, and damage. Yet, for reasons canvased above, large-scale attacks remain highly improbable—and not because extraordinary measures have made us safer.

## II. OTHER CAUSES FOR THE EMBRACE OF AUTHORITARIAN LEGALITY

Chapters 2 to 4 sought to demonstrate that a fear of a short-term recurrence of large-scale terror played a key role in legal and political justifications for extraordinary measures. The argument for reform in later chapters has been premised upon the assumption that reforms are more likely to be made if a wider public, together with lawmakers and jurists, can be persuaded that current threats are not qualitatively different from those we faced before 9/11. Yet, no part of the book has yet offered argument or evidence in support of the validity of this premise, and it can be challenged on a number of grounds.

In what follows, I briefly explore two, and then attempt to defend the merit of critiquing the harbinger theory as more persuasive and possibly effective basis for advocating reform.

### Racism, Xenophobia, or Fear of a Foreign Other

Sherene Razack, among others, has suggested that something more than a calculus of potential risks posed by terrorists is at play in much of the public support for authoritarian measures in North America.[12] As a consequence, one might argue from this perspective, a case for reform that target fears about large-scale terror would seem, for many, beside the point. For Razack and others, the politics of counterterrorism is best understood within a larger set of sociological or cultural trends, which invite a whole other order of complexity into the project of reform—or at least call for greater sensitivity to some of the underlying ideas and assumptions driving support for security law and policy.[13] In Razack's view,

> [t]hree allegorical figures have come to dominate the social landscape of the "war on terror" and its ideological underpinning of a clash of civilizations: the dangerous Muslim man, the imperiled Muslim woman, and the civilized European. [... T]hese figures animate a [contemporary] story about a family of white nations,

---

12 Sherene Razack, CASTING OUT: THE EVICTION OF MUSLIMS FROM WESTERN LAW AND POLITICS (Toronto: University of Toronto Press, 2008).

13 Other lines of inquiry to consider here include Giorgio Agamben, HOMO SACER: SOVEREIGN POWER AND BARE LIFE, transl. Daniel Heller-Roazen (Stanford CA: Stanford University Press, 1998); Edward Said, ORIENTALISM (New York: Vintage, 1979) and COVERING ISLAM: HOW THE MEDIA AND THE EXPERTS DETERMINE HOW WE SEE THE REST OF THE WORLD (New York: Vintage, 1997); and Judith Butler, PRECARIOUS LIFE: POWERS OF MOURNING AND LIFE (London: Verso, 2004) and FRAMES OF WAR: WHEN IS LIFE GRIEVABLE? (London: Verso, 2010).

> a civilization, obliged to use force and terror to defend itself against a menacing cultural Other. The story is not just a story, of course, but is the narrative scaffold for the making of an empire dominated by the United States and the white nations who are its allies. Supplying the governing logic of several laws and legal processes, both in North America and in Europe, the story underwrites the expulsion of Muslims from political community, a casting out that takes the form of stigmatization, surveillance, incarceration, abandonment, torture, and bombs.[14]

Thus, for Razack, broad public support for authoritarian measures in western nations after 9/11 forms part of an earlier history of Anglo-American or European racism and imperialism. This can be gleaned from the fact that contemporary support for extreme measures coincides with a rise of anti-Muslim sentiment that engages an older set of "Orientalist" stereotypes of violent and radicalized Muslim or Arab men.[15] On this reading, neither the support for the measures, nor the public's indifference to the state's failure to take accountability for serious violations of human rights, should come as a surprise. This is because the measures are not primarily motivated by fears of a catastrophic attack, but are impelled by an evolving set of beliefs about the nation-state itself—one in which "a national community [is] organized increasingly as a fortress, with rigid boundaries and borders that mark who belongs and who does not."[16] These beliefs both draw upon and maintain "old notions of the nation as a racial kin group," and are a symptom of the larger-scale persistence of a "racially ordered world."[17]

Support for authoritarian measures is not therefore grounded on assumptions about the magnitude of the threat, but on a "denial of a common bond of humanity" among racial groups. It also involves a "logic of exception" and the use of camps and other spaces in which "rightless peoples" are being separated and abandoned.[18] A case for reform targeting assumptions about outstanding threats would be misguided. It would fail to see the indifference to or support for extraordinary measures as a reflection of a deeper set of racist attitudes and beliefs.

A still further challenge to the case for reform advanced in this book is posed by a version of the same criticism, without attributing an underlying racial motive. The wider public, on this view, is indifferent to the measures because they affect so few people.[19] The measures were therefore entrenched not because of public support for the "growing threat" theory, but because of public indifference to the government's actions. And given the majority's indifference to the cause of a tiny minority of people affected, it is not likely to mobilize in support of change—whatever arguments are offered in favor of it.

---

14 Razack, CASTING OUT, *supra* note 12, at 5.

15 Ibid. at 6.

16 Ibid.

17 Ibid.

18 Ibid.

19 I am indebted to Professor Robin Elliot for raising this point.

## Counterterrorism Law as Part of an Older "Culture of Control"

Chapter 2 referred briefly to the work of contemporary criminologists David Garland, Lucia Zedner, and Jonathan Simon. Each has identified trends in law, politics, and culture that pre-date 9/11 and serve as important antecedents to authoritarian legality. Support for extraordinary measures is seen here as involving much more than a set of beliefs about the potential threat posed by terrorism. The beliefs are a contemporary form of a much older and deeper cultural phenomenon that cannot be easily addressed by dealing with only one of its more recent manifestations.

The reader may recall that, for Garland, the fear of violent crime has served as a "prominent cultural theme" since roughly the 1970s.[20] It gave rise to "a settled assumption on the part of a large majority of the public in the US and the UK that crime rates are getting worse, whatever the actual patterns, and that there is little public confidence in the ability of the criminal justice system to do anything about this."[21] Law and policy have moved further away from a sympathetic view of "the delinquent as a disadvantaged, deserving, subject of need," and replaced this with "stereotypical depictions of unruly youth, dangerous predators, and incorrigible career criminals."[22] This has enabled a deeper shift toward a more controlling, punitive, authoritarian style of law and government on a range of matters pertaining to crime and security. Garland described this shift in a passage written just before 9/11, which shows how the groundwork for a transition from a liberal to an authoritarian form of legality was already firmly in place:

> There [has been] a relaxation of concerns about the civil liberties of suspects, and the rights of prisoners, and a new emphasis upon effective enforcement and control. The call for protection *from* the state has been increasingly displaced by the demand for protection *by* the state. Procedural safeguards (such as the exclusionary rule in the USA and the defendant's right of silence in the UK) have been part-repealed, surveillance cameras have come to be a routine presence on city streets, and decisions about bail, parole or release from custody now come under intense scrutiny. In these matters the public appears to be (or is represented as being) decidedly risk-averse, and intensely focused upon the risk of depredation by unrestrained criminals. The risk of unrestrained state authorities, of arbitrary power and the violation of civil liberties seem no longer to figure so prominently in public concern.[23]

Thus, the cultural logic for a wider public acceptance of extreme measures was embedded well before 2001, and a key part of this was a growing risk-aversion to violent crime.

---

20 David Garland, The Culture of Control: Crime and Social Order in Contemporary Society (Chicago: University of Chicago Press, 2001), at 10.

21 Ibid.

22 Ibid.

23 Ibid. at 12.

In light of this diminished tolerance for violence, it would seem futile for rights advocates to quibble about the likelihood of mass terror if significant future acts of terror cannot be ruled out altogether. This inference is bolstered by the fact that increasingly, over the past three decades, North Americans have tended to value their security, however vaguely understood, over their liberty *regardless of evidence that violent crime has diminished.*

Jonathan Simon and British criminologist Lucia Zedner provide further corroboration of the depth and intractability of these trends. For Simon, a major obstacle to reform of authoritarian measures is the degree to which a punitive, risk averse, victim-centered thinking has transformed both local and national politics in the United States, along with prevailing styles of lawmaking. From the Johnson administration onward, Simon argues that to be elected, presidential and gubernatorial candidates have had to demonstrate a solidarity with victims, a punitive spirit, or an effectiveness in an earlier role as either a prosecutor or a legislator of pro-prosecutorial law.[24] A punitive, authoritarian style of lawmaking has become prevalent, marked by a sense of the crime victim as the "dominant model of the citizen."[25] For Simon, the goal of catering to the victim's interests has become central not only to criminal law and policy, but also to the very "mission of representative government" itself. For this reason, the style of lawmaking in the "war on terror" was to a large extent less a response to claims about growing threats and more a continuation of the approach taken in the "war on crime."

For Zedner, recent counterterrorism measures are part of a larger and earlier shift toward a pre-emptive or what she calls a "pre-crime" society.[26] Rather than having to wait for serious threats to materialize, law enforcement agencies are now permitted to employ a wider range of precautionary measures. These include "anti-social behavior orders," "travel restriction orders," and "control orders" against terror suspects (pursuant to the Prevention of Terrorism Act of 2005). Less emphasis is placed on the goals of "social prevention" or the task of "identifying the fundamental causes of social disorder and sexual and political violence."[27] These are displaced by "a move towards secondary prevention [or] a focus on forestalling the risk posed by known or suspected offenders."[28] For Zedner, then, pre-emptive control measures in criminal law, and the logic to support them, are not a consequence of 9/11. Both are best understood as facets of a deeper embrace of a precautionary, risk-averse approach that stems from a larger set of fears than terror alone.

---

24 Jonathan Simon, GOVERNING THROUGH CRIME: HOW THE WAR ON CRIME TRANSFORMED AMERICAN DEMOCRACY AND CREATED A CULTURE OF FEAR (Oxford: Oxford University Press, 2007), Kindle edition, location 629.

25 Ibid. at location 175.

26 Lucia Zedner, *Seeking Security by Eroding Rights: The Side-stepping of Due Process*, in Benjamin J. Goold & Liora Lazarus, eds., SECURITY AND HUMAN RIGHTS (Oxford: Hart Publishing, 2007).

27 Ibid.

28 Ibid.

Thus, the view from contemporary criminology suggests that even if large-scale terror attacks can be shown to be improbable, a good portion of the public would still support a compromise of civil liberties because the risk of at least some form of terrorism remains. The fact is that for much of the public in developed Western nations, security has become a major preoccupation.[29] The fear that drives the desire for greater security, harsher penalties, and fewer liberties may be inchoate, irrational, and mostly imagined. But rights activists cannot easily counter it. The project of reform is therefore much more complex and daunting than the model in Chapter 6 would suggest.

## III. TWO RESPONSES

### Conceding Obstacles

The arguments put forth in the previous section are complementary. They expose further layers of the cultural logic in support of authoritarian legality. These in turn serve as major obstacles to reform that liberal advocates will need to overcome. But the prospect of overcoming them should not be the only measure of the merits of any given approach to reform. Some arguments for reform might be more persuasive than others, despite the fact that certain obstacles render the prospect of meaningful reform in the short term unlikely.

One response to these arguments, then, is to simply concede them. A widespread animus for a foreign other or an increasing culture of control may indeed be obstacles to reform of counterterrorism law and practice. In this case, the model set out in Chapter 6 might be qualified in the following way. While it may offer the basis for a more persuasive case for reform than some earlier approaches, it may be no more effective in advancing the cause of reform—at least in the short term.

### Official Reasons Matter

Perhaps a more crucial argument in support of the approach in Chapter 6 is that aiming to critique the harbinger theory remains a potentially powerful tool for seeking reform because it aims to address the *explicit* and official justification consistently given for extraordinary measures. It offers a means of a more direct challenge to fundamental assumptions in the debate about rights and security.

Put otherwise: although the beliefs explored above may form an essential part of the cultural context for recent measures, none of them appears explicitly in public policy discussions around national security. As canvassed in Chapters 2 to 4, the single recurring claim among politicians, jurists, and security experts is that illiberal measures are necessary due to a change in the nature of the threat that terror poses. And the claim is specific: threats of unprecedented gravity oblige us to revisit older ideas about absolute or

[29] Ulrich Beck, Risk Society: Towards a New Modernity (London: Sage Publications, 1992).

non-derogable rights, due process, and accountability, to allow for greater discretion, force, and secrecy.

Therefore, while racism, xenophobia, or facets of a prevailing "culture of control" may inform public and political support for authoritarian measures to some degree, they have not been *officially* defended in these terms. The defense has been and continues to be based on a variation of the harbinger theory. Thus, whatever other grounds there may be in support of extreme measures, the official version serves as a crucial set of beliefs to challenge. And to the extent that there is a *public* (non-academic) debate about the measures going forward, it will not likely be focused on larger abstract trends, such as a culture of control, or an "Orientalist" tendency in relations with Arab or Muslim populations. Instead, the argument in support of extreme measures has been—and will likely continue to be—*practical, empirical, quantitative* and *qualitative*. It stands to reason that an effective way to respond to such claims is to address them directly.

## Part 2. Recommendations for Reform

### I. RESTORING LIBERAL LEGALITY

If terror on the scale of 9/11 is not likely to occur in North America in the foreseeable future, what changes should be made to counterterrorism law?

As a general proposition, any measures that mark a clear departure from liberal legality should be reassessed. If a case cannot be made for them without recourse to claims about the imminent possibility of mass terror, they should be rescinded or abandoned. What follows is not an exhaustive or detailed account, but an overview of some of the more salient measures that might be reformed and how.

### Reinstating Absolute or Non-Derogable Human Rights

The use of targeted killing, or drone strikes, should be exceptional rather than routine. It should be permitted only in strict conditions of necessity and proportionality, and be subject to the oversight of an independent and impartial tribunal. The criteria for inclusion on a list of targets should be made public, and the decision to carry out a killing should be reviewed independently *before* it takes place—unless strict criteria of temporal imminence are satisfied. The test upon review for authorization to carry out a killing should function in a manner similar to the test for a search warrant.[30] A tribunal should decide whether the evidence

---

[30] In a response to Attorney General Eric Holder's March 2012 speech on targeting killing at Georgetown Law, David Cole points out that U.S. citizen Anwar Al-Awlaki had been on a "kill list" for almost two years prior to his assassination. Cole writes: "[S]urely the minimal burden of making one's case to an independent judge in camera would be worth the time and effort required. Notice and an opportunity to be heard may not be realistic, but Holder did not explain why it would be impossible for the executive to make its case to an independent judge, much as it does for 'foreign intelligence' searches and wiretaps under the Foreign Intelligence Surveillance Act. We have long recognized that those charged with law enforcement or security are at risk of

provides reasonable and probable grounds to believe that a target is directly involved in a specific plot or a criminal act which poses an imminent danger to human life, defined as "substantially likely to occur in the near future," rather than "possibly occurring at some point in the near future." A second part of the test should ask whether the suspect can be otherwise apprehended without undue risk to the lives or safety or others. This review may take place in secrecy, but not necessarily. Justified exceptions to the need to seek prior authorization should be similar to those allowing for the use of deadly force in conventional policing. Officers may use such force in the course of their duty where suspects pose an *immediate* risk of death or serious bodily harm to the officers or to those around them, and the killing is necessary in self-defense or the defense of others.

Other extreme practices should also be prohibited, including torture, rendition, and coercive interrogation, or the use of information obtained in the course of them. Also, the *Suresh* exception should be overturned. (This allows courts in extraordinary cases to defer to the Minister's discretion to deport a person despite the risk of torture upon return to his or her country of origin.)

The practice of indefinite detention without charge on secret evidence should cease—in all its forms. This could be done by imposing a strict limit on the length of administrative detention in whatever form it assumes—for example, the detention of foreign terror suspects under the National Defence Authorization Act of 2012, or under Canada's security certificate regime in the Immigration and Refugee Protection Act.[31] After a substantial but limited period of time—six months to a year—a detainee should either be charged with a criminal offense or released.

If charged criminally, the accused ought to receive *full disclosure* of all relevant evidence in the case against him. If the court grants the state's request to maintain secrecy over certain evidence, and fair trial rights are substantially impaired as a result, a judicial stay should be mandatory. (This is in contrast to the current provision in the Canada Evidence Act, which gives judges the *discretion* to grant a stay where fair trial rights are violated.[32]) The Supreme Court of Canada's decision in *Charkaoui*, recognizing the concept of a "substantial substitute" for disclosure (special advocates) in security certificate cases, should be overturned. In a liberal conception of legality, there can be no "substantial substitute" for disclosure, because there can be no substitute for knowing the *specifics* of the case to meet.[33] (Put another way, one cannot know "the case to meet" without "knowing the specifics" since the two cannot be distinguished.) Similar changes should

---

overestimating their own certainty, and have therefore required that the government obtain a warrant from an independent judge before conducting a search, unless there is not time to do so. If we require such process even for the search of a backpack, shouldn't we demand at least as much before the President orders the non-battlefield killing of a human being?" David Cole, *An Executive Power to Kill?* N.Y. REV. OF BOOKS, Mar. 6, 2012.

[31] *See* discussion of each of these acts in Chapter 2.

[32] Section 38.14 of the Canada Evidence Act, R.S.C., 1985, ch. C-5.

[33] *See* discussion in Chapter 2.

be made to afford full disclosure to detainees seeking *habeas corpus* in U.S. military detention cases, or to accused persons in trials held by U.S. military tribunals.

At this point in time, there can be no plausible "security" justification for refusing full disclosure of evidence in cases where the state seeks a life sentence or the death penalty on the basis of evidence gathered over a decade ago. For more recent cases, where a plausible claim about privilege may be made, the state ought to strike a balance between disclosure and prosecution. That is to say, it should seek to prosecute terror suspects—or persons it deems dangerous—using whatever evidence it can afford to disclose for whatever conviction that may support. What ought to be abandoned is the view—expressed by President Obama in April of 2009 with respect 48 Guantanamo detainees, and still current—that certain persons are too dangerous to release but not indictable or triable, due to concerns about tainted evidence, a lack of evidence, or a reluctance to disclose. If there is evidence to believe a person to be dangerous, that person should be tried for an offence such as conspiracy or attempt, and otherwise released.

## Raising Thresholds for Granting Privilege and Lawful Surveillance

The reader will recall from Chapter 2 that the Anti-terrorism Act of 2001 amended the Canada Evidence Act to allow the government to assert privilege over "potentially injurious information" or "sensitive information." It also allows the executive to second-guess or trump the court's decision by issuing a certificate that prevents disclosure in cases where this was ordered. New categories of privilege, along with the power to issue a certificate, should be repealed.

The use of privilege in litigation might also be reformed, in both Canada and the United States, by the exercise of less deference on the part of the courts. In the various tort actions for state complicity in torture currently under way, U.S. and Canadian courts should fashion a higher standard for applying the state secrets or privilege doctrines. This would serve to counteract the present tendency on the part of both governments to invoke privilege primarily as a shield from accountability and transparency in cases involving state complicity in serious rights violations.

Chapter 2 surveyed changes to U.S. surveillance law after 9/11. These included the Attorney General's order permitting secret wiretapping of solicitor and client relations, and the expansion of the authority to issue warrants under both the Wiretap Act of 1968 (for warrants in ordinary criminal cases) and the Foreign Investigations Surveillance Act of 1978. The changes allow for secret surveillance on lower thresholds, over a wider range of territory, and over any medium. When surveying these measures, I made the point that many of them individually are not inconsistent with liberal legal principles, but together, they contribute to a broader shift toward an authoritarian legal framework. The question of how to reform these measures to bring them into closer conformity with liberal legality is beyond the scope of this discussion. Suffice it to say that certain features of these new laws are justified and consistent with liberal legality. These would include the grant of warrants to carry out surveillance over a wider area, involving various new media, or pertaining to persons whose identity is unknown. But liberal legal principles would support a return to higher and clearer standards for deciding when to grant a warrant, what its purpose or object should be, and how long it should last. In short, tests for granting warrants should function in closer conformity with the standards that apply in conventional criminal search warrants, which are meant to safeguard liberal expectations of privacy and dignity.

### Codifying Rules for Compensation

This point is closely related to the suggestion above that courts should exercise less deference in granting privilege in tort actions involving victims of torture or cruel and inhumane treatment. Greater judicial oversight of privilege is not enough. Just as both Canada and the United States have passed legislation in recent years in support of victims of terror,[34] so too should both governments pass law that addresses the position of innocent victims of counterterrorism measures. The United States has enacted legislation providing a basis for torture victims to sue *foreign* individuals or governments in tort.[35] But both governments should assist victims of torture or cruel treatment by passing laws that accomplish two ends: enable litigants to hold domestic officials (or the state itself) liable in tort, and provide a basis for finding in favor of plaintiffs in cases where state secrecy would otherwise serve to prevent redress or accountability.

Jasminka Kalajdzic has proposed that Section 38.14 of the Canada Evidence Act be amended to extend to civil trials a parallel form of relief allowed for in criminal cases (i.e., an acquittal where a fair trial is impaired by secrecy).[36] More specifically, the section might be "extended to empower civil trial judges to find in favour of a plaintiff where the claim of national security privilege frustrates the litigation."[37] Kalajdzic also notes that a similar provision was contemplated in a bill before Congress in 2009, which did not pass but might still be tabled.[38] In light of a finding of privilege in favor of the state, the State Secret Protection Act would have allowed a court to find in favor of a party on a factual or legal issue, exclude evidence, dismiss a claim or counter-claim, or make any "appropriate orders in the interest of justice."[39]

---

34 *See* Bill C-10, 41st Parliament, 1st sess., Safe Streets and Communities Act, which contains provisions to enact the Justice for Victims of Terrorism Act. *See also* USA PATRIOT Act, tit. VI: Providing for Victims of Terrorism, 115 Stat. 272 (2001).

35 *See* Torture Victim Protection Act (102nd Cong.), H.R. 2092.

36 Jasminka Kalajdzic, *Access to Justice for the Wrongfully Accused in National Security Investigations*, 27 Windsor Y.B. Access Just. 171 (2009), at 204.

37 Ibid.

38 State Secret Protection Act of 2009, H.R. 984 (111th); cited in Kalajdzic at 204, ibid.

39 Ibid. §7(d).

### II. WHICH MEASURES SHOULD BE KEPT?

The model set out in Chapter 6 also supports keeping in place a number of less invasive but effective *preventive* measures. These include laws and regulations meant to safeguard sensitive sites and materials, and their transport and trade.[40] Greater surveillance, tracking, and restrictions on access and use of nuclear, biological, or radiological materials and sites can be easily justified, given the danger at issue. It is precisely through the effective regulation of these materials that the danger they pose can be managed and significantly reduced.

The same argument extends to the practice of information sharing among government agencies and with other nations—a practice that has increased considerably since 2001. While there is certainly a risk of sharing faulty information, or enabling access to personal information too widely and too readily, those risks can be addressed through practical improvements and safeguards.

In short, the model set out in Chapter 6 supports the reform of pre-emptive measures that amount to gross violations of liberal legal principles. It does not, however, preclude all pre-emptive measures per se. A pre-emptive approach is necessary and prudent. But I join many other rights advocates in suggesting that this does not have to mean that core human rights or liberal legal principles should be dispensed with.

## Part 3. Challenging the Harbinger Theory in Practice

This book has focused in large part on the case for and against extreme measures. Yet the entire debate has unfolded against the backdrop of a much larger and older set of problems, including questions about how to conduct more accurate threat assessments, and make law and policy, in times of perceived crisis or "moral panic."[41] The research in this book may therefore be relevant to debates about lawmaking in moments of apparent urgency involving something other than terrorism. In this final section, I suggest three ways in which the approach to rights advocacy set out in this book might be used in such moments to promote a more careful, considered approach to lawmaking.

### Intervening at the Legislative and Policy-Making Stages

In ways explored in Chapters 3 and 4, for much of the post-9/11 period, politicians and security officials have frequently made statements in parliamentary or congressional hearings and debates, and in speeches or media appearances, in which the public was asked

---

40 The Public Safety Act (2002), S.C. 2004, ch. 15, made a number of amendments to various acts for this purpose including the Explosives Act, R.S.C., 1985, ch. E-17; the Hazardous Products Act, R.S.C., 1985, ch. H-3; the Radiation Emitting Devices Act, R.S.C., 1985, ch. R-1; and the Biological and Toxin Weapons Convention Implementation Act, S.C., ch. 15, s. 106.

41 Stanley Cohen, Folk Devils and Moral Panics (St Albans: Paladin, 1972); Stuart Hall, Policing the Crisis: Mugging, the State and Law and Order (London: Macmillan Press, 1978).

to accept at face value the validity of claims about the catastrophic nature of pending threats. In much of this discourse, often no effort was made to seek a balance of opinion, and for the most part, neither the media nor the academic or expert community helped to raise a public expectation that there was a balance to be sought. The most vocal experts on current threats—Harvard's Matthew Bunn, Graham Allison, and others—tended only to bolster the validity of a belief in the undeniable likelihood of a possible mass terror attack. There was, in short, no prominent set of public voices consistently offering a contrary assessment—especially in the places where it mattered most: in political rhetoric and congressional or legislative debates.

This points to the most conspicuous and potentially critical space for more effective advocacy in defense of rights when law is being made in times of crisis. Rights advocates might be more effective in these moments by using a form of argument that they have not consistently employed in these spaces. That is to say, when speaking in legislative hearings, debates, or in the media, rights advocates have often tended to focus—at least in the field of counterterrorism—primarily on ways in which the proposed measures will violate constitutional rights and principles, and why this ought to be avoided.[42] Yet they might make an even stronger case in these moments by explaining, if possible, that extreme measures are unnecessary because the threats that are said to justify them have been overstated and are unlikely. In the post 9/11 period, liberal jurists and activists generally fell short of this approach by limiting their practical critique of extreme measures to the *investigative* or *preemptive* merits of "coercive interrogation," indefinite detention, and other measures. Advocates generally argued that such measures are less effective than many assume. But, as the survey in Chapter 5 has sought to demonstrate, the argument was rarely tied to a critique of the nature of the threat itself. Extending the argument in this way might render the case against a proposed set of invasive measures more forceful by provoking members of the public to question the need for the measures at a more fundamental level.

One important caveat to this suggestion is that it is best suited to cases where the threats that serve to justify invasive measures are indeed overstated or unlikely. Threat inflation is certainly not unique to the discourse around terrorism. But that discourse may be unique in terms of both the scale of the threats invoked in defence of invasive measures, and the extent of those measures. By contrast to this, many of the threats invoked in the near future as a rationale for employing invasive measures may well be less striking, or less likely to engage the public imagination with the same force.

One example of this is the threat to public safety that serves as a basis for "lawful access" provisions in the realm of cyber security. Governments are now beginning to insist that much greater surveillance of online activity and identity is necessary on the basis of the threat posed by pedophiles, members of organized crime, and terrorists who

---

42 *See*, e.g., Ateqah Khaki, *The Patriot Act, 10 Years Later*, American Civil Liberties Union (Oct. 24, 2011), at https://www.aclu.org/blog/national-security/patriot-act-10-years-later.

seek to exploit online anonymity to shield their activity.[43] The fear invoked here is less one of a pending catastrophe of existential import for the state and more a kind of growing menace of concerning though moderate proportions. (The Canadian government has not, to this point, explicitly tied the threat of *mass* terror to its arguments for lawful access provisions.)

Interventions in Constitutional Litigation:

A largely unspoken but central assumption that runs through all major post-9/11 decisions of the supreme courts of Canada and the United States that touch on counter-terrorism is that the threat of terror has become so grave that a much greater degree of deference to the executive on national security matters is now warranted. The assumption takes a different form in the United States and Canadian cases, but in each context, it remains unquestioned. Calling the belief in a "grave threat" into question, or making it a more central issue in future litigation, is one way that right activists might undermine the court's rationale for assuming an excessively deferential posture to the executive in times of perceived crisis.

Rights Advocacy Among NGOs, Scholars, and Activists.

As noted in Chapter 5, much of the reform advocacy on the part of NGOs, activists, scholars, and jurists since 9/11 has dealt with questions of legality or with demonstrations of how certain measures are excessive or unjust. The case for reform might be bolstered by also engaging some of the more ambitious claims made about pending threats to national security. Advocates need not make an extensive or decisive case against the prospect of mass terror. Simply *debating* the question would change the tenor of the discussion around extreme measures in significant ways.

Rights advocates might begin to do this by becoming more conversant with the critical literature around threat assessments. By more frequently invoking some of these critical perspectives in the course of their work, rights advocate could help a larger public come to appreciate at least the debatable or unsettled quality of many claims made about terrorism. This would help to contribute to a more informed public discussion of the nature of outstanding threats and proportionate responses.

## Conclusion

Throughout the modern history of authoritarian government, leaders have argued that extraordinary measures are necessary because today's emergency is new and different.

[43] *See*, e.g. Public Safety Canada's press release rationalizing the tabling of bill C-30, 41st Parliament, 1st Session: *Harper Government Introduces* Protecting Children from Internet Predators Act, Public Safety Canada, at: http://www.publicsafety.gc.ca/cnt/nws/nws-rlss/2012/20120214-eng.aspx.

With the death of bin Laden and al Qaeda in evident decline, the sense of crisis is receding. New configurations of militant extremism are emerging in the Middle East and central Asia, but these appear to be primarily regional in their focus. Yet states still continue to insist on the need to retain extraordinary post-9/11 powers, based at least in part on a belief in the possible imminent recurrence of terror on the scale of 9/11. The task for rights advocates moving forward is to expose this gap in rhetoric and reality as a central part of its case for the return to a more robust form of the rule of law.

# Bibliography

I. LEGISLATION


Authorization to Use Military Force, Pub. L. 107–40 (S.J. Res. 23)

National Security; Prevention of Acts of Violence and Terrorism, 66 Fed. Reg. 55,062 (Oct. 31, 2001), codified at 28 C.F.R. 501.2, 501.3 (2003).

Biological and Toxin Weapons Convention Implementation Act, S.C., ch. 15.

Canada Evidence Act, R.S.C. 1985, ch. C-5.

Canadian Charter of Rights and Freedoms, Part I of the Constitution Act, 1982, being Schedule B to the Canada Act 1982 (U.K.), 1982, ch. 11.

Canadian Security Intelligence Service Act (R.S.C., 1985, ch. C-23).

Charter of the United Nations (1945), Ch. VII, Art. 51.

Convention against Torture and Other Cruel, Inhuman or Degrading Treatment or Punishment, Dec. 10, United Nations, Treaty Series, vol. 1465, 85.

Criminal Code of Canada (R.S.C., 1985, ch. C-46).

Criminal Code, R.S.C., 1985, ch. C-46.

Detainee Treatment Act of 2005 (H.R. 2863, Title X).

European Convention on Human Rights, 213 U.N.T.S. 221.

Explosives Act, R.S.C., 1985, ch. E-17.

Foreign Surveillance Act of 1978 Amendments Act of 2008, H.R. 6304.

Geneva Convention Relative to the Protection of Civilian Persons in Time of War, Aug. 12, 1949, 6 U.S.T. 3516; 75 U.N.T.S. 287.

Geneva Convention Relative to the Treatment of Prisoners of War, Aug. 12, 1949, 6 U.S.T. 3316; 75 U.N.T.S. 135.

Hazardous Products Act, R.S.C., 1985, ch. H-3.

Immigration and Refugee Protection Act, S.C. 2001, ch. 27.

International Committee of the Red Cross (ICRC), Geneva Convention Relative to the Treatment of Prisoners of War (Third Geneva Convention), Aug. 12, 1949, 75 UNTS 135.

International Covenant on Civil and Political Rights, Sept. 19, 1966, 999 U.N.T.S. 171, Can. T.S. 1976 No. 47, 6 I.L.M. 368.

International Covenant on Economic, Social and Cultural Rights, Dec. 16, 1966, 993 U.N.T.S. 3; S. Exec. Doc. D, 95–2 (1978); 6 I.L.M. 360 (1967).

National Defense Authorization Act for Fiscal Year 2012, H.R. 1540, 112th Cong. (2011).

Protecting Children from Internet Predators Act, Bill C-30 (41st Parliament, 1st Sess., Spring 2012).

Radiation Emitting Devices Act, R.S.C., 1985, ch. R-1.

State Secret Protection Act of 2009, H.R. 984 (111th).

Torture Victim Protection Act (102nd Congress) H.R. 2092.

United Nations Convention against Torture and Other Cruel, Inhuman or Degrading Treatment or Punishment, 1465 U.N.T.S. 85 (entered into force June 26, 1987).

United Nations Security Council S/Res/1373 (2001).

Universal Declaration of Human Rights, G.A. Res. 217A (III) 1948, U.N. Doc. A/810 at 71.

## 2. JURISPRUDENCE

*A and others v. Secretary of State for the Home Department* [2004] UKHL 56.

*Abdelrazik v. Attorney General of Canada and Lawrence Cannon*, Federal Court of Canada (T-1580-09).

*Abdelrazik v. Canada*, 2009 FC 580.

*Al-Bihani v. Obama*, USCA for District of Columbia Circuit, 2010.

*Al-Haramain et al v. Obama*, US District Court for Northern District of California 2010.

*Al-Haramain v. Obama et al*, 507 F.3d (2009) at 1203.

*Almrei v. Canada (Minister of Citizenship and Immigration)*, 2005 F.C.A. 54.

*Application under s. 83.28 of the Criminal Code (Re)*, [2004] 2 S.C.R. 248.

*Boumediene v. Bush*, 476 F. 3d. 981 (2008).

*Canada (Citizenship and Immigration) v. Harkat*, 2014 SCC 37.

*Canada (Prime Minister) v. Khadr*, 2010 SCC 3, [2010] 1 S.C.R. 44.

*Canada v. Almalki*, 2010 FC 1106.

*Canada v. Almalki*, 2011 FCA 199.

*Charkaoui (Re)*, 2004 FCA 421, [2005] 2 F.C.R. 299.

*Charkaoui v. Canada (Citizenship and Immigration)*, [2007] 1 S.C.R. 350.

*Charkaoui v. Canada (Citizenship and Immigration)*, 2007 SCC 9, [2007] 1 S.C.R. 350.

*Doe v. Tenet*, 329 F.3d 1135 (9th Cir. 2003).

*Ellsberg v. Mitchell*, 709 F.2d (1982) at 58.

*Hamdi v. Rumsfeld*, 542 U.S. 507 (2004).

*Hamlily v. Obama*, 616 F. Supp. 2d 63 (D.D.C. 2009).

*Harkat v. Canada (Minister of Citizenship and Immigration)*, [2004] F.C.J. No. 1104.

*Canada (Minister of Citizenship and Immigration) v. Mahjoub*, 2004 FC 1028.

*Hedges v. Obama*, 12 Civ. 331 (S.D.N.Y. 2012).

*Nlandu-Nsoki v. Canada (Minister of Citizenship and Immigration)*, [2005] F.C. 17.

*R. v. Ahmad*, [2011] S.C.C. 6.

*Rasul v. Bush*, 542 U.S. 466 (2004).

*Re: Application under s. 83.28 of the Criminal Code*, [2004] 2 S.C.R. 248.

*Re: Jaballah* 2005 FC 399.

*Suresh v. Canada (Minister of Citizenship and Immigration)*, [2002] 1 S.C.R. 3.

*Totten v. United States*, 92 U.S. 105 (1876).

*United States v. Reynolds*, 345 U.S. 1 (1953).

*Weinberger v. Catholic Action of Hawaii/Peace Education Project*, 454 U.S. 139 (1981).

## 3. MONOGRAPHS AND EDITED COLLECTIONS

Ackerman, Bruce. *Before the Next Attack: Preserving Civil Liberties in the Age of Terror* (New Haven CT: Yale University Press, 2006).

Agamben, Giorgio. *Homo Sacer: Sovereign Power and Bare Life*, Daniel Heller-Roazen transl. (Stanford CA: Stanford University Press, 1998).

Agamben, Giorgio. *State of Exception*, Kevin Attell trans. (Chicago: University of Chicago, 2004).

Allison, Graham. *Nuclear Terror: the Ultimate Preventable Catastrophe* (New York, Henry Holt: 2005).

Alvarez, Luis W. *Adventures of a Physicist* (New York: Basic Books, 1988).

Baker, Stewart & John Kavanagh, eds., *Patriot Debates: Experts Debate the USA PATRIOT Act* (Chicago: American Bar Association, 2005).

Baker, Stewart. *Skating on Stilts: Why We Aren't Stopping Tomorrow's Terrorism* (Stanford CA: Hoover Institution Press, 2010).

Barnaby, Frank. *How to Build a Nuclear Bomb and other Weapons of Mass Destruction* (London: Granta Books, 2004).

Beck, Ulrich. *Risk Society: Towards a New Modernity* (London: Sage Publications, 1992).

Blum, Gabriella & Philip Heymann. *Laws, Outlaws, and Terrorists: Lessons from the War on Terrorism* (Boston: MIT Press, 2010).

Bunn, Matthew. *Securing the Bomb 2010: Securing All Nuclear Materials in Four Years*. (Cambridge MA & Washington, DC: Project on Managing the Atom, Belfer Center for Science and International Affairs, Harvard Kennedy School and Nuclear Threat Initiative), April 2010.

Butler, Judith. *Frames of War: When is Life Grievable?* (London: Verso, 2010).

Butler, Judith. *Precarious Life: Powers of Mourning and Life* (London: Verso, 2004).

Clark, William. *Bracing for Armageddon: the Science and Politics of Bioterrorism in America* (Oxford: Oxford University Press, 2008).

Clarke, Richard A., & Robert K. Knake. *Cyber War: The Next Threat to National Security and What to Do About It* (New York: Ecco Press, 2010).

Cohen, Stanley. *Folk Devils and Moral Panics* (St. Albans: Paladin, 1972).

Cole, David, & Jules Lobel. *Less Safe, Less Free: Why America is Losing the War on Terror* (New York: The New Press, 2007).

Cole, David. *Enemy Aliens: Double Standards and Constitutional Freedoms in the War on Terrorism* (New York: The New Press, 2003).

Committee on Research Standards and Practices to Prevent Destructive Application of Biotechnology and National Research Council of the National Academies. *Biotechnology Research in an Age of Terrorism* (Washington DC: National Academies Press, 2004).

Daniels, Ronald, Patrick Macklem, & Kent Roach, eds. *The Security of Freedom: Canada's Anti-terrorism Bill* (Toronto: University of Toronto Press, 2001).

Daubney, David, ed. *Terrorism, Law and Democracy: How is Canada Changing Following September 11?* (Montreal: Themis, 2002).

de Leon, Peter, et al. *The Threat of Nuclear Terrorism: A Reexamination,* N-2706 (Santa Monica CA: RAND, January 1988).

Dershowitz, Alan M. *Preemption: A Knife that Cuts Both Ways* (New York: W.W. Norton, 2006).

Dershowitz, Alan M. *Why Terrorism Works: Understanding the Threat, Responding to the Challenge* (New Haven CT: Yale University Press, 2003).

Diab, Robert. *Guantanamo North: Terrorism and the Administration of Justice in Canada* (Black Point NS: Fernwood Publishing, 2008).

Dicey, A. V. *Introduction to the Study of the Law of the Constitution* (London: MacMillan and Co, 1889).

Drell, Sidney, et al, eds. *The New Terror: Facing the Threat of Biological and Chemical Weapons* (Stanford CA: Hoover Institution Press, 1999).

Dworkin, Ronald. *Is Democracy Possible Here? Principles for a New Political Debate* (Princeton NJ: Princeton University Press, 2006).

Dworkin, Ronald. *Taking Rights Seriously* (Cambridge MA: Harvard University Press, 1977).

Dyzenhaus, David, ed. *Civil Rights and Security* (Farnham, Surrey: Ashgate, 2009).

Dyzenhaus, David. *The Constitution of Law: Legality in a Time of Emergency* (Cambridge: Cambridge University Press, 2006).

Falk, Richard. *The Great Terror War* (New York: Olive Branch Press, 2003).

Ferguson, Charles D., & William C. Potter. *The Four Faces of Nuclear Terrorism* (London, Routledge: 2005).

Forcese, Craig, & Nicole LaViolette, eds. *The Human Rights of Anti-terrorism* (Toronto: Irwin Law, 2008).

Fuller, Lon Fuller. *The Morality of Law* (New Haven CT: Yale University Press, 1964).

Gardner, Dan. *Risk: Why We Fear the Things We Shouldn't—and Put Ourselves in Greater Dangers* (Toronto: McLelland and Stewart, 2008).

Garland, David. *The Culture of Control: Crime and Social Order in Contemporary Society* (Chicago: University of Chicago Press, 2001).

Gerges, Fawaz. *The Rise and Fall of Al-Qaeda* (New York: Oxford UP, 2011).

Ginsburg, Tom, & Tamir Moustafa, eds. *Rule By Law: the Politics of Courts in Authoritarian Regimes* (Cambridge: Cambridge University Press, 2008).

Goold, Benjamin, & Liora Lazarus, eds. *Security and Human Rights* (London: Hart Publishing, 2007).

Graff, Garrett. *Threat Matrix: the FBI at War in the Age of Global Terror* (New York: Litle, Brown and Company, 2011).

Graham, Robert, et al. *World At Risk* (New York: Vintage Books, 2008).

Greenberg, Karen. *The Least Worst Place: Guantanamo's First 100 Days* (Oxford: Oxford University Press, 2009).

Gross, Oren, & Fionnuala Ni Aolain. *Law in Times of Crisis: Emergency Powers in Theory and Practice* (Cambridge: Cambridge University Press, 2006).

Hall, Stuart. *Policing the Crisis: Mugging, the State and Law and Order* (London: Macmillan Press, 1978).

Hart, H. L. A. *The Concept of Law* (Oxford: Clarendon Press, 1965).

Hirschl, Ran. *Constitutional Theocracy* (Cambridge: Harvard University Press, 2010).

Humphreys, Stephen. *Theatre of the Rule of Law: Transnational Legal Intervention in Theory and Practice* (Cambridge: Cambridge University Press, 2010).

Ignatieff, Michael. *The Lesser Evil: Political Ethics in an Age of Terror* (Princeton: Princeton University Press, 2004).

Jenkins, Brian. *Will Terrorists Go Nuclear?* (New York, Prometheus Books, 2008).

Jenkins, Brian. *Would-Be Warriors: Incidents of Jihadist Terrorist Radicalization in the United States Since September 11, 2001* (Santa Monica CA: RAND, 2010).

Deutch, John, et al. *The Future of Nuclear Power* (Boston: MIT Press, 2003).

Mueller, John, ed. *Terrorism Since 9/11: the American Cases* (Columbus OH: Mershon Centre, 2012).

Kahn, Paul. *Cultural Study of Law* (Chicago: University of Chicago Press, 1999).

Kahn, Paul. *Sacred Violence: Torture, Terror, and Sovereignty* (Ann Arbor: University of Michigan Press, 2008).

Kellman, Barry. *Bioviolence: Preventing Biological Terror and Crime* (Cambridge: Cambridge University Press, 2007).

Langewiesche, William. *The Atomic Bazaar: The Rise of the Nuclear Poor* (New York: Farrar Straus and Giroux, 2007).

Laqueur, Walter. *No End to War: Terrorism in the Twenty-first Century* (New York: Continuum, 2004).

Laqueur, Walter. *Terrorism* (New York: Little, Brown, 1977).

Laqueur, Walter. *The New Terrorism: Fanaticism and the Arms of Mass Destruction* (Oxford: Oxford University Press, 1998).

Leventhal, Paul, & Yonah Alexander, eds. *Preventing Nuclear Terrorism: the Report and Papers of the International Task Force on Prevention of Nuclear Terrorism* (New York: Lexington Books, 1987).

Levi, Michael. *On Nuclear Terrorism* (Cambridge: Harvard University Press, 2007).

Maras, Marie-Helen. *Computer Forensics: Cybercriminals, Laws, and Evidence* (Sudbury, MA: Jones and Bartlett, 2012).

Mayer, Jane. *Dark Side: the Inside Story of How the War on Terror Turned into a War on American Ideals* (New York: Random House, 2008).

Miller, Judith, et al. *Germs: Biological Weapons and America's Secret War* (New York: Simon and Schuster, 2001).

Mueller, John. *Atomic Obsession: Nuclear Alarmism from Hiroshima to Al Qaeda* (London: Oxford University Press, 2009).

Mueller, John. *Overblown: How Politicians and the Terrorism Industry Inflate National Security Threats, and Why We Believe Them* (New York: Free Press, 2006).

Mueller, John & Mark Stewart. *Terror, Security, Money: Balancing the Risks, Benefits, and Costs of Homeland Security* (Oxford: Oxford University Press, 2011).

National Research Council of the National Academies. *Making the Nation Safer: The Role of Science and Technology in Countering Terrorism* (Washington DC: National Academies Press, 2002).

Oliver, Dawn, & C. Fusaro, eds. *How Constitutions Change: a Comparative Study* (Oxford: Hart Publishing, 2011).

Posner, Eric, & Adrian Vermuele. *Terror in the Balance: Security, Liberty and the Courts* (Oxford: Oxford University Press, 2007).

Posner, Richard. *Catastrophe: Risk and Response* (Oxford: Oxford University Press, 2004).

Posner, Richard. *Preventing Surprise Attacks: Intelligence Reform in the Wake of 9/11* (Maryland: Rowman and Littlefield, 2005).

Posner, Richard. *Not a Suicide Pact: the Constitution in a Time of National Emergency* (Oxford: Oxford University Press, 2006).

Posner, Richard. *Countering Terrorism: Blurred Focus, Halting Steps* (Maryland: Rowman and Littlefield, 2007).

Rajah, Jothie. *Authoritarian Rule of Law: Legislation, Discourse, and Legitimacy in Singapore* (Cambridge: Cambridge University Press, 2012).

Ramraj, Victor V., ed. *Emergencies and the Limits of Legality* (Cambridge: Cambridge University Press, 2012).

Raz, Joseph. *The Authority of Law*, 2nd ed. (Oxford: Oxford University Press, 2009).

Razack, Sherene. *Casting Out: The Eviction of Muslims from Western Law and Politics* (Toronto: University of Toronto Press, 2008).

Rhodes, Richard. *Twilight of the Bombs: Recent Challenges, New Dangers, and the Prospects for a World Without Nuclear Weapons* (New York: Vintage Books, 2010).

Roach, Kent. *September 11: Consequences for Canada* (Montreal: McGill-Queen's University Press, 2003).

Roach, Kent. *The 9/11 Effect: Comparative Counter-Terrorism* (Cambridge: Cambridge University Press, 2011).

Rossiter, Clinton L. *Constitutional Dictatorship: Crisis Government in Modern Democracies* (Princeton: Princeton University Press, 1948).

Said, Edwarad. *Covering Islam: How the Media and the Experts Determine How We See the Rest of the World* (Vintage: New York, 1997).

Said, Edward. *Orientalism* (Vintage: New York, 1979).

Schell, Jonathan. *A Hole in the World: An Unfolding Story of War, Protest and the New American Order* (New York: Nation Books, 2004).

Schell, Jonathan. *The Seventh Decade: the New Shape of Nuclear Danger* (New York: Henry Holt, 2007).

Schmitt, Carl. *Political Theology: Four Chapters on the Concept of Sovereignty*, George Schwab (trans.) (Chicago: University of Chicago Press, 2005).

Simon, Jonathan. *Governing Through Crime: How the War on Crime Transformed American Democracy and Created a Culture of Fear* (Oxford: Oxford University Press, 2007).

Sunstein, Cass. *Worst Case Scenarios* (Cambridge MA: Harvard University Press, 2009).

Tenet, George, & Bill Harlow. *At the Center of the Storm: the CIA During America's Time of Crisis* (New York: Harper Collins, 2007).

Tucker, Jonathan B. *Biosecurity: Limiting Terrorist Access to Deadly Pathogens*. Peaceworks, No. 52 (Washington DC: United States Institute of Peace, 2003).

Tushnet, Mark, ed. *The Constitution in Wartime: Beyond Alarmism and Complacency* (Durham: Duke University Press, 2005).

Yoo, John. *War by Other Means: An Insider's Account of the War on Terror* (New York: Atlantic Monthly Press, 2006).

Younger, Steven. *Endangered Species: How We Can Avoid Mass Destruction and Build a Lasting Peace* (New York: Harper Perennial, 2008).

4. ARTICLES AND BOOK CHAPTERS

"Text: Obama's Speech on National Security" (May 21, 2009) *New York Times*.

Ackerman, Bruce & Oona Hathaway. "Did Congress Approve America's Longest War?" (Jan. 27, 2011) *The Guardian*.

Ackerman, Bruce. "The Emergency Constitution" 113 *Yale Law Journal* 1029 (2004).

Ainscough, Michael. "Next Generation Bioweapons: Genetic Engineering and Biological Warfare," in Jim A. Davis and Barry R. Schneider, eds., *The Gathering Biological Warfare Storm* (Westport CT: Praeger, 2004).

Allison, Graham. "Is Nuclear Terrorism a Threat to Canada's National Security?" (2005) 60:3 *International Journal* 713.

Allison, Graham. "Must We Wait for the Nuclear Morning After?" (Apr. 30, 1995) *Washington Post*.

Allison, Graham. "The Ongoing Failure of Imagination" (2006) *Bulletin of the Atomic Scientists* September/October: 36.

Arthurs, H.W. "Rethinking Administrative Law: A Slightly Dicey Business" (1979) 17:1 *Osgoode Hall Law Journal* 1.

Baker, Peter. "Cheney Back Delivering the Grim Campaign Speech" (Oct. 8, 2006) *Washington Post*.

Bellinger, John. "A Counterterrorism Law in Need of Updating" (Nov. 26, 2010) *Washington Post*.

Bergen, Peter, & Paul Cruickshank, "The Unraveling: The Jihadist Revolt against bin Laden" (June 11, 2008) *New Republic*.

Booth, Robert. "The Killing of Osama bin Laden: How the White House Changed Its Story" (May 4, 2011) *The Guardian*.

Broad, William. "Among Gingrich's Passions, a Doomsday Vision" (Dec. 11, 2011) *New York Times*.

Brody, Reed. "No Real Justice in Guantanamo" (Apr. 19, 2012) *Human Rights Watch*.

Bronskill, Jim. "Ottawa Tells Spies to Use Possible Torture Info in 'Exceptional' Cases" (Feb. 7, 2012) *The Globe and Mail*.

Bunn, Matthew, Anthony Wier. "Terrorist Nuclear Weapon Construction: How Difficult?" (2006) *Annals of the American Academy of Political and Social Science* 607: 133.

Bunn, Matthew. "Reducing the Greatest Risks of Nuclear Theft and Terrorism" (2009) 138:4 *Daedalus* 112.

Cameron, Gavin. "Weapons of Mass Destruction Terrorism Research: Past and Future" in Andrew Silke, ed., *Terrorism: Trends, Achievements and Failures* (London: Frank Cass, 2004).

Carson, Mark. et al. "Can Terrorists Build Nuclear Weapons?" in Paul Leventhal & Yonah Alexander, eds., *Preventing Nuclear Terrorism: the Report and Papers of the International Task Force on Prevention of Nuclear Terrorism* (New York: Lexington Books, 1987).

Censer, Marjorie. "Richard A. Clark to Focus on Cybersecurity, Counterterrorism at SRA International" (May 6, 2012) *Washington Post*.

Cheney, Richard. "Vice President Cheney's Remarks at the American Enterprise Institute" (May 21, 2009) *Council on Foreign Relations*.

Chevrier, Isabelle. "Why Do Conclusions from the Experts Vary?" in Andreas Wenger and Reto Wollenmann, eds., *Bioterrorism: Confronting a Complex Threat* (London: Lynne Rienner Publishers, 2007).

Cole, David. "An Executive Power to Kill?" (Mar. 6, 2012) *New York Review of Books* (NYR Blog).

Committee on Science and Technology for Countering Terrorism, *Making the Nation Safer* (Washington DC: National Academies Press, 2002).

Cornwell, Susan. "FBI's Mueller: Al-Qaida Has Intent to Use Nuclear Weapons" (June 11, 2007) *Prison Planet.com*.

Cotler, Irwin. "Thinking Outside the Box: Foundational Principles for a Counter-Terror Law and Policy" in Ronald Daniels, Patrick Macklem & Kent Roach, eds., *The Security of Freedom: Canada's Anti-terrorism Bill* (Toronto: University of Toronto Press, 2001).

Cushman, John. "Sept. 11 Suspects to Be Tried by Military" (Apr. 4, 2012) *New York Times*.

Danner, Mark. "The Red Cross Torture Report: What It Means" (Apr. 30, 2009) *New York Review of Books*.

Danner, Mark. "US Torture: Voices from the Black Sites" (9 April 2009) *New York Review of Books*.

David, Jim A. "A Biological Warfare Wake-Up Call: Prevalent Myths and Likely Scenarios", in Jim A. Davis & Barry R. Schneider, eds., *The Gathering Biological Warfare Storm* (Westport CT:, Praeger, 2004).

Denbeaux, Mark & Joshua Denbeaux, et al. "Report on Guantanamo Detainees: A Profile of 517 Detainees through Analysis of Department of Defense Data", Seton Hall Law School, 2006.

Donadio, Rachel. "Italy Convicts 23 Americans for C.I.A. Renditions" (Nov. 4, 2009) *New York Times*.

Dreazen, Yochi, Aamer Madhani & Marc Ambinder. "The Goal Was Never to Capture bin Laden" (May 4, 2011) *The Atlantic*.

Dworkin, Ronald *et al.* "On NSA Spying: A Letter to Congress" (Feb. 9, 2006) *New York Review of Books*.

Dworkin, Ronald. "Terror and the Attack on Civil Liberties" (Nov. 6, 2003) *New York Review of Books*.

Dworkin, Ronald. "The Threat to Patriotism" (Feb. 28, 2002) *New York Review of Books*.

Editorial Board, New York Times. "Justifying the Killing of an American" (Oct. 11, 2011) *New York Times*.

Ellis, Brent. "Countering Complexity: An Analytical Framework to Guide Counter-terrorism Policy-Making" (2003) 6:1 *Journal of Military and Strategic Studies* 1.

Falconer, Sara. "Mohammad Mahjoub: the Life of a Security Certificate Detainee" (June 1, 2011) *Rabble.ca*.

Finn, Peter, & Del Quentin Wilber. "Guantanamo Detainees See Legal Process Reversed" (5 July 2011) *Washington Post*.

Finn, Peter, & Greg Miller. "Anwar al-Awlaki's Family Speaks Out Against His Son's Death in Airstrike" (Oct. 17, 2011) *The Washington Post*.

Forcese, Craig. "Is Bill C-3 the Security Way to Go?" (Feb. 6, 2008) *Globe and Mail*, A17.

Forcese, Craig. "Assessing Secrecy Rules" (2009) Institute for Research on Public Policy: *Choices*, 15:5.

Gellman, Barton & Jo Becker, "A Different Understanding with the President" (June 24, 2007) *Washington Post*.

Goldsmith, Jack. "The New Vulnerability" (June 7, 2010) *The New Republic*.

Goodspeed, Peter. "Ongoing Nuclear Threat Looms Over Seoul Summit" (Mar. 24, 2012) *The National Post*.

Gordon, Robert. "Some Critical Theories of Law and Their Critics," in David Kairys, ed., *The Politics of Law: A Progressive Critique* (Basic Books: New York, 1982).

Greenberg, Linda. "Gitmo Fatigue at the Supreme Court" (Apr. 6, 2011) *New York Times.*

Greenwald, Glenn. "The Killing of Awlaki's 16-year-old son" (Oct. 20, 2011) *Salon.com.*

Glenn Greenwald, *No Place Left to Hide: Edward Snowden, the NSA, and the U.S. Surveillance State* (New York: Metropolitan Books, 2014).

Gross, Oren. "Chaos and Rules: Should Responses to Violent Crises Always Be Constitutional?" (2003) 112:5 *Yale Law Journal* 1011.

Gross, Oren. "The Prohibition on Torture and the Limits of the Law," in Samuel Levinson, ed., *Torture: a Collection* (Oxford University Press, 2004).

Harris, John, Mike Allen, Jim Vandehei. "Cheney Warns of New Attacks" (Feb. 2, 2009) *Politico.com.*

Hathaway, Oona & Samuel Adelsberg, Spencer Amdur, Philip Levitz, Freya Pitts, Sirine Shebaya. "The Power to Detain: Detention of Terrorism Suspects After 9/11" (2013) 38 *Yale Journal of International Law* 123.

Human Rights First, "Some Key Facts on Military Commissions v. Federal Courts" online: http://www.humanrightsfirst.org/wp-content/uploads/pdf/Fact_Sheet-Key_Facts_Military_Commissions_vs_Federal_Courts.pdf.

Human Rights Watch, "By the Numbers: Findings of the Detainee Abuse and Accountability Project" April 2006, online: http://www.hrw.org/en/node/11352/section/1.

Human Rights Watch, "Getting Away with Torture: the Bush Administration and Mistreatment of Detainees" July 2011, online: http://www.hrw.org/en/node/100262/section/1.

Ignatieff, Michael. "Lesser Evils" (May 2, 2004) *New York Times Magazine.*

International Committee of the Red Cross, "Report on the Treatment of Fourteen 'High Value' Detainees in CIA Custody," February 2007, online: http://www.nybooks.com/media/doc/2010/04/22/icrc-report.pdf.

Jacobs, Stanley. "The Nuclear Threat as a Terrorist Option" (1998) 10:4 *Terrorism and Political Violence* 149.

Johnson, David. "U.S. Says Rendition to Continue, but With More Oversight" (Aug. 24, 2009) *New York Times.*

Johnston, David, & Charlie Savage. "Obama Reluctant to Look Into Bush Programs" (Jan. 11, 2009) *New York Times.*

Kalajdzic, Jasminka. "Access to Justice for the Wrongfully Accused in National Security Investigations" (2009) 27 *Windsor Year Book of Access to Justice* 171.

Kalajdzic, Jasminka. "Outsiders: The Sources and Impact of Secrecy at the Iacobucci Inquiry" (2010) 36 *Queen's Law Journal* 160.

Kamp, Karl-Heinz. "Nuclear Terrorism is Not the Core Problem" 40:4 *Survival,* 170 (Winter 1998–1999).

Kaplan, Eban. "Q&A: Targeted Killings" (Jan. 25, 2006) *New York Times.*

Kasinof, Laura, Mark Mazzetti, & Alan Cowell. "U.S.-Born Qaeda Leader Killed in Yemen" (Sept. 30, 2011) *New York Times.*

Landler, Mark. "Obama Presses Netanyahu to Resist Strikes on Iran" (Mar. 5, 2012) *New York Times.*

Laqueur, Walter. "Postmodern Terrorism: New Rules for an Old Game" (1996) *Foreign Affairs* September/October.

Laqueur, Walter. "The Terrorism to Come" 126 *Policy Review* 49 (August 2004).

Lawson, Philippa. "Moving toward a Surveillance Society—Proposals to Expand 'Lawful Access' in Canada" (Vancouver BC: British Columbia Civil Liberties Association, 2011).

Levi, Michael, & Henry Kelly. "Weapons of Mass Disruption" (November 2002) *Scientific American* 77.

Levinson, Sanford. "Escaping Liberalism: Easier Said Than Done" (1983) 96:6 *Harvard Law Review* 1466.

Lichtblau, E., J. Risen. "Bush Lets U.S. Spy on Callers Without Courts" (December 16, 2005) *New York Times*.

Lichtblau, Eric, & Eric Schmitt. "U.S. Widens Inquires Into 2 Jail Deaths" (June 30, 2011) *New York Times*.

Lightcap, Tracey. "Review of Kent Roach's *The 9/11 Effect: Comparative Counter-terrorism*" (2012) 22:1 *Law and Politics Book Review* 129.

Linzer, Dafna. "Nuclear Capabilities May Elude Terrorists, Experts Say" (Dec. 29, 2004) *Washington Post*.

Lobel, Jules. "The War on Terrorism and Civil Liberties" (2002) 63 *University of Pittsburgh Law Review* 767.

Luban, David. "The War on Terrorism and the End of Human Rights" (2002) 22:3 *Philosophy and Public Policy Quarterly* 9.

Luban, David. "Eight Fallacies About Liberty and Security", in Richard Ashby Wilson ed., *Human Rights in the "War on Terror"* (New York: Cambridge University Press 2005).

Luban, David. "Liberalism, Torture, and the Ticking Bomb" (2005) 91 *Virginia Law Review* 1425.

Lynn, William, "Defending a New Domain: the Pentagon's Cyberstrategy" (2010) *Foreign Affairs* September/October.

Mayer, Jane. "Outsourcing Torture: The Secret History of America's 'Extraordinary Rendition' Program" (Feb. 14, 2005) *The New Yorker.*

Mazzetti, Mark, Eric Schmitt & Robert Worth. "Two-Year Manhunt Led to Killing of Awlaki in Yemen" (Sept. 20, 2011) *New York Times*.

Mcleod, Ian, & Andrew Duffy. "A Question of Balance: Canada's Justice Minister Says New Anti-terror Laws Protect Human Rights. Critics Beg to Differ" (Dec. 11, 2004) *Ottawa Citizen*.

Meisels, Tamar. "Torture and the Problem of Dirty Hands" (2008) XXI:1 *Canada Journal of Law & Jurisprudence* 149.

Mell, Patricia. "Big Brother at the Door: Balancing National Security with Privacy Under the USA PATRIOT Act" (2002) 80 *Denver University Law Review* 375.

Meselson, Matthew. "The Myth of Chemical Superweapons" *Bulletin of the Atomic Scientists* (April 1991) 13.

Mooney, Alexander. "Obama Says Time to Rid World of Nuclear Weapons" (July 16, 2008) *CNN Politics.com*.

Mowatt-Larssen, Rolf. "Al Qaeda Weapons of Mass Destruction Threat: Hype or Reality?" (Cambridge MA: Belfer Centre for Science and International Affairs, Harvard, 2010).

Mueller, John. "Is There Still a Terrorist Threat?" (2006) *Foreign Affairs*, September/October.

Mueller, John. "The Atomic Terrorist: Assessing the likelihood" (2008), online: http://polisci.osu.edu/faculty/jmueller/APSACHGO.PDF.

Mueller, John. "The Truth About al Qaeda: Bin Laden's Files Revealed the Terrorists in Dramatic Decline" (Aug. 2, 2011) *Foreign Affairs* (blog).

Mueller, John, 7 Mark Stewart. "Civil Liberties, Fear, and Terrorism" (2012) 2:2 *Notre Dame Journal of International & Comparative Law* 282.

Mueller, John, Mark Stewart. "The Terrorism Delusion: America's Overwrought Response to September 11" (2012) 37:1 *International Security* 81.

Nir, Ori, & Marc Perelman. "CIA-Linked Study Warns of Bio-Terrorst Attacks During Next 15 Years" (Jan. 21 2005) *Forward.*

Perlstein, Deborah. "More on the New AUMF" (26 June, 2011) *Opinio Juris*, online: http://opiniojuris.org/2011/05/26/more-on-the-new-aumf/.

Peter Baker, Helene Cooper and Mark Mazzetti. "Bin Laden is Dead, Obama Says" (May 1, 2011) *New York Times.*

Pluta, Anna, & Peter Zimmerman. "Nuclear Terror: A Disheartening Dissent" (2006) 48:2 *Survival* 55.

Podgor, Ellen, & John Wesley Hall. "Government Surveillance of Attorney-Client Communications: Involved in the Name of Fighting Terrorism" (2003–2004) 17 *Georgetown Journal of Legal Ethics* 145.

Posner, Richard. "Torture, Terrorism and Interrogation" in Sanford Levinson, ed. *Torture: A Collection* (Oxford: Oxford University Press, 2004).

Priest, Dana. "US Military Teams, Intelligence Deeply Involved in Aiding Yemen on Strikes" (Jan. 27, 2010) *Washington Post.*

Pue, W. Wesley. "Protecting Constitutionalism in Treacherous Times: Why Rights' Don't Matter" in A. V. Narsimha Rao, ed., *Constitutionalism: an International Perspective* (Hyderabad: Amicus Books, 2008).

Pue, W. Wesley. "The War on Terror: Constitutional Governance in a State of Permanent Warfare?" (2003) 41:2&3 *Osgoode Hall Law Journal* 267.

Richey, Warren. "Supreme Court Rejects Guantanamo Detainees' Appeals for Better Protections" (Apr. 4, 2011) *Christian Science Monitor.*

Roach, Kent. "*Charkaoui* and Bill C-3: Some Implications for Anti-Terrorism Policy and Dialogue between Courts and Legislatures" (2008) 42 *Supreme Court Law Review* (2d) 281.

Roach, Kent & Gary Trotter. "Miscarriages of Justice in the War Against Terror" (2005) 109 *Penn State Law Review* 967.

Roach, Kent. "Better Late Than Never: the Canadian Parliamentary Review of the Anti-Terrorism Act" (2007) Choices (Montreal: Institute for Research on Public Policy) 13.

Roach, Kent. "Must We Trade Rights for Security? The Choice Between Smart, Harsh, or Proportionate Security Strategies in Canada and Britain" (2006) 27:5 *Cardozo Law Review* 2151.

Roach, Kent. "Sources and Trends in Post-9/11 Anti-terrorism Laws" in Benjamin J. Goold & Liora Lazarus, eds., *Security and Human Rights* (Oxford: Hart Publishing, 2007).

Sabulis, Tom. "Ex-senator Nunn Warns of Nuclear Terror Threat" (Feb. 15, 2010) *Atlanta (Ga.) Journal-Constitution.*

Sadat, Leila. "Extraordinary Rendition, Torture and Other Nightmares from the War on Terror" 75:05/06 *George Washington Law Review* 105.

Savage, Charlie. "Accused al-Qaeda Leader is Arraigned in U.S.S. Cole Bombing" (Nov. 9, 2011) *New York Times.*

Savage, Charlie. "Secret U.S. Memo Made Legal Case to Kill a Citizen" (Oct. 8, 2011) *New York Times.*

Savage, Charlie. "Suit Over Targeted Killing Is Thrown Out" (Dec. 7, 2010) *New York Times.*

Scahill, Jeremy. "The CIA's Secret Sites in Somalia" (July 12, 2011) *The Nation.*

Scheppele, Kim Lane. "Law in a Time of Emergency: Terrorism and States of Exception", 6 *University of Pennsylvania Journal of Constitutional Law* 2004.

Schmitt, Eric, Thom Shanker. "Qaeda Trying to Harness Toxin, Ricin, for Bombs, U.S. Says" (Aug. 12, 2011) *New York Times.*

Smith, Jeffrey, & David Hoffman. "No Support Found for Report of Lost Russian Suitcase-Sized Nuclear Weapons" (Sept. 5, 1997) *Washington Post.*

Stewart, Hamish. "Public Interest Immunity after Bill C-36" (2003) 47 *Criminal Law Quarterly* 249.

Stewart, Hamish. "Rule of Law or Executive Fiat? Bill C-36 and Public Interest Immunity" in R. Daniels & P. Macklem, eds., *The Security of Freedom: Essays on Canada's Anti-Terrorism Bill* (Toronto: University of Toronto Press, 2001).

Stober, Dan. "No Experience Necessary" (2003) 57 *Bulletin of the Atomic Scientists* (March/April).

Timmerman, Ken. "FBI Director Mueller: Al-Qaida Still Wants Nuclear Bomb" (Mar. 18, 2010) *Newsmax.com.*

Tossutti, Livianna, Osvaldo Croci & Amy Verdun, "National Threat Perception: Survey Results from Canada" (Garnet Working Paper, 18.2; May 2007).

Tushnet, Mark. "Defending Korematsu?: Reflections on Civil Liberties in Wartime," (2003) *Wisconsin Law Review* 273.

United Nations' Commission on Human Rights, "Situation of the Detainees at Guantanamo" (February 2006), UNHCR, E/CN.4/2006/120.

Wald, Matthew. "Suicidal Nuclear Threat Is Seen at Weapons Plants" (Jan. 23, 2003) *New York Times.*

Waldron, Jeremy. "Security and Liberty: The Image of Balance" (2003) 11:2 *Journal of Political Philosophy* 191.

Waldron, Jeremy. "Torture and Positive Law: Jurisprudence for the White House" (2005) 105 *Columbia Law Review* 1681.

Wenger, Andreas, & Reto Wollenmann. "Bioterrorism: A Complex Threat" in Wenger & Wollenmann, eds., *Bioterrorism: Confronting a Complex Threat* (London: Lynne Reinner Publishers, 2007).

Whitehead, John, & Steven Aden. "Forfeiting 'Enduring Freedom' for 'Homeland Security: A Constitutional Analysis of the USA PATRIOT Act and the Justice Department's Anti-terrorism Initiatives" (2001–2002) 51 *American University Law Review* 1081.

Wier, Anthony. "Terrorist Nuclear Weapon Construction: How Difficult?" (2006) 607 *Annals of the American Academy of Political and Social Science* 133.

Wilson, Scott, Jon Cohen. "Poll Finds Broad Support for Obama's Counterterrorism Policies" (7 February 2012) *Washington Post.*

Wirz, Christoph, & Emmanuel Egger. "Use of Nuclear and Radiological Weapons by Terrorists?" (2005) 87:859 *International Review of the Red Cross* 497.

Wispinski, Jennifer. "The USA PATRIOT Act and Canada's Anti-terrorism Act: Key Differences in Legislative Approach" (Ottawa: Parliamentary Information and Research Service, 2006).

Zedner, Lucia. "Seeking Security by Eroding Rights: The Side-stepping of Due Process," in Benjamin J. Goold & Liora Lazarus, eds., *Security and Human Rights* (Oxford: Hart Publishing, 2007).

Zimmerman, Peter, & Cheryl Loeb. "Dirty Bombs: the Threat Revisited" (January 2004) 38 *Defense Horizons* 1.

5. REPORTS, POLICY STATEMENTS, AND HEARINGS

Alston, Philip. "Report of the Special Rapporteur on Extrajudicial, Summary or Arbitrary Executions" (UN General Assembly, Human Rights Council 14th Session) A/HRC/14/24/Add.6 (28 May 2010).

Canada, Department of Public Safety. "Building Resilience Against Terrorism: Canada's Counter-terrorism Strategy" (February 2012), online: http://www.publicsafety.gc.ca/cnt/rsrcs/pblctns/rslnc-gnst-trrrsm/index-eng.aspx.

Canada, Parliament. House of Commons. Standing Committee on Justice and Human Rights. *Evidence.* (Meeting No. 31, Oct. 24, 2001) 37th Parliament, 1st Session.

Canada, Parliament. House of Commons. Subcommittee on Public Safety and National Security of the Standing Committee on Justice, Human Rights, Public Safety and Emergency Preparedness. *Evidence.* (Meeting No. 8, Mar. 23, 2005) 38th Parliament, 1st Session.

Canada, Parliament. House of Commons. Subcommittee on Public Safety and National Security of the Standing Committee on Justice, Human Rights, Public Safety and Emergency Preparedness. *Evidence.* (Meeting No. 28, Nov. 16, 2005) 38th Parliament, 1st Session.

Canada, Parliament. Senate. Special Senate Committee on the Subject Matter of Bill C-36 *Evidence.* (Meeting No. 31, Oct. 24, 2001) 37th Parliament, 1st Session, issue 3.

Canadian Security and Intelligence Service. "2008–2009 Public Report."

Canadian Security and Intelligence Service. "2009–2010 Public Report."

Commission of Inquiry into the Actions of Canadian Officials in Relation to Maher Arar. "Report of the Events Relating to Maher Arar: Analysis and Recommendations" (Ottawa, 2006).

Commission of Inquiry into the Investigation of the Bombing of Air India Flight. "Report of the Commission of Inquiry into the Investigation of the Bombing of Air India Flight 182" (Ottawa, 2010), online: http://epe.lac-bac.gc.ca/100/206/301/pco-bcp/commissions/air_india/2010-07-23/www.majorcomm.ca/en/reports/finalreport/default.htm.

Department for Communities and Local Government (UK). "Improving Opportunity, Strengthening Society: One Year On—A progress report on the Government's Strategy for race equality and community cohesion" (West Yorkshire: DCLG Publications, 2006).

Gilmore Commission (Advisory Panel to Assess Domestic Response Capabilities for Terrorism Involving Weapons of Mass Destruction), "First Annual Report: Assessing the Threat," (Dec. 15, 1999), online: www.rand.org/nsrd/terrpanel.

H.M. Coroner (UK). "Coroner's Inquests into the London Bombings of 7 July 2005" (Office of H.M. Coroner, May 2011).

Human Rights Watch and the American Civil Liberties Union, *With Liberty to Monitor All: How Large-Scale US Surveillance Is Harming Journalism, Law and American Democracy* (New York: Human Rights Watch, 2014).

International Bar Association. "International Terrorism: Legal Challenges and Responses", International Bar Association, "Task Force on International Terrorism" (Ardsley NY: Transnational Publishers, 2003).

International Commission of Jurists. "Assessing Damage, Urging Action: Report of the Eminent Jurists Panel on Terrorism, Counter-terrorism and Human Rights" (16 February 2009), online: http://www.refworld.org/docid/499e76822.html.

International Commission of Jurists. "Upholding Human Rights and the Rule of Law in Combating Terrorism" (Geneva: International Commission of Jurists, 2004).

International Committee of the Red Cross. "ICRC Report on the Treatment of Fourteen 'High Value Detainees' in CIA Custody" (February 2007), online: http://www.nybooks.com/media/doc/2010/04/22/icrc-report.pdf.

National Commission on Terrorist Attacks upon the United States. *The 9/11 Commission Report* (New York: Norton, 2004).

Office of Homeland Security. *The National Strategy for Homeland Security* (Washington DC: Office of Homeland Security, July 2002).

Office of Homeland Security. *The National Strategy for Homeland Security* (Washington DC: Homeland Security Council, October 2007).

President's Review Group on Intelligence and Communications Technologies. "Liberty and Security in a Changing World: Report and Recommendations of The President's Review Group on Intelligence and Communications Technologies" (Dec. 12, 2013).

The Honorable Frank Iacobucci, Commissioner, *Internal Inquiry into the Actions of Canadian Officials in Relation to Abdullah Almalki, Ahmad Abou-Elmaati and Muayyed Nurredin: Final Report* (Ottawa: Ministry of Public Works, 2008).

The White House. *National Strategy to Combat Weapons of Mass Destruction* (Washington DC: December 2002).

The White House. *The National Security Strategy of the United States of America* (Washington DC: September 2002).

The White House. *The National Security Strategy of the United States of America* (Washington DC: September 2006).

The White House. *The National Security Strategy of the United States of America* (Washington DC: May 2010).

UK House of Commons. "Report into the London Terrorist Attacks on 7 July 2005" (CM 6785; The Stationary Office, 2006).

UK House of Commons. "Report of the Official Account of the Bombings in London on 7th July 2005" (HK 1087; The Stationary Office, 2006).

U.S. Department of Homeland Security. "Mass Transit System Threat Assessment" (DHS, Transportation Security Administration Office of Intelligence, February 2008).

U.S. Department of Justice, *Amerithrax Investigative Summary* (Feb. 19, 2010), at http://www.justice.gov/archive/amerithrax/docs/amx-investigative-summary.pdf

# Index

www.ingramcontent.com/pod-product-compliance
Ingram Content Group UK Ltd.
Pitfield, Milton Keynes, MK11 3LW, UK
UKHW020926180926
475595UK00034B/143

9 780190 243227